The Red Church
or
The Art of Pennsylvania German Braucherei

by C. R. Bilardi

The Red Church
or
The Art of Pennsylvania German Braucherei

by C. R. Bilardi

PENDRAIG PUBLISHING, LOS ANGELES

© 2009 C. R. Bilardi. All rights reserved. No part of this publication may be reproduced, stored in a retrieval system or transmitted in any form or by any means, electronic, mechanical, photocopying, recording or otherwise without the prior written permission of the copyright holder, except brief quotations used in a review.

Pendraig Publishing, Sunland, CA 91040
© C. R. Bilardi 2009. All rights reserved.
Published 2009.
Printed in the United States of America
ISBN 978-0-9820318-5-8

Disclaimer

The material presented herein serves two roles: primarily, for the presentation of traditional methods of Pennsylvania German magical folk healing for their preservation and continuance; secondarily, for potential (but cautious) use by readers wishing to supplement/augment scientific, modern medical intervention and therapies. Therefore, the contents of this book are by no means a substitute for professional medical intervention. Neither the author nor the publisher assumes *any* responsibility for the use of these traditional remedies, methods, or formulae by the reader or their outcomes. Please use common sense.
Caveat medicus.

Note: Throughout *The Red Church* the term "patient" (and alternately "client") is used to designate any individual who comes to see a braucher (Pow-Wower) for "treatment". None of these terms: "patient", "client", "treatment", etc. are meant to indicate any sort of licensed or accredited statuses for any and all practicing this modality of folk medicine. These terms are used only for the ease of communication of various concepts in this text.

The Binding and Blessing

In the name of God the Father, and of the Son, and of the Holy Ghost. Amen.

By Michael, Salatheel, Raphael, and Uriel- by the witness of the Four Evangelists, and by the might of Metatron and Sandalphon:

Whoever takes possession of this book is bound to do good alone, to the glory of God and for the well-being of Man and Beast. No part of this work of mercy shall be abused. All who make proper *use* of the contents of this book shall be blessed and held in Adonai's protective hands, safe from enemies seen and unseen, and from all malign Witchcraft.

Anyone who abuses this work shall be bound: this book and its contents shall be forever *closed* and *sealed* to him.

All this by the grace, mercy, goodness, and power of Adonai: Elohim, YHVH Tetragrammaton, Eloha, El Elion, Shadai El Chai, Sabaoth, Soter, Emanuel, Jesus Christus, Alpha et Omega. Amen.

Dedication

This grammary is dedicated to Dr. Frederick LaMotte Santee, and Edna (Janie) Kishbaugh-Williams. May your memory be eternal, and may the Lord God give you Light, Peace, and Rest.

Acknowledgments

First, I give thanks to the One Power for having created me, and having given me the gift of a good mind, and for any and all healing for which I have been the instrument.

In this world:
My heart-felt gratitude and thanks goes to Mr. Mark Stavish, whose friendship, prodding, patience and mentorship made this book possible. Gratitude and thanks also goes to my Pow-Wow teacher "Daisy Dietrich"; and also to Dr. David W. Kriebel for taking the time and interest to facilitate me in my desire to learn the art of brauching in a traditional manner. I also wish to here acknowledge my wife and best friend, Kelly. Like the wives of so many other occultists and esotericists, she has endured many strange journeys, meetings, and tedious arcanae with unflinching grace and loving support.

My thanks go to all the spirits of the Pow-Wow doctors of old. I like to think that you are with me and standing by with guidance and assistance in the continued Work of Mercy in the service of The Highest. May the Lord God give you all Light, Peace, and Rest in His Kingdom. Amen.

Table of Contents

Disclaimer   5

The Binding and Blessing   7

Dedication   9

Acknowledgments   9

Foreword by Mark Stavish   17

Introduction to The Red Church   21
Ich bin Braucher: a brief explanation of Braucherei and its background; "Christ has no hands but our hands" – in healing work our hands become God's: *"Dei Hand un mei Hand iss Gottes Hand"*; a brief overview of Sympathetic Medicine; The Italian-Irish-English Dutchman, or How I became a Braucher: Pennsylvania Dutch culture and "cultural conservationism"; My Braucherei: an explanation of involvement; Daisy, a Braucherin: an introduction to "Daisy Dietrich," a longtime practitioner; A soapbox for a braucher: a brief discussion of Braucherei's pre-Christian roots.

Part I: The History of Braucherei   39
Section Overview: Who the Pennsylvania Dutch are; where they came from; why they came; the differences between "The Plain" Dutch and "The Church" Dutch; the different denominations that still comprise the mainstays of Pennsylvania Dutch identity, with a brief outline of each; an overview of Braucherei and its cultural context; The premise of "Sympathetic Medicine" will be discussed in further depth, being the differences between sympathy, antipathy, and contagion; some research into the power of prayer; The differences between Braucherei and traditional notions of Witchcraft.

Chapter 1: A History of the Pennsylvania Germans   41
1683 and the 'Plymouth Rock' of the Germans; Tumult in the Old World; New Sweden; William Penn; Germantown; Is it *Deutch*, *Deitsch*, or *Duits*?; overviews of the Church People and the Plain People: the Lutherans, the Reformed, the Catholics, the Moravians, the Mennonites, the Amish; the Brethren, the Schwenkfelders.

Chapter 2: An Overview of Braucherei Practice   69
Some Context: The Problem of Braucherei: the cultural setting of Pow-Wow practice – religio-magical healing, the issue of origins and the importance of the Christian religion; Ethnicity, the Land and Roots: ethnicity and its connection to the land – "folk religion is always ethnic"; Community; Doing it by the books: an introduction to the more prominent texts used in old Braucherei practice: *The Long Lost Friend, Albertus Magnus' Egyptian Secrets, The Sixth and Seventh Books of Moses, Three Books of Occult Philosophy, Secrets of Sympathy, The Wolfsthurn Manual, The Munich Handbook, The Bible*; "What's love got to do with it?": Love and the power of Christ is a necessity in healing work; Some Ancient and Contemporary Comparisons: a further look at the relation of Braucherei's Christian and pre-Christian elements along with a brief comparison of charms and amulets from the 1st Century to the present; The Historical Threads of Braucherei: a diagrammatic chart.

Chapter 3: Sympathy and Prayer   107
An Old View of the World: Sympathy, "magic" and the obsolete materialist notions of the Victorian era; the interconnection between all things; modalities of practice; the similarity of Mesmeric hand passes to those in brauche work; Oskar Estebany and his magnetized cotton; Etheric Fluid and Magnetization: Franz Anton Mesmer's *animal magnetism* and Paracelsus' *mumia*; energy dams; "Magnets" and Contagion: Sympathy, magnetization, contagion, and Paracelsian methods of removing disease; the *zwischentrager*; Active Prayer: Another name for Pow-Wow; "*Nothing fails like*

prayer"?; A few studies on prayer; Sovereign God and the power of healing

Chapter 4: The Damned "W" Word -- Witchcraft: The Relationship between Hexerei and Braucherei   119
The Power that Binds: idioms of power; The Degrees of Power: the different levels of Pow-Wowing and witching power; The Etymological Origins of *Witch*; Literal or Figurative? – being the realness or illusion of the witch; The Venusberg: witch mountains and spirit flight; The Bible and Spiritual Discernment – Old Testament and New Testament explanations of Witchcraft; The Black Art in the Flesh: traditional notions of hexerei and spiritual degradation.

Part II: The Practice of Braucherei   145
Section Overview: The use of "the General" technique of brauche healing: the specific hand-motions and charms needed to affect this; additional healing charms and prayers that can be used alone or within "the General" technique – also, instruction on how to create personalized charms and prayers in a traditional way; the use of some traditional healing herbs and herbal mixtures with instructions on their use and application; instruction on making amulets and talismans of protection and defense against illness, danger, and malign Witchcraft; the use of the himmelsbrief and various "Fire and Pestilence letters" to protect home and person.

Chapter 5: The Operation of Braucherei   147
A brief overview of some modalities; a note concerning 'tools' of the trade; An Apologia; The "General" Operation of Pow-Wow; a few final notes before you begin: Protection, Semi-audible prayers; a note on patient proximity; the Commonwealth of Pennsylvania.

Chapter 6: The General Brauche Circuit   157
A step-by-step analysis of hand movements needed to Pow-Wow illness.

Chapter 7: The Details of Pow-Wowing -- Timing and Sympathetic Alignments for Healing Work 177
A consideration of planetary energies and astrological timing – the "Zodiac Man" or "Almanac Man"; General Lunar Influences; Lunar Phases; General Planetary Influences; General Zodiac Influences; Adam Kadmon – the Universal Man and the Tree of Life; additional Names of God with explanations.

Chapter 8: The Cyclopedia of Working Braucherei -- The Prayers, Charms, and Formulae 193
Verbal charming: Abscesses, Boils, Sores, and Ulcerations; Blood, and Bleeding (*Blutschtille*); Colds, and Illnesses of the Throat, Lungs, Ears, and Mouth; Colic, and "the Livergrown" (*Aagewachse*); Atrophy (*Abnemmes*); Eye Troubles; Fevers (*Fiewer, Kaltfiewer, Hitz*); Headache (*Koppschmaerz, Koppweh*); Heart Troubles (*Haerzschlaek*), Apoplexia, and Convulsions; Snakebite, and Other Animal Bites; Sores, Tetter, Herpes (Gschwaer/Schlier); Sprains (*Verrenkder*) and Rheumatism; Stomach and Bowels; Swellings (*Gewecks, Heisch*), Tumors, and Erysipelas (*Rotelauf*); and also Burns; Teeth, Toothache: *Zaeweh, Zaeschmaerze*; Urinary; Warts, Corns (*Gewecks, Gewax, Warz*); Women's Ailments; Worms; Miscellaneous. Verbal Charms for Protection, Exorcism, and Allied Needs – Various Charms of Protection and Defense; charms and prayers for exorcism.

Chapter 9: The Talismantia of Working Braucherei -- The Talismans, Briefe, and Written Charms 261
The Annängsel and the Zauberzettel; Reviving the art of the Zauberzettel; A Written Charm of Exorcism; Fire and Pestilence Charms; The Sator Square; Written Charms of Protection; Anti-theft Amulets; The Brauche Bag; The Petschaft; Divination and Miscellaneous Operations: procedures against Witchcrafts; Various Exorcisms and Wardings; The Himmelsbriefe: The Koenigsberg Fire Brief, 1714; The Magdeburg Himmelsbrief, 1783; Letter of Protection (William Wilson Beissel); What about "Hex Signs"? – The Hex Grex.

Chapter 10: A Braucher's Pharmacopeia   323
Overview of herbal usage in Braucherei; the following herbs, vegetables and plants are treated here: agrimony, angelica, beets, birch, blessed thistle, burdock, chamomile, camphor oil, celandine, chickweed, cloves, coltsfoot, comfrey, coriander, coxcomb, dandelion, devil's bit, dragon's blood, elder, elecampane, fennel, ferns, garlic, gentian, ginger, ground ivy, horehound, horseradish, horsetail, juniper, lungwort, magic balsam, marigold, masterwort, moss, mouse ear, mugwort, mullein, mustard seed, nettle, pipsissewa, prickly ash, pumpkin, sanicle, sarsaparilla root, sassafras, scorpion oil, snakeroot, speedwell, St. John's wort, radish, rain-worm oil, rhubarb, thornapple, tormentil, turpentine, vervain.

Conclusion   349

A Chapter of Dedication and Remembrance: 351
Dr. Frederick LaMotte Santee, and Edna (Janie) Kishbaugh-Williams -- A Ship Called "Fredna"

Appendix I:
A Glossary of Braucherei and Related Subjects   365

Appendix II:
Use of the Psalms and the Names of God from Scripture   467

Appendix III:
Pennsylvania German and Standard German Pronunciation Guide   473

Appendix IV:
Table of Planetary Hours   481

Bibliography   483

Index   495

Foreword

It is with great pleasure that I introduce to you, the Red Church, or the Art of Pennsylvania German Braucherei. Not only is it Chris Bilardi's first book, but is also one that since its inception I have eagerly awaited seeing in print. When Chris first mentioned to me several years ago that he intended to write a book on German folk magic, or pow-wow as it is commonly known, I was thrilled for several reasons. First, I knew that after having Chris's editorial assistance with four of my own books, that he would do a job worthy of publication. It would be a book that once bought would stay in a reader's collection forever. Secondly, I knew that in addition to a fine academic understanding of the material, he would also bring it to life with a host of historical and modern examples of how pow-wow is still alive in parts of the United States and Canada among the descendents of the first German immigrants and their neighbors. Thirdly, despite several popular books on the subject of pow-wow being in print, few have any real value as they miss entire areas of study important to not only understanding the historical context of this peculiar form of folk magic, but also its spiritual context as well. Without both of these parts, pow-wow is reduced to an academic study for folklorists and not a living practice of healing, magic, and spiritual unfoldment.

Having read and been asked to review several popular books on pow-wow over the years I have been both pleased and shocked at what was being presented to the public regarding this traditionally Christian form of qabala and magic. One book in particular, written by an internationally known author of books on wicca, who wrote a book on pow-wow in the early 1990s that I was sent to review, and it actually made personal history as being the first book I ever threw into the garbage. Its misrepresentation of facts and historical revisionism demonstrated that the author had only the most superficial understanding of pow-wow. Despite this, the book has been in print for over ten years under several titles, and remains one of the few books easily available to the new student on German folk magic. With the release of The Red Church this problem is now remedied.

My reason for being so concerned about this small and obscure area of occultism and spirituality is simple: I come from a family of pow-wow practitioners, and not just your average granny wart or burn healer, but full-blown zaubermeisters. Magicians in possession of occult secrets, complete with the oral traditions, books, and tools of the trade. The first article I ever published was entitled, Pow-wow, Psalms and German Magical Folklore and first appeared in one of the last issues of Mezlim, one of the foremost, small journals on occultism that existed in the 1980s and 1990s. The story around how this article came to be is strange enough to encourage any student of synchronicity to believe that there is truly no such thing as 'coincidence' but that on some strange level, everything is interconnected. This is in fact the underlying notion of magic, for without it, scribbles on a piece of paper and poorly pronounced Hebrew prayers would have no effect on the health and well-being of man or beast, outside of the consciousness of the magician.

Because of the lack of material in this subject area I planned to write a book on pow-wow myself and began collecting research materials. A sizable portion of correspondence was amassed from ageing residents of eastern Pennsylvania, from the hard coal regions of the Blue Mountains on the edges of Pennsylvania Dutch Country, as well as communities in Luzerne and Columbia counties. For several weeks I went to the mail box wondering what treasure would be sent to me by someone who was replying to my "letter to the editor" that had appeared in their local newspaper asking for stories about pow-wow. Meetings were arranged and magical pilgrimages undertaken to meet with these, the last of their kind, willing to pass on information to me – and as you will read, to Chris as well as he undertakes his magical quest – on their Art.

Without hesitation I handed over to Chris my research, knowing that since I had yet to start writing my planned book it might be delayed too long, so my supply of research was added to his cornerstone, and as you will read, Chris quickly added the needed materials to build a temple dedicated to the Art of pow-wow. I say this because, not only is this book the book I would like to have written, but I am so glad that someone, and Chris in particular, has written. It is a genuine contribution as well as a monument to one of the most influential forms of folk magic.

In today's culture of disposable everything, including those 'inconvenient truths' of spirituality and occultism and their role in history, it is not well known that in the 18th and 19th Centuries, what we now call occultism played a major role in popular culture. Among the most widely respected and feared texts, a book in my family's possession was the so-called Sixth and Seventh Books of Moses. While it has undergone many reprints, or more rightly mutilations, its contents have inspired many a would be magus as well as sorcerer for over two and a half centuries. Compiled from the medieval and renaissance writings of Albetus Magnus, Trithemius, Cornelius Agrippa, and various kabbalistic rites, the reach of The Sixth and Seventh Books of Moses can be found in African-American Hoodoo, West African shamanism, and emulators of Faustian magic alike. For the serious student of pow-wow, the most recent redaction of The Sixth and Seventh Books of Moses, compiled, edited, and graphically restored by Joseph Peterson and published by Ibis Press is the definitive edition and will make a fine companion to those who wish to study and practice the contents of The Red Church, and simply read about them.

May God bless you in this Work, and all who see, hold, touch, or hear of in any manner whatsoever the contents of this book.

Elohim+Elohim+Elohim+

Mark Stavish, Wyoming, Pennsylvania, March 29, 2009

good many houses and outbuildings from the 18th and 19th centuries were made of stone, and later of brick. Here is a home sporting a tin roof and gothic third floor windows, features commonly found on many such older homes in these parts.

Introduction to The Red Church[1]

ICH BIN BRAUCHER. I am a braucher. That is to say, I am a Pow-Wower, or modern-day 'witch doctor'. This book is the culmination of many years of research, study, and practice. It is not a book to take lightly and contains some of the rarely published "occult" healing practices of the people know as the Pennsylvania "Dutch" or Germans. It has been my desire during the process of writing this book, to compile as many useful pieces of this art as possible for those who may be interested in keeping these practices alive in a traditional manner.

Decade after decade since the turn of the 20th Century, these practices have been consigned to the grave. *Braucherei, Pow-Wow, hexerei* -- the Witchcraft, magic and faith healing of the Pennsylvania Dutch, have been described as either "dead" or "dying". This is not so. However, it would be overly optimistic to say that these are thriving. They are not. Our so-called "Information Age" is a Faustian bargain. On the one hand, it gives us tools like the Internet that can send information across the globe in the blink of an eye. On the other, half-truths and outright falsehoods are more easily disseminated; Truth and historical accuracy take a backseat in a chaotic market place of 'information' to historical revisionism and fantasies. In this type of atmosphere, it is quite easy to mistake traditional systems of magic and faith healing as "dead", and ripe for picking on their bones.

---

[1] My choice of title for this work was inspired by the predominance of the use of the color red in pow-wow work, and the phrasing comes directly from a charm to banish rotlauf by way of invoking 'redness' *"...and in the red wald I saw a red church..."*. Red is the color of life, and therefore of protection, and healing. It is the color of the braucher's craft. Braucherei has been described as "white magic", but it could well be argued that we are "red magicians"! Mark Stavish writes the following regarding the color red: "Red is also the color of victory, success, divine blessing, and the energy of the Original Being (Adam). In traditional Kabbalah, red strings were given as a means of keeping evil away." *Kabbalah for Health and Wellness*, p.172. Stavish also states that red clothing was also worn during Kabbalah healing work.

When most folks hear or see the word "Pow-Wow", images of teepees and befeathered American Indians engaged in tribal ceremonies come to mind. However, within the culture of the Pennsylvania Germans, is the practice of the folk magical healing art called Pow-Wow, or sometimes seen spelled as "Powwow."

The proper German name for this practice is *Braucherei*. The origin of the former term is still rather vague. Some have opined that the origin can be found in the word "powan"[2], a word belonging to some of the Native American languages of the Northeast, with inference to a practitioner of magic and medicine. The later German term is derived from the word *brauchen*; this has been translated as meaning "to use". Whereas, the word *brauche* has the meaning of "use" or "custom", this is reminiscent of the translation of the word *kabbala*[3].

Braucherei is not to be confused with another term, *hexerei*, which means "Witchcraft" -- a "hex" or "hexe" being a witch. This Witchcraft is not the polite, kind-hearted Witchcraft of Wiccan circles. Hexerei, in its lowest octave, is simply mean-spirited, spiteful, greed driven psychic violence and violation. It is malice and mischief. The problem of "Witchcraft" will be treated separately later on.

It is a fashionable modern convention to disbelieve in *evil*[4] as a power

2 To my knowledge, this etymology for the word pow-wow comes from A. Monroe Aurand Jr.

3 The word *kabbalah* comes from the Latin *cabbala*, which in turn comes from the Hebrew *qabbalah*, meaning received lore or tradition. It is related to the Hebrew verb *qibbel*, meaning "to receive". Braucherei comes from the German verb *brauchen*, meaning "to use". Its etymology can be traced back to the Proto Indo-European base *bhrug*, meaning "to make use of, to enjoy"; it is related to the Latin word *fructus*.

4 There are three categories of evil: physical, moral, and metaphysical. Physical evil: e.g., natural disasters, famine, etc.; moral evil: deviation from moral precepts -- e.g., cruelty, malevolence, etc.; metaphysical evil: conditions of limitation -- e.g., blindness, deafness, birth defects, etc. In the realm of the supernatural, spiritual forces can partake of all three categories. For example, elementals, which are generally seen as being little more than semi-conscious forces, may contribute to various physical (natural) evils in the life of man; whereas, spiritual beings that are conscious

or a definite quality in life; we have all in one way or another been anesthetized to evil by media-induced sensory over-stimulation and tainted by a frightening relativism that places all deeds and ideas on an equal and level playing field. Braucherei, Pow-Wow, is an antidote to evil, as surely as that of the rite of exorcism found in the *Rituale Romanum* of the pre-Vatican II Catholic Church.

It seems that every culture has some sort of magical or folk religious answer to human suffering, both small and great. In Mexico, a sister-practice to Braucherei is called *curanderismo*; in some parts of Italy it is called *benedicaria*[5]. In all of these there is the acknowledgment of powers both human and 'spiritual' that are hell-bent (as it were) to cause as much woe as possible. As a result of the New Age movement there is a horrid mistake being made in regard to non-physical creatures (that is to say, what we call spirits, ghosts, angels, demons, etc.): that these beings are all sweetness and light; all-good, all knowing, whose intentions are always enlightened and noble. This is definitely not the case according to a host of traditions. Some of these creatures are, in fact, just as malicious, cunning (alternately, stupid), petty, conniving, and violent as any flesh-and-blood human being. Our physical world, called Malkuth[6] in the kabbalah, acts to some extent as a protective barrier between us and the Other[7]. We only need to take a cursory glance at our current state of affairs to see that something in our world has gone horribly wrong. Can mere creatures of clay take full 'credit' for the situation?

---

and aware are able to impact human beings to their good or to their detriment.

5   Benedicaria (benedictus) is a term that is said to be in use in Sicily and some parts of Southern Italy. The only place I have come across this term is from the works of Vito Quattrocchi. Generally, these folk systems tend not to have proper names, but various euphemisms used to refer to them.

6   There are ten spheres or realms on the kabbalistic Tree of Life: Malkuth being the nethermost of the ten, with the top most called Kether (the "Crown").

7   Our world is a crossroads for various realms of existence. The northern European (heathen) concept of Middle Earth demonstrates this. Medieval models of the universe also show the Earth at the center of the heavenly spheres. Despite the liminal potential of our physical realm, the density of energy at this level of creation acts as a filter or barrier to the other realms. For as much as human beings are oppressed by natural and metaphysical evils, we are also sheltered from many others.

Evil can only grab a foothold when it is first *invited*. In age-old folk beliefs, there is also the acknowledgement of the *contagion of evil*. Taking a slightly more philosophical (or if you wish, theological) view of this phenomenon, the very first doorway to be traversed by evil is the threshold of the *human heart*. This is where it all really begins. It starts with our own perversity. In magic-speak, the Heart can be referred to as the true and primal triangle of manifestation[8].

To be sure, this is not a "politically correct" book, and throughout there will be numerous instances where this issue of the contagion of evil will be explored in further depth, where appropriate.

Another issue that needs to be addressed is the question of superstition[9]. It has been said that one man's snake-oil is another man's religion. Indeed, there will be some who will pick up this book and find its contents "snake-oil" from one perspective or another. In the current social climate of both America and Europe (more so the latter), it is the fashion to see the Christian religion as such superstitious humbug. On that score, what you will see with Braucherei is that either you have *faith*[10] or you do not. Either there is an acceptance of Christ *at some level*, or there is not. It's really that simple. If you are inclined to the opinion that Christianity, esoteric or otherwise, is 'bogus' then the practice of Braucherei is *not* for you.

---

8   In ceremonial magical practice a triangle is set apart from the circle, which the magician steps within for protection. Outside of this circle, the triangle acts as a 'ground zero' for any spiritual manifestations that the magician may call upon. However, here I use the term a little more figuratively. The human "heart" is a doorway. It is a medium through which various spiritual principles may manifest as a result of the heart's moral and spiritual condition.

9   Esotericist Mark Stavish defined "superstition" quite succinctly: "Superstition is a magical or religious act performed without an understanding of the inner principals it invokes or that are at work. It is aping the original and hoping for the same results." (Private e-mail communication between Stavish and author 17 October, 2007.)

10 In order to do brauche one must be open to being a conduit for the Christ's healing energies. Without that, there is no brauche -- the *besprechen* (verbal charm) won't work.

Folk magic is primitive. That can be its strength as well as its Achilles' heel. In the hands of a skilled and knowledgeable magician, or a person of great religious faith, Pow-Wow can be a source of true wonderworking. The 'primitiveness' of this manner of working is beautiful for its simplicity and utility, much like the old stone farm houses that still dot the landscape of southeastern Pennsylvania. On the opposite side of this coin there are a few practices that probably tried the patience and belief of past practitioners.

I remember the first time reading the *Egyptian Secrets of Albertus Magnus*, one of the more popular books used by brauchers in the past. After flipping through the book a few times, there was found a "recipe" for increasing one's strength and physical vitality. The directions stated that in order to regain one's strength, he is to go out before sun rise and find a large, black spider; then proceed to take the creature *alive* back to one's kitchen and apply it between two slices of buttered bread: in other words, a spider sandwich for breakfast. Who would like to try this? It is very much doubted that there were too many folks who tried this out even 100 years ago.

Of course, for those with even a brief acquaintance with folk magic, a recipe such is this is based upon the idea of sympathy, which is closely allied to the notion of contagion: where one absorbs *desired qualities* or virtues through a like substance -- that is why such remedies are named "sympathetic". In the above case, the spider is thought of as powerful creature, with desirable qualities to be ingested. Also in this category, there is the example of using "evil" to scare away evil -- like stone gargoyles on medieval cathedrals, or the use of pre-Christian demon masks, grotesque statuary, and the like. Another variant on this practice would be the use of nasty odors to scare away disease bearing spirits. While there are many who will see this sort of principle as superstition in its own right, there are some usages that are a little more gullible than others.

A much less repugnant charm than our spider sandwich can be found in the use of the herb asafetida in the curing of colds, sore throats and other ailments. The most common manner in which it is used is to take the herb and place it in a woolen sock and wrap it around the patient's throat (assuming a sore throat). Now, in lieu of the herb, it was felt by some that the only requirement for the cure was that of a stinky sock. My dear friend, Edna (to whom this book is in part dedicated), now deceased, was half Pennsylvania Dutch and half Lenne Lennape; her mother was a Pow-Wow. She had relayed a story that when she had sore throats as a little girl (circa 1920), her father would apply his sweaty socks around her neck: obviously the belief in the power of 'stinkiness' was enough. This manner of practicing ignores the past occult virtues assigned to the herb asafetida[11]. Outside of the more educated, schooled practitioners of the art, these details were often not known.

Witchcraft, hex healing, witchdoctors, white magic and black. The bottom line for most is: Does any of it *work*? For readers who have been intimately involved in occult matters, the answer is probably "yes". My answer is: Yes and No. There are a lot of factors that go into making "magic" work. First and foremost, Braucherei is not strictly magical. In fact, there are some practitioners who want nothing to do with the subject of "magic" as in their view magic[12] is synonymous with hexerei. Many such brauchers or Pow-Wow doctors will call what they do "Active Prayer" or "faith healing". As for my take on it, magic can indeed be a process outside of religion, but in the context of traditional Braucherei, that is not entirely the

---

11   Generally assigned to the planet Mars, asafetida (*ferula foetida*) is an herb of exorcism and protection. Its presence can destroy or inhibit the manifestation of spirits when burned as incense.

12   Magicians, witches, anthropologists, and many others have attempted to define just what is meant by "magic" (See Glossary entry for MAGIC). All of them tend to fall short because magic defies all boundaries. My utilitarian definition of magic: *the employment of the little known laws of nature to affect the patterns of causality in accordance to one's desires*. In a way, the common act of prayer can be a type of magic when done in conjunction with various techniques such as visualization, the use of repetition, and body movements. The Catholic Rosary, or the Eastern Orthodox prayer rope are two examples of prayer that use physical motions and repetition in order to engender a certain state of consciousness. Prior to Vatican II the exercises of Rosary prayer were quite intensive: the devotee is supposed to visualize Christ's passion and crucifixion through the "decades" of beads. See Agrippa's eloquent definition of magic in his Chapter 2, p5 of *The Three Books of Occult Philosophy*. Donald Tyson (ed), Llewellyn Publications, St. Paul, MN. 2000. For the reader's convenience, this has been reproduced in this book's appendices.

case. Faith healing, by my estimation, is quite magical -- that is to say, it is a process or event that unveils/reveals the entry of the numinous and the Divine into mundane life. These things reveal God's imminence: the action of the Holy Ghost. For Christians who see magic as idolatry and devil-worship, despite the existence of innumerable, devout Christian practitioners[13] of the magical Art over the past 20 centuries, nothing that can be written here will be of use to convince such a person otherwise.

"Christ has no hands but our hands."
The above old maxim nicely drives home the point any braucher would make in regard to charges of "devil's work". When you get into the Practice section of this book, you will see that all brauche formulae rely upon this sympathetic principle: **our hands become God's hands**: *Dei Hand un mei Hand iss Gottes Hand*. Not surprisingly, this sort of sympathy is not at all different from the work of the true *teufelsdiener* (devil's servant) whose sees his or her actions as being a medium for the unholy ghost[14]: "It is not my hand that does this, but that of ___" fill in the blank with any demon's name and you get the idea.

We all have at least one gift given to us by God. Some people are wizards in the kitchen; some can't even boil water. Some are artistic; others are great speakers, etc. Some gifts are uncanny, because God is uncanny too. A person who is able to heal by the slightest touch, see spirits, instinctively know which plants and herbs can heal, or foresee various strings of events is a special person indeed. Not everyone who is gifted in this way can do all of those things mentioned. Some, in fact, have far more than those as well. When we are given a gift it is meant to be used for the good of others and

---

13   It comes as a shock to some that devout Christians have been (and are) practicing magicians. The roots of many magical practices current in folk magic throughout the Western world can be traced back to the ancient Coptic Christians of Egypt. Their magical formulae, in turn, emerged out of the Greco-Egyptian hermetic matrix of the first and second centuries *Anno Domini*.

14   This term is used in a very figurative sense. In no manner is it to be accepted as a theological statement -- i.e., as a part of a rival satanic trinity. No such thing exists. Here it is used to illustrate the *negativity* that can build up within the "heart" displacing the Holy Ghost.

to the glory of God.

> For God, who commanded the light to shine out of darkness, hath shined in our hearts, to give the light of the knowledge of the glory of God in the face of Jesus Christ. But we have this treasure in earthen vessels, that the excellency of the power may be of God, and not of us. **2 Corinthians 4:6-7** (KJV)

A Pow-Wow doctor is usually one who gains the "doctor" title from being recognized as talented in Braucherei treating many different illnesses. Community recognition comes from success, not from a shingle hung outside of an office. Usually the practitioner of Braucherei is an individual who shows an aptitude for at least one sort of healing. For example, some brauchers are only good at removing warts, others fevers; others are only good at "unwitching" rifles and other firearms. You could say that these sorts of folks are specialists. More often, this specialization is due to their abilities being limited to that one sort of brauching. Now, this limitation may be self-imposed: perhaps that person didn't want to take his or her brauching further; maybe that decision was based on fear. Or, perhaps they made attempts to do brauche for other ailments and found that they had *no ability to do so*. Some methods of Braucherei work for some people and not for others. This is the reason that you, the reader, will not receive a concrete answer regarding Braucherei's efficacy. For someone new, it is a matter of experimentation. It is also a matter of faith. *Faith* is a damned "F" word for some (see footnote above), but it is what really makes the difference between a genuine healing and merely kind thoughts and wishes. Braucherei can bust your faith like a hat-pin if you go beyond what you believe; deep down, that you are capable of dealing with. Brauching is a constant process of reminding the braucher that she or he is not the source. Truly, Christ[15] has no hands but our hands, but we have no hands (i.e., Power) beyond Christ. When we Pow-Wow (brauche) we tell the patient that we will *try* for them. There are no guarantees made, for it is the Holy Ghost that does the work. For the would-be braucher I say: enthrone the Holy Ghost in your heart, have an open mind, be willing to help,[16] **and *will nothing* from your own self**. If the healing occurs, give thanks to God[17].

The Italian-Irish-English Dutchman or How I became a Braucher
As some have already guessed from my surname, I have Italian ancestry. My ancestry is also Irish, English, and Welsh. Perhaps from my northern Italian family, I have Germanic 'blood'; most certainly from my English antecedents (Anglo-Saxon, Danish, and Frisian). Ireland was also a recipient of the Viking raids, and eventually Scandinavians settled in mixing with the Irish Gaels. There is even a Palatine German settlement in Ireland, which is not that far from where my ancestors come. However, as far as I know, there's not a "Dutchy" bone in my body. But, I am a native Pennsylvanian. As will be seen in the first part of this book, the designation of "Pennsylvania Dutch" can be claimed by only a few – it is a very specific ancestry.

All of us who are of European descent share some very important things in common. Despite the differences in ethnicity and language, there are some overarching, pan-European things that glue us all

---

15　　Please see the Glossary entry for **CHRIST**. It is not the author's desire for this work to be bogged down by any sectarianism. Christ means many different things to many different Christians. The vast number of denominations attests to this. By formulated theology of traditional Creeds (such as accepted by PA Dutch Christians), Jesus is the Anointed One (the Christ), Son of God, and the Divine Redeemer of fallen humanity. For as true as this expression of faith is, within the context of this healing work *Christ is the incarnate and visible love of God*. This Love is the Power that is 'channeled' through the pow-wower. The healing Power needs to be *felt*. It is imminent and permeates all things.

16　　When considering braucherei theologically, please keep the motto "Sola Fide" (by faith alone) in mind. The good works of braucherei are not a substitute for faith in Christ; but like any good works, they are a result of that faith -- like good fruit that comes from a healthy tree.

17　　That is to say, the ego is to remain out of the way before, during, and after the healing event. When the healing takes effect, the braucher cannot allow himself to get a 'swollen head' over the success, as it was not *he* who did the healing.

together. One of them, to the chagrin of some, is Christianity -- a Christianity that is peculiarly European. It matters little whether we are talking of Catholicism, Protestantism, or Anabaptism. There is an 'over soul' we share, and various ancestral streams knotted into a common root. A good portion of this "root" pre-dates our Christianity by thousands of years. We are a deep well. We have also sometimes (all too often) hated one another intensely on those very same grounds. Now, we come to a point in our history where we need to reflect upon who we are, where we've come from, and then figure out where we want to go from here. It is no secret that we are loosing our identities to a globalism only interested in the financial bottom-line, bulldozing through thousands of years of culture and history to make way for Babylon. This unholy "new order" is not a done-deal. There's still time for a rescue or a rebirth.

The Commonwealth of Pennsylvania is a very interesting. Of the original Colonies, it is one that did not have a so-called witch-craze[18] due to the indulgent and liberal nature of William Penn, a Quaker. All manner of religious flora and fauna existed in Penn's Woods. Elsewhere, these same mystics, magicians, and utopian communards would have languished. Many today look to Massachusetts as the "witch" State due to the unfortunates who suffered in Danvers and Old Salem Village. I tell you, truly, that magic and Witchcraft was *never* so ensconced in *any* of the Colonies as it was in Pennsylvania. The State seal really ought to have a conical hat and broomstick on it, but I digress...

Penn actively solicited for the immigration of persecution-beleaguered Anabaptists (being the Amish and Mennonites). Of course, not all of these Germans were Anabaptists; many more were Lutheran and Reformed, along with a minority of Catholics. These were top-notch farmers from the Palatine and Switzerland who quickly brought agricultural order to the then existing Western frontier. They brought with them folkways that took firm root in

---

18   This is not to say that witch hunts were totally unknown in Pennsylvania. This shall be treated further in Part I, Chapter 3.

the Commonwealth's soil. Braucherei is part of this heritage. Since their arrival in Philadelphia, the Germans who came to be called the "Pennsylvania Dutch" soon developed a culture uniquely their own. More of the history of the Pennsylvania Germans (Dutch) shall be treated later on in Part I, Chapter 1.

As for me: I am a cultural conservationist. Some seek to conserve rare specimens of flora; others look to protect endangered species. It is my feeling that the culture of the Pennsylvania Germans is not quite dead, but definitely fading. This is sad. Ever since I was a teenager, I was fascinated by images of the Amish and Old Order Mennonites. Of course, these are the exact stereotypical images that come to mind when thinking of the Pennsylvania Dutch. But the Dutch are so much more than just Anabaptists. They are Lutheran, Reformed, Moravian, and Catholic; they are farmers, artisans, factory workers, and office workers, just like anyone else. But, there is a distinctive culture that has been loosing focus and waning. Over the years, I have studied the many different phases of Pennsylvania German culture and have fallen in love with it. I was born a Pennsylvanian Italian-Irishman, but I am a Dutchman by osmosis. As a Pennsylvanian, I want to see this very unique expression of my State's heritage not just survive, but flourish; as a Pan-Europeanist, I want for this expression of European identity be hale and hardy, with good, strong roots finding rich, fertile soil from Pennsylvania into the Old World. I look forward to a renewed Europe, and a re-born European people. I look to our *Lilienzeit*[19].

My Braucherei
For nearly 25 years I have been a student of the occult. My focus has been primarily on traditional systems, such as folk magic. Coupled with an interest in traditional PA Dutch culture, it seems that my interest in Braucherei would have been a natural and direct progression. However, in the esoteric realm there is little that is

---

19   That is, the Time of the Lily. It refers to the new golden age of Christ's reign after the end of this cycle of time. Here I am using the term figuratively to denote a possible second renaissance for Europe.

direct in the usual sense. It was actually many years before I became cognizant of Pow-Wow/Braucherei as anything more than a set of rude "house-wife" remedies -- and, even in these, there is much that I did not appreciate at the time. However, I do now appreciate even the simplest remedies, and no longer dismiss the old wisdom of the *hausfraa*. It's easy to over look these treasures because they are not big and shiny; the more exotic, gaudy baubles of esotericism tend to shift a student's focus from these homely arts.

Some years back, my wife, mother-in-law, and I were in Gettysburg doing some antique shopping. It was a very nice time, and I was especially sensitive to the unseen presences around us. It is difficult to be open in a place like Gettysburg, without feeling "something" -- something quite akin to static electricity. As we browsed through one of the many antique shops, we came upon an old family Bible, which I was immediately drawn to. After fondling it for sometime, my wife and mother-in-law bought it for me, seeing that I was so attached to it. Here is the odd thing about that Bible: on first holding it in my hands, I received the *call* to Pow-Wow. It came, seemingly, out of no where. There was a distinct directive for me to practice, and at that time I still knew surprisingly very little about Braucherei. At that point, I just knew that I had to practice. The sensation grew as the day wore on, as I lugged around that 35 lb Bible from shop to shop. From that time forward, I have delved into Braucherei studying every detail and haven't stopped yet. I also developed a mania for collecting *Heilige Schrift*.

I had known about Hohman's infamous *The Long Lost Friend*, and wasted no time acquiring a copy. It was from that, as well as *The Egyptian Secrets* book, that I developed some basic ideas and techniques, combined with previous knowledge of other strains of folk magic, and personal intuition (or as some call it, *personal gnosis*) that I worked my Braucherei. Much later on, I came across an on-line article by Dr. David Kriebel: "Powwowing: A Persistent Healing Tradition", which originally appeared in the Pennsylvania German Review[20]. This was an absolutely fascinating article, which I read over several times, while making copious notes. In that article, Dr. Kriebel had several sources in the persons of living brauchers, one of whom he identified by the pseudonym of "Daisy Dietrich". After several false starts, I managed to locate Dr. Kriebel, and asked if he would place me in contact with "Daisy". As it turned out, he was delighted by my interest and put me in contact with her.[21]

Daisy, a Braucherin[22]
When we finally met, it was a sloppy late winter day bordering on spring. My wife, who has so kindly indulged me in my wild esoteric goose chases and research sprees, accompanied me to Daisy's that day. The visit had a dubious start, when I parked the newly washed car down on a slope of mud, which was otherwise a real driveway when dry. Between my less than happy wife in the muddy car and the tire-gouges in Daisy's driveway I was wondering if this was a good idea. Happily, Daisy didn't mind the butchered driveway. Pleasant, but business-like, there was little small talk, and she got down to the reason for my visit. Here was the thing: if I were meant to learn Pow-Wow, there would be a test. Her enclosed front porch serves as her reception and workroom for her patients. We sat at her work table, and she said very matter-of-factly, "I am going to say some words to you. I won't repeat them. If you can say them back to me, then you are meant to go further." The implication, of course, is that if I could not repeat what she said to me, then the teaching stopped, as I would not be meant to learn. The first set of brauche words was not hard. However, after each piece or section is learned, there is yet another, until the

---

20   Dr. David W. Kriebel. "Powwowing: A Persistent Healing Tradition" The Pennsylvania German Review: A Journal and Newsletter of The Pennsylvania German Cultural Heritage Center at Kutztown University and The Pennsylvania Dutch Folk Culture Society. Fall 2001, pp14 - 22.
21   In 2005 Dr. Kriebel interviewed me for his book *Powwowing Among the Pennsylvania Dutch*. I appear in that book under the pseudonym "Tom Barrone".
22   This would be the female form of the word "braucher", but to make things simple I have used the word throughout (in most instances) in its masculine form to refer to both sexes.

whole series is memorized and repeated (again, she only spoke the words once). Daisy's lessons form the core of what I call here "The General Circuit" of Brauching. After two such visits, I was on my own. Daisy's teaching was very basic, and she passed along what she had. The real complexity of what she taught lies within the actual application and the nuances that happen with each individual patient. Daisy is very good, very sensitive to the ailing and hurting spots on a person. She does her brauche very well, indeed, and has the clientele to vouch for that. Therefore, I trace my Pow-Wow lineage to "Daisy Dietrich" and from her, to her husband "Julius"; and from him, to Ruth Strickland Frey[23] (deceased). Daisy is still available to me for consultation, and for 'backup' when I (and her other students) run into rough spots. My practice is a combination of what Daisy taught me, and what I have learned through many years of research and delving into old records, books, articles, and consulting with various individuals who have Pow-Wow in their families. I have also combined many of the older forms of magical art that were a few of the fountainheads of later Braucherei practice: the work of Paracelsus, and Agrippa. Along with these, there are also the writings of Hildegard von Bingen, Jacob Boehme, Conrad Beissel, Johann Kelpius, and others that have influenced my way of doing things. Of course, my Catholic upbringing and the use of sacramentals were of great help too. These things and many more have shaped my Braucherei.

There is one more source that I would like to mention, as his book caused a major breakthrough in my attitude and approach: *Hex and Spellwork: The Magical Practices of the Pennsylvania Dutch*, by Karl Herr (pseudonym). Mr. Herr defines the spiritual 'situation' of Pow-Wow: that Christ is the bedrock for all true works of mercy: indispensable to Pow-Wow practice, and not a non-option or an inconsequential add-on in a happy mix of deities and god-forms. There is no way to get around the very essence of what constitutes

---

[23] My teacher's name shall remain anonymous, as this protects her privacy. However, I have freely used the real names of her husband's teachers as they were previously given in Dr. Kriebel's published article.

traditional brauching practice.

A Soap-box for a braucher
As for the so-called pagan roots of Braucherei, here is a personal opinion, which may not leave me endeared: our heritage is a combination of both the Christian and the non-Christian in as much as our ancestry precedes the coming of Christ and His teaching. Some of the threads of brauching can be seen in fragments turned up by scholars and antiquarians, such as the Merseburg Incantations. A fuller treatment of the pre-Christian roots of Braucherei will appear in Part I of *The Red Church*.

It must also be pointed out that the roots of what we now call Pow-Wow or Braucherei are not a simple "Christianizing" of pre-Christian practices of the ancient Germanic tribes. There is a movement led by some who seek to remove the Christian content, thereby exposing the bones of a heathen practice. In fact, this is a gross misunderstanding. Whatever the Teutonic peoples of old may or may not have specifically practiced, any attempt to "reconstruct" these practices out of Braucherei will only lead that person down the garden path. The reason for this is that the roots of Braucherei (or Pow-Wow) are not entirely Germanic. You will see in the foregoing chapters the evidence for this art's complex roots, some of which can be traced directly back to Coptic Christian Egypt, and possibly further back to Demotic sources. However, this is not to say that brauche practice is not Germanic. Much like Christianity, a religion native to first century Palestine, the strains that make up this ancient healing art were synthesized and reified in a uniquely Germanic way, making the practice every bit as "native" as the straight heathen praxis that preceded it.

"Pagan" and Christian elements comprise our heritage. I am not in favor of one obliterating the other, as that denies our ancestors (the pagan and the Christian). By no means do I condone the horrors that have been done in the name of Christ, as the conversions of our ancestors were not always peaceful. It is my belief that true conversion is a matter of the heart, and this cannot occur at sword-point. True conversion is not a wholesale acceptance of any dogma, sect, or denomination, as it is the giving place to Christ in one's heart. I have seen some truly Christian actions on the part of non-Christians; and I have witnessed some very un-Christ-like behavior on the part of "believers". With that said, I have also witnessed some very scary behavior by a few latter-day neo-pagans and non-Christian magical practitioners who see fit to vilify, slander, debauch, pervert, and undermine any and all things Christian, laboring as some of them do under ignorance and really bad revisionist history.

Climbing down off of my soap-box, I would like to leave you with this quote from *Meditations on the Tarot: A Journey into Christian Hermeticism*,

> With respect to Christian Hermeticism, it cannot see otherwise than that as the coming of Jesus Christ was an event of universal significance, it had its universal preparation, i.e. that just as the prophets of Israel until John the Baptist prepared the coming of Jesus Christ in the flesh, so did the initiates, sages and righteous men of the whole world prepare the world for his Word and his Spirit. The incarnated Logos was awaited everywhere wherever one suffered, died, believed, hoped, loved... The Jews prepared for the Incarnation; the pagans prepared themselves to recognize the Logos. Thus Christianity had its precursors everywhere -- the "choir" of precursors included not only the prophets of Israel, but also the initiates and sages of paganism.[24]

Magic is real, because Nature is real. Nature is One, because God is One. Through root in the deep soils of God's Love, all things find

---

24   P 428. Anonymous. Meditations on The Tarot: A Journey into Christian Hermeticism. Element. Rockport, MA. 1985.

their being. To restate the Hermetic doctrine, what is Above mirrors what is Below, and all things proceed from The One. According to biblical teaching, we are made in God's image. *This* is the ultimate in *Sympathy*. Here is the bottom-line of why "magic" works. Those folks who say that these matters are "of the devil" give Satan far too much credit (their *fear* is a stunning display of a lack of faith in Christ). Satan is *neither* the root nor the soil. Diabolus' works are illusions, though devastating in their effects. And, if by Satan we speak in truly biblical terms, he is God's *servant* who tries the worth of mankind before the Almighty. When Christians end up more 'devil fearing' than 'God fearing', there's a problem indeed.

It is my hope that you will find this book useful, and that its contents may be a blessing to you and yours.

In the name of the Lord of Heaven and Earth, YHVH, Elohim, Shadai El Chai, Sabaoth, Adonai, and our most glorious Lord Jesus Christus Soter Emmanuel Adonai and the blessed Holy Sophia; may the Lamp of the Ever-Living God light your way. Amen. Amen. Amen.

+ + +

C.R. Bilardi
Braucher

Part I: The History of Braucherei

Section Overview: Who the Pennsylvania Dutch are; where they came from; why they came; the differences between "The Plain" Dutch and "The Church" Dutch; the different denominations that still comprise the mainstays of Pennsylvania Dutch identity, with a brief outline of each; an overview of Braucherei and its cultural context; the premise of "Sympathetic Medicine" will be discussed in further depth, being the differences between sympathy, antipathy, and contagion; some research into the power of prayer; the differences between Braucherei and traditional notions of Witchcraft.

The pentagram design is surprisingly common in older church architecture. Unlike the dramatic carved pentagram and hexagram on the dormers of the Lutheran "Marktkirche" of Ss George & James in Hanover, Germany, this Church of Christ house of worship displays a humble, but noteworthy pentagramic steeple window.

1: A History of the Pennsylvania Germans

1683 and the 'Plymouth Rock' of the Germans

TUMULT IN THE OLD WORLD: The people who were to become the "Pennsylvania Dutch" where not a single group or an entirely homogeneous folk. At the time of their arrival in the New World, the Germany that we know today did not exist, and would not exist until 1871. The "Germany" of that period was, in fact, "the Germanies" – many German principalities and duchies under the Holy Roman Emperor. The majority of these people came from the area known as the Palatine, which is now located in the southwestern corner of present-day Germany. It is from the Pfälzisch dialect of this area of the Rhine Valley, between the cities of Neustadt, Grünstadt, and Mannheim, that the Pennsylvania German language finds its root.[1]

Many of these people came to Pennsylvania from areas that are presently not recognized as being "German" such as Silesia, which is now in Poland; and Alsace, in France.[2] They also came from Hesse and Baden. From Switzerland came the Mennonites and Amish who migrated to the Palatine and stayed for a short time until moving on. A few families and individuals came from the Netherlands too, although this is not why the Pennsylvania Germans are known as the "Dutch." The question of what is "Dutch" is addressed shortly.

---

1   Much of the information for this chapter comes from Andrew's *History of the United States*, and Eshelman's *Historic Background and Annals*.

2   The Holy Roman Empire encompassed many areas of Europe and the Mediterranean at different points in its history. Silesia, Pomerania, & Neumark are now in Poland; Artois, Savoie, Alsace, Lorraine, & Franche-Comté: France; Lombardy, Tuscany, Alto-Adige, Emila-Romagna, & Piedmont: Italy. On another note, the Kingdom of Prussia occupied portions of what are now Lithuania, Poland, & Russia.

Religious conflict and perpetual war were the extreme motivators that drove vast amounts of the Germanic population to America. These were primarily the Thirty Years War (1618 – 1648) between Catholics and Protestants[3], and the incursion of French imperialism under King Louis XIV in the Palatinate. The latter is known as either the War of Augsburg or the War of the Palatinate of 1688, and it came to an end with the Treaty of Ryswick (1697), but not before the French decimated the cities and the countryside. The year 1702 saw the beginning of the War of Spanish Succession, and once again the French pressed the natives into a distressed refugee status. The Napoleonic Wars, especially in regard to the War of the Fourth Coalition (1806 – 1807), also drove many more Germans from the Old World.

Between these military horrors were sandwiched the persecutions of Anabaptists, who were hounded from one principality to another. The torments that these peaceful Christians endured are well documented in Thielman van Braght's Martyrs Mirror of 1685. The Peace of Westphalia (1648) empowered the princes to determine the religious affiliation of their principalities. However, it must be understood that this "choice" on the part of the princes was enforced upon all their subjects. Therefore, if the people were Catholic and were under a Lutheran prince, they all had to convert to Lutheranism. If, at some point that prince decided to become a Calvinist (Reformed Church), the people had to change yet again. Any religious dissent was seen as treason. The only other answer was for people to move. It was out of this nasty matrix that the war-weary Germans came to Colonial America.

New Sweden

Before the Germans came to what was to become "Pennsylvania" the British, Dutch, and Swedes held a stake in the area of the Delaware watershed. The Dutch were mainly interested in trading, and their

---

[3] In fact, The Thirty Years War was a very complex affair, although its genesis was religious conflict. This War alone was responsible for killing off 30% of the German population.

claim on the land stemmed from Henry Hudson's exploration under the Dutch West India Company in 1609. However, the British held a claim by way of John Cabot's exploration in 1497. The Dutch referred to this area as "New Netherlands" while the Swedes invited by the Dutch Director-General, came in greater numbers than the Dutch.

By the mid 1600's Swedes and Finns were populating the territory and established their own trading post Fort Christina (now in Wilmington, Delaware). They called this area which occupied parts of what are now New Jersey, Delaware, and Pennsylvania "New Sweden." The Dutch attacked the Swedes and forced the area back into the colony of New Netherlands. It was not long after this that the British reasserted themselves under the Duke of York. Thus began the British colonial period.

If we consider the English (Anglo-Saxons) as part of the greater Germanic ethnic group, along with the Holland Dutch and Scandinavians, there has then been a Germanic presence in the New World for well over 500 years. There is also archeological evidence that Vikings settled in North America (Vinland/Vineland)[4], which pushes back the date on this presence even further yet, at least to the 10th Century.

---

4   Newfoundland, Pistolet Bay.

Map of Pennsylvania circa 1698, Gabriel Thomas

William Penn

The Commonwealth's founder William Penn (b. 1644 – d. 1718) was the son of the distinguished Admiral Sir William Penn of the British Navy. Britain was strapped for money and could not remunerate the elder Penn for his services, which amounted to £16,000. In 1680 Admiral Penn petitioned King Charles II to grant him letters-patent *"for a tract of land in America, lying north of Maryland, on the east bounded with Delaware river, on the west limited as Maryland, and northward to extend as far as possible."*[5] This request for colonial territory was for Penn's payment instead of the monies owed him, which was in turn given to the younger Penn. On March 4th, 1681, the King signed over the tract and named the land "Pennsylvania" in honor of Admiral Penn. William was now the Proprietary.

---

5   Egle, p. 45

In 1667 William converted to Quakerism, and was quite active as a preacher and writer. As a result of these activities, Penn was arrested several times. His booklet *The Sandy Foundation Shaken* earned him imprisonment in the Tower of London. While in prison he wrote *No Cross, No Crown*. Not long after, he was arrested again for street preaching. During his imprisonment in 1674 he wrote another pamphlet *England's Present Interest Considered*. Only Penn's friends and political connections saved him from doing 'hard time' while others less fortunate languished for the same offense.

Quakers were not his only concern, for in 1674 Penn corresponded with the magistrates of Emden pleading for tolerance towards Mennonites. These letters were originally written in a mix of Latin and English, which were then translated into German and circulated among Mennonite congregations. By 1677 William Penn and a few associates made their way into Holland and Germany in order to preach.[6] Despite the fact of his imprisonments, he was actually well-liked by the King (this time James, Duke of York – Charles II had passed away). William was successful using this access to James to have "liberty of conscience" granted to all religionists, with special consideration given to Quakers in 1687 under the "Toleration Act." The previous year saw Penn's success in liberating 1,200 Quakers. Unfortunately, this was not the end of Penn's troubles as he was tried for treason in 1688, but was acquitted. One more imprisonment came in 1708 for past financial debts, but was released by his friends.

Because of the persecutions faced by William and fellow Quakers, he conceived of what has been dubbed "the holy experiment" of religious liberty for his colony. Aside from this ideal, Penn needed to ensure that his colony would be successful; to that end, Penn's toleration worked toward attracting more industrious and talented individuals from Europe.

---

6   In 1678 Holland Mennonites help Swiss Mennonites into the Palatinate.

When Penn was granted the colony, he had shown himself to be a model gentleman in his dealings with the American Indians. Before implementing any of his plans for the colony, he made certain to first purchase the land.

> One of the first acts was a treaty with the Indians, whom he recognized as the rightful owners of the soil. He did not pretend to make any title to lands before he procured the relinquishment of the Indians' title by treaty and purchase. The treaties made by Penn with the Indians were sacredly kept by him, and they stand out in honorable relief, when contrasted with a century of violated treaties, broken promises, and bad faith of the United States Government, in its dealings with various Indian tribes.[7]

The above is not to claim sainthood for William Penn. Even though there was freedom of conscience in Pennsylvania, Roman Catholics were restricted in their political participation, and he tended to favor his own 'sect' or denomination. Beidelman describes the first Colonial Assembly of Pennsylvania on 10 January, 1683, as being dominated by Penn and his Quakers, where strange laws were proposed (and some passed) for the new colony. He gives examples of such "queer" laws as those proposed to encourage matrimony, to make illegal the wearing of more than two different types of clothing, to change the names of the days of the week, and to fine at half a crown per incident anyone caught lying in conversation.[8]

Germantown

There are in fact two Germantowns: one in New York State and the other is now a suburb of Philadelphia.[9] As the name attests, these

---

7   Beidelman, pp 38-39
8   Beidelman, pp 171-72
9   That is to say, there are two Germantowns that we are interested in here; others exist:

areas were settled by Germans. Most of these people emigrated from the Palatinate, and for quite some time the name "Palatine" was used by the English to designate all Germans, regardless of their actual place of origin. Several other groups came from Alsace, Silesia, Holstein, Franconia, Baden, Nassau, and Württemberg. As noted above, religious and political warfare drove the Germans out of their homelands, but along with that was also the hardship of bad weather in the Old World.

> The unfavorable conditions in their homelands would probably not have induced the Palatines to leave if it had not been for the strong attractions of the New World. William Penn had visited western Germany and apparently influenced the dissidents who settled in Germantown in 1683. After Penn's visits there appeared brochures and books in which various writers sang the praises of the English colonies in North America. Two of these, both written by Lutherans and both widely circulated in Germany, were Daniel Falkner's *Curieuse Nachricht von Pensylvania* (1702)
> and Joshua Kocherthal's *Ausführlich und umständlicher Bericht von…Carolina* (1706)[10]

When the first Germans made their journey over to the New World, they were out numbered by Swedes, Finns, English, Welsh, and Scotch-Irish. Yet, by 1709 nearly 13,500 Germans tried to emigrate. Germantown, PA (or perhaps more accurately, Philadelphia as their actual port of entry) is the equivalent of "Plymouth Rock" for the first German peoples in America. This group consisted of 13 Mennonite families who sailed over on the *Concord*. The area that became Germantown was cut up into 14 divisions for the settlers. At the out-start, the Germans were so poor that the

---

[10] Germantown, Ohio, was founded by migrating Pennsylvania Germans in the early 19th Century; there are also Germantowns in Wisconsin, Maryland, Tennessee, and Illinois.
Nelson, p.23

settlement was know as "Armentown" (*armen* meaning "poor").[11] Eventually, this group established themselves, prospered, and the settlement became known as "Germantown." The next waves of settlers were not so fortunate, as all of the better pieces of land were taken and land costs driven up. Rents were also exorbitant; and a combination of these factors drove the newer arrivals out into what was then the frontier. The English used the Germans settlers, the *Iwwerbariyaleit*,[12] as a buffer between the English areas and the French and Indians. In 1737 another group of Mennonites came over on the *Charming Nancy*.

Earlier, in 1708, Lutheran minister Joshua Kocherthal brought over a small group, which later launched an avalanche of German migration. Between 1709 and 1710 Germans from Switzerland immigrated into the Palatine, and were then moved into Rotterdam, Holland, before being transported to London. Not all of these people made it to America. It was Queen Anne's wish that some remain in England, and that others were sent to Ireland in order to offset any Roman Catholic presence. It was for this reason that the Queen had sent back to the Continent most German Catholics, as she wanted the colonies to be predominantly Protestant. Catholics who wanted to immigrate to the Colonies had to find another way there, as they would not receive help from the English.

Approximately 2,000 Germans were sent to America, and settled about 80 miles up the Hudson River in New York: Newburgh, West Camp, Rhinebeck, and Germantown. The English had desired them to be in those areas in order to make tar and pitch for

---

11   Henry Muhlenberg, the "godfather" of American Lutheranism, found the state of Lutheran German immigrants deplorable. These were some shockingly poor people, who Muhlenberg described as *"some of them are growing up wild and have no further interest in churches or schools."*(Muhlenberg pp 18 – 19) This sad state of affairs was circa 1747. It was equally unfortunate for the Lutheran immigrants that they were subject to itinerant quack-ministers who posted as legitimate clergy and often charged for the Sacraments. Previous to Muhlenberg's arrival, there were legitimate Lutheran clergy among the Swedes and Finns, however, the German settlers were often far outside of their territories, and many of these could not serve them in anything but Swedish. The German Lutherans were in a desperate state for some one to preach to them and administer legitimate Sacraments in their mother tongue.

the Royal Navy, in addition to being the aforementioned human buffers. The English were not pleased when the bulk of these immigrants decided to move down into Pennsylvania. The bulk of German immigrants who arrived in the New World did so through Philadelphia, others (such as from New York) found their way into the Commonwealth. It was these primary settlers who came between the mid-to-late 17th Century and early 19th Century who are called the "Pennsylvania Dutch." Later German immigrants do not belong to this grouping and have not identified themselves with it. From Pennsylvania and New York, some immigrated to Canada and others to surrounding colonies such as the Carolinas, Virginia (West Virginia), Maryland, and Delaware.

Within a forty year period between 1725 and 1775 there were 321 ships that carried German immigrants to the Port of Philadelphia. In 1738 alone there were 16 ships that transported 3125 souls to Pennsylvania. Below is the breakdown.[13]

Name of Ship	Date of Arrival	No. of Passengers
Catherine	July 27	15
Winter Galley	Sept. 5	252
Glasgow	Sept. 9	349
Two Sisters	Sept, 9	110
Robert and Oliver	Sept. 11	320
Queen Elizabeth	Sept. 16	300
Thistle	Sept. 19	300
Nancy and Friendship	Sept. 20	187
Nancy	Sept. 20	150
Fox	Oct. 12	95
Davy	Oct. 25	180
Saint Andrew	Oct. 27	300
Bilender Thistle	Oct. 28	152
Elizabeth	Oct. 30	95
Charming Nancy	Nov. 9	200
Enterprise	Dec. 6	120

---

13   Diffenderffer, p 47

Is it Deutsch, Deitsch or Duits?

It seems that there has been some confusion concerning the term "Pennsylvania Dutch." As mentioned above, this term designates a number of very specific groups of people who arrived in America between the 1600's and the early 1800's. As we have seen, these were mainly Germans from the Palatine. However, as we have also seen there was also a much earlier Holland Dutch presence in the New World in addition to some who came over later on. Moreover, some of the Germans who came over to America were from Saxony; therefore, they were speakers of Low German dialects (*niederdeutsch*). These dialects are closely related to the Holland Dutch language. The Germans from the Palatinate were speakers of the **High German** (*hochdeutsch*) Pfälzisch dialect. Over the years of interaction between this dialect which acted as the foundation, English and those of other German dialects, the Pennsylvania Dutch language was born. This language, along with the original dialect, as it currently exists in the Palatine today, is called the *mudderschprooch*, or mother tongue. As late as the end of the 19th century, the dialect was still widely spoken as a first language (or with very little knowledge of English).[14]

In standard High German, the word for the language is *Deutsch*. In the dialect it is *Deitsch*. Meanwhile the Holland Dutch name for their language is *Duits*. In older forms of the Hollander language, the word is *Dietsch*. In the Low German dialects this latter word is the one used, as in the term *Plattdietsch*. Although it is not a totally clear cut matter, "Deitsch" is the typical southern German pronunciation of the word "Deutsch" and it is therefore not an indication this cultural group is "Dutch" in the sense of being Hollanders. Alternative to "Pennsylvania Dutch" is the term "Pennsylvania German."

---

14   *"There are still many thousands of people in Pennsylvania, who speak no other language. They are found in nearly all counties in Pennsylvania lying east and south of the Blue Mountain, and in some of the counties beyond..."* Beidelman, p 102

In this present work these two terms are used interchangeably. This has not always been the case, where some people have used the latter as a designation for High Germans who came *after* the early 19th Century (and who happened to find their way to the Commonwealth). Today, the more generic hyphenated "German-Americans" is used in this more general sense, and can cover a large number of people such as the Germans from Russia who immigrated to the Dakotas, or those who immigrated to Texas.

The German language was a bone of contention with the state up until the mid to late 20th century. There were various incentives and punishments doled out for incompliant Dutchmen and their children who persisted in speaking the mother tongue. For example, corporal punishment was used on schoolchildren who spoke German in public school. Prior to the First World War, there was a general prejudice against the PA Dutch. So much so, that a news writer with the *Public Ledger*, circa the 1870's or 1880's, wrote an editorial on the 'backwardness' of the Germans and that "We behold a picture of the dark ages" as they "came over here with their priests, a fragment of the middle ages, uncultured and uncultivated."[15] Next edition there was a rather humorous response in defense of the Germans.

> To be plain, if some of our crotchety, one-idead dyspeptic, thin cadaverous, New England brethren would emigrate to our German counties; follow for a generation or two, the open air life of our German farmers; and last of all marry into our vigorous anti-hypochondriacal German families, they would soon cease to die by scores of consumption, to complain that there were no longer any healthy women left...[16]

Once World War I arrived, a new wave of anti-German sentiment

15 Beidelman, pp 173-74
16 Ibid.

took hold, which is ironic considering how much of American culture is German. Sauerkraut became "liberty cabbage" and other such moves to de-Germanize the culture and marginalize the actual ethnic Germans themselves. Twenty years later WWII commences and places a further aura of suspicion upon German speakers. Today, in Pennsylvania, we can still occasionally hear comments "the dumb Dutch".

Overviews of the Church People and the Plain People

The Pennsylvania Dutch are mainly a Protestant people. The largest group is the Lutherans, followed by the Reformed Church. In the past when clergy where spread thinly, and congregations were clumped together out of necessity due to their rural locations, there were a number of mixed or "union" churches that were Lutheran-Reformed. Along with these two churches are the Moravians. Anabaptists represented by the various sects of Amish and Mennonites are not the majority among the "Dutch," but are over-represented, because of how they stand out from the rest of the surrounding society. Not all Anabaptists are "Old Order" and the more liberal Mennonites are indistinguishable from others in modern American society. The pietistic Church of the Brethren is also represented in the Anabaptist mix of people.

Traditionally, the smallest religious group among the Pennsylvania Dutch is Catholicism. Yet midway between the Lutherans and Anabaptists is "the Middle Way" practiced by the small Schweckfelder congregations who number less than the Catholics. During the 18th Century, there were smaller sects represented by individuals such as the mystical Pietist Conrad Beissel and the Ephrata Cloister. Although these utopian communards no longer exist, the German Seventh-Day Baptists represent the remnant of the Cloister, or to be more exact, the "householder" congregations that were satellites of the Cloister and its offshoots. The "Church" people are traditionally the members of the Lutheran, Reformed, and Moravian churches; these have also been known as the "Gay" or "Fancy" Dutch. Those few are far between Catholic Dutchmen would also go under these headings. Mennonites, Amish, Brethren, and Schwenkfelders are the "Plain" Dutch. However, in regard to the Schwenkfelders today, this designation does not apply.

The Lutherans

Of all the religious groups represented by the Pennsylvania Dutch, the Lutheran Church is the most ubiquitous. Early on there were various "union" churches that were Lutheran-Reformed that served both denominations. As previously mentioned, Lutheranism, in one form or another, has been in North America almost since the beginning of European settlement. In the area that was to become Pennsylvania, this presence came in the form of Swedish and Finnish immigrants. Afterwards the Germans came, and it was not until their coming that the Lutheran Church found a solid foundation through the efforts of Henry Melchior Muhlenberg. Previous to Muhlenberg, the widely spread Lutheran Christians were mainly pastorless, and were sometimes ill served by itinerate lay preachers.

The primary split between Lutherans and the Catholic Church revolve around the doctrine of justification before God. Justification is by grace (*Sola Gratia*), faith (*Sola Fide*), and Christ alone (*Solus Christus*). Good works do not satisfy God, as even when we are at our best we are still quite shabby when compared to God's goodness and justice. Yet good works do hold a place in the life of a Lutheran, for they are the fruit of faith. Incidentally, Martin Luther did not have any intentions of creating a new church – it was his desire to reform the one that already existed. He was also opposed to such labels as "Lutheran," believing that a Church ought to be named after Christ.

Amongst Lutherans, the Bible is divinely inspired and is the source of all spiritual knowledge (*Sola Scriptura*). *The Book of Concord* (1580) has ten treatises with explanation of Scripture; also included are the Ecumenical Creeds, and seven creedal statements on Reformation theology. Although Lutherans do not accept the Catholic belief in transubstantiation, they do accept the Real Presence: that Jesus Christ is indeed present within and under the Eucharistic elements. Some churches differ in their approach to liturgy. Many place great importance on the liturgical worship service, whereas others place the importance of the pulpit ahead of the altar. Reformed churches see the communion as symbolic, which explains the minimization of the Lord's Supper. However, Lutherans do accept that the communion is more than a mere memorial, regardless of the emphasis on pulpit or altar.

The Pennsylvania Ministerium

This was the first real Lutheran church body in North America. It was officially known as The Evangelical Ministerium of North America, but was changed to The Evangelical Lutheran Ministerium of Pennsylvania and Adjacent States in 1792. In 1918 the Ministerium was succeeded by the United Lutheran Church in America. The ULCA was then succeeded by the Lutheran Church in America (1962), and reorganized yet again in 1988 as the Evangelical Lutheran Church in America (ELCA). The Lutheran Church exists in synod form, and there are several of these. Currently, the Wisconsin Synod and the Missouri Synod represent a more conservative Lutheranism in America. Women are able to be ordained in the ELCA, whereas in the Missouri Synod, they are not.

The Reformed

Among the Pennsylvania Dutch, the Reformed church accounted for nearly half of the religious congregations. The Reformed churches were structured like Presbyterian congregations and were adherents of the Heidelberg Catechism (1563), the Belgic

Conference (1566), and the Canons of Dortrecht (1619). Huldrych Zwingli (b. 1484 – d. 1531) was a contemporary of Martin Luther and a fellow initiator of the Reformation. Like Luther, Zwingli believed that a strong government was needed to implement the reforms sought and to enforce them since Rome's central authority was now out of the way. Papal authority was now superseded by the authority of councils and princes for the Reformed and Lutheran churches.[1] In the Reformed Church the Eucharist was of symbolic value only, and infant baptism was affirmed *via* the church-state union. The Anabaptists, who did not believe in the value of infant baptism, quickly became anathema to the Reformed states and provinces. However, the Reformed Church saw baptism as simply a covenantal sign and not having any further virtue beyond that.

Holland Dutch Reformed minister Paul van Vlecq established a Reformed congregation at Skippack, Pennsylvania in 1710. Layman Conrad Templeman conducted services in Lancaster County where he services seven congregations. In 1727 the ordained minister George Michael Weiss arrived in Philadelphia to serve the Reformed congregations there. The American congregations looked to Holland for authority. The Classis of Amsterdam sent Michael Schlatter to America in order to organize a synod. On 24 September, 1747, the Coetus of the Reformed Ministerium of the Congregations of Pennsylvania was born. In Carlisle, Pennsylvania, the German Reformed Seminary was established in 1825; it was then moved to Lancaster in 1871 to become the Lancaster Theological Seminary. Franklin College (1787) merged with German Reformed Marshall College in 1853 to create Franklin and Marshall College.

The mid-19th century saw the development of the Mercersberg Movement which attempted to create a more altar-centered worship within the Reformed churches in order to unify congregants and to resist sectarianism. Pietism and revivalism were something of a thorn in the side of the Reformed Church; the latter especially was called "inauthentic." Reformed minister Philip William Otterbein

---

[1]   Nolt pp 8-10

was also a Pietist and founded the United Brethren Church, which was later merged into the United Methodist Church. The Reformed Church affirmed the supremacy of Scripture, the absolute sovereignty of divine grace, and radical moral reform. The Mercersberg Movement eventually lead to a schism; the dissenting body that rejected the altar-centered liturgical movement became the "Old Reformed" and founded Ursinus College in 1870.

The earlier Reformed churches were gradually merged into larger bodies such as The Evangelical and Reformed Church of 1934, which in turn was merged with the Congregational Christian Churches in 1957 to form the United Church of Christ (UCC). The UCC recognizes two sacraments being baptism and communion. It accepts the Apostles' Creed, Nicene Creed, the Heidelberg Catechism, Luther's Small Catechism, the Kansas City Statement of Faith (1913), the Evangelical Catechism (1927), and the Statement of Faith of the UCC (1959). The present-day UCC is noted for its liberal/progressive stances on a variety of social issues, but individual congregations have their own authority and may differ from the national body.[2]

The Catholics

The story of Roman Catholicism in Colonial America is unfortunately not an extensive one. Prior to the American Revolution, anti-Catholic sentiment kept their numbers low in the Colonies. During the exodus from their homelands 13,000 souls made their way to England from Rotterdam. Queen Anne returned 2,207 of them back to the Continent, all Roman Catholics.[3] The census of 1757 counted 1,365 Catholics in Pennsylvania out of population of 200,000 + colonists.[4] Of that number of Catholics, only 949 were German.

---

2   www.ucc.org
3   Stoudt, p. 31
4   John T. Ellis, *Catholics in Colonial America*, 1965.

Nineteenth century Pennsylvania German historian William Beidelman paints a better picture of the Roman Catholics' situation.

> Before the Revolution many German Catholics had settled in Pennsylvania, and they were prompt in enlisting on the side of freedom, and their blood mingled with their Protestant compatriots on many a sanguinary field of the Revolution.
>
> In German Catholic emigration to America, may be found an argument showing that the direct cause of the great exodus of Germans to America was not altogether the result of persecution, but rather the desire to get away from the incessant European wars and its desolations. It was not an unusual thing during the later years of the German emigration, for the Protestant and the Catholic to cross the ocean in the same ship, and upon their arrival settle in the same neighborhood...[5]

This sentiment does have some backing as demonstrated by Steven Nolt's research.

> Anti-Catholicism long had been a staple of American Protestant thought, thought Pennsylvania German Protestant and German-American Catholic relations were not always as antagonistic as they would become after 1817. During the late eighteenth and early nineteenth centuries, in fact, as German-speaking Pennsylvania Catholics asserted their identity against an English hierarchy, they evinced sympathy from their Pennsylvania German Protestant neighbors, some of whom assisted

---

5   Beidelman, p 97

Philadelphia German Catholics in constructing their own church building in 1789.[6]

The Catholic Church began to make roots for itself in Colonial Pennsylvania: at St. Paul's Mission, Goshenhoppen, was a 500 acre Jesuit farm, and St. Francis Regis Mission at Conewago.[7] Among the Pennsylvania Germans, Catholics were rare, but they did exist. German Catholics who wanted passage to the New World often had to make their own arrangements. Those who could not afford the passage, just as with their Protestant brethren, often opted for indentured servitude. Such a German Catholic was Braucher, John George Hohman, whose *The Long Lost Friend* has been consistently in print since 1820 and is the archetypal Pow-Wow manual. Despite the prejudice surrounding Catholicism, Pennsylvania was a relative haven of religious liberty compared to the repressiveness experienced in other colonies. Yet, for all of William Penn's tolerance, after 1700, Catholics experienced restrictions in their social and political participation. The root of anti-Catholicism has been the fear of the Papacy as a foreign power, and the suspicion that Catholics would have divided loyalties.

Although not Pennsylvania Germans, the later German immigrants from Russia were (and are) largely Roman Catholics. At around the same time that the Palatines were leaving the Old World, many other Germans were leaving for Russia at the invitation of Czarina Catherine II to relocate along the Volga River (1764 – 1767). Later on more relocated to the Ukraine, the Crimean Peninsula and Bessarabia. With the coming of the 19th century, the Russian government made several and increasing attempts at Russification of the Germans. Most of the preferential rights enjoyed by the settlers were removed by Czar Alexander II, despite the earlier Czarina's promise that these rights would pass "to their descendants forever."[8]

6   Nolt, p 112
7   Joseph L. J. Kirlin, *Catholicity in Philadelphia*, 1909.
8   This information can be found at http://library.ndsu.edu/grhc. North Dakota State University's Germans from Russia Heritage Collection is a wonderful resource to learn more

"Forever" was quite a short time indeed for the Germans. As a result of these pressures, many left for the United States (Colorado, Kansas, Nebraska, and North Dakota) and Western Canada.

The Moravians

Count Nikolaus von Zinzendorf und Pottendorf – born in Dresden, 26 May 1700 (d. 1760). It is not possible to discuss the Moravian Church in America without first making a brief overview of Count Zinzendorf. This highly motivated, intelligent, and temperamental bishop helped to root the Moravian community in Pennsylvania, and is currently on the Evangelical Lutheran Church's Calendar of Saints (ELCA). Zinzendorf grew up in a deeply religious household; both parents were Pietists and moved their family from Austria after the Reformation.

Dissatisfied with Lutheran orthodoxy, Zinzendorf desired a free association of Christians that would have no state connections. The Count was deeply influenced by the Bohemian Brethren (Moravians) when he gave them asylum on his estate of Berthelsdorf in Saxony during the early to mid 1700's. There, the settlers established the village of Herrnhut. For his particular religiosity, Zinzendorf was banished from Saxony in 1736, which was rescinded in 1749.

He was consecrated a bishop on 20 May, 1737. His efforts in Pennsylvania were directed towards the creation of a new universalist Christian order where all spiritually illuminated ("awakened") people would come together under Christ the Lamb. August Gottlieb Spanenberg (b. 1704 – d. 1792), a member of the Associated Brethren of the Skippack[9], returned to Germany and informed Zinzendorf that the ground in Pennsylvania was fertile for great spiritual work and conversions. In 1739 Zinzendorf conferred with the Moravian Synod in Gotha regarding his ideas

---

about these fascinating people. They have a great set of catalogues for educational materials on the Germans from Russia: cookbooks, music, history books, etc. They can also be reached at P.O. Box 5599, Fargo, ND 58105-5599.

9   He was later a Moravian bishop who led a survey party to North Carolina.

for a mission in Pennsylvania. The Count renounced his rank when coming to the Colonies. Brother Ludwig, as he was known, would find only frustration to his plans in Pennsylvania.

> Strong personalities clashed in Pennsylvania: Conrad Beissel with his nihilist, quietist mysticism, who was meeting his call and building his own fellowship along the Conestoga; Johann Adam Gruber – *Ein Geringer* – who had led the awakenings in southern Germany during the 1710s and was a fully charismatic personality; and Count Nicholas von Zinzendorf, imperious, commanding, dedicated, devout, and stubbornly loyal to his "plan" for Pennsylvania. In the end the failure may have come from this clash of personalities.[10]

Be this as it may have been, Zinzendorf was successful at planting the Moravian Church in Pennsylvania, with Bethlehem and Nazareth as its two main settlements. Truly, Brother Ludwig was an inspired man; along with his moves to organize Christian communities, he also possessed a strong mysticism. Just as with the earlier mystics of the Catholic Church, Zinzendorf recommended devotion to the Wounds of Christ, and visualization of these in prayer. Some have found his visualizations and devotions to be a bit 'graphic'. More unsettling to those not familiar with this sort of mysticism was his belief that sexual intercourse was a transcendent act which foreshadows the union of the soul with Christ.

What of the Moravian Church itself? Sixty years prior to Luther's reforms was the formation of the Unitas Fratrum (Unity of Brethren), being the earliest name of the Moravian Church in Bohemia and Moravia, now the Czech Republic. Prior to its organization was the life of reformer Jan Hus (b. 1369 – d. 1415), rector of the University in Prague. Hus wanted reform in many

10   Stoudt, pp 54-55

of the practices of the Roman Catholic clergy. He was accused of heresy and burned at the stake.

After the persecutions of the 16th and 17th centuries, Count von Zinzendorf grew into the role of being one of the Moravian Church's greatest patrons in the 18th century. The first attempt at settlement started in Georgia (1735), but fizzled out after only five years. Bethlehem (1741) was the next attempt at settlement, which proved fruitful. A sister settlement in North Carolina was created at what is now known as Winston-Salem.

The motto of the Moravian Church is "In essentials, unity; in nonessentials, liberty; and in all things, love." The Church recognizes two sacraments: Trinitarian baptism of infants and adults, and communion. With regard to the elements of the communion, the Moravian Church does not try to analyze exactly how Christ's presence is manifested in these.[11]

The Amish and the Mennonites

Now we come to address the two groups that are not only conflated with one another, but are believed *to be* the Pennsylvania Dutch in their entirety by those on the outside. Amish and Old Order Mennonites have been the objects of a large tourist industry that has glommed onto these quiet Christians. Their 'quaint' clothing, horse drawn buggies, and their lives without electricity have caught the imaginations of the people who go to 'see' them (as if they were zoo exhibits). In part, this fascination may have to do with our own disenchantment with "modern" life and its incessant "progress". We recognize older models of community and family that we have long lost, which they have mysteriously preserved, against the odds.

For some of us, that loss makes us heart sick, an extreme case of *heemweh*,[12] that seemingly only a time-machine could cure. Then,

---

11   www.moravian.org
12   Pennsylvania German for "homesickness".

of course, there are those who travel around "Dutch Country" just to be rude and gawk. It must be pointed out, however, that the Plain People are not entirely adverse to this, as it draws in revenue for those businesses owned by Mennonites. The quilting 'industry' alone draws in a good amount of tourist traffic.

The story of the Anabaptism, the religious grouping to which the Amish and Mennonites belong, is quite involved. Numerous books of varying degrees of scholarliness have been devoted to the study of Anabaptists. To make this history fit within the short confines of this book, a good deal of abridgement and truncation is needed. Please look to the bibliography at the back of this work to find sources of greater detail.

Anabaptism was 'born' in Zurich, Switzerland. During the time of the Reformation, there were some groups of people who felt that the Reforms did not go far enough. Although the political power of the Vatican was cancelled out by those areas of Europe that reformed, the power vacuum was filled in by local counsils and nobility. More than ever the State was married to the Church as a result. Certain groups among the "radically" reformed wanted to do away with all Church-State unions and desired the Church to be free of all political involvement.

On 21 January, 1525, a group of individuals met together in defiance of the Zurich Counsil in order to rebaptize one another. Part of the "radical" agenda was the belief that infant baptism was useless. Only when one was old enough to make an informed, conscious decision to follow Christ, did baptism have any meaning. Therefore, the belief of these dissenters was that the act of baptism imparted no special grace on its own as a sacrament without the conscience directly engaged. The word "Anabaptism" literally means "second baptism". Technically, then, only one who has been baptized twice could literally be known as "Anabaptist". Yet, to this day, despite the fact that most "Anabaptists" are only baptized once in their lifetime are still refered to by this name.

Baptism during this era was not only an induction into the Church membership, but also a means to citizenship. To be rebaptized as an adult, or to not have one's children baptized, were subversive acts. As a result, Anabaptists were relentlessly pursued and persecuted at every turn. At first the measures were simply coercive: jail time, fines, exile, and threats. Later on in the next century, the sanctions escalated to torture, beheading, burning at the stake, and being sold into slavery. Special "Anabaptist hunters" were used by some city-states at that time in order to root out Anabaptism. Despite these horrors, the religious movement spread from Switzerland into southern Germany, northern Germany, the Alsace, the Austrian Tyrol, Moravia, and Holland.

The Anabaptists became known as "Mennonites" through the conversion of the Dutch Catholic priest Menno Simons (b. 1496 – d. 1561). Simons was quite a prolific writer, and sympathized with the Anabaptists for some time before converting in 1536. Simons came onto the 'scene' in time to do 'damage control' for Anabaptism after the rebellion of the non-pacifist branch of the Church in Münster, 1534. For those who know the beliefs and natures of Anabaptists, the Münster episode might come as a bit of a shock. In belief and practice most practitioners were pacifists. The northern German Anabaptists had different ideas, and took the city in a violent uprising. However, the Protestants and Catholics raised a joint army and took the city back. The post-Münster atmosphere was ill favored for the Anabaptists, and Simons did what he could to reverse their tarnished image.

Even among their enemies, the Anabaptists were known for their martyrdom and their gentleness. Thielman J. van Braght detailed the martyrdom and sufferings of this people in his mammoth *The Bloody Theater; or Martyrs Mirror of the Defenseless Christians*, 1660. With the engravings of Mennonite artist Jan Luyken, this book is a gruesome testimony to their suffering. Dioletian's persecutions could not have been any worse than what these Christians endured.

From their travail also came the *Ausbund*, which was the Mennonite hymnal until 1800, but is still in use by the Amish today. In 1535 a group was captured on the Barvarian border and held prisoner for five years in Passau castle. The original 53 hymns were composed during their time spent there. By 1564 the hymns were printed in book form. Unlike most hymnals, there are no music notes. All of the musical settings for these hymns have been handed down orally through the centuries.

Eventually, the movement needed some codification and structure. On the Swiss-German border in Schleitheim a group met to unify their beliefs and practices. The codifying of belief during this meeting is known as the Schleitheim Confession. In 1632, another meeting to further discuss the use of "shunning" in church discipline took place in Dort, Holland; the result being known as the Dortrecht Confession.

"Shunning" is perhaps one of the more sensational aspects of Anabaptist life for the non-Anabaptist. In German, this discipline is called *meidung*. In essence this is excommunication, where the offending member is literally not allowed to take part in communion, which for Mennonites took place only once a year. Wrapped up in meidung was the question of the degrees of social ostracism that were permissible. Much agonizing took place of this issue and eventually led to the schism that created the Amish. The purpose of the meidung was not (and is not) "hate". By excommunicating a church member it was hoped that this discipline would manifest in the reform of the individual. For the Anabaptists, this was a critical thing: to be *in* the world, but not *of* it. By breaking church discipline and order, one ejects himself from community by being *of* the world. This is the real reason for the rejection of electricity, telephones, and modern conveniences among the Old Order Mennonites and the Amish. Electrical power lines and telephones connect a person to dependence on the outer world (of the worldly), and the modern conveniences lead to sloth and worldly behavior.

Jakob Ammann (b. circa 1656 – d. circa 1730) was a Swiss Mennonite elder who was the most stringent in his interpretation of the meidung. The persecutions of the Anabaptists pressed some families to leave the movement and rejoin one of the state churches. These people, along with those who were favorably disposed to the Mennonites were known as "Half-Anabaptists" or the "True-Hearted". The True-Hearted would help the Mennonites whenever possible, intervening on their behalf with the authorities. Ammann was opposed to any reliance on these individuals as they were part "of the world" and outside of the genuine Church, as he saw it. It was his conviction that God would see them through any situation and were in no need of outside intervention. This was linked to the larger issue of laxness in Church discipline among the faithful, and it was to the end of enforcing this discipline that Ammann pushed the issue of a more stringent meidung. Ammann mercilessly hounded elder Hans Reist for a 'showdown' regarding these issues, and caused no end of ill feelings; this was the source of the split between those who agreed with Ammann and the mainstream Mennonites. The former then became know as the "Amish".

Jumping ahead, as noted earlier, the Mennonites settled Germantown in the late 17th century. From Pennsylvania, the Amish and Old Order Mennonites have spread to other states in the Union: principly in Ohio, Indiana, and Illinois; although, there are also settlements in other states such as Delaware, Tennessee, Georgia, Florida, Iowa, Kansas, Texas, Minnesota, Montana, Missouri, New York, Virginia, Wisonsin, Kentucky, Maryland, North Carolina, Michigan, and Oklahoma. Outside of the U.S., they can also be found in Ontario. As of 1991, there were also congregations in Costa Rica, El Salvador, and Paraguay.[13]

Over the past 200 plus years, the Amish and Mennonite Churches have split into many different branches. As previously remarked, the non-Old Order Mennonites are practically indistinguishable

13   Nolt, 1992, p 281

from the non-Mennonites around them; whereas the Old Order people keep to their plain dress and various limitations on certain devices and conveniences.

The Brethren

There are actually several denominations that exist under the umbrella of "Brethren." All of these emerged out the Pietism of the 17th century under the Schwarzenau German Baptist Brethren founded by Alexander Mack (b. 1679 – d. 1735) in Schwarzenau, Germany. Like many radical Protestants of that era, they were under intense pressure in their homeland and left for Holland to escape the persecution. Peter Becker brought the first group of Brethren to Pennsylvania in 1719, who later founded the first congregation in Germantown on Christmas Day, 1723. In 1729 nearly forty other families immigrated to Pennsylvania.

The River Brethren, under the leadership of Jacob and John Engle, were baptizing people in the Susquehanna River in 1770. Martin Boehm, the initial leader of this sect, was later bishop of the Church of United Brethren in Christ.

Nicknamed by their neighbors "Dunkers"[14] or "Dunkards" after their manner of baptismal practices, they are Baptists, yet not in the usual sense.[15]

The hallmark beliefs that define the Brethren are trine immersion baptism of adults, foot washing, and a communion service/dinner, which is sometimes referred to as a *Love Feast*. They reject infant baptism, and they believe in universal salvation, anointing with oil, pacifism, and subscribe to the inerrancy of the New Testament

---

[14]   This is an Anglicization of the German verb *tunken* (to dip) – and, of course, our English word "dunk" comes from the German.

[15]   The first schism among the German Baptists was a disagreement about the Sabbath. Conrad Beissel and his followers broke company with the other Brethren over this issue and formed the monastic society at Ephrata. The householder congregations of the Seventh-Day Brethren eventually formed the core of the later German Seventh-Day Baptists. This latter denomination considers itself fully Baptist while not being in the English Conference.

in all matter of faith. Much like the Mennonites and the Amish, they are among the Plain People. The present day Church of the Brethren members are often indistinguishable from the rest of society, as with non-Old Order Mennonites. The Old German Baptist Brethren are an example of an Old Order group among the present day Brethren.

As mentioned above there are currently many different Brethren denominations, and six of these meet under the Brethren World Assembly: Church of the Brethren, Dunker Brethren, Fellowship of Grace Brethren Churches, The Brethren Church, Old German Baptist Brethren, and the Conservative Grace Brethren Churches, International. This Assembly is a relatively recent development of the early 1990's. Other Brethren groups include the Brethren in Christ, Old Order River Brethren, the Calvary Holiness Church, and the United Zion Church.

The Schwenkfelders

The Confessors of the Glory Christ – the followers of the Silesian nobleman Caspar Schwenkfeld von Ossig (b. 1489 – d. 1561). During the fervor and excitement of the Reformation, thinkers such as Schwenkfeld were attempting to formulate different paths back to primitive Christianity, or at the very least, an elemental Christianity without any of the "bells and whistles" associated with either Lutheranism (and the Catholicism before it) or the Reformed Church. These two churches, along with the Catholic Church, had state support and were the source of much persecution of these smaller sects. In 1518 Schwenkfeld had a "visitation from God" and was passionate for the recovery of the Christian fellowship of all believers in Christ.

Count Zinzendorf gave refuge to the followers of Schwenkfeld on his estate in 1726. However, they feared for their safety after the death of the Elector of Saxony in 1733, and came to Pennsylvania in 1734. Prior to this there was an earlier group that came to Philadelphia three years earlier. The 1734 group arrived in Philadelphia on 22 September; on the 23rd they made their oath to the Crown, and on the 24th they held a day of thanksgiving, the *Gedächtnestag*, which has been celebrated by the Schwenkfelders ever since.

It was not Schwenkfeld's desire to create a new church, but to make a reformation by the "Middle Way". This particular path "stressed the supremacy of the spirit over the letter and the spirituality of the Christian religion over literalism and externalism."[16] He was deeply concerned that the spirit of the Faith was being buried underneath a blanket of "intolerant orthodoxy." Originally the sect was Plain, but the present church does not require that lifestyle.

Between 1907 and 1961 his works were gathered together in the *Corpus Schwenkfeldianorum*. Early individual works include Christopher Schulz's *Compendium of Dogmatic Theology*, which existed only in manuscript form until 1836; and the 1762 hymnal *Neu-Eingerichtetes Gesang-Buch*, published by Christopher Saur.

The year 1782 saw the formation of the Society of Schwenkfelders, but it was not until 1909 that they incorporated into a church organization. At present there are only five Schwenkfelder churches, in addition to one retirement home and a school. The Apostles' Creed is the foundation of their belief; they practice open communion, which is symbolic in nature – as it is in many Protestant churches.

---

16   www.centralschwenkfelder.com/history.htm

2: An Overview of Bruacherei Practice

It has been said by Christ that His true followers would do the same things and still greater ones; but it would be difficult to find at present one Christian minister who can do anything Christ did. But if any one who is not a man-made minister comes and cures the sick by the power of Christ acting through him, they call him a sorcerer and a child of the devil and are willing to burn him upon the stake. – Paracelsus (p. 30 *The Life of Phillipus Theophrastus Bombast of Hohenheim*)

But when the Pharisees heard *it*, they said, "This *fellow* doth not cast out devils, but by Beelzebub the prince of devils." And Jesus knew their thoughts and said unto them, "Every kingdom divided against itself is brought to desolation; and every city or house divided against itself shall not stand: and if Satan cast out Satan, he is divided against himself; how shall then his kingdom stand? And if I by Beelzebub cast out devils, by whom do your children cast *them* out? Therefore they shall be your judges. But if I cast out devils by the Spirit of God, then the kingdom of God is come unto you."
Matthew 12:24-28 KJV

My grandmother was a devout and practicing Lutheran. Her Lutheran Book of Worship, in the German language, lies on a shelf in my study. But grandmother was also what the Pennsylvania Dutch call a "Pow-Wow" doctor. She was a practitioner of folk medicine. I can decide that she was a

> superstitious person who was a heretical Lutheran, or I can observe that her folk medicine and her Lutheranism were both part of her religiousness, perhaps even part of her Christianity. – Richard E. Wentz, *Pennsylvania Dutch Folk Spirituality*, p.17

𝕾ome context

THE PROBLEM OF BRUACHEREI – actually, Bruacherei has several problems and they are **all** *contextual*. Let's first define what is meant here by the word 'problem.' A thing can be perfectly good and also perfectly problematic when it is juxtaposed to seemingly contradictory positions, creating a "cognitive dissonance" for those who entertain more than one view of the situation. This is Bruacherei's situation. It has been praised as the work of the Holy Ghost and equally condemned as the work of the devil. Within Pennsylvania German culture there are these two strains of thought that stem from a rigid "Churchianity"[1] on the one hand and a true folk-understanding and practice of Christianity on the other. The Pennsylvania Dutch are not unique in this. Mexican, Spanish, Italian, Portuguese, Irish and Polish Catholics find themselves in this bind as well; Serbian, Greek and Russian (etc.) Orthodox are in the same boat. If any of these people practice a folk medicine and folk Christianity alongside of their church attendance, they are peas in the same pod. Richard Wentz' recollection of his grandmother (quoted above) poignantly demonstrates this division in comprehending a practice such as Bruacherei. The 'problem,' it must be pointed out, is not on the end of the Bruacher, but from the vantage point of one looking 'in' from the outside. That Wentz' grandmother had no trouble squaring her orthodox Lutheranism with her Pow-Wow is quite clear; Wentz, however, is not without understanding when he analyses that:

---

1   I wish to apologies for the use of this rather polemical term. It is not a condemnation of mainstream Christianity, but of a rigidness of spirit that all too unfortunately infects our potentially efficacious practice of the Christian religion.

> An interest in folk spirituality emerges from the realization that all of us are involved in what seems to be extra-ecclesial religion. We discover that there are spiritual resources which do not always conform to what synods, councils and systematic theologians define and prescribe as normative. There are things that we think, do and believe that are not officially religious, yet may in many instances have been hundreds, even thousands, of years in the making.[2]

Another layer in the heap of 'issues' is the contention of some who would take those "even thousands" of years and attempt to redefine Bruacherei as a purely heathen practice that (unfortunate by their accounts) had a light sprinkling of Jesus powdering the top of it in order to make the modality socially acceptable. They claim that the Jesus 'powder' can be blown or dusted off the top to reveal the glory of a pre-Christian method of healing. Elsewhere in *The Red Church* copious mentions are made of Bruacherei's pre-Christian roots. Nothing emerges from a vacuum. Every art, craft and science of the human race predates the Christian era. Yet, we do not refer to architecture, medicine, carpentry, masonry, farming, etc. as *de facto* heathen provinces. It is an error to confuse a sincerely held folk Christianity, which in its non-specifically Christian components *may* ante-date the religion, with genuine heathenism.

In the minds of clergy who have struggled with folk spirituality, charges of paganism (or worse) have sometimes been leveled – especially among the charismatic evangelical believers today who are still reeling from the aftershocks and paranoia of the "Satanic Panic" of the 1980's. However, it is equally true that more than a few Bruachers of yesteryear were also clergy of the Lutheran, Reformed and Anabaptist (and Pietistic) churches. A bone of contention with folk spirituality among clergy can be called the problem of

---

[2] Wentz, p. 11

"unofficial grace;" that is, accessing God's creative energies without the sanction or medium of official clergy.

A minister or priest is one who (in theory at least) has Apostolic Succession and is charged via The Great Commission[3] to heal, bless nd exorcize. An old woman living up in the hills dispensing herbs and the grace of the Holy Ghost does not 'count' by this line of thinking.[4] She is thus a "Witch" by her unofficial mediumship of Christ's healing Work. That is a shame and a travesty, especially when one understands what constitutes genuine *hexerei* (see Chapter 3). On the other hand, it is also a species of cultural violence when the paganistically-inclined wish to forcefully redefine *what* that old lady was doing up in her little woodland cottage. Then, of course, there is the argument of whether this "Commission" extends only to those with succession, or extends to all believers. For clergy with an ax to grind, this is perhaps the crux of their protest. Bruacherin Ruth Weil Kusler, describes in her book, how her mother, Katherine, had to modify her charm-prayers as her work spooked the local North Dakotan ministers.

> ...they harassed Katherine for her work. But she continued helping people when needed and at times, risked her life to save others. After a time, even though she didn't understand how healing and praying to God could be wrong, Katherine learned to do things differently. She changed the chants to sound more like prayers...[5]

A rather cynical note can be struck by speculating that their complaints hinged upon an unconscious envy that someone like

---

[3] Mark 16:14-18; Matthew 28:16-20; Luke 24:44-49

[4] Such is the case with "Mountain Mary" (Maria Jungin) of Oley, who during the American Revolution, was a source of Christian mercy, healing and comfort to all who came to her in need. She has been seen as a "saint," canonized such by the unofficial medium of the people who loved her. Thus is the way of folk Christianity.

[5] Kusler p.8

Katherine could fulfill the *healing mission of Christ*, while they (in all likelihood) could not.

The roots of Bruacherei are indeed quite long, some of which can be traced to pre-Christian Germanic heathenism.[6] Other roots are equally pre-Christian and stem from older forms of Judaism and the many strains of religion and medicine of the Roman Empire. Without overreaching too much, the sometimes blurry lines between what constituted a "Germanic" tribe versus a "Celtic" tribe or a "Slavic" tribe, make it quite possible that there are Slavic and Celtic pre-Christian elements in Bruacherei. The truly unique thing about Bruacherei is that it is a wholly Germanic synthesis of all these cultural strains. Anyone looking for a purely heathen Germanic healing-way *via* Bruacherei is in for a major disappointment. To take Bruacherei and reshape in this manner is to make a *brand-new* practice out of it. Therefore, it would no longer be Bruacherei as it has been practiced for nearly 900 years and most certainly not as it has been practiced for the past two centuries in America. Whatever the old heathen Germanic tribes were practicing prior to Christianization are now only dim memories – for good or ill.[7]

[6] Incidentally, the word "heathen" used throughout this book is **not** employed in its pejorative sense. In fact, this is the description of choice among practitioners of *Asatru* and *Vanatru*, who are the careful reconstructionists of pre-Christian Germanic religion. This author, although Christian, has respect for the folks who have gone through the laborious effort of trying to reconstruct the ways of their ancestors. There is currently a group of individuals who are trying to do this sort of reconstruction via the Pennsylvania Dutch identity, which they call *Urglaawe* (that is, "primal belief"). This is an interesting development, but the Pennsylvania Dutch were never heathens as they did not exist as a unique ethnic group until the different German ethnicities mixed after coming to early America. Perhaps in *Urglaawe* they are looking for the heathen roots of Southern Germans, but that still places us well outside of these Germans *as* the PA Dutch. As with braucherei itself, PA Dutch culture has many threads within it, some of which are heathen, but other which are not – but all of which have been molded and shaped into a unique culture under various strains of the Christian religion for hundreds of years. It is this author's opinion that to extract a pure heathenism or remake one out of this culture is to unravel the ball of twine.

[7] As can be seen in the diagram entitled "The Historical Threads of Bruacherei", it has been 1,600 + years since the beginning of Germanic Christianization. That is a long time. In terms of a real, solid grasp on the passage of time, most people today can possibly get their minds around a century or two of human history with all of its nuances, changes, etc. Beyond that, without the help of the written word and oral tradition, everything beyond that becomes very fuzzy. Today, where we are further separated from the sorts of lives our great-grandparents lived than previous generations, even a century can seem an awfully long time. Sixteen centuries of not engaging in a paleoheathen life-style or religious observance is more than enough time to make the gulf between now and then insurmountable for the full recovery of any whole "ur" tradition.

Here we come to the "Merseburg Incantations," so-called as they were housed in the library of the cathedral chapter of Merseburg. Discovered in 1841 by Georg Waitz in a theological manuscript from Fulda written *circa* the 9th or 10th centuries, these charms are the closest things we have to seemingly genuine pre-Christian charms. However, John Jeep, the editor of *Medieval Germany: An Encyclopedia* makes the following comment regarding these charms:

> Since the charms are recorded in a theological manuscript, most likely by a monk and are followed by a liturgical prayer, even the question of whether or not they are pagan has been disputed by some modern critics. Indeed, it would be more accurate to say that the charms are not clearly Christian, than to state that they are pagan.[8]

Here are the two charms recorded in the Jeep collection. The first is a charm to liberate prisoners and the second is to heal a horse's sprained hoof. The charms were written in Old High German. The first entries are in that tongue, followed by an English translation. The "pipes" between the stanzas are placed here in order to preserve the original meter while conserving space.

> *Liberation of prisoners*
> Eiris sazun idisi | sazun hera duoder. | suma hapt heptidun, | suma heri lezidun, | suma clubodun | umbi cuoniouuidi: | insprinc haptbandun, | inuar uigandun! H.[9]
>
> Once the Idisi set forth, | to this place and that. | Some fastened fetters, | Some hindered the horde, Some loosed the bonds | from the brave: | Leap forth from the fetters, | escape from the foes.

---

8 Jeep p. 113
9 Jeep p. 112

Horse cure
Phol ende uuodan | uuorun zi holza. | du uuart demo balderes uolon | sin uuoz birenkit. | thu biguol en sinthgunt, | sunna era suister; | thu biguol en friia, | uolla era suister; | thu biguol en uuodan, | so he uuola conda: | sose benrenki, | sose bluotrenki, | sose lidirenki: | ben zi bena, | bluot zi bluoda, lid zi geliden, | sose gelimida sin.[10]

Phol and Odin | rode into the woods, | There Balder's foal | sprained its foot. | It was charmed by Sinthgunt, | (so did) her sister Sunna. | It was charmed by Frija, | (so did) her sister Volla. | It was charmed by Odin, | as he well knew how: | Bone-sprain, | like blood-sprain, | Like limb-sprain: Bone to bone, | blood to blood, | Limb to limb, | As though they were glued.

If a charm from a 19th century Pow-Wow book is placed along side of either of these charms, it can be seen that they are not a million miles apart from one another. Thoroughly Christian charms of the same period as the above incantations, display the same meter and rhyming patterns. Truly, the English translations of the old Pow-Wow manuals lose the original rhymes and puns contained in the German copies. The narrative quality of the second charm is quite interesting, especially when compared to the standard inflammation charms that begin by describing a journey though a "red wood," or "red woodland," or a "red wald." There are other examples, of course, that describe journeys "over the land" or "across the sea."

The foregoing is only the beginning of Bruacherei's contextual issues. Regarding those who wish to heathenize Bruache practice, the tendency to the same is linked directly to a much larger issue being the increasing secularization of society. More than perhaps at any other point in past 20 centuries of Western Civilization, today

10   Jeep pp 112-113

we find major swaths of un-churched people. Even many who describe themselves as "Christian" are only so in a nominal sense. It is not unusual at all to even find people within the churches themselves that have a minimal knowledge of Scripture, tradition, or the history of the Church. Not all the "modern" or "contemporary" Divine Services in the world can help this if people are not paying attention or comprehending what they read. The fault for this latter condition lies with the clergy[11] whose sermons usually boil down to simply *"Jesus loves you"* therefore *"be nice."* "Folk" Christianity is a remedy to this problem, because it places the action of the Holy Ghost imminently within one's everyday life. Making Christianity a mere matter of doing "church" on Sunday has led to boredom and a matter of convention; and leaving everything to a priest or minister has led to a separation or alienation from the Christian's sacred duty to perform our common priesthood.[12]

In an effort to combat this trend mainline churches have taken to innovations that range from the silly to the blasphemous. A case in point would be the infamous "clown" Masses such as were celebrated at Trinity Episcopal in New York City. For those who don't know, a clown Mass is where the clergy dress up as mimes, clowns and jugglers and proceed to conduct a service by pulling the Eucharist out of magician's hat – along with rabbits and whatever else. There are variations on this, but that is the gist of it. So, Jesus is a clown. It's all a joke – what else can be learned from such doings? Liturgy is a teaching tool and this is what they are teaching. Antics such as this couldn't be more blasphemous than if a nude woman lay upon the altar, presided over by old Anton LaVey[13] himself. Then they wonder why the pews are growing cold and empty.

[11]   By itself this statement is a half-truth. Parents need to be the first line of any sort of education, whether that education is religious or secular. Today we seem to be addicted to the cult of "professionals" where the education and well-being of children is entrusted to the school, the state, the church, etc. Regarding homilies and sermons, it must also be pointed out that this example is not the norm, but unfortunately it happens and is not limited to any particular denomination.

[12]   How many today are aware that lay people are able to baptize others, so long as they have received a Trinitarian baptism themselves?

[13]   Anton Szandor LaVey (Harold Levey) was the founder of the Church of Satan back in the mid 1960's. He used a naked female as an "altar" when conduction group rituals.

Ethnicity, the Land & Roots

When the Germanic tribes began their journey into the Christian faith (willingly or otherwise), they did so by Germanicizing it.[14] They took what essentially was an alien religion borne of 1st century Palestine and made it their own. Every culture recipient of the Christian creed has done this. ***Folk religion is always ethnic.*** The mainstream churches, in an effort to cater to the current Golden Calf of multiculturalism have been trying to wash away any ethnic taint to their denominations.

This approach is not helpful. Using the Catholic Church as an example, there have always been individual churches within the RCC that are "ethnic:" the Italian Catholic Churches, the Irish, the Polish, etc. There is nothing wrong with this and it is from this mix of culture and Church that folk Christianity arises. The only error in any of this is when the ethnic component becomes more important than Jesus Christ and His message. All of the Orthodox Churches are strongly ethnic in character, but that does not change the *message* from church to church. Lutherans historically are mostly of Germanic and Scandinavian stock, yet there are also Latin Lutherans and Ethiopian Lutherans too (among many others). **When the churches try to do away with the ethnic component of their individual congregations, they kill the seed of a living folk spirituality.** It is also an error to believe that non-members of any given ethnic group are 'unwelcome' in such churches. This author has *never* been the recipient of such prejudice and he has attended services in a great many churches of highly 'ethnic' flavor.

---

[14] The process of Germanicization was also undertaken by the early missionaries in an attempt to make Christianity less alien and more appealing. Germanization consisted of harmonizing Church holy-days with a few key heathen ones, along with framing the Biblical narrative in terms of Germanic values, such as bravery, heroism, loyalty and depicting Christ as the ultimate heroic King or tribal Chieftain. Indeed, Christ's life has parallels to the myths of Germanic deities such as Woden and Balder. Therefore, the life of Jesus of Nazareth, as a First Century Palestinian Jew, was not nearly as alien to the Germanic peoples as might appear at first glance. Once the Faith took hold, the ordinary people refashioned their Christianity further to fit their ethnic reality. All Christianized peoples the world over have done this and it is a perfectly natural and desirable development.

Therefore, folk spirituality is the set of ideas, beliefs and practices that are close to the ordinary lives of people, yet not usually considered to be part of the normative traditions, of which the people may or may not be members.

When the people tell tales of the miracles of a saint and of the spiritual power of a sacred place, they are engaged in ritual expression which provides continuing order and meaning to an otherwise meaningless and sorrowful existence.

[Folk spirituality is] to live with the folk in their struggles to perceive the whole of existence as ultimately meaningful and intimately ordered and permeated with spiritual power.

Since the emergence of Protestantism and the Enlightenment of the eighteenth century, there has arisen in Christendom a puritanizing and rationalizing process that seeks to eliminate or ignore folk spirituality. The religiosity of the folk is disdained as magic and superstition and assumed to be meaningless or regressive.[15]

In the United States, ethnic identity among those of European stock is waning. So, to some extent passages such as the above may be puzzling to people with low ethnic identity. **Being rootless is unhealthy**. It opens a person up to being easily manipulated and homogenized to the selfish ends of others. A contemporary case in point is what is happening in Mexico. Protestant missionaries have been making incursions into Mexico over several decades. As a result, those who have been converted have taken to iconoclastically tearing apart key components to Mexican identity:

15   Four powerful paragraphs from Wentz pp. 15 & 17

the Catholicism and its 'cults' of Saints, especially Guadalupe and a total horror of the practice of curanderismo, which is reinterpreted through the new lens as a form of Satanism. Meanwhile, Wal-Mart has insensitively built a "superstore" adjacent to an ancient step-pyramid and certain movers and shakers in Mexico, the U.S. and Canada are seeking to conglomerate the three countries into a humongous Leviathan tentatively called "the North American Union." It all adds up to massive destruction, an insensitive and greedy bulldozing of centuries worth of culture and identity.

What is written above is illustrative of one major point in regard to Bruacherei and is not merely an indulgent soap-box rant. Bruacherei cannot be understood outside of two things: 1) Christianity – especially German folk Christianity and 2) Pennsylvania German culture. The charms and healing modalities of Bruacherei are completely incomprehensible without these contexts. An "un-churched" person will not grasp the significance of faith next to the act of healing; the Bible is then just a name for a book as foreign to such a person as the *Gathas* and the *Avesta* are to most everyone else.[16] As for Pennsylvania German culture, it has been suffering the fate that Mexican culture is just now experiencing. The farmstead has been the focal point of PA Dutch culture since the 18th century. Today, Pennsylvania is being plundered of its farmlands by developers and the Pennsylvania Department of Transportation (PENDOT). It is a common, not to mention jarring, sight to see complex daisy-looped superhighways nestled up against Amish farmland: eighteen wheelers and horse-drawn buggies. It ought to go without saying that that same farmland is greedily eyed-up by land brokers who can sell it to someone who will pave it all over and make more cookie-cutter, high-end housing developments.

In the book of Genesis, the human race is commissioned to be stewards of creation. It is unfortunate that these passages are so misunderstood and misinterpreted:

---

16   That is not to say that the Bible is 'unknown' to such people, but that it is ignored and taken for granted due to its ubiquity.

> So God created man in his own image, in the image of God created he him; male and female created he them. And God blessed them and God said unto them, "Be fruitful and multiply and replenish the earth and subdue it: and have dominion over the fish of the sea and over the fowl of the air and over every living this that moveth upon the earth." And God said, "Behold, I have given you every herb bearing seed, which *is* upon the face of all the earth and every tree, in the which *is* the fruit of a tree yielding seed: to you it shall be for meat. And to every beast of the earth and to every fowl of the air and to every *thing* that creepeth upon the earth, wherein *there is* life, *I have given* every green herb for meat: and it was so. **Genesis 1:27-30**

This first commission from God to humanity did not include the wanton use of the bulldozer and concrete mix. Then the Fall occurred, which changed the situation. This time, humanity had to suffer and toil to keep stewardship:

> In the sweat of thy face shalt thou eat bread, till thou return unto the ground; for out of it wast thou taken: for dust thou art. And unto dust shalt thou return. **Genesis 3:19**

> Therefore the LORD God sent him forth from the garden of Eden, to till the ground from whence he was taken. **Genesis 3:23**

And these are only two reasons why the Plain People farm and work as hard as they do.[17] The Fall not only changed our relationship to God, but also to "the beasts" who were not our original food sources.

---

17   The "Church Dutch" work just as hard, but with modern conveniences.

To destroy a people, you destroy their land. By destroying the land, not only is the identity destroyed but the 'soul' as well. The ruin of the land is a blasphemy and crushes the life out of what it means to be truly human. When that is gone, dignity is gone; it is impossible to relate to one another when the green and living things that we have been charged to oversee have been destroyed. The souls of all our ancestors live in the land as much as in Heaven and surely the Spirit of God moves through them both. The paving over of arable land, housing developments, strip malls, box stores, uber-highway systems and all of the trash and cigarette butts that litter them are as much a slap in God's face as that clown Mass at Trinity Episcopal. It's also one of the instruments that are destroying the Pennsylvania German culture. To understand PA Dutch culture, you have to understand *the land.*

When speaking of "roots" or being "rooted" it is not entirely a metaphor. To be closely connected with a certain area or patch of earth is essential to good mental, spiritual and physical well being which is hand-in-hand with ethnic consciousness. Every tribe or people leave an energetic imprint on the area of land they inhabit. Centuries of this inhabitation binds the people with the land. We only have to cast a cursory look at the situation of the American Indian, who has been reduced to poverty and alcoholism as a result of their internal rootlessness and spiritual disconnection.

Tribalism or ethnicity aside, practices such as Pow-Wow are closely connected to the natural world. In fact, a good deal of what a Bruacher does falls under the heading of "Natural Magic," which is the knowledge and manipulation of the wholesome, but unseen spiritual, energetic, or preternatural processes of the visible aspect of earthly Creation and our immediate little corner of the solar system. With so many people now living in cities and suburbs, there has been an attempt by some writers to market to these individuals by way of books geared towards "urban magic" or "city magic". Despite the fact that one can practice any sort of magic in a city, the fact remains that cities are *not natural* and they are sources of stress, anxiety and alienation. They are places un-conducive to a *whole* and genuinely human way of life. Man makes cities, but God made the country and wild open spaces. We may think that we are very cleaver in manipulating DNA, but no human being has the power to create even so much as a flower *ex nihilo*.

Community

Today, in the 21st Century, we are very individualistic people; the past two centuries have seen
the eroding and increasing atomization of the Western family. Other parts of the world have not fared nearly as badly, having intact extended families. The main reason for this atomizing is the shift from a traditional society to a functional society, from holistic human communities to specialized ones. This movement occurred as Western society became increasingly technological and industrialized. Previous to specialization, work was done at home and goods of value were made in small towns and villages, and consanguineal family formed the foundation of society. Once industrialization occurred, the functionalism of "work" shifted the focus of family from the consanguineal extended clan to that of the conjugal unit. Functionalism is a tool to create specialized tasks to maximize efficiency. Each person that occupies a functional slot is interchangeable with any other person with those "skill sets" as it is the function that matters and not the person. In other words, this process of "efficiency" has *dehumanized* us, making us less 'natural'. The Devil is in the details, indeed. The Pennsylvania Dutch have traditionally, largely been farmers. These were not the corporate mega-farms that we know today, but the small family farms that were the norm in the Commonwealth and throughout the United States. This way of life allowed for the continuance of traditional modes of society.

Two major challenges befall the family in technological society. The first change involves the gradual weakening of kinship ties and supportive

> neighborhood-type groupings. In traditional society, the family consists of more than the nuclear unit of husband, wife and offspring. The traditional family consists of a sizable group of people and includes many conjugal units linked through some structure based on common descent.
>
> Technological society changes the relationship between conjugal unit and both the wider kinship and village-neighborhood networks. The bonds within a kinship grouping begin to weaken and the family group as a whole becomes smaller. Village-neighborhood relationships lose much of their familiarity, stability and interdependence.[18]

The Pennsylvania Dutch, even when not being farmers were[19] very family and home oriented. Beidelman gives a glowing appraisal of this situation circa the 1890's.

> A marked characteristic of all Germans everywhere, is their "home life." Nowhere do we find such cheerful sunny homes, as among the Germans. No matter how humble the home, or how poor the family may be, the first consideration always is, to live for home and family where cheerfulness and affection reign supreme.[20]

---

18   These two paragraphs come from the on-line article "The Family in Technological Society" by Howard King, which can be found at www.patriarch.com. In this article, King attempts to digest for his readers the complex ideas in the eighteenth chapter of Stephen B. Clark's *Man and Woman in Christ: An Examination of the Roles of Men and Women in the Light of Scripture and the Social Sciences.*

19   Past-tense; this quality can still be found, especially among those with a heightened sense of ethnic identity; however, today ethnic identity among the PA Germans is relatively low. The demise of the family farms have led to the atomization described above, making the "Dutch" little different than their "English" brethren. This, of course, does not apply to the Old Order Anabaptist groups.

20   Beidelman, p 139

It was normal for a pre-mid 20th Century people to be connected to a certain community and area of land their whole lives – being born, living and dying within a radius of a mere five miles; our current mobile life style was highly unusual and far from the norm.[21] If one was born Lutheran, or Catholic, or Reformed, he stayed that way because it was the way of his family. Seldom did anyone travel outside of these social boundaries. The world of the pre-1950's traditional Bruacher was bound up with community and all of its accompanying privileges and limitations. *And the Bruacher and his Pow-Wow were defined by that community.* "Witches" were individuals whose magic went outside of the community's norms and was not worked in its interests. Witches, in this instance, were not just eccentrics, but malefactors. Bruachers, on the other hand, may or may not have been eccentric, but whose labors reified communal norms.

The life of a Christian exists within the greater life of community. The Holy Trinity is a community of Three Divine Persons of One Holy God. A Christian community is, therefore, individual persons united within the single Body of Christ, even as the Father, Son and Holy Ghost are one. We come together in worship to celebrate and to forget about our small-selves and to pray for one another. Our traditional communities were *not* utopias to be sure. Yet, a closely knit agricultural Christian community is (and was) second-to-none for giving its members a sense of well being, rootedness and wholeness, such as has been described about the lives of the Amish.[22] *Faith, family, community* and the *land* have defined and shaped the practice of Pow-Wow. Outside of this context, Bruacherei is a fish out of water.

---

21   Of course, this does not include those events that have pressed people to move, such as natural disasters, previous pioneer expansionism and the hiving off in order to set up new communities – such as the Amish and Hutterites currently do.

22   Yoder & Duncan 1999

Doing it by the books

> I say: any and every man who knowingly neglects using this book in saving an eye, or the leg, or any other limb of his fellow-man, is guilty of the loss of such limb and thus commits a sin, by which he may forfeit to himself all hope of salvation. Such men refuse to call upon the Lord in their trouble, although He especially commands it. If men were not allowed to use sympathetic words, nor the name of the MOST HIGH, it certainly would not have been revealed to them; and what is more, the Lord would not help where they are made use of. God can in no manner be forced to intercede where it is not his divine pleasure.[23]

The Pow-Wow manual is a staple of the lore attached to Bruacherei. The above quote comes from one of the most well known, if not infamous, Pow-Wow texts of all time – being, John George Hohman's *Pow-Wows: or Long Lost Friend* or *Der Lange Verborgene Freund* in German, the book's original language. *Pow-Wows* has been consistently in print since 1820, with numerous plagiarized editions – a backhanded complement if there ever was one. One of the earliest pirated versions of *The Long Lost Friend* came into print in 1837 under the title of *Der Lange Verborgene Schatz und Haus Freund*.[24] Yet, according to extensive research done on the text by Don Yoder shows that Hohman himself took great license in culling from other manuals without any mention of credit to his sources. Bits and pieces of *The Long Lost Friend* have been traced to *The Romanusbüchlein*, or simply *The Romanus*. Other charms can be located in *Albertus Magnus Egyptian Secrets*.

---

23   Hohman p.4
24   Heindel p.132

Interestingly, the word "freund," which is usually translated into English as "friend" also has the double meaning of "familiar" – as in a Witch's "familiar." Indeed, this text functioned in that manner as generations of American Bruachers felt 'naked' without their copy of Hohman's book. Some wrongly believed that their power derived from the book and not from God Himself. The belief in books having a power and influence of their own is very ancient. We take the written word for granted as we are literally surrounded by the printed word everywhere we look. It wasn't until the invention of the printing press during the Early Modern period that books could be mass produced and placed within reach of the common person. For most of humanity's history, we have been illiterates.

The written word was mysterious and held in awe. Books of magic, especially, were pure magic in themselves as a result. A *grimoire* or book of sorcery could even act as a vessel for holding spirit powers, just like the brass vessel in which King Solomon was said to have trapped 72 *genii*. Despite the borderline idolatrous regard for these books, the fact is that such a book can function as a holding vessel or even as a 'battery' of sorts. Books can be charmed and bound shut so unwanted prying eyes cannot gawk at things better left private. Some books are charmed in such a way so that their contents, no matter how plain and well written, become inscrutable and opaque to those not prepared to read them. Aside from the Hohman book, a Bruacher's best *friend* is a book kept in his or her own handwriting. Often, this book was no more than a common notebook with recipes, charms and formulae jotted down in case the memory failed – or in case it was to be passed on so the legacy would continue. To this day there are Pennsylvania Dutch families who have an heirloom century-old copy of Hohman's, or a notebook written by the hand of one or more ancestors. Some of these heirlooms are not books at all, but merely scraps of paper tucked away into a family Bible.

As for the man Hohman (or Homan), he was born somewhere around 1778 and left for God in 1845 or there about. No one really knows as he was "essentially a mystery man" according to Don Yoder in his work *The Pennsylvania German Broadside*. Also according to Yoder's research, Hohman arrived with his wife and son on the ship *Tom* on 12 October 1802. He was a talented publisher by trade and came to America in poverty. He and his wife Anne paid off their debt of passage by indentured servitude. After gaining their freedom, John George tried to make a living by way of selling printed birth and baptismal certificates (*geburtscheine, taufscheine*), himmelsbriefe among many other things. His *Land und Haus Apotheke* (The Field and House Pharmacy Guide) was produced in 1818 and by 1819 Hohman was completing *The Long Lost Friend*.

Due to his impoverished circumstances, some have opined, cynically, that Hohman produced his *Friend* in order to doctor-up his meager income. However, Hohman was never wealthy and *"The Friend"* was plagiarized remorselessly within his own life-time (and afterward). Unlike most of the German folk who came to Pennsylvania, Hohman was a Roman Catholic. His last known printing project was *Aufblick der Seele in den Himmel* (The Soul's upward Glance into Heaven), 1842. Ned Heindel speculates that Hohman passed away in Reading on 19 April 1845.[25] Nothing is known about his earlier life in the Old World. During his lifetime he (and most likely his wife too) was a Bruacher and treated many people. Regardless of whatever flaws can be pinned on old Johann, one of them is not insincerity.

The Long Lost Friend had a staring role in one of Pennsylvania's more sensational moments, being the York "hex murder" back in 1928. One of the pitfalls of Witchcraft history books is the constant rehashing of all the trials, tortures and executions suffered by the victims of the justice systems of those eras. It is not my wish that *The Red Church* falls into this category, so the treatment of this infamous episode will be rather light-weight, but will guide the reader to more extensive sources of information.

25   Heidel p.46

Nelson D. Rehmeyer: the victim of a Witch hunt

On the 27th of November, 1928, sixty-six year old Bruacher Nelson D. Rehmeyer, the so-called "Witch of Rehmeyer's Hollow," was wrestled to the ground and bludgeoned to death. His corpse was tied up in a mattress and blanket then set on fire. It is said that the intention was not to kill Rehmeyer, but to procure a lock of his hair or force him to give up his copy of *The Long Lost Friend*. John Blymire, John Curry and Wilbert Hess thus went to pay a call on this unsuspecting fellow at his secluded home nestled in Rehmeyer's Hollow, Hopewell Township, near Red Lion in York County. At that time John Blymire was 32 years old. He has been described as a not very bright young man, perhaps a little on the 'slow' side. Yet, by the testimonies of those who knew him before the trouble began, he was a good Pow-Wow. Blymire worked odd jobs and part-time work; his zeal for Pow-Wowing prevented him from keeping down a full-time normal occupation.

According to the principal writers who researched this case (Ammon Aurand and Arthur Lewis specifically), Blymire's troubles began after he had charmed a rabid dog. From there his luck turned sour; he lost weight, he had "the take off" (*opnema – abnemmes*); he felt debilitated, possibly depressed and highly fatigued. He found that he could not Pow-Wow himself and that he lost the ability to try for others too. This began his grail-like quest for the ultimate Pow-Wow doctor who could lift the malaise. His search was interrupted for a time when he married. The trouble began anew in earnest when his two infant children passed away and he slipped down into a deeper 'hole' than previously. Blymire's two cohorts, Hess and Curry, joined their friend in his relentless search for a cure; they, too, felt the weight of a "hex" on their shoulders and were equally determined to find a remedy for themselves as well. The three covered a good swath of Dutch territory and no Bruacher they visited proved efficacious. They consulted with the dubious "Dr." (or "Professor") Andrew Lenhart, whose answer to all his clients' ills was that they were *verhext*. The remedy usually involved some advice that the client might have to *kill* the spell-caster. Right around 1922 or 1923, one of Lenhart's clients murdered her husband, perhaps after being advised by the "doctor" that he had 'Witched' her. Blymire got a does of this "advise" too and began suspecting his own wife of Witchcraft. It was his wife, then, who got the legal ball rolling against him – needless to say, she didn't want to be on the receiving end of Dr. Lenhart's suggested remedies. However, it was not this hex doctor that finally got Blymire's head all wrapped around the idea of having been *verhext* and in need of hunting down his tormenter. This role was filled by either a "Mrs. Noll" or a "Mrs. Knopt," depending upon whose version is read. According to the court transcripts for *Commonwealth v. John Blymire*, it was the latter. Mrs. Knopt kept Blymire on a hook, charging him for each of the six visits it took in order to find the identity of his hexer. On his final visit, she had shown him the identity of the "Witch" when she directed him to take a dollar bill and lay it in his hand; after doing so, the Bruacherin pulled the bill out of his hand and within his palm he saw a vision of Nelson Rehmeyer – or so we're told.

Rehmeyer was a family friend of the Blymires. According to Kriebel (who cites Lewis, Aurand and the court transcripts)[26] Rehmeyer had Pow-Wowed for John when he was a child, perhaps more than once. It is perplexing why such a man would have wanted to "hex" John Blymire. If Rehmeyer truly was an out-and-out *hexe* and the dictum regarding a Witch's existence is true enough (*fa die lied gwele*), then perhaps there would have been no real reason needed. Such a person would hex simply to make innocent people miserable. However, this author's impression is that Rehmeyer was nothing of the sort.

On the evening of November 27th, the trio found their way to the old fellow's house. If they could get a clip of his hair and bury it six or more feet under ground, that would have been enough; alternately,

[26] Kriebel 2007, p.119

by demanding his copy of Hohman's, that would break his power too. Why they thought that Nelson Rehmeyer would go along with either is astonishing. Rehmeyer is described has having been a hulk of a man, three grown men could not completely subdue him. In the struggle, one of the three dealt the death-blow (Blymire thought John Curry did it). Ironically, when they turned Rehmeyer's house inside-out searching for the dreaded tome, they found *nothing*. In a panic and in order to make the murder look like it was a robbery in progress, they took a little cash that was lying around and then proceeded to burn the corpse in order to hide the crime. As with most of their actions that evening, they hadn't thought out the situation very well, because Rehmeyer wasn't lighting up – it takes temperatures in excess of 4,000 degrees to truly cremate a body. At his trial, John Blymire showed not a jot of remorse. His friends said at trial that at Rehmeyer's actual expiry John exclaimed in a wash of relief: *"Thank God! The Witch is dead."*[27]

It is truly amazing that Blymire and company did not get the electric chair. In 1953 his sentence was commuted and he was released from prison on parole. Hess served his sentence and returned home; Curry was paroled in 1939, served in WWII and became a dairy farmer. John Blymire lived quietly into the 1960's, no one hearing so much as a peep from him. All of these men are now returned to dust; and Nelson Rehmeyer's secrets, if he had any, lay down with him in the quiet, good earth of Dutch country. Because of the misdeeds of John Blymire, John Curry and Wilbert Hess, the Commonwealth started a rolling juggernaut of "education" and "science" to wipe out the so-called superstitions of the Pennsylvania Dutch. The trial caused an embarrassing whirlwind, not just within the State, but literally throughout the Western world – wherever there was a newspaper printed, folks knew of the murder and its dramatic, sensationalistic circumstances. This was egg on the face of Harrisburg and they did not want Pennsylvania known as the second "Salem" comprised of "dumb" Dutch and other 'bumpkins.' World War II accelerated anti-German feeling,

27   Lewis, p.71

which was still lingering from the previous World War only a mere 20 plus years prior. All of these factors combined helped along the deterioration of not just Pow-Wowing, but Pennsylvania Dutch culture as a whole – the dialect especially suffering horribly.

Come November 27th; say a prayer for the soul of Nelson Rehmeyer.

Albertus Magnus' Egyptian Secrets

The historical saint Albertus Magnus, Count of Bollstädt, was born in Lauingen, Swabia in 1193 and died in 1280. It is a certainty that the above named book was never written by him. Another much earlier book *The Book of Secrets of Albertus Magnus*, despite its closer proximity to Albertus' era was not a product of his pen either. Works such as these have historically been ascribed to famous holy men in order to bolster their credibility. However, it is equally certain that the Dominican hieromonk, who taught in the schools of Ratisbon, Cologneand Hildesheim, was also highly knowledgeable in the arts of natural magic, such as all learned men of that day were.

Natural magic is the result of how God has put together the natural world; it is the utilizing of its hidden and little understood laws. For this reason, the medieval clergy saw nothing untoward in its study and application. It is this type of "magic" that forms part of the foundation for Bruacherei. The other part is charming and prayer in God's name. Albertus influenced a great many people and produced remarkable students such as St. Thomas Aquinas, who had no small amount of esoteric knowledge himself. His scientific probing and deep knowledge of chemistry (for that time) was what really earned him the reputation of being a sorcerer. *Egyptian Secrets*, along with *The Long Lost Friend*, was another key charm book on the shelves of Bruachers. Several charms in *The Red Church* are directly from both of these texts. Both books are treasure troves of well-used Bruache charms that have traveled through the centuries.

The Sixth and Seventh Books of Moses

Here is the granddaddy of all hex books, traditionally dreaded, with Bruachers seldom admitting to owning a copy themselves. The authors of old grimoires such as the *Sixth and Seventh Books of Moses* (herein abbreviated TSSBM), were mainly anonymous. Besides the safety of anonymity, attributing one's book to the authorship of an illustrious ancient gave it authority – just as in the case of Albertus Magnus (above). There is no doubt whatever that Moses had nothing to do with the writing of TSSBM.

The first five books of the Old Testament, called The Pentateuch, hold a strong mystical allure; but, they have been considered to be wholly 'exoteric' texts. Over the ages it has been suspected that there are another five books attributable to Moses, but that have been left out of the canonical grouping. The Sixth through the 10th books are said to contain Moses' secrets given to him by the angels and by God Himself. By these secrets, Moses was able to bring on the plagues, part the sea and confound Pharaoh's priests.

The magic contained in TSSBM harkens to these legendary powers by offering seals and sigils that correspond to the vestments of the High Priest of the old Temple in Jerusalem. Also among these are signs that are named after the acts of Moses, such as *"Moses Changes Water into Blood"*[28] This author's original opinion of TSSBM was that it is largely useless. Until Joseph Peterson came along and cleaned up the text, the sigils were completely unusable, the Hebrew illegible and the organization awful. The book was translated out of German and into English and more or less the same imprint was reproduced *ad nauseam*, mistakes and all.

---

28   Peterson version of TSSBM, p. 84

The so-called Eighth through 10th books are also available, but these are no more Mosaic than TSSMB. Early 20th century occult writer Henri Gamache cobbled together the latter text, weaving bits and pieces of Coptic Christian magical texts with interesting speculations of his own. Gamache's book never really became popular with Pow-Wowers, but was seized upon more by Southern black hoodoo practitioners and root workers. It is an interesting aside that Hohman's book became popular in the South among hoodoo practitioners.

Because of the satanic aura that still hangs around TSSBM, most traditional practitioners today do not own a copy. The hex doctors of yesteryear are another story. The sinister reputation of TSSBM derives from its blatant conjurations of various infernal agencies. But, these sorts of magical operations need to be kept in context. On the one hand, some such workings of magic have a definite "Faustian" character, where the magician swaps his soul for knowledge, power, or whatever. On the other hand, conjurations of this type often have 'higher' purposes such as is found in the grimoire called *The Book of Abramelin*, where a magician will deliberately call upon satanic powers <u>in order to defeat</u> them, thereby strengthening his will and spiritual character.

The magical operations in TSSBM are mainly in the latter category. It must be said that these sorts of 'operations' are not the whole of the text. According to Peterson, the very first mention of this book appeared in 1734. Then the antiquarian Johann Scheible collected together various related texts, which he then published in 1849, with TSSBM as its sixth chapter.

> The core of 6/7Moses can be traced back to the Latin magical text Liber Razielis, in a section ascribed to Moses. It is related to the well-known Hebrew magical text Sefer Raziel HaMalach [*The Book of the Angel Raziel*], thought

to have been composed or compiled in the thirteenth century.[29]

and

6/7Moses is in fact based largely on Books 6 and 7 of the Latin Raziel.[30]

According to some traditions of Kabbalah, Raziel is the archangel (or one of the cherubim) who is the keeper of divine secrets; he taught Adam and Eve the holy magic after their ouster from Eden so that they would have a sort of spiritual 'road map' back to paradise and also to have a tool of survival in a new, harsh post-Fall world.

For the work taught in *The Red Church*, this depth of esoteric study is not necessary and books such as TSSBM are deep waters, indeed. It was believed (and still is by some) that books such as these lead one into "being read fast," and therefore bound to powers of darkness. It takes much spiritual discernment to wade through texts such as TSSBM, which are best left alone by most. The TSSBM has an appended section entitled *Sepher Schimmusch Tehillim*, translated from the Hebrew by Godfrey Selig, is of great value and highly recommended for those wishing to pursue more advanced work with the Psalms.

The Romanus

Also known as the *Romanusbüchlein* is said to be the main text that Hohman freely borrowed from when compiling *The Long Lost Friend*. The best commentary on *The Romanus* that this author has come across was done by Adolf Spamer: *Romanusbüchlein: Historisch-philogischer Kommentar zu einem deutschen Zauberbuch*, 1958. In Johanna Nickel's introductory chapter to the subject "*Zur Tradition der Romanusbüchlein*", an early print date for *The Romanus* seems to be 1788. Johann Scheible included *The Romanus* in his *Das Kloster*; this is the same book in which Scheible placed

---

29   Peterson, p. IX brackets mine
30   Ibid.

TSSBM. As already pointed out, to have the Hohman book is to also have a good portion of *The Romanus*.

Three Books of Occult Philosophy

Written by Henry Cornelius Agrippa of Nettesheim, *Three Books of Occult Philosophy* (TBOOP), written in draft form around 1510, did not make it into print until the year 1531 *via* the press of John Graphaeus of Antwerp.[31] For over 470 years TBOOP has influenced the work and thought of English and European occultists. It is the root of the content of many "magical" books today and therefore a great debt is owed to Agrippa. For those who are sincerely interested in the magical art and in the roots of past and present practice, it is well worth the price and effort to acquire Donald Tyson's reworking of TBOOP. It is unknown to this author as a certainty if any Pennsylvania Dutch Bruachers owned a copy of Agrippa's book; no such mention has been found thus far. However, due to the influence of TBOOP some manifestation of this work has had to touch upon the more complex workings of the master Bruacher or hex doctor. TBOOP is almost wholly a study of "natural magic" – whereas the work of conjuration lays within *The Fourth Book of Occult Philosophy*, which is separate from TBOOP. There is some dispute as to whether or not Agrippa authored *The Fourth Book*, but at the very least it was written by one of his students.

Secrets of Sympathy

William James Beissel, 1938. *Secrets of Sympathy* is one of the few published Pennsylvania Dutch Bruacherei manuals since the works of Hohman and the "copy cats" (out-right plagiarists really) who followed in his wake.[32] What makes this little booklet more amazing is that it was published not even a whole decade after the

---

31 Tyson p. xxxiii

32 According to Kriebel, Don Yoder was able to trace Beissel's charms to an earlier manual by *Dr. G. F. Helfenstein's vielfatig erprobter Hausschatz der Sympathie; oder, Enthullte Zauberkrafte und Geheimnisse der Natur*, 1853.

"hex murder" of Nelson Rehmeyer. *Perhaps* it was because of the charged aura of mistrust surrounding Pow-Wow that Bill Beissel published his booklet, so as to make Pow-Wow less mysterious. SOS contains many of the same charms contained in Hohman, Albertus, *The Romanus*, etc. The booklet forms a discrete chapter in the book *Powwow Power* by James D. Beissel. *Powwow Power* had a very limited printing and circulation; therefore copies are exceedingly rare or otherwise awfully expensive. But much the same as the other books cited here, it is well worth tracking down.

The Wolfsthurn Manual

Manual's author unknown. Historian Richard Kieckhefer gives a brief history of this household manual, which is quite obviously a 15th century ancestor of the much later 19th century Pennsylvania German *hausmittel* books.

> The Wolfsthurn handbook shows the place magic might hold in everyday life.[33]
>
> It recommends taking the leaves of a particular plant as a remedy for "fevers of all sorts"; this in itself would count as science, or as folk medicine, rather than magic. Before using these leaves, one is supposed to write certain Latin words on them to invoke the power of the Holy Trinity and then one is to say the Lord's Prayer and other prayers over them; this in itself would count as religion. There is no scientific or religious reason, however, for repeating this procedure before sunrise on three consecutive mornings. By adding this requirement the author enhances the power of science and religion with that of magic.[34]

---

33   Kieckhefer p. 2
34   Kieckhefer p. 3

A few of the *Wolfsthurn* formulae have been included in *The Red Church* for possible use by those interested. The charms in the manual mirror every bit the ones in the well-know Pow-Wow books of later centuries.

The Munich Handbook

Kieckhefer also documents the existence of a more sinister volume simply known as *"The Munich Handbook"* (Bayerische Staatsbibliothek, Munich). The handbook is written in Latin and gives directions on demonic conjuration, replete with whole passages taken from Roman Catholic liturgy.[35] The book describes the uses of swords, daggers, circles, etc. which probably places it on the same level as TSSBM (above). However, from reading Kieckhefer, an impression is made that this handbook has more of a 'watered down' folk element to its use, than the other books which were aimed at priests and other learned individuals of the time.

The Bible

Lastly, but certainly not the least of these is *Die Bibel oder die ganze Heilige Schrift des alten und neuen Testaments*. The Bible is the mother of Bruacherei. There are Bruachers who will use **nothing** but the Bible. *"Either you serve one, or you serve the other,"* to paraphrase Daisy Dietrich.[36] The Bible is present during every treatment. Some practitioners have a tradition of opening the Bible to specific books or chapters when Pow-Wowing, such as **Mark 16**, or **James 1**. It may also be opened to any other significant chapter when trying for an illness covered in those passages. *The Book of Ruth*, for example, is used when performing a sort of divination involving a key (see Part III, Chapter 5, Divination and Miscellaneous Operations). The best Bruache charms and prayers are passages directly from Scripture, the most famous example

---

35   Kieckhefer p. 4

36   I had asked Daisy about the use of the old Pow-Wow books during my trainingand this is more or less her opinion of any brauche book other than the Bible.

being **Ezekiel 16:6** for the stopping of blood. Other charms will incorporate passages of Scripture, or make allusions to events in the Bible. When all the other manuals and charm books fail, nothing works like these verses. In some regards, it is almost redundant for a Bruacher to use anything else. But, for whatever reason, each practitioner finds what passages in the Bible work best for them; or what non-Biblical charms are the most efficacious. Some people can stop blood with *nothing but* Ezekiel 16:6; and some find that they are quite capable when using the other charms, which are also included here in *The Red Church*.

"What's love got to do with it?"

Further regarding Scripture, it is good to keep in mind that the primary meaning and reason for its existence is as a tool towards Salvation. Church tradition also functions in this way. When people wonder about Jesus' "lost years" and wring their hands over what the primitive Christians may or may not have been doing in the minutia of their daily lives, Scripture is silent. Those who insist that all of the 'machinations' of Bruacherei are not completely attested for in Scripture are on shaky ground. The use of herbs and healing foods, the use of lunar phases (planet earth's time-clock), the intricate knowledge of natural processes and patterns of disease, etc. have *nothing* to do with the Bible's core message.

> Methods such as Bruache are a practice rooted in devotion, they are if you will, a magic of the heart (metaphorically and literally). Without the devotion prayers are empty and no amount of imaging will fix that. Devotion by its nature requires the emotion of love, as well as abstraction, since it is a love directed to something greater than one's current experience of 'self'. Papus said, "Magic is love."
>
> What is most interesting about the Fourth Book of Occult Philosophy by Agrippa is its clear emphasis

> on the use of Scripture and related stories (even Saints) *as a means of anchoring the devotion into a historical reality*. I do not believe this is simply a 'X-tian cover' or convention but a serious and important technique.[37]

The Bible does not teach us how to make a gourmet dinner. Gourmet dinners, for however lovely they are, do not pertain to Salvation. Neither are they prohibited. Just because Haute Cuisine is not located in the *Heilige Schrift* does not mean that God forbids it. All of the prohibitions of "sorcery" in the Bible can be traced back to crimes against *Love* – the Love and Charity that binds humanity to God and that binds each of us to one another. It is hoped that you, the Reader, having journeyed thus far through this book, have come to the conclusion that Bruacherei is a tool in service of that Love and not in defiance of it.

> I know that without me, God can no moment live; were I to die, then He no longer survive. I am as great as God and he is small like me; He cannot be above, nor I below Him be. In me God is fire and I in Him its glow; in common is our life, apart we cannot grow. He is God and man to me, to Him I am both indeed; His thirst I satisfy, He helps me in my need. God is such as He is, I am what I must be; if you know one, in truth you know both him and me I am the vine, which He doth plant and cherish most; the fruit which grows from me; is God the Holy Ghost.
> --Johann Scheffler (Angelus Silesius) 1624-1677

---

37   Mark Stavish; from a letter posted on his private mailing list: July 29, 2006. The original e-mail was much more extensive. Stavish's mention of "imaging" refers to a previous commentary on contemporary magical techniques that rely wholly upon visualization. Incidentally, "X-tian" is a pejorative spelling of the word "Christian"; where as "Christianity" is snidely shorthanded as "X-tianity". It seems that this practice might have started as a spin-off of the habit of spelling "Christmas" as "X-mas". However, its usage today is to belittle the Christian religion; it is in popular use amongst many Neo-pagans, Wiccans and other non-Christian occultists with an ax to grind. Here Stavish is highlighting this prejudice and throwing it back. The italics are mine.

Some Ancient and Contemporary Comparisons

Previously, we have taken a look at the Merseburg Incantations that may point to the forms taken by late Germanic heathen charms. The date of these incantations or charms is late enough that their contact with the Christian religion may have influenced their structure – that is to say, these charms *may* be an instance of *Christian incantations heathenized.*

There is evidence from around the Mediterranean that the pagans[38] of the First Century and onwards had enough contact with Christianity that the final forms of paganism were no longer examples of what we might call "paleopaganism." At the same time these forms were not syncretistic either – that is to say, these late forms of paganism were not examples of "Christo-paganism" as it was that these cults and Mystery Religions (such as *the later forms* of Mithraism) took Christian concepts and ideas and fitted them onto the older strata of any given cultus.

If this is true, this process would have been the exact opposite of what is usually claimed: that Christians from the Second Century onward borrowed (or by some accounts "stole") concepts from paganism and heathenism.[39] Before any readers object to this notion, please bear in mind that the author is *suggesting* that this sort of cultural interchange is a good *possibility*, but not a dogmatic certainty.[40]

---

38   The term "pagan" and "paganism" in this context refers to the pre-Christian religions of the Mediterranean area. "Heathenism" is now the preferred term for Germanic pre-Christian religions.

39   *The Case for Christ*, pp161-162

40   This possibility will be unthinkable and akin to blasphemy for those married to the idea that early Christians were "thieves" and borrowers of pagan religion. We have seen that missionaries to the Germanic tribes did, in fact, use elements of the Teutonic worldview in order to make the new religion less alien; this later technique was a far cry from using elements from pre-Christian religion in order to create Christianity. We must look at the probability that (at least in terms of the Greco-Roman Mystery Religions) there was an influence in the opposite direction. Julian the Apostate made several reforms in the pagan religion of Rome that were borrowed from Christianity in order to make the older cults more competitive with the new religion. Christian writer and apologist Glenn Miller answered to this issue on his website "A Christian Think-tank" http://www.christian-thinktank.com/copycatwho1.html; another similar discussion can be found

When considering the many roots of Bruacherei, a look at the state of early Christianity and late pagan religions becomes a part of the puzzle and worthy of inquiry. Some of the earliest roots of Pow-Wow charms can be demonstrated as deriving from Coptic Christian Egyptian healing incantations of the Second Century and onward. In this first example, we can see the narrative-type charm that is so common to Pow-Wow.

> [Three men] met us in the desert [and said to the lord] Jesus, "What treatment is possible for the sick?" And he says to them, "[I have] given olive oil and poured out myrrh [for those] who believe in the [name of the] father and the holy [spirit and the] son."[41]

This charm is called "narrative" as it tells a story (and in this case gives directions) as a part of its recital. As with Pow-Wow charming, it is concluded in "the Three Highest Names." Compare with Hohman's charm for scurvy and sore throat.

> Job went through the land, holding his staff close in the hand, when God the Lord did meet him and said to him: Job, what art thou grieved at? Job said: Oh God, why should I not be sad? My throat and my mouth are rotting away. Then said the Lord to Job: In yonder valley there is a well which will cure thee and thy mouth and thy throat, in the name of God the Father, the Son and the Holy Ghost. Amen.[42]

Another Coptic device, which closely resembles a Bruacherei *zauberzettel*, is this amulet for protection from fever. The name of the individual for whom it was made was written into the text.

---

at: http://www.tektonics.org/copycat/mithra.html.

41   Meyer & Smith, p. 31; this charm is part of the *Oxyrhynchus* text, Fifth Century.

42   Hohman, p. 33

	† † †	
Jesus Christ wolf,	ERICHTHONIE	Let the white
heals wolf,	RICHTHONIE	the white
the chill wolf	ICHTHONIE	the white
and the shivering	CHTHONIE	heal the
and every Joseph.	THONIE	fever of
disease of the quick! ††	ONIE	They are
body of Joseph,	NIE	
who wares	IE	
the amulet daily	E	
and intermittently.		
They are quick! Amen,		
Alleluia. †††[43]		

A fever amulet from Albertus' *Egyptian Secrets* works with a similar word device, which is to be hung around the patient's neck.

```
H B R H C H T H B R H
H B R H C H T H B R
H B R H C H T H B
H B R H C H T H B
H B R H C H T H
H B R H C H T
H B R H C H
H B R H C
H B R H
H B R H
H B R
H B
H[44]
```

---

[43] Meyer & Smith, p. 37; *Cologne* text, Seventh Century; the Word of Power, ERICHTHONIE (Erichthonios, a Greek hero), is in the shape of a heart. The "white wolf" is Christ. The Words of Power in Coptic charms and amulets derive from the Greek and Coptic languages. Some are considered 'nonsense' words by scholars, derived from a type of glossolalia.

[44] *Egyptian Secrets*, Empire Publishing Company, p. 44

The verbal charms of Britain and Europe have some very consistent features. One of these is *narration* (i.e., telling a story), such as we see with the Coptic charms. Narration is not always present, however. Another is *instruction* and is often found tucked into narration. These charms also have *number*, often having "three-ness" – there are often three beings or characters refered to or addressed. The charms are usually to be spoken three times, but not always. Odd numbers are more common than even ones. The English charm for burns demonstrates some of these features. This particular charm has many different variations depending upon the locality where it was recorded. The following was recorded in 1911 in Devon, England.

> Three Angels came from North, East and West,
> One brought fire, another brought frost,
> And the third brought the Holy Ghost
> So out fire and in frost
> In the name of the Father, Sonand Holy Ghost[45]

In her book *Tender Hands: Ruth's Story of Healing*, Ruth Weil Kusler describes a prayer for shingles:

> The prayer *Es genngen drie young frauen, Aus England die druken die Rosen in ehera hand, Die Rosenfar swantera the Blumen far swanten* was used to heal shingles, as nothing seemed to work as well for this affliction. The chant told the story of three young girls who came from England to Germany and carried flowers in their hands. They brought the flowers to the sick. If the flowers wilted, the person had shingles.[46]

---

45   Jonathan Roper does an exceptionally good poetical analysis of this and other verbal charms from the Anglo-Saxon to the Serbo-Croatian in his article "Towards a poetics, rhetorics and proxemics of verbal charms" which can be viewed at www.folklore.ee/folklore/vol24/verbcharm.pdf. This article is of great interest as there are comparisons of the structures of German *beschprechen*, Anglo-Saxon charms, East Slavic *zagovo* and many others.

46   Kusler, p. 7

THE HISTORICAL THREADS OF BRAUCHEREI

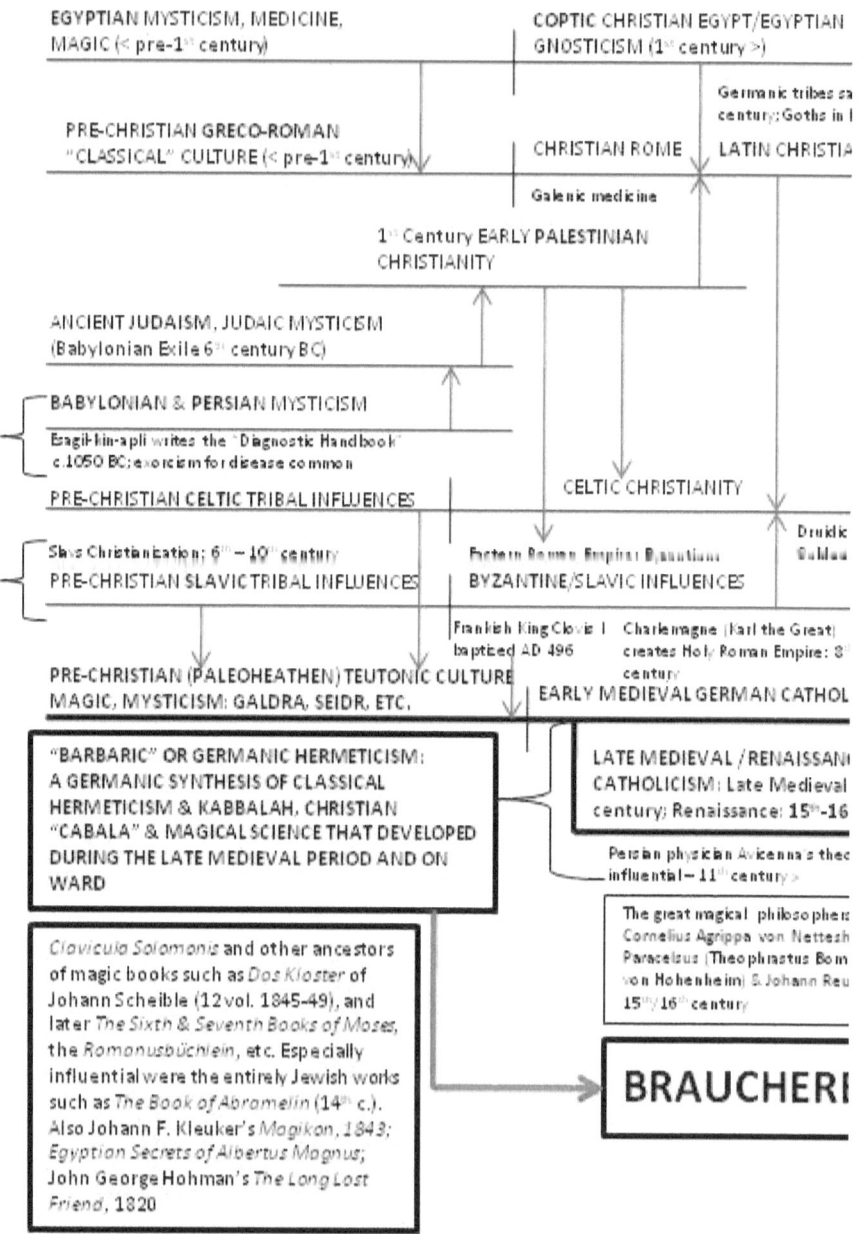

The practice called "Braucherei" or "Pow-Wow" did not emerge from a vacuum. It is the uniquely Germanic synthesis of many cultural influences and religio-magical streams that have merged into the healing-ways of German folk Christianity. Braucherei is not necessarily a unified system, and it has many redactions that vary by locality and individual practitioners. This is identical to the situation of the "Cunning Art" found in the British Isles. Some variations are more influenced by mystical currents such as Behmenism and Rosicrucian thought. Others are not. Pow-Wow doctors of the past have ranged from simple charmers to full-blown magicians skilled in the occult sciences of astrology, Kabbalah, and alchemical medicine. Like its sister practice of English Cunning Art, braucherei is mostly representative of a homey, folkish, treatment of some of these more complex practices. Braucherei is a thoroughly Christian folk healing art, and it has been so for many centuries (even if the orthodoxy of some practices is questionable). This situation of braucherei is beyond doubt especially in its American form for nearly 330 years. That's a long time — at least long enough for most of us.

ck Rome 3ʳᵈ – 6ᵗʰ
Rome 3ʳᵈ century

NITY
The Eastern Germanic tribe of the Goths are some of the first Germans to be Christianized. They were led by the Chalcedonian Bishop Wulfila (or Ufilas) in the 4ᵗʰ century. AD 476 the Western Roman Empire falls to Odoacer who proclaims himself "King of Italy" – Western Rome becomes an Ostrogothic kingdom under Arian Christians. Eastern & Western Church split in AD 1053.

ic Christianity: Monastic
e church   Irish
                    missionaries
                    sent to the
                    Germanic
                    tribes 6ᵗʰ – 7ᵗʰ
                    century

LICISM

St. Boniface fells the Saxon's Donars Oak AD 723; Saxon nobility officially converts AD 785 (8ᵗʰ century). Meister Eckhart: 13ᵗʰ c.; St. Hildegard of Bingen: 12ᵗʰ c. St. Albertus Magnus: 12ᵗʰ c.
6ᵗʰ – 11ᵗʰ century

CE ERA GERMAN   EARLY MODERN PERIOD GERMAN RELIGION:
Era 11ᵗʰ – 13ᵗʰ   CATHOLICISM & REFORMATION: 15ᵗʰ – 18ᵗʰ
century   century

GERMAN FOLK CHRISTIANITY DURING THESE PERIODS: AN AMALGAMATION OF ALL FOREGOING RELIGIO-MAGICAL CURRENTS

PIETISM, ANABAPTISM, LUTHERANISM
Luther's 95 Theses 1517

MODERN PERIOD: ROSICRUCIANISM, THEOSOPHY, BEHMENISM, MESMERISM: 18ᵗʰ century to present⁸

Germanic Theosophists/Pietists: Boehme: 16ᵗʰ/17ᵗʰ century; Gichtel, Beissel, Kelpius: 18ᵗʰ century; also Lutheran minister & astrologer Valentin Weigel: 16ᵗʰ century

The Germanic peoples were undergoing Christianization from the 4ᵗʰ century (Goths) until the 18ᵗʰ century: a time span of 1600-years.

EI

Healing magic has universal appeal as disease and accidents unfortunately touch everyone from time to time. It is little wonder that so many of these charms and amulets have spread far and wide throughout Europe and the British Isles. A blood-stopping charm such as the *"Jesus Christ, dearest blood, who stops the pain and stops the blood"* can be found from England to Germany and appears in the old Bruache books too. Tracing the culture of origin for any of these incantations is a very tricky business.[47] It is hoped that the examples given here will jogg the reader's interest and encourage others to take up this line of research.

Indeed healing rituals and charming are very ancient. The later Christian forms have been built upon a foundation of very old ideas and verbal/ritual conventions (meter, rhyme, etc.). During the transitional period between the Christian and pre-Christian eras, it is clear that these cultures influenced eachother in many peculiar ways. The pre-Christian content of Bruacherei then exists as the survival of *ideas* and *forms* – not any specific pagan or heathen theology or cultus.

The diagram on page 100-101, "The Historical Roots of Bruacherei," illustrates the many different possible cultural interactions that may have contributed to this healing art. Some streams are unquestionable the further in time the diagram goes; the farther back, the more speculative it becomes.

---

47   Eastern Europe is a little different. The folk magic of those regions has retained a good deal of pre-Christian Slavic religion. Latvian, Estonian, Finnish and Lithuanian folk magic retains more of that sort of content than has that of Central/Western Europe.

3: Sympathy and Prayer

And these signs shall follow them that believe; "In my name shall they cast out devils; they shall speak with new tongues; they shall take up serpents; and if they drink any deadly thing, it shall not hurt them; they shall lay hands on the sick, and they shall recover." **Mark 16:17-18 KJV**

Indeed, I told myself that Elisha would come out to greet me; that he would stand and call on the name of his God; and that he would put his hand upon the place and heal the leprosy. **4 Kingdoms 5:11 The Orthodox Study Bible**

An Old View of the World

There are many practitioners of Brauche work that will not use the word "magic" to describe what they do. Indeed, it's a loaded term just was with the word "Witch" (discussed below). In fact, there is much justification for a repugnance or resistance to the description when the magical art is understood in the common way as either illusion, trickery, or the works of the Devil. What is not commonly seen or understood by many is the "sympathetic" world-view of healers past and present – an ancient view of the way in which God, creation, and each creature one with the other interact and are connected. Countless cultures have referred to the matrix of Nature as a "web" and depicted the Supreme Being as a weaver, whose symbolic emblems were spiders, spindles, looms, and such.

When we understand that all aspects of creation are energetically connected together in largely unseen ways, the concept of "sympathetic medicine" becomes not only understandable, but rational. Despite living in the 21st century, most people today still have what we might describe as materialistic 19th century view of how the world works – a form of scientific knowledge that passed away with the theories of Albert Einstein after the beginning of the previous century. Indeed, the advances in Quantum Mechanics, String Theory, Chaos Theory, etc. shows up this gulf or knowledge-gap when people express surprise or disbelief that healing can be had outside of a hospital, or that prayer can actually affect another at a distance. This "new" knowledge of how the world works is not new at all, and would be quite familiar to the shamans of the past. When we retreat from the mechanistic, materialistic, Victorian-scientific view of how creation operates, sympathetic medicine no longer appears as "superstition".

There are various "modalities" of Braucherei practice. Many of these are covered in this present work. Aside from the 'mystical' charms and 'odd' prayers, perhaps the most eye-catching modality is the use of various hand gestures to affect healing. Presented later on is one of the more extensive and complex methods of this variety of Pow-Wowing. This manner of working closely resembles Reiki, Therapeutic Touch, as well as old-fashioned Mesmerism. Other varieties of the Pow-Wow laying-on of hands are less complicated, and may resemble the form of laying-on that is done in the churches. One form of Brauche work is very much a form of intense massage and has elements of what we now call "Reflexology".

The practice of the laying-on of hands is quite ancient – that is to say, laying-on in the general sense of using the hands to touch or 'go-over' the body of an ill person. Yet, it may very well be possible that complex means of affecting this work, such as "The General Brauche Circuit" provided later on, was a result of popular movements such as Mesmerism during 18th and 19th centuries.

George Barth, in his book *The Mesmerist's Manual of Phenomena and Practice* (1850), describes the hand motions undertaken in Mesmerist practice. These gestures come very close to the gestures of Brauche work, which have a general top-to-downward motion with sweeps away from the patient. The Mesmerist places the hands no closer than three inches to the surface of the patient's body, and often much farther away than this. Little physical contact is made with the patient, which is the method of the Brauche work presented in this volume.

Other forms of the laying-on of hands are more directly physical, such as was practiced by the healer Oskar Estebany. Dr. Dolores Krieger studied Estebany's methods and was pleasantly surprised to meet a gentle and sincere healer, with none of the arm-waving and bombast of the stereotypical Mesmerist.

> Oskar Estebany had been a Colonel in the Hungarian cavalry. He loved horses; and one day, when his own horse became ill, he stayed all night in the stable with the horse. He knew the horse would be shot if it did not recover, and so he did everything he could think of to help the horse: He massaged it, he caressed it, he talked to it, he prayed over it. The last, in particular, he did not do lightly, for he was a man of deep religious beliefs. In the morning, to the surprise of all, including himself, Estebany found that the horse was well.[1]
>
> His healing ability carried with it a deep sense of commitment, and he did not spare himself in its practice: He frequently worked on the healees sixteen hours a day; more often than not he worked until Dora [Kunz] took away his patients and made him relax. Even then, he would take with him rolls of cotton batting to "magnetize" for the healees, and in the morning he would be up before sunrise, ready to start healing again. He would distribute the magnetized cotton to the healees after having it near his person during the night; some of these

---

1   Krieger, p. 4

patients have told me that, even after nearly a year, they could still feel an energy flow from the cotton.²

Estebany's magnetized cotton is not dissimilar to the Brauche bags and *zauberzetteln* given to patients by Pow-Wow doctors. These, too, are given to patients not just as "prophylactic"³ magical agents, but as devices to transfer healing energy to patients in the Braucher's absence. This is a form of what we might call "automated remote healing," for a lack of better terminology.

Etheric Fluid and Magnetism

Franz (Friedrich) Anton Mesmer (b. 1734 – d. 1815) may have coined the term "animal magnetism" in order to describe the energetic interchange between the healer and patient, but he was definitely not the first to have discovered the use of *magnetism* or to use such a term for this style of medical treatment. Paracelsus (see Glossary), in fact, was working with magnetism and sympathies 200 years before Mesmer came along. It is interesting to observe that a good deal of the practitioners of early energetic medicine were Germans. Paracelsus wrote the following.

> Man possesses a magnetic power by which he can attract certain effluvia of a good or evil quality in the same manner as a magnet will attract particles of iron. A magnet may be prepared from iron that will attract iron, and a magnet may be prepared out of some vital substance that will attract vitality.⁴

According to Barth, Mesmer was mainly influenced by the magnetic work of John Baptist von Helmot ("The Magnetic Cure of Wounds" – 1617), and Dr. Robert Fludd (*Mosaical Philosophy* – 1659)

2	Krieger, p. 5
3	That is, "protective" – amulets for protection
4	Hartmann, p. 187

Mesmer's animal magnetism is the same as Paracelsus' "mumia". Mesmer chose the word "animal" as it relates to the Latin *animus*, meaning "spirit". In the East this same "fluid" is known as *prana*. A century prior to Wilhelm Reich, Mesmer was attempting to build devices that would accumulate and concentrate this mysterious power. This power or energy was conceived of as being an etheric fluid that connected all things. Mesmer believed that disease was an unnatural event, and it arose from a knotting-up (or damming-up) of the flow this fluid. Those who are familiar with the concept of *chi* will automatically understand this notion. The much earlier Paracelsian diagnosis of disease was identical to this.

> Philosophy informs us that the world is made out of the will of God. If, then, all things are made out of will, it logically follows that the causes of all internal diseases are also originating within the will. All diseases, such as are not caused by any action coming from the outside, are due to a perverted action of the will in man, such as is not in harmony with the laws of Nature or God.[5]

The Lutheran pastor and psychologist William Backus makes the interesting observation that spiritual healing can lead to physical healing; the 'energy dams' that are created by a perversity in our will and ill-perception can be released through *repentance*, which in the New Testament literally means to change one's mind.[6] The healer, according to Therapeutic Touch pioneer Dr. Dolores Krieger, is an activator or booster to the "healee" in order to remove these blockages or misalignments of energy.

"If evil elements exist in the sphere of our soul, they attract such astral influences as may develop disease." – Paracelsus

---

5   Hartmann, pp 200 - 01
6   Backus, p. 117

"Magnets" and Contagion

Seemingly "witchy" substances such as hair, nails, and blood, etc. are sympathetic elements that can be used to great affect in the healing of disease. The Brauche manuals of the past are based entirely on the twin engines of verbal charming (prayer), and sympathetic remedies. It is unfortunate, however, that some of the *raison d'être* for many of these practices were forgotten and the void filled in with genuine superstition (e.g., see the Introduction regarding *asafetida*).

Some Paracelsian methods of sympathetic healing include the use of what is sometimes called a *zwischentrager*, or "go-between"[7] to take up the disease or other malady from the patient and transferred elsewhere. Now, the Paracelsian method is a little different in some respects to a straight-forward go-between devise. To sympathetically cure a person of a certain disease, it is necessary to know the planetary rulership of the illness; next some physical substance such as nails, skin, blood, etc. is to be dried out if it is a wet material. Once the material is desiccated, it is placed in the area of the affliction and acts as a sponge to draw out the illness. It works this way because the material still contains the energetic signatures of the patient's body and is therefore still linked to the patient. The desiccated material (called a "magnet") will lack its original *mumia*, and because of its connection to the body, it will draw out the illness in a 'vampiric' manner. The "magnet" is then mixed with dirt and an herb of the same planetary signature as the illness is to be grown in this earth. As the plant grows, it transmutes the energy of the disease and relays back health to the patient through the sympathetic connection.

In folk magic and medicine *contagion* is the analogue of sympathy. The Paracelsian "magnets" are examples of vehicles for contagion. The *zwischentrager* carries the contagion from one thing to another.

---

7   *Zwischentrager* is not an entirely correct term for the "magnets" used in Paracelsian practice, but these magnets function nonetheless as go-betweens or vehicles for contagion just as the more 'primitive' devices of folk magic do.

In some Pow-Wow practice, pennies, potatoes, pieces of meat, etc. are used to remove warts, for example; that is, they are used to draw out the energy of the wart and carry its contagion. This concept is explored in further depth throughout later on. It is a practice in some cultures to take the contaminated items and leave them where they will be found by another, who will then take up the illness and relieve the original sufferer.

Active Prayer

This is what a few Braucher's call their practice – not Pow-Wow, not Braucherei. It is a way to distance the practice from overloaded concepts such as "magic" and especially "Witchcraft," as mentioned at the beginning of this chapter. Truly, "active prayer" is a great term for what a Pow-Wower really does.

All prayers are active, *if they come from the one's heart-center*. "Prayers" such as "Oh God, if you let me hit the Power Ball tonight, I swear that…" Those don't count.

One disgruntled ex-minister, now professional atheist, likes to say "Nothing fails like prayer." He's wrong, and now there is a growing body of evidence that demonstrates it. Of course, when it comes to scientific, quantitative analysis, prayer can be a little slippery to study. When creating an experiment, all factors need to be considered; and in prayer, some variables are not measurable. Divine intervention, for example, is not measurable. Even when prayer is demonstrated to work, scientists can come up with dozens of reasons for its success outside of considering intervention by Divine Providence.

When testing new medications, scientists can control the dose – there are beakers and scales and other instruments that can measure the precise amounts in each dose for each test subject. When testing prayer, how does a researcher measure the 'dosage'? If a prayer for healing by one person works more strongly than that of another, can it be conclude that the first person prayed more vigorously, or that there is some 'quality' possessed by that individual lacked in the other? And, these sorts of questions are just the beginning of the types of variables that need consideration in the scientific study of prayer.

Sir Francis Galton during the late Victorian era wished to determine if prayer had any effect on the life expectancies of clergy as opposed to materialists; or if frequently prayed for individuals (such as the Queen) lived longer than others. This first attempt at a scientific study of prayer was a disappointment. The conclusion he reached was that prayer had no affect on longevity.

Since the time of Sir Francis, numerous studies have been conducted under varying degrees of scientific rigor; some of these have show promise. The National Institute for Healthcare Research (NIHR) has compiled a mammoth three volume compilation of abstracts for 1200 studies on the subject of spirituality, prayer, and healing entitled *The Faith Factor: An Annotated Bibliography of Clinical Research on Spiritual Subjects*. A well know double-blind study was conducted by Dr. Randolf Byrd, and appeared in the *Southern Medical Journal* in December 1988.[8] Over a period of ten months 393 patients were studied; 192 were randomly selected for prayer, and 201 were in the control group. Those who prayed were not physically in the hospital, while neither the patients, nor the doctors, were aware of who was being prayed for. The patients that received prayer had significant recovery compared to those patients in the control group. None in the prayed for group was in need of intubations, and were less likely to need antibiotics. In another piece of research; *The effect of "distance healing": a systematic review of randomized trials*,[9] 23 studies were conducted of 2,774 patients that met inclusion criteria. Different modalities of "distance"

---

8   Byrd, R.C. (1988). Positive therapeutic effects of intercessory prayer in a coronary care unit population.

9   Astin, J.A., Harkness, E., Ernest E. *The efficacy of "distant healing": a systematic review of randomized trials*. Ann Intern Med 2000 June 6; 132: 903-10.

healing were tested: Therapeutic Touch, prayer, paranormal healing, psychokinetic influence, and remote mental healing. Eleven trials tested non-contact Therapeutic Touch; of the 11, seven showed positive treatment. Of the 23 studies, 57% showed positive treatment. In 1969, J.P. Collipp's, *The efficacy of prayer: a triple-blind study*, appeared in the *Medical Times*. Of the 18 children in the study, 10 were randomly selected to receive prayer; the control group of eight did not receive prayer. After 15 months of the study, seven children in the prayer group were still alive; and of the eight in the control group, only two remained.

Different explanations have been proposed for the success of prayer: placebo effect, self-hypnosis, and the power of suggestion, the strengthening of the immune system due to lower stress levels as a physiological benefit of prayer; also spontaneous remission, and pure coincidence. Among those interested in psychic phenomena the explanations include various theories on the projection of energy or mental power. The last thing that seems to be considered is Divine Intervention of one manner or another. It is true that these sorts of healings can (and do) fall under any one of these categories at any given time. It is true that there is a placebo effect that sometimes kicks in when someone knows they are on the receiving end of a healing; yet not all healings are done with the knowledge of the patient. The metaphysically minded will say that the subconscious mind of the patient 'picked up on' the psychic intent of the healer and responded, thereby yet again eliminating Divine Intervention. Then again, our old friend Paracelsus had something to say about these invisible, yet natural functions of which we are capable of influencing each other for good or ill:

> In the Mumia there is a great power, and the cures that have been performed by the use of the Mumia are natural, although they are very little understood by the vulgar…They therefore look upon such cures as having been produced by 'black art,' or by the help of the devil…and even if the devil had

caused them, the devil can have no power except that which is given to him by God, so it would be the power of God after all.[10]

It is hoped that Paracelsus' point is not lost. By extension, the Devil aside, even our own psychical powers are not totally our own, and are really just on loan as it were. Therefore, when researchers go on an Easter Egg hunt for 'causes' in spiritual healing and avoid the God-question, such as Dolores Krieger does with Therapeutic Touch, it's really all the same difference whether they realize it or not, as all power ultimately comes from the One Power. God is Sovereign. William Backus in his *Healing Power of a Christian Mind*, a very good book incidentally, goes on a small rant against "New Age" beliefs. The problem with belief in the powers of the mind, by his estimation, is that they remove God from the Sovereign position and negate any Divine influence to be had as a result of prayer. The so-called psychical powers we possess as human beings are no different than any of the other abilities or gifts we have been given. However, because psychic phenomena seems to encroach a bit more closely on numinous holy ground (i.e., the "spirit realm"), it appears to some folks that it ought to be *verboten* as it may lead to some form of idol-worship. Unfortunately, that point is sometimes too close to the mark. We tend to allow our egos to make gods of ourselves; in our hubris we sometimes forget who the Land Lord is, and really think that we own the place.

---

10   Hartmann, p. 185

4: The Damned "W" Word

Witchcraft -- the relationship between Hexerei and Braucherei

When composing this book there was originally no intention to devote an entire chapter to the subject of hexerei. However, a book on Braucherei would really be incomplete without a more thorough discussion on the subject. Witchcraft is not always a titillating thing to write about, as it is a maelstrom, a hornet's nest chalk-full of all sorts of problems. Despite this, here needs to be discussed the vexed (hexed?) question of what constitutes a "Witch" and, therefore, "Witchcraft". Since this is a book on Pennsylvania German folk magic and healing, the field is narrowed a bit, thereby cutting down on some of the dissonance. Within the context of traditional Pennsylvania German culture, *Witch-ness* (that is, to be a Witch, a "hex") takes on a specific set of meanings.

In the Introduction, some rather harsh things are said about hexerei. As this chapter develops, you will see why.

> In Pennsylvania Dutch tradition:
>
> Is a Witch a devil-worshipper? A: Maybe, but not really, not always. Many times, never.
>
> Is a Witch a Pagan religionist (such as a Wiccan)? A: No.
>
> Is Witchcraft the practice of malevolent magic? A: Yes, mostly.
>
> Can a Witch ever be good? A: No, mostly. But it really depends.

𝕿𝖍𝖊 𝕻𝖔𝖜𝖊𝖗 𝖙𝖍𝖆𝖙 𝕭𝖎𝖓𝖉𝖘

While exploring hexerei, keep this one precept foremost in your mind: Witchcraft is an idiom for ***power***.[11] It's all about power: how it is used, to what *extent* it is exercised, and to what *degree* the practitioner possesses it (or as the Dutch would say, *to what degree **it** possesses the practitioner*). Power is the bottom line in the struggle between what is good and what is evil.

Power possesses. It's rarely possessed. In a way, that is true of Braucherei too, as the Braucher is an instrument of Providence. It is the Deity that *is* the Power and the source of all power, not the little homosapien conjuror calling on Power. In Christian (Catholic/Orthodox) terms this can be seen in the fact that even the Virgin

---

11   James Martin Nyce. *Convention, Power, and the Self in German Mennonite Magic.* Thesis. May 1987 pp73-98.

Mary is not divine *in herself*, but has taken on divine Light or Fire by her grace from, and proximity to God. The Eastern Orthodox Churches refer to that burning nearness to God as *theosis*[12]. Even Lucifer does not shine with his own Light, but only that given to him.

Now, with hexerei a Witch can almost always be described as a *teufelsdiener* -- that is to say, a "devil's servant". What this actually means really depends upon the Witch. As mentioned above, a Witch is not necessarily a person who is a devil-worshipper. By devil-worshipper, this means one who consciously and willingly gives divine honors and worship to Satan, following him even as a devout Christian would follow Christ. However, a Witch is often a devil's servant nonetheless, despite the possibility of that missing element of *latria*[13].

The "Faustian" class of magicians, who make pacts with demonic powers, or the Devil himself, are such servants. Even though the pact is a business deal of sorts, they have placed themselves in vassalage, in direct possession *by* that power wielded by the Devil. In classical theological thought, that is to say that the Devil himself only obtains the power God allows him *to borrow* and exercise. The Devil is not a Power in his own right. The Faust-type magician, therefore, need not worship the Devil but only enjoy what benefits that may be had from such an arrangement.

---

12 *Theosis* is also called "deification". This is the process of becoming more like God through His grace. See 2 Peter 1:3,4. *Theosis* is not to be confused with another term *apotheosis*, which is the soul *becoming* a god *per se*. In Christian theology this is not possible, because all things are by nature what they are and cannot become something else outside of that nature. For example, an acorn always grows into an oak tree; it can never grow into a spruce. The Greek word *theos* (God) comes from a verb meaning "run," "see," "burn" --all of which have energetic connotations.

13 *Latria* is a Latin term used in theology referring to the worship that is due to God alone. In Catholic theology there are two other forms recognized: *dulia* and *hyperdulia*. The former is the respect and honor that is given to saints and angels; the latter is a special 'extra' veneration reserved for the Virgin Mary. Neither of these is classed as "worship", which is only *latria*. True devil or demon-worship then is diabolatry, or demonolatry.

According to the folklore of the demonic pact the goods delivered by Hell are not always what the magician expects, or at least *how* he expects them. In fact, this en-vassalage need not occur as a result of a tacit or planned pact, but may happen according to a process referred to as "being read fast". To be "read fast" is to be consumed by (or "locked into") what are considered "forbidden" magical writings, otherwise called *grimoires* or *grammaries*. A Braucher is not immune to being caught in this trap and thereby cross over into the realm of Witchdom.

Gradually, the power takes over the life of the conjuror until little is left. He or she ends up having no control over the magic itself. Every act of magic twists, becomes twisted, reverses, or has otherwise wholly unexpected results. The Witch then entirely slips down the hellish slope becoming little more than a transmitting device for malice -- even if the Witch has no desire to harm, that harm will radiate off of him or her anyway. At this stage in the degeneration it is said that little can be done for such an affected person. However, if caught in time, a *read fast* practitioner can be rescued. The process of *reading-out* is tedious: the Braucher needs to read backwards each and every word in his forbidden books[14]. This is quite literally like finding the way out of a labyrinth tracing steps backwards.

Betty Snellenburg in "Four Interviews with Powwowers" receives a description by an informant of the severity of being "locked into" Witchcraft:

> The children of a certain family were dying, one by one, of tuberculosis. Mr. D. took the parents to see Mr. O. Mr. O., after while, "looked the mother right in the eye and said, 'If I were you, I'd leave my children alone'". The woman was very upset because she hadn't known she was bewitching her

---

14   Bill Ellis, *Lucifer Ascending: The Occult in Folklore and Popular Culture*. The University Press of Kentucky, 2004. In chapter four, "Satanic Bibles", Ellis carefully describes the tradition of forbidden magic books and the phenomenon of being "read fast", pp 70 - 79 being the most germane.

children. Afterward, the members of the family still kept dying of tuberculosis. Mr. O. explained to Mr. D. that even though she now realized what she was doing, the mother "would not stop until every last member of her family was dead" because she was "locked into" being a Witch. And, sure enough, Mr. D. explained, not one member of the family survived, not even the grandson. [15]

Regarding the issue of "black magic": in the old sense this is the conjuring and binding of spirits towards earthly ends. The old black magicians were often conventionally religious, calling upon God to bind demonic entities for their use. Many Churchmen were *de facto* black magicians. This magic did not verge into the realm of heresy unless the magician ordered the spirit to perform deeds outside of what God allows such spirits to do, or what would be lawful for the magician to possess.

This process of binding spirits is called evocation. Meanwhile the invocation of angelic powers of the heavenly realm were considered above-board and respectable. Of course, not everyone saw it this way. Cornelius Agrippa was once run out of the University of Dole[16] when a monk accused him of heresy. In those days, a magician would have little to worry about when under the patronage of a prince, king, or "prince of the Church". However, it took only one condemnation to send a conjuror packing. Sometimes even the strongest patrons could not entirely intervene once the heresy-hunting machinery was set into motion. Occultist Arthur Edward Waite had this to say,

> The presumed possession of the secret of this art [domination over spiritual powers] made Magic formidable, and made therefore its history.

And

---

15   Snellenburg, p. 41

16   Skinner p229. This was only one of many instances of Agrippa having to take flight.

It was the fascination of this process which brought men and women --all sorts and conditions of both-- to the Black Sabbath and to the White Sabbath, and blinded them to the danger of the stake.[17]

Power binds, and magicians both dubious and otherwise are bound by their deeds. Our Germanic ancestors would have referred to this as laying deeds in the Well of Wyrd, creating one's fate for better or worse.

The Degrees of Power

Degrees of power have been mapped out by Don Yoder cited by James Martin Nyce.[18] These degrees are reminiscent of a sort of paranormal Fujita Scale in their intensities and potentials for destruction. The classifications are given as: charmers, Powwowers, hex doctors (or witch doctors), and Witches. According to Yoder all of these practitioners are "Powwowers of different sorts and status."[19] It may seem that, at the end of the day, 'a Witch is a Witch is a Witch' -- a rose by any other name, etc. What class a practitioner falls into depends upon his or her degree of seriousness and involvement with the Art.

The Charmer

Charmers, being the least involved, are "respectable" individuals who may know a *besprechen* or two for the occasional bleeding cut or obnoxious wart. Such charmers are the most numerous of the Braucherei folk. Many of you reading this book will fall into the

---

17   Arthur Edward Waite. *The Book of Black Magic and of Pacts: Including the Rites and Mysteries of Goetic Theurgy, Sorcery and Infernal Necromancy.* The de Laurence Company, Inc., Chicago. 1940. p7. Waite's "Black" and "White Sabbath" refer to varying theories as to the nature of the Witches' Sabbath: was it truly infernal (Satanic worship), or just an excuse for a sex orgy ("Venus" worship)?

18   Nyce pp 78-80.

19   Ibid.

first category, as very few wish to go beyond this *level of use*.

The Powwower

A Powwower by Yoder's classification is one, who by his or her deeper involvement and competency, moves closer to the realm of the professional practitioner, and also enters a new level of doubtfulness.[20] Outside of Pennsylvania Dutch culture a parallel to this extent of *using* would be the Scots-Irish "granny women" of Appalachia. However, no gender in these degrees of power is implied here. Familial terms of endearment are found for both sexes of the "Powwower" level. "Grandmas", "uncles", and "*old* So-&-So's" abounded.

The Hex Doctor

A Braucher who takes this competency to full-time using of Powwow is re-classed as a hex doctor. A hex doctor's skill set is that of a ceremonial magician. That is not to say that he or she is an actual ceremonial magician in practice (although he may be), but that such a person has that full range of skill. These would include: divination, angelic invocation, spirit conjuration, the making of amulets and talismans, counter Witchcraft 'spells', and Witch finding (which falls under the heading of divination, but was often enough a principal activity in its own right). If the Powwower is a dubious figure, the hex doctor's reputation is off the charts. *"These figures were feared, avoided and resorted to only for their healing and to counter the magic of a Witch."*[21]

Now, in fact, an hex doctor will usually be a decent person, despite the dread attached to the occupation by non-practitioners. Such a figure may very well attend services every Sunday, coach Little League, belong to the PTA, and hold down a regular job in addition to more-or-less on-call brauching. Community distrust of the hex

---

20   That is to say, the powwow is regarded as "less respectable" because the power possession makes not only the practitioner's personal motives less transparent, but the degree of power possession more opaque as well. Such a professional magic user may be a Witch unknown.

21   Op. Cit. p80.

doctor is not always automatic or a given. Many communities of the past have loved and valued a really good hex doctor, such as Brauchers[22] from the family lines of the Saylors[23] or Wilhelms of 19th and early 20th century Williams Township, Pennsylvania.[24]

A prerequisite for Braucherei treatment is that one believes in God. By tradition, specifically this means that one needs to be a Christian. Some scholars have made *this* particular point yet another theoretical dividing line between common Pow-Wow practitioners and the professional hex doctors. To consult with a hex doctor religious faith was not seen as prerequisite. *"The very fact that they were bewitched and being tormented was realistic enough for them to believe in the existence in a God and a Devil."*[25] In some manner, the hex doctor's powers would seem to be independent of 'faith' for the client and perhaps the hex doctor himself. But, this seems to me to be an almost arbitrary categorization. Past practitioners who have been labeled 'hex doctors' or 'hexenmeisters', or who have labeled themselves such do not seem to always fit this rule of thumb.[26]

The Witch

This is the final degree of power in Yoder's classification, and the subject of this chapter. Nyce observes that Yoder's categories "come apart" when attempting to define what a Witch is. Oddly enough, this is where our subject comes together with the Witch as the yardstick.

Although this is the final level in the Yoderite classing, the powers and potentials of the Witch and the hexenmeister[27] are roughly

---

22   Unlike Yoder and Nyce, I use the terms *hex doctor* and *powwow doctor* interchangeable with *braucher*.

23   Also spelled Seiler, or Sailor.

24   Heindel 2005.

25   Shaner 1963, p9.

26   Such public examples of not fitting this description by Shaner would be the authors Karl Herr (pseud.) and Lee R. Gandee.

27   Literally, "Witch master". This designates that one is skilled in overmastering the malevolent spells of others. Some have claimed that this title might indicate one who is a "master" in the sense of being a Witch *leader*. However, this has never been its real meaning. A similar

equal. This is why the hex doctor is ideal for fighting true cases of malevolent magic. Sociologically, the hexenmeister and Witch diverge from one another in their degree liminality or 'otherness' in comparison to the ways of the community. To put it shortly, a Witch is a Witch because he cannot be trusted, his values are alien and his motives and goals unknown. Despite this, the figure of the Witch acts to reify and define community boundaries. The hexenmeister, by this model, sits on the edge of being trustworthy or touchable.

The Etymological Origins of Witch

It is hoped that the next few paragraphs will enlighten and not cause the eyes to glaze over. Etymology, the study of the origins of words, can have that latter effect. All of the hoopla surrounding *the Witch* cannot really be accounted for without some explanation of the terms surrounding the idea.

The English:
The word 'Witch' derives from much earlier English. In Middle English this would be *wicche*; in Old English (Anglo-Saxon) *wicca*[28] (male) and *wicce* (female). To 'beWitch' was *wiccian*[29]. The practice itself was *wiccecraeft*. This particular set of English words comes from the Low German word *wikken* or *wicken* (to use Witchcraft); while a *wikker* or *wicker* is a soothsayer. It is possible that these words may be related to yet another ancient term, *wigle* (meaning divination), or *wig/wih* (an idol -- a *wiglaer* being an idol worshiper). All of these may be the children of the Proto-Germanic *wikkjaz*, being a sorcerer.

---

term such as "devil's master" is hardly synonymous with a devil's disciple, but a folksy term for an exorcist (hence, someone who is skilled in kicking a demon's arse and not in kissing it).

28 All of the foregoing etymologies can be found in the Online Etymology Dictionary: www.etymonline.com.

29 Some like to believe that wicca means 'wise' and that Witchcraft, therefore, means "craft of the wise". This is total nonsense, as any good etymological dictionary will show. Incidentally, the double *cc* in Old English is pronounced "ch" or "tch".

The German:

Now, *hex*, *hexe*, *hexen* (plural) and *hexerei* descend from the Middle High German *hexse*. Farther back *hex* is traceable to the Old High German word *hagazussa*. This last word is directly related to another Old English word for 'Witch' being *haegtessa*. It is from this constellation of Germanic words that we get our modern English word 'hag'. Haegtessa literally means one who is a "hedge rider". The words 'hedge' and 'hag' are related. The Havamal speaks of *"hedge riders witching aloft"*. A Witch, in this archaic sense, is a shamanistic[30] boundary traverser. It is from this most ancient conception that we have our notions of Witches flying on broomsticks and pitchforks.

The Hedge:

The hedges (or hedgerows) were literally the boundaries of our ancestors' villages, and all that lay outside of these hedge-walls was the unknown, the wild. A "Witch" traveled beyond the spiritual hedge in a condition akin to out-of-body travel or "astral projection". These hedge riders were not always literal members of a community in a physical human sense. The Witch, here, is a dual figure: it can be a real flesh and blood human being skilled in the so-called shamanistic arts, or (more often) it was a phantasmal presence: an image of an uncanny or pestilential spiritual power plaguing an individual or entire community. The human practitioner eventually merged with the spectral powers in the minds of non-practitioners, as both way-fared in unseen ways in wild spirit-scapes. The Navaho *skin walkers* are such creatures as well.

---

30   I have never liked using this word. Shaman properly refers to a specific sort of aboriginal Siberian spiritual practitioner. Modern English and Romance languages tend to have limited ways of speaking on archaic spiritual and magical practices, so it is little wonder that "shaman" has been used so indiscriminately. Our vocabulary needs to become more precise as "shamanism" is now such an umbrella that it means next to nothing.

Literal or Figurative?

The duality of the Witch figure, therefore, has informed Germanic culture since times long past. It is not to be wondered that Pennsylvania Dutch culture would carry these hoary notions to the New World. This is why it is often difficult to assess the literalness of Pennsylvania Dutch Witch-tales, or reports of bewitchment. Is the Witch a literal person, or a convenient image for an unknown spiritual malady? One can just as easily be "Witched" by a spirit as by a human practitioner. Outside of the mythic dimension, it was not uncommon to hear of someone loosely speaking of "Witching" in a mundane way. Divining for water has often been called "water Witching" or "Witching for water". *To Witch*, being a common way of describing a utilitarian act of magic, without carrying the negative baggage of actually calling someone a Witch. It is in this latter sense that we derive our notions of the "white Witch". This is a person who is a Witch that is not ***a Witch***. That is to say, a person who uses magic with none of the diabolatry and evil usually attached to actual *maleficia*[31].

By this definition even a Braucher or British cunning man is a Witch. *But*, it must be made clear that this is a very loose and imprecise usage and only serves to confuse matters when speaking about **hexerei** proper. We can take ourselves around in circles arguing about how hexerei is really just 'hedgery' and, therefore, simply a misunderstood innocuous discipline. The bad reputation of hexerei started from somewhere, and usually that bit of baggage has been unfairly dropped at the doorstep of the Church. This, when our heathen ancestors knew very well about evil magic and *burned Witches* long before Jesus was a twinkle in Mary's eye[32].

31   Latin for evil-doing by way of magic. It is *maleficia* (and another term *veneficia* -- poison making) that is truly what is meant by the words *Witch* and *Witchcraft*. In Latin a "Witch" would therefore be a *malefica* or *venefica*. The Romans had a similar concept to the Germanic *hagazussa* in the figure of the *strix* or night owl. It is from the latter that Italian has its word *strega* (Witch). This is very close to the old Hebrew beliefs in the *Lilith*, a Witch-vampire-owl creature that sucks the blood of infants, and by one account, the first wife of Adam.

32   Heathen Witch hunting was not an organized affair as it was with later Christians,

The Venusberg

In the Old World many localities had their very own Witch mountain, generically known as "Venusberg". The Herz Mountain range in Germany, for example, harbors the Brocken, a peak infamous for its Witch assemblies[33]. It was here that Witches and evil spirits would hold court with Satan during the diabolic Sabbath. In older lore it was not the Devil who held sway, but "Dame Venus" who later was figured in as Satan's Sabbath Queen. "Venus" was a pseudo-classical reference to a female divinity or spirit who was an echo to the more primitive (or primal) night flying hag or hedge rider. "Diana" is another Latinate reference to this spirit. Of course, this divinity is neither the Classical Diana nor Venus. Her native Germanic names have been Holda[34], Hulda, Perchta, etc.

As a night flyer, she led a train of the dead that rode through the sky called the Wild Hunt. Among spirit leaders, she shares this distinction with Woden (Odin) who also flew with the spirits of the dead on certain nights, acting in his role as psychopomp. Later it was the Devil who took his place in the *Wild Hunt*. The spectral Sabbath fires burned and the spirit-winds roared upon the Venusberg on special nights such as Walpurgisnacht[35], being the night of April 30th, May Eve. The southern Germans who came to Pennsylvania carried this idea of Witch-mountains with them. Throughout Dutch country there have been a few hills reputed

---

especially in Germany during the Thirty Years War. Ancient Rome was a little more intense in this regard with several pagan Emperors who made round-ups of sorcerers. Rossell Hope Robbins in his comprehensive *The Encyclopedia of Witchcraft and Demonology* (Crown Publishers, Inc., NY. 1959) notes in his entry under "Germany" that *"A common fallacy imagines Witchcraft to be of popular origin. But ordinary people never took revenge on sorcerers by bringing them to trial. Certainly, some baleful sorcerers were lynched here and there, but there was no organized persecution."* p218. Kieckhefer notes on p. 41 of his book that the pagan Ammanus Marcellinus believed that the death penalty was due for anyone practicing *folk magic and healing charms*.

33 Sweden had an equally sinister mountain called the Blokula.
34 Holda may be an ancestress to our Mother Goose.
35 In Germany this night was named after St. Walburga.

to be Witch haunted, but none so as the Hexenkopf in Williams Township.

The Hexenkopf is basically a thankless hulk of stone with a very bad reputation, surrounded as it has been by tragedies, losses, insanity, and just plane bad luck. It gained its name from the curious shape of one of its most prominent outcroppings, shaped as it is like the outline of a stereotypical Witch's head (i.e,. a *hexenkopf*). Most of these unhappy occurrences took place soon after settlers made their way into what was then considered to be the Western frontier. Legend has it that the Hexenkopf was sacred to certain Indian tribes, with almost ghostly sightings of Indians appearing out of nowhere reported well into the 19th century. During the late Victorian and early Edwardian periods it was not unusual for the un-superstitious to go on picnic outings to the rock, apparently with little or no incident. Due to the presence of mica in the stone, the mountain emits an eerie glow when bathed in moonlight. This effect probably did not help its reputation for those with active imaginations. It was this Witch's Head that was the center for the lively revels of evil spirits in that locale. When reading over some of the accounts, the duality of the Witch figure becomes prominent. Back to the former question: is the Witch real or just figurative?

> In an interview a Lehigh Valley lawyer recalled how the Walpurgisnacht dances figured in a divorce action brought by one of his clients at the end of World War I. A farmer sought the advice of his lawyer after making the terrifying discovery that his wife was a Witch. It seems that on Walpurgisnacht he had gone to bed, but because of excessive coffee consumption he could not fall asleep. His wife, thinking him asleep, arose from bed just before midnight, anointed her face with an ointment from her dresser drawer, mounted a broomstick, uttered, "*Uber Stock und uber Stein,*" and flew out the window. Curiosity prompted the farmer to grab

a broom and to repeat the procedure. Immediately he found himself flying through the air on a broom which took him to the Hexenkopf summit on which blazed a huge bonfire.[36]

After arriving at the mountain his wife showed no sign of surprise, leading him to a banquet table attended by "little black men with long tails"[37] who served him an intoxicating brew. According to the lawyer, the husband remembered little more, awaking as he did in his neighbor's pig pen. Interestingly, the lawyer helped smooth things out between the farmer and his wife, thereby avoiding an embarrassing debut in court for all. This is more or less how many of these stories go. The account came from an attorney. Could it all have been made up? Was the farmer delusional; was he having a bad nightmare; was he going senile? Or, did something untoward and uncanny truly occur that May Eve?

St. Paul tells us in Ephesians 6:12 (NKJV),

> For we do not wrestle against flesh and blood, but against principalities, against powers, against the rulers of darkness of this age, against spiritual hosts of wickedness in the heavenly places.

There is little doubt that some Brauchers actively take on wicked spirits when fighting for the health and sanity of a client or even an entire community. And for these spirits, their human janissaries are the hexen with whom the Braucher will also do battle against their pernicious influence.

The Hexenkopf was the contagion-target for one Dr. Peter Saylor (1770 - 1862) of Raubsville, Williams Township. Dr. Saylor's method of brauching involved the transference of disease and malign Witchcraft from the patient to the passive receiver, Hexenkopf. The Bible gives a good example of this sort of transference when Christ

---

36 Heindel 2005, p67.
37 Op. Cit.

ordered the spirits out of the demoniac and into a herd of swine (Matt 8:32).

A favorite activity of rural Witches was the enchanting of farm animals, magically stealing milk, or otherwise spoiling milk and butter. Franz Hartmann recalls a modern day (circa early 20th century) instance of this sort of Witchcraft. It is worth quoting in full.

> Several cases of "bewitched cattle" and "blue milk" are known to me personally, of which I will mention the following as an example: -- At a farm-house not far from Munich the milk became one day "blue"; after having been deposited in the usual place it began to darken, became lightly blue, and that colour after a while deepened into an almost inky darkness, while the layer of cream exhibited zigzag lines, and soon the whole mass began to putrefy and to emit a horrible odour. This occurred again and again every day, and the farmer was in despair. Everything was attempted to find out the cause of the trouble; the stable was thoroughly cleaned, the place where the milk was kept was changed, a different food was given to the cattle, and samples of the milk were sent to Munich to be examined by chemists; the old milk-pots were replaced by new ones, &c., but nothing produced a change in the existing state of affairs.
>
> At last my sister, the Countess S---, who resides in the neighbourhood, hearing of these things, went to that farm-house to investigate the matter. She took with her a clean, new bottle, and filled it with the milk as it came from the bewitched cows. This milk she took home with her and deposited it in her own pantry, and from that day the trouble in

the house of her neighbor ceased, and all the milk in her own house became blue.

Here again everything was tried to find out the cause, but without any success, until, about three months afterwards, some old lady – living about 300 miles distant – effected another spell by her own occult powers, using some slips of paper, on which she wrote something, and in consequence of which the trouble ceased. Before it ceased, however, something strange happened. Before daybreak, as the milkmaid was about to enter the stable, some black thing like an animal rushed out of the half-opened door, knocked the milk-pail and the lantern out of her hands, and disappeared. After this all went well again.

On another occasion, in a similar case which too place in the same neighborhood, the owner of the bewitched cattle was advised to take a sample of the milk from each cow, to mix them in a pan, to boil it over a slow fire, and to whip it with a rod while it was boiling down, and to throw the rest away. This advice he followed, and on the next day a person of ill repute was met, having his face covered with bloody streaks, as if they had been inflicted with a rod. This man could give no satisfactory account of the origin of his marks, and it is supposed that he was the punished sorcerer.[38]

So, here is instance with some proof (albeit anecdotal) that such things still take place and are not the imaginings of mistaken, or uneducated superstitious minds. Hartmann was a medical doctor as well as an Esotericist. There are numerous tales such as this

[38] Hartmann pp. 154-155

one describing the effects of anti-Witch charms. The Witch is connected to his or her magical works in the same manner that hair and finger nails are connected to one's person. The magic is an extension of the self, like an appendage. If something happens to that 'appendage' it transfers to the whole Witch. That's another danger of Witchcraft. Should the afflicted figure out what is being done to them, all they have to do is know the proper way in which to 'slap' the invisible hand. For the Witch it can be much worse than this -- that 'slap' can lead to death. *Remember that Witchcraft, in this context, is unprovoked spiritual violence and molestation.*

The animal shape that is sometimes encountered, such as in the above story, can be pegged to one of two sources. It is either 1) the projection of a part of the Witch's soul (in English Witchcraft, it is called the "fetch") that can take on an animal shape, or 2) it is an independent spirit in the Witch's service. Either of these two things can be described as the Witch's "familiar."[39]

There are times that are more propitious for the working of Witchery than other. Just as in Braucherei, lunar phases are observed (and in the work of a Witch, possibly more so). To make this grow, the waxing phase is observed; but the black work is best done during the waning phase or the dark of the moon. Various planetary constellations are also conducive to works of poison and malice. In regard to Böhme's *De Signatura Rerum*, Arthur Versluis writes that Witchcraft has certain specific "signatures."

> …which is Mars beside Saturn, Venus under Mars, and Jupiter under Venus, all together under the influence of the Moon, a signature of corruption poison, and evil. Böhme's spagyric medicine,

---

[39] It should also be pointed out that brauchers can have "familiars" too. In the annals of pow-wow doctoring can be found instances of brauchers who claimed to have been given "guides" and spirit helpers. A popular type of guide is the "Indian" guide – a being said to be the soul of a deceased American Indian. If there truly is any Native American influence in braucherei, aside from some native herbal remedies, the continuing visitation of these spirits to brauchers can be a case in point.

therefore, exists in a moral context that determines its meaning; it is a medicine of the soul. – Versluis, p. 16

Witchcraft, like Braucherei, exists on – and utilizes – a spectrum of energy peculiar to it. It has its own type of "frequency" that can be apprehended by the non-physical senses when there is enough openness and sensitivity present to do so. The "energy" of hexerei has a much different feel to it than that of Braucherei. You know it when you are near it.

The Bible and Spiritual Discernment

The Red Church is, indeed, a book on "magic," but it is not a book of Witchcraft. From the foregoing you can see that magic, like any other human endeavor: art, craft, or technology can be perverted and abused. Some of the most common Christian objections to "magic" stem from the Bible itself; however, what are often not taken into consideration are two things: 1) the contexts, and 2) the original language of these texts. When the matter is more closely explored, it becomes rather apparent that it is not "magic" that is being condemned *in toto*, but rather certain types of acts and motivations that have clearly deleterious effects upon those who practice and are practiced upon.

Earlier on a rather light-weight personal definition of magic is given in a foot note stating that my definition is utilitarian, with magic being "the employment of the little known laws of nature to affect the patterns of causality in accordance to one's desires." This is a bare-bones way of defining what previous ages knew as "Natural Magic." The latter is the discovery and application of these laws, which are instituted by God in His continuous act of recreating the Universe and all things in it at every moment. Indeed, a few Rabbis have described God as a "verb" rather than a "noun" because the Almighty is always in action. If God were to truly withdraw from creation, all things would cease to exist.

There are moral laws instituted by God for the good of humanity. We are not simply beasts in the field. So, much more is expected of us. These are statements of personal faith, and are not, therefore, able to be subjected to quantifying on scales and or tested in beakers.

The most often quoted passage in the Old Testament regarding Witchcraft is **Exodus 22:18** *"Thou shalt not suffer a Witch to live."* In our currently "politically correct" culture this passage ruffles a lot of feathers. If we look at this passage measured against the laws, taboos, and mores of other cultures, we see that non-Abrahamic peoples have similar treatments for "Witches." Among the Navajo, for example, Witchcraft is seen as an abominable practice, because it is a craft used for deadly and perverted ends – they are considered murderers. Indeed, the Navajo, being a highly moral people, consider the Witch to be one who has left all standards of human decency; such a person is said to have forfeited their status as a human being. The Witches then are considered a threat to the community and could be killed with impunity.

Out of a sense of moral obligation, I wish to state that most people today who chose to refer to themselves as "Witches" are not the individuals that are being described here. In the above quoted passage from Exodus, the Hebrew word that translates into the English word "Witch" is *kashaph*. The meaning of this word is "enchanter," or "one who mutters incantations." On the surface this would look like a description of what a Braucher does! However, we have to also look at the contexts that word is used in. *Keshaphim*, being the practice of a *kashaph*, is seduction through sorcery. Semitic languages such as Hebrew, Aramaic, and Arabic are called "root languages." These languages are not written with vowels, but only consonants. From a single constellation of consonants come a multitude of words with related meanings. In the case of kashaph there is the word *kasaph*, which has the meaning of "longing," "burning desire," and also "greed." The word implies covetousness. Witchcraft, in this sense, is the working of a burning covetousness, which enchants and blinds. In **2 Kings 9:22** Queen Jezebel's actions are described as *keshaphim*, using seduction to selfish, destructive ends.

The next most quoted Witch-passages in the Old Testament are **1 Samuel 28:3-25**. This is the chapter contains the recounting of King Saul's infamous trip to see the "Witch of Endor." King Saul had purged Israel of all its magicians, sorcerers, and necromancers. Contemporary Jewish commentary on this chapter suggests that these passages are a satire on King Saul. The king, who purged his land of Witches, now ends up consulting with one. Saul was preparing for a battle with the Philistines and had received no counsel from his dreams, or from the Urim (an oracular device used in the Temple), and was about to go into battle blind. Out of desperation he consults with "a woman that hath a familiar spirit." In the King James Version of the Bible, this woman is called a "Witch." The actual Hebrew is *ob*, which has a meaning close to our modern word "medium" – as in a spiritualist medium. Some older commentators refer to her as a "Pythoness."

The Biblical injunctions against speaking with the dead are very clear. In the Jewish religion, especially in its older phases, it is considered "unclean" to come in contact with the dead. This taboo is usually in regard to corpses. Yet, what we are seeing in 1 Samuel is perhaps the extension of this taboo to the souls of the dead themselves. To practice necromancy is to place oneself in a ritual state of uncleanness, unfit for prayer to God.

> Do not have recourse to the spirits of the dead or to magicians, they will defile you. I am Yahweh your God. **Leviticus 19:31**

As a result of the taboo against speaking with the dead, Brauchers do not conduct such activities. To speak with the dead means specifically to ritually conjure a deceased person's spirit. This ought to not be confused with praying for the dead, or even "speaking to" dead relatives when thinking about them. Some Brauchers carry this taboo even to the length of never speaking to ghosts when they manifest. When ghosts come they usually do so on their own volition, and not because they were forced by way of sorcery. If you encounter spirits ("ghosts") it is perfectly legitimate to query them in order to discern if they are from God or from the Devil. This is what is known as discerning spirits. It is one of the gifts of the Holy Ghost listed by Paul in the book of *Acts*.

Other prohibitions in the Old Testament extend to acts of divination that occur without the aid of God, such as *'anan* (divination by clouds), and *qesem* (divination by intuition). In the New Testament the cluster of words used for "magic" are *mageia*, *pharmakeia*, and *perierga*. The first of these is where we get our modern words "magic" and "magician." The word magos (Greek, magician) is often translated as "wise man" or "wise men" (*magoi*). Originally, the magoi were practitioners of the Oriental religion of Magism. One of their disciplines was what is now called astrology. These were the people who visited Jesus after His birth.

The second of these words is where the modern terms "pharmacy" and "pharmacist" derive. Pharmakeia is the use of unguents and herbal compounds used to blind, stupefy, subvert, or otherwise kill. The last of these is translated as "curiosities" – implying a sort of impertinent or vain, idle mental laxity concerning spiritual things that leads into error.

When taken into context, all of the mentions of magoi, such as Simon Magus, or Barjesus, are not condemnations of "magic" in themselves, but of the individual whose mageia is secondary to their actual offense. In the case of Simon, he was condemned because he wanted to buy his way into holy orders – an offence now named "Simony." Offenders such as Simon also demonstrated one other thing common to all of them, *they wanted to fool and dazzle people.*

Magic, being a *holy science* among the ancients of both the Hebrew religion and the Orient, such behavior is inexcusable. It debases the art. Of course, the same occurs with common religion too, hence Jesus' condemnation of religious hypocrites who love putting on a show for others. So many of these instances condemned in the Bible boil down to people being harmed, deceived, killed, poisoned, subverted, or otherwise being sinned against by violations of love, charity, goodwill, and common decency.

A whole separate book could be written concerning Biblical notions of magic and sorcery. The above ought to suffice in order to give a sense of orientation for those unfamiliar with the background.

The late hexenmeister Lee Gandee wrote the following concerning the discernment of spirits when commenting on the Witch of Endor:

> I think that they were wrong in calling the woman a Witch. To be sure, King Saul was wise in seeking to prevent communication between his people and the dead: for the soil of Israel was full of the bones of their enemies. The psychic atmosphere still contained the presences of the old heathen gods of Canaan. Their influence, plus the malice of the dead, would have produced some tragic results had the people asked discarnates for advice. Lying spirits, still burning with desire for vengeance upon the Jews, would have answered them, trying to lead them to their utter undoing. Later, St. Paul would not have enumerated discerning of spirits as one of the great spiritual gifts, had the danger of contacting malevolence not been great. It still is.[40]

Another reason for not contacting the dead: for those who say that they trust in Lord of the Universe and believe in His availability to

---

40   Gandee, p.67-68

them, why go to any other spirit than the Holy Ghost? When one has access to the ultimate Power, why go to an inferior source?

To discern either spirits or living people:
1) Observe what they do (Matthew 7:15-20)
2) Observe and listen if that person exalts Jesus Christ (1 Corinthians 12:3, 1 John 4:1-3)
3) If encountering a spirit, greet it with a salutation such as *"Praise the Lord, the Almighty King."* If it answers in the affirmative, it might be trustworthy. If it does not answer, or prevaricates, then immediately shut off communication and call upon God to expel the spirit from the place.
4) "Toys" such as Ouija boards ought to be avoided; not because the boards themselves are "evil," but because the spirits that these devices bring through are almost *always liars*. This comment is based upon personal experience.

And remember the following points. These apply to all areas of life, not just "magic" –

- There is a price for everything
- Nature abhors a vacuum
- God calls us to be conscious of what we do, and to be faithful stewards of our gifts
- All gifts and abilities are subject to abuse or perversion
- Stay alert and aware that the above does not happen

The Black Art in the Flesh

As for the flesh and blood Witch (aside from the mythological beings), this chapter has outlined a few ways in which various folk have stumbled into or sought out the path of hexerei. Shaner also gives three different variations on how one becomes a hexe. The first involves boiling a black cat alive, collecting the bones, and floating them in a stream. A special bone will appear to float against the current. This bone will allow a person to work Witchcraft. This method is identical to another procedure utilizing a toad. The second is a classical satanic denial of Christ, but while standing on a mound of manure and swinging a manure hook. The third method requires one to draw a circle with some coal. Having had drawn the circle the would-be Witch steps into it while holding out her hand. The Devil is supposed to appear and place his mark on the palm, thereby giving her the ability to hex[41].

Given the nature of this book you shall not find any solid instructions to become an operator of hexerei. The above "methods" are listed for informational purposes only. If, for whatever reason, this is what you want you shall have to find your own way. Needless to say, by pursuing the options given by Shaner, option 1 would make you an evil sadist; option 2 would make you look funny and smell bad while being naughty; and option 3 would probably just make you stand around in your coal circle for a long time while feeling stupid.

Genuine evil is not something to seek out. The demonic forces[42] are agents of chaos, destruction, and degradation. By invoking the Holy Ghost, relying upon Christ, and calling upon His angels, one calls upon the Powers of order: Life, Light, Logos, the powers of holiness and sanctity. That Power shall give you a peaceful and blessed life, an ordered mind, heart, and soul. The Black Art consumes like a fire, but unlike a holy fire it does not purify. It leaves nothing left but a gutted out shell. That is why you shall find in this book instruction on how to make a himmelsbrief but not a *teufelsbrief*, although such is possible. By omitting the latter I have not made

[41]   Shaner 1963, p5.

[42]   Some magicians see the demonic realm as being little more than semi-conscious elemental-type beings whose role it is to take things apart with a blow torch. Perhaps some of these "demons" are really nothing more than this sort of entropic force, like the "black stage" in alchemical work. The evils wrought by such demonic forces would then not be moral evils, as they would be as impersonal as a tornado. However, there is little doubt that there are highly intelligent spiritual powers that are warped and wicked, even as are some human beings. These seek the undoing and misery of whatever unfortunate that comes to their notice.

that decision for you, but decided for myself that I shall teach only the good. And, it is the Supreme Good that the Braucher serves.

VIII.

The older homes of Southeastern Pennsylvania are typically made of field stone, however, as can be seen in this photo, many of these had their stone plastered over at an early point in time. The tall, narrow build of this home is a prevalent architectural type.

Part II: The Practice of Braucherei

Section Overview: The use of "the General" technique of Brauche healing: the specific hand-motions and charms needed to affect this; additional healing charms and prayers that can be used alone or within "the General" technique – also, instruction on how to create personalized charms and prayers in a traditional way; the use of some traditional healing herbs and herbal mixtures with instructions on their use and application; instruction on making amulets and talismans of protection and defense against illness, danger, and malign Witchcraft; the use of the himmelsbrief and various "Fire and Pestilence letters" to protect home and person.

THIS SECTION IS THE HEART OF THE BOOK, divided in what is hopefully a reader/practitioner friendly format. In the traditional Brauche books such as *The Long Lost Friend*, and *Egyptian Secrets of Albertus Magnus*, there is no particular order to the charms, formulae, and recipes. Maneuvering through those old books is only possible with the aide of their indexes; and thank God (or the publisher) for them! Otherwise, not a blessed thing could be found in a pinch. In addition to an index, you will find all of the work organized in alphabetical subsections thusly:

- Abscesses, Boils, Sores, Ulcerations
- Blood, and Bleeding (*blut schtille*)
- Colds and Illnesses of the Throat, Lungs, Ears, and Mouth
- Colic and "the Livergrown" (*aagewachse*)
- Atrophy (*Abnemmes*)
- Eye Troubles
- Fevers (*fiewer*, and *kaltfiewer*)
- Headache (*koppschmaerze*)
- Heart Troubles (*haerzschlaek*), Apoplexia, and Convulsions

- Snake Bite, and Other Animal Bites
- Sores: Tetter, Herpes (*gschwaer/schlier*)
- Sprains (*verrenkder*) and Rheumatism
- Stomach and Bowels
- Swellings, Tumors, and Erysipelas (*gewecks, heisch, rotlaufe*)
- Teeth, Toothache (*zaeweh, zaeschmerze*)
- Urinary
- Warts, Corns (auswachs -- also, *gewecks*)
- Women's Ailments (*"ihre zeit", mutterweh*, etc.)
- Worms
- Miscellaneous

At the back of Part III there is a separate chapter on charms and formulae for protection (various himmelsbriefe, and other "letters", etc.)

I hope that you will find the above arrangements to be helpful. The categorizations are not scientific by today's standards, but ordered in a general enough manner for you to find what you need. When first starting to put together the materials for this book, I had high hopes of raking together as many Brauche formulae as possible. It's not possible, and even if it were it would probably be too overwhelming to be of practical use. Please see the Appendix I Glossary for term definitions, which may come in handy for referencing the old Brauche manuals.

5: The Operation of Braucherei

There are many different styles of practice among practitioners of Braucherei. I have both learned of, and known people who only utter charms and prayers; there are some who incorporate a few hand movements with their charms. There are others who go through far more complex forms of ritualism.

Lee R. Gandee in his book *Strange Experience*[1], tells of how he would wear a special hat for Pow-Wow work. Throughout the literature on Brauche you can find a few instances where a Braucher will wear hats or bonnets in order to practice. Karl Herr (pseudonym), author of *Hex and Spellwork*[2] likens this latter practice to that of Orthodox Jewish men who wear their black, wide rimed hats during prayer. On my end, I honestly do not know where this practice hails from, although it would not surprise me if this is truly a carry-over from Judaism[3], as aspects of Kabbalism permeate a good deal of Pow-Wow work. Further, I do not do this myself, as I was never instructed to do so. Adopting it would seem sort of artificial to me anyway.

There are Brauchers who employ more than just chants and hand movements in their work. Depending upon the illness (or other problem) and the expertise of the worker, there are any number of other possibilities for use. Some will use blessed oil[4], or even a series of specialized blessed oils, applying them to the patient in a ritual manner, tracing out crosses or other symbols upon

---

1   Gandee, Lee R. *Strange Experience: The Autobiography of a Hexenmeister -- Personal Encounters with Hauntings, Magic and Mysticism.* Prentice-Hall, Englewood Cliffs, 1971, p130.
2   Herr, Karl. *Hex and Spellwork: The Magical Practices of the Pennsylvania Dutch.* Red Wheel/Weiser, Boston, 2002, p23.
3   On the other hand, it could be a throwback to the sorcerer's cap, which may be related to the Phrygian cap seen on statues of Mithras. However, this is just a personal observation.
4   Blessed oils: these are either oils that have been prayed over by the Braucher (usually these prayers are Psalms, along with traditional formulae), or they have been blessed by a minister or priest. In the latter case, a Catholic Braucher will use this sacramental oil, along with holy water. This is a very common practice in other types of folk magic and healing such as found throughout Catholic countries.

traditionally predetermined parts of the patient's body. Such places are innocuous enough: the crown of the head, forehead, back of the neck, the back, shoulders, hands, and feet just to name the more usual spots of application.

Other practitioners will use more involved tools. Two possible practices are called *annängsel* and *petschaft*. Gandee mentions these two practices in his book[5]. The former term refers to written talismans that are placed upon the patient's person. Such talismans consist of written prayers accompanied by various special signs and symbols. My teacher used such devises very sparingly. In fact, as far as I know, there is only one such talisman that she regularly employs, which will be given later.

In this section you will find many more talismans for your use in the healing art. These papers are often (mostly) placed in Brauche bags/pouches and hung around the patient's neck, or sometimes tied around the specific ailing body part. This book will show you how to make these talismans, which is very easy to do. The *petschaft*, on the other hand is a bit more difficult. A *petschaft* is a basically a stamper tool that transfers the talismanic image it bears upon the patient's body. The hardest part about this usage is to actually make one. Later on there will be some ideas on how this can be done -- one method will be traditional, whereas the other may not be. (That is to say, I thought up the alternative application, but someone else may have done the same unbeknownst to me.) Many of the practices that I use today were not taught to me by my teacher, but adopted through research. The techniques and methods disclosed here are not exhaustive. Over the centuries there have been many, many practitioners of this art who have adopted and modified these *uses* as needed -- the forms these practices take will, therefore, be legion. However, you will notice common threads or denominators through all of them, and this is where the tradition lies.

Most of what you will find here are techniques for healing both

---

5   op. cit.

humans and animals. What applies to one can be applied to the other. There are herbal mixtures (which are not specifically a part of Pow-Wow *per se*, but exist traditionally in close proximity to it) for various problems. But, aside from healing work, there are instructions for various charms, prayers and talismans for protection and defense: to either ward off malign magic and paranormal events, or to actively counteract them when they occur.

Braucherei is easy to do; however, it will take some work and persistence -- just like anything else. Through practice, you will learn what techniques will or will not work for you. Presented next is what I was taught by Daisy. Among the main instructions, there are side notes on how this technique can be modified in a way that is sensitive and consistent with traditional use. The modifications that you may wish to make will depend upon your abilities, the patient's need, and any specializations you may need to make to accommodate the situation.

A note concerning 'tools' of the trade:

Considering what you have read thus far, if you figure that there is no 'regular' set of tools for a Braucher, you are correct. Beyond the occasional red string, rocks, pennies, plants, bits of metal, handwritten talismans, etc., there is little that is standard, beyond the presence of the Bible. Some Brauchers **never** use any "secondary" elements in healing work. It's just a triangle of God, the patient, and the Braucher. Period. There was an author who once wrote about making Pow-Wow "altars". There's no such thing. This cannot be said enough: Braucherei is NOT a religion. Traditional Brauchers have a religion, and it is Christianity. Braucherei is *a way* of manifesting Christ in the world; it is just something that is done, like rubbing iodine on a cut. It is a craft and a gift, *but it does not take the place of religion*. If a Christian wants to have a special place for prayer, that is fine, but Braucherei is not dependent upon that locus. During a Brauche session, the only real ritual-tool and focal point that exists is the Bible. Catholic Brauchers may also employ any number of sacramentals in their brauching as well.

𝔄n 𝔄pologia

> Neither do men light a candle, and put it under a bushel, but on a candlestick; and it giveth light unto all that are in the house. **Matt. 5:15 KJV**

Before presenting this technique for Pow-Wow healing, there is something that needs to be disclosed. When Daisy taught me how to Pow-Wow, she said that if I should reveal what she taught me to one not ready or fit to learn, then I would forfeit my ability to *use*. The traditional manner in which to teach Brauche is by word of mouth, and only after the potential new Braucher is put through a test to see if he or she is able (or meant) to do the work. The teaching is almost always done cross-gender: from male to female, female to male. An exception to this is when the transition is familial: father to son, mother to daughter, etc. A friend of mind who has Braucherei in his family was told that one way around the taboo of same-sex transmission was for the teacher to teach an inanimate object, or a pet, while the other person of the same gender "accidentally" over heard the instructions through an act of fortuitous eavesdropping.

There have been many other Pow-Wow manuals written over the past two centuries. So, consider this book a sort of literary eavesdropping. In earlier drafts of *The Red Church* it was originally decided to provide only reworded charms for "The General Brauche Circuit". However, in order to be consistent with my feelings on 'secrecy' (see next paragraph), this approach was reconsidered. The "Circuit" prayers are, therefore, given *as is*, or 'straight up'. Outside of the context of this particular "general" working of Pow-Wow, all of the other chants, charms, and prayers provided are also *as-is* -- that is, as I have found them in my rummaging through various antediluvian tracts, pamphlets, notes, and papers, etc. Only the directions for employing the latter have been altered at times in order to provide greater clarity.

Braucherei is *not* an oath bound tradition. These matters, as indicated above, have been committed to pen and paper many times over the centuries. Pow-Wower Aunt Sophia Bailer, back in the 1950's, had no qualms with having her inherited charms printed for all to see in *The Pennsylvania Dutchman*. We live at a time in history where there are no more secrets. That is to say, like it or not, many things previously hidden for their preservation are now out in the open.

It is the author's honest opinion, along with that of several others that while secrecy may have been a 'good thing' in its time, it is now a detriment to long-term survival. **When a practice such as Braucherei is brought out into the open by those who know it best, true and reliable information can supersede any previous falsehoods and misinformation** (see Introduction). The time for our "hiding light under a bushel" has come to an end. Either Braucherei practice can take its proud and rightful position next to humanity's other great folk medicinal practices, for the good of all, or it shall remain a curious phenomenon known only locally to the "Dutch" and their friends – and possibly die out.

Pow-Wow is now gaining in popularity, more folks have heard of it than before, but it has yet to attain the status of Reiki, Therapeutic Touch, Shiatsu, and various Amerindian healing ways. As of this writing, Mexican Curanderismo, while more vital than Braucherei, is experiencing the ravages of commercialization due to New Age incursion. A friend of this author, "Eduardo" Bryant Holman, and many native Mexican Curanderos, have been at the forefront of halting this kudzu weed-like parasitism upon that noble healing art. They realize, too, that in order for their folk medicine to survive, it has to be brought out of the closet before it ceases to exist. If practices such as Braucherei and Curanderismo cease to exist in their traditional manner, they will be superseded by animals, that neither of our ancestors would recognize.

So, where does this place the traditional methods of transmission? It places them squarely where they always have been. Learning from a book is no substitute for learning from a real teacher. There is a dynamic present, a synergy, when a living teacher transmits these teachings mouth-to-ear that you will not experience by way of a book, no matter how good or thorough a work it may be. Despite this, a book such as *The Red Church* will give you the tools you need in order to practice in a traditional manner, assuming that you haven't recourse to a teacher. ***It will give you a place to start.***

One objection received, regarding the publishing of this material, is that it is dangerous to give people such tools in order to teach them how to "move energy" without direct apprenticeship. One answer to that is two fold: 1) as noted above, these charms and modalities have been written and published before; and 2) the New Age section of every book store absolutely groans with titles that teach readers how to nothing but "move energy" – sometimes in not very nice ways. Yet another objection received was that these charms are the embodiments of "the ancestors", and that writing them down "kills the Spirit" (and also the unspoken statement that it cheapens them both). The response: see point "1" above. As for "the ancestors" and "the Spirit" – the Holy Ghost goes where it wills to. If the printed word "kills" the Spirit, then that Spirit would hardly be God. If "the ancestors" are killed off so easily when their words are written down, then they are not all that powerful to begin with. Is anything that weak worth surviving? Please re-read the bolded statement in the preceding paragraph.

In part, that anything written down is necessarily "dead" or at least 'dehydrated' in a literary sort of way. However, like boxed mashed potatoes they instantly reconstitute themselves when the 'water' of the Spirit infuses the Brauche. As for the ancestors, much like God's Living Spirit and the Land itself, *they are always around us.* They, too, will infuse the Pow-Wow with power when in the hands of a genuine practitioner. And, what makes a practitioner 'genuine' is what resides in the heart and that one remains *true* to the traditions of Braucherei and the culture of the Pennsylvania Dutch, while having the gift (ability) of healing.

The "General" Operation of Pow-Wow

Daisy has called this modality of her practice "The General". This pretty much means what it seems: the 'general', over-all method you employ in order to *use* or *try* for someone. This method of praxis is outlined as best as possible in order to make it intelligible and user friendly. The most difficult aspect of this particular technique is the hand movements, which are done in a very specific sequence. Before getting to the meat of doing this work, there are some preliminary things that need to be addressed.

Be direct with your patient
German people tend to be very direct, at least by American standards. When Pow-Wowing, it is necessary that the Braucher gets to the 'brass tacks' of the person's situation. Some Brauchers are often as busy as doctors, with their homes or offices as the sites of much hub-bub and coming and going. If, in your practice, you build up a steady base of patients, you will want to schedule them carefully. Further on in this section there will be a discussion regarding issues of personal power, fatigue, and potential psychical contagion.

When someone comes to see you, allow them a little time to discuss what's wrong with them (or, at least what they *think* is wrong with them). Don't allow the session to become a social call. It has been my experience that a long social call can be a potential drain on a Braucher's energies. This is especially so if the person is needy (and possibly hypochondriacally oriented). There are exceptions to this. But, as a general rule, try to keep to that. Aside from Pow-Wowing, the author found this to be especially true as a card reader. People will come simply to 'dump' and siphon off the reader's energies.

Belief in God

Furthermore, this directness comes in the form of being frank with your patient in regard to what Braucherei can or cannot do for them. This applies most definitely with people who have never been Pow-Wowed before. You need to tell them from the outset that you will *try for* them; that you cannot promise the result; and that it is *from God* that the healing ultimately comes.

This latter point needs to be driven home to the patient. The very first question that needs to come off a Braucher's lips is: *"Do you believe in God?"* If the answer is in the negative, then the appointment ends right there. No exceptions. Traditionally this question has referred to whether or not a person is a believing and practicing Christian. However, this attitude has lightened up a bit among various practitioners. Basically, it really is an inquiry more about a person's acceptance of a "Higher Power" than it is about affiliation and theology.

Get the patient's full name

It has been traditional that old-time practitioners would only heal for Christians. The reason for this has to do with the Braucher's conceptualization of the origins of Power. Jesus Christ, in the words of Karl Herr, "is the foundation of hex work". Therefore, if one is baptized into Christ, then that spiritual connection will be activated when the Braucher blesses in 'the three Highest Names' of Father, Son, and Holy Spirit.[6] After the initial question regarding the acceptance of the Divine, the Braucher needs to ask for the patient's full name. Names have power; they bear identity and personal energies. In all works of conjuration and exorcism, it is crucial to know the name of the spirit to be called or banished. The individual's name becomes a part of the living charm that exists *between* the Braucher and the patient. However, despite the above,

---

6   *"For ye are all the children of God by faith in Christ Jesus. For as many of you as have been baptized into Christ have put on Christ."* Galatians 3:26-27

in times of emergency a Braucher can substitute the phrase "a child of God" or "a creature of God" in lieu of a proper name (such as when happening upon an accident involving strangers, or animals without personal names).

Seat the patient
After all of the above is taken care of, seat the patient in the chair that you will set aside for this practice. The patient will need to face east. Some practitioners have their patients stand or sit facing north. There are others who have no particular direction that they insist upon. Of course, each and every direction has much symbolism attached to it. The east is symbolic of light, the rising sun, new beginnings, resurrection (and, therefore, Christ), birth, etc. On the other hand, north is traditionally a place of mystery, darkness, and cold, the Pole Star, the hidden and the uncanny. Old time churches and cathedrals were *oriented* (literally meaning being faced eastward) so that the altar and the priest/congregation faced east. The church was generally built in the form of a cross, having doors in the west, south, and north. The dreaded "North Door" of these old churches was often symbolical of the Devil and other uncanny creatures, and therefore bolted permanently shut, or otherwise bricked up, being a door in symbol only.[7]

Once seated, you will take your Brauche Bible --that is, a regular Bible that you have set aside for Pow-Wow practice-- and have the patient hold it in his or her lap. While the patient is facing east, you will be facing the patient while kneeling in front of him/her. It is strongly suggested you obtain a comfy, small pillow just for this occasion, as you will be on your knees for what would otherwise be an uncomfortable duration. Make sure the patient is quite comfortable. If he or she needs a pillow to support the back or cushion the spine, please provide one. The patient needs to keep an upright, but *relaxed* posture with feet and legs together.

---

7 The north side of some old churches also contained a second altar that was reserved for the Heathen gods. This practice occurred during the initial conversion period when many European Christians were still quasi-pagan. It was probably from this ancient practice that the North Door received some of its uncanny associations.

Don't allow the patient to slouch. If the person is too tense and rigid, encourage them to relax with positive affirmations. Let them know when their posture is 'good'; softly encouraging rhythmic, deep breathing. While closed eyes are ideal for relaxation, they can remain open. In fact, when you learn this method well, your eyes can be closed too in order to aid concentration on the feeling out of the person's energies. This can help you discover where the patient might have an energy imbalance.

A few final notes before you begin:

Protection:
Before undertaking Braucherei work, make sure that you are wearing something to protect yourself. Traditionally this would be a cross or crucifix. A hexenfoos (pentacle) may also be used as well. Please note that the pentacle/pentagram *is not* an exclusively Pagan or Wiccan symbol, and has been used by Christians for many centuries (See Glossary entry for HEXENFOOS). Some well-meaning Christians see this sign as devilish, but they are mistaken. If you are a Christian (which a practitioner of Braucherei **needs** to be, at least on some level), but you are not comfortable with the hexenfoos as an amulet, then you need not employ it. The author uses a cross of iron that he made himself. Iron is a protective metal in its own right, and combined with the symbol of the cross (in its many meanings) is a powerful tool to protect the areas of the Heart and the Solar Plexus.[8] In the chapter covering protective charms, tools, and prayers this will be discussed further.

Semi-audible prayers:
Traditionally, all Brauche charms and prayers are repeated in semi-silence, barely audible to the patient. There are different schools of thought on this, however. Don Yoder's Pow-Wow consultant, Aunt

---

[8] Iron is also the metal of Mars. Iron can thoroughly break a magical current, which is why some systems of traditional practice forbid the use of iron in certain operations. Wearing iron frequently (daily) is not recommended. While the metal has the virtue of breaking spells, it can also draw in strange and sometimes hostile situations due to its 'Martial' sympathy.

Sophia Bailer: *"When I call a blessing on some one I will speak my words loud any person can hear me..."*[9] The way Aunt Sophie saw it, if a person spoke their charms secretly, then they might be up to no-good – that is to say, Hexerei. There are two other ways (and possibly more) to look at the repetition of semi-audible charms: The first is that secrecy provides a powerful psychological 'kick' for the patient (and for the practitioner). The introduction of the 'mysterious' will activate a person's subconscious. The downfall there is that the patient's subconscious may, in fact, close more tightly rather than open up. This is a fear reflex. **Anyone who fears Braucherei should not get Pow-Wowed**. The negative beliefs and suggestions that they have internalized will either negate any effect the Brauche will have, or will produce contrary results. In other words, a person can 'hex' himself by way of his own negative beliefs. If a person comes to you looking for Braucherei treatment and you are getting some strongly mixed signals or fear responses, it is suggested that the session goes no further. In the past, such self-induced psychic indigestion was responsible for good Brauche doctors being labeled "Witches". That label sometimes earned them a beating or worse. The second explanation for semi-audible charming and prayer is one of humility. The Braucher is not the source (this point cannot be drilled enough) of the healing. To speak prayers in silent conforms to scripture:

But thou, when thou prayest enter into thy closet, and when thou hast shut thy door, pray to thy Father which is in secret; and thy Father which seeth in secret shall reward thee openly. **Matt. 6:6 KJV**

Daisy's instruction was to speak these quietly. But, this is a matter for you to decide if you wish to take up Pow-Wowing. Of course, those who feel strongly that "their" ability to Pow-Wow will be reduced if the prayers are made audible are another reason for speaking semi-audible blessings.[10]

---

9   "Witches...I have known", *The Pennsylvania Dutchman*, vol. IV, No. 1, May 1952, p. 8

10   Yet another reason for semi-audible chanting is well know among practitioners of the

A note on patient and practitioner proximity:
This style of Braucherei practice presented here is almost wholly 'energetic' in the sense that the Braucher 'cleans' the patient with Divine energies. In this method there is next to no physical contact with the patient. There are some modalities of Brauche that are more like therapeutic massage. This note on proximities is especially important for male practitioners. In order to avoid potential 'scandals' and misunderstandings, it is my suggestion to all male Pow-Wowers that you insist on your female patients to have a 'chaperone'. Such a person need not be sitting right on top of you during a session, but at least a few feet away. Men, this is especially important when treating new (and therefore unknown) female clients. Until you get to know very well those who come to you, it is always preferable that there ought to be someone else in the house (or office) besides the patient and you. Conversely, female Pow-Wowers ought to consider not being alone while treating new male patients. The author makes sure that his wife is home when people come to see him – this is for both sexes, as sometimes visitors are strangers. This advice is not intended to make new Brauchers paranoid. It is, however, something to keep in mind.

The Commonwealth of Pennsylvania:
Back in 1999 Pow-Wower Marie May was arrested for fortune telling after a sting by Officer Andrea Kohut. "Mrs. May" as she was known to some of her clients, had a complaint against her through the State Attorney General's Bureau of Consumer Protection. Lebanon County police then proceeded to "dust off" a 137-year-old anti-fortune telling law in order to make the arrest.[11] As of this writing, many occult shops across the state no longer offer card readings and other such services of divination. After the York "hex murder" of Nelson D. Rehmeyer back in 1928, and the trial of his

---

magical art: power shared is power lost. However, since the power for this style of healing doesn't come from you directly then there ought to be no fear of "loosing" anything. No one has a monopoly on the Deity.

11   "Psychics have trouble foretelling when state law may be used against them" Post-Gazette.com, Tuesday, January 19, 1999. http://www.post-gazette.com/magazine/1999011psychic1.asp

murderers, John Blymire and John Curry in 1929, Pow-Wowing has been a target for law enforcement and also for much social condemnation (please refer back to Part I or to the Glossary for further details on the York Hex Murder Trial). Before Pow-Wowing for anyone outside of your family and friends, please check into your state's laws on alternative medical practices, and also on such activities as 'faith healing'. ***Remember that you are not a doctor*** – unless, of course, you actually are an M.D., or D.O.[12] ***You cannot make diagnoses. You cannot charge***, at least not in Pennsylvania. If you do, you can find yourself in a world of hurt with the law. These are the same exact restrictions that apply to anyone in the alternative medical trade who does not possess state approved credentials and licenses. ***Always remember that you are only a "consultant"***. According to Karl Herr, the Commonwealth of Pennsylvania did issue licenses to Brauchers:

At one time the state of Pennsylvania used to license hexenmeisters. They did this to be certain that they had at least a grade school education. They also gave the aspiring hexenmeister a written test on the subject, although what it could consist of I do not know. Licensing of hexenmeisters is no longer done by the state.[13]

We have not been able to find out any further information on these old licenses as of this writing. The only work you may charge for are material endeavors that involve time and personal skill, such as the physical by-hand creation of himmelsbriefe. This would be no different than charging someone for creating a piece of art. A few Brauchers in the past did, in fact, charge for their services. Some would-be Pow-Wowers still do, although they are playing with fire by doing so. The laws of Man aside, religiously and spiritually, it is an affront to God to charge for this work because it is not your power, it's His.

---

12   *"Another reason has also been advanced for the nonacceptance of payment, namely, the Medical Practices Act of Pennsylvania, which specifically forbids anyone not meeting the definition of a medical doctor from practicing medicine (Aurand 1929, 10-14)."* Kriebel, 2008, pp32-33.

13   Herr p.23

Just one more note before you begin:

As you have discovered from the previous chapters, sympathetic treatment deals also in the transference of disease – or to be more specific, the transference of 'disease energy' (to coin a term). Many, many Pow-Wowers over the years have emphasized the demanding and sometimes stressful nature of Braucherei – for the Braucher. This is due to the above-mentioned 'energy' coming off of the patient and transferring (theoretically at least) into the healer. God then removes that 'disease' energy from the healer. Some Brauchers in the past, such as the Saylors and Wilhelms of Williams Township, transferred the energetic essence of the disease from themselves to a 'contagion target' such as a tree, an animal, a stone, string, eggs, wood, metal or some natural feature.[14] Daisy decontaminates herself by way of shaking and wiping down her arms and hands – as if shaking off contagious water or dirt. However, despite this process of decontamination there are still some side effects. Fatigue can be one of these; or it is also common for Brauchers to feel 'phantom' pains of the illness that they removed from the patient a little while after the treatment. *But, to be frank, some Brauchers do get genuinely ill after treating people.* This is why there have been (and still are) many people who have the knowledge and the ability to Pow-Wow, but will do so very seldomly because of this. Pow-Wow practitioners are not alone in this. Practitioners of other folk healing methods from Europe, Mexico, and South America mention these very same after-effects. [15] Therefore, when performing the General Brauche Circuit, make certain to at least shake off your arms and hands after the performance of each movement. Observe this practice along with the suggestions in the paragraph above

---

14   In the case of the Saylor and Wilhelm brauchers, that target of transference was the Hexenkopf in Williams Township.

15   Hermeticist Mark Stavish is of the mind that if one is truly drawing energy from outside of one's self, then that alone ought to keep a person from being drained and feeling the effects of contagion. However, if there is a true transference of the 'sick' energy (if not the actual illness) to the healer, then that person needs to decontaminate him or herself by brushing off the energy, or transferring it to another creature or object. PA Dutch witches (practitioners of hexerei) know that they work with deadly spiritual poisons and are always at pains to decontaminate and shield themselves from the effects of their own sorcery.

labeled "Protection". These warnings are not to scare anyone away from brauching. The worst this author has experienced thus far is fatigue and some minor aches. The good news is, unless you really do get a full-blown 'bug' you are not likely to feel ill for very long. But, your general health and constitution play a large role in how you will deal with such 'fallout'. This is a heads-up so you will be neither frightened nor surprised ought this happen to you after Pow-Wowing. In an interview with an unnamed Pow-Wower Robert Dluge was informed that,

> ...when I work on those cases [contact dermatitis/*rotlaufe*], I will just turn fiery red and I'm gasping for my breath – I will also sweat. That means it's coming from the patient into me, and the Lord is then taking it away from me, if he so wills. But I am knocked out some times, for a short period. Any person that does this work and doesn't tell you that, well, then they're not working.[16]

And, of course, Jesus Christ Himself could sense power leave Him when healing:

> And Jesus said, Who touched Me? When all denied, Peter and they that were with him said, Master, the multitude throng thee and press thee, and sayest thou, Who touched me? And Jesus said, Somebody hath touched me: for I perceive that virtue is gone out of me. **Luke 8:45-46.**

NOTE THE FOLLOWING: 1) *"Powwowing is good for only what you get in the world, not what you bring."*[17] **2) You cannot Pow-Wow for direct blood relatives (your parents, and children): that is,** *those that you come from or who come from you.*[18]

---

16   "My Interview with a Powwower" p. 41, *Pennsylvania Folklife*, Summer 1972.

17   Snellenburg p.42 A key component in understanding braucherei is that it is only good for ailments and diseases acquired while in this life, *but it cannot be used on congenital diseases and other problems.*

18   Daisy Dietrich

"The Powwow-Doctor" Courtesy of the Roughwood Collection

6: The General Brauche Circuit

I) The General Brauche Circuit

1) First sweep of the head
While kneeling in front of the patient, take both hands and start with the top of the head. Hold your hands side-by-side at the top of the head. Bring the hands down on either side in a sweeping motion down to the shoulders, while continuing the sweeping motion away from the shoulders, as if pushing something away. This is done three times. *Please remember that **everything** in Braucherei is done three times.* As you are making these motions you say in a low, inaudible tone with each sweep:

> *"Es Wasser un es Feier"*
> *"Es Wasser un es Feier"*
> *"Es Wasser un es Feier"*

(If you are unfamiliar with Pennsylvania German, please see the pronunciation guide in the appendices.)

That is, say this phrase once per sweep. The words mean "The water and the fire". You are now calling upon the powers of water and fire to clear the person's head. For a further explanation, see the end notes to this chapter.

2) The first sweep of the body
After the first sweeps of the head, there is next the general cleansing of the body by continuing the sweeps along the sides of the patient (you are still kneeling). Start at the sides of the shoulders (not at the tops of them where you left off), and bring your hands down along the shape of the patient in one, long graceful sweep. When you get down to the area of the feet, send your arms and hands outward in as if you are pushing something away from the patient's person.

To some extent what you are doing is, indeed, pushing something way. You are assisting to brush away blockages and clutter in the patient's energy body. You are assisting, because it is truly God that does the healing. Before proceeding further, please keep The Power foremost in your mind. Allow the procedure to be worked physically by your hands, but place no effort in willing the healing yourself. This will only serve to drain your own energy. Rely utterly upon The Power to do this. God knows best how and where to heal. Unlike other healing techniques you may have come upon, there is nothing to visualize. There is no need for visualization here. If you decide to concentrate on anything at all, let it be toward *being aware* and *feeling*.

As always, this general sweeping of the body is done three times. While making the sweeping motions, you will again speak the following charm in a low tone, audible to the patient only as mumbling:

„Datt so grosse Ding iss in dem heilige Scheide unser scheeni Jungfraa Maria."

„Datt so grosse Ding iss in dem heilige Scheide unser scheeni Jungfraa Maria."

„Datt so grosse Ding iss in dem heilige Scheide unser scheeni Jungfraa Maria."

With this charm you are calling upon the Virgin Mary for assistance. The Pennsylvania German here is exactly as it was given to me. It means something close to this: *"Thank God for the miracle of the womb of our beautiful Virgin Mary."*[1]

II) <u>The Narrowed Brauche Circuit</u>
    1) <u>The second (closer) sweep of the head</u>

You will now notice that we are going from sweeping the body in a general sense, to narrow down spots where you will now work more intensely. Periodically make sure that your patient is

---

1   This is, indeed, a loose translation. Literally: "There so great thing is in that holy womb [of] our beautiful Virgin Mary."

comfortable: good breathing, good posture with legs together and feet flat on the floor. If he or she is tending to cross the arms or legs, gently remind them to keep them uncrossed. Crossing limbs restricts blood flow.

You are still kneeling. Your patient remains sitting with the Bible in the lap and the hands resting upon it. In this sort of Brauche, we always start at the top of the body, working our way down to the feet.

2) <u>Working on the face</u>

Start the circuit by first working on the head, specifically the face. To do this, take your right hand and make counterclockwise circular motions over each member of the face: eyes, nose, and sinus area. Do this left to right (meaning your patient's left, not yours). Each facial part is gone over three times. That is, three counterclockwise circular motions over the left eye, then the right; three over the nose; three over the sinus area on the left, then the right. With each motion you speak inaudibly the Brauche:

„Dei Hand un mei Hand iss Gottes Hand."
„Dei Hand un mei Hand iss Gottes Hand."
„Dei Hand un mei Hand iss Gottes Hand."

This means "Your hand and my hand is the Hand of God".
After you are finished with each part (that is, each eye, the nose, etc.) 'seal' it with the traditional blessing of three crosses. To do this, take your right hand and ball it up into a fist. But, unlike a real fist, your thumb will be sticking up (like giving the thumbs-up sign). Make a small, equal-armed cross + over each part, making it in a right to left direction. In other words, start at the top of the cross, and then go down, then over right, then left. You make three of these crosses in the air over each body part. It is traditional to invoke the Trinity: *"In the name of God the Father, God the Son, and God the Holy Spirit. Amen"* with the making of each cross. You can say this in English or German if you'd like: *„In namen Gottes des*

Vaters, und des Sohnes, und des Heiligen Geistes. Amen. *"* In the charms that will follow this part of the chapter, you will see many of these concluded with three crosses like this: + + +. This indicates the Trinitarian invocation.

3) Working on the thyroid

Right after working on the face, proceed to the thyroid area of the neck. With the same small, counterclockwise circles go over this area *three times.* You are still chanting the "Dei Hand" charm while doing this. When you are finished doing your passes around the thyroid area, seal it with the *three crosses.*

This will finish the second sweep of the head.

4) Sweep of the digestive tract

Everything above the collar bone is considered to be your 'head/hand'. Everything below the collar bone is said to be your 'foot/foundation' (i.e., the rest of the body). Now we move down below the shoulders to focus on the digestive system. Throughout this Brauche, you will be making counterclockwise circles unless otherwise directed. When working on this aspect of the digestive system you will **not** be using the circles.

Starting at the collar bone, slowly drag your right hand down over the area of the esophagus, down to the stomach area. Stop when you reach the navel point. This dragging motion is done three times. During each motion say the Brauche charm:
„Dei Fuss un mei Fuss sin gleich."
„Dei Fuss un mei Fuss sin gleich."
„Dei Fuss un mei Fuss sin gleich."

Here this means "Your foot and my foot are alike". In other words, this is to say that you and your patient are in sympathy[12] with one another. Once you have finished the motions, proceed to seal the area with *three crosses.*

5) <u>Sweep of the arms</u>

After finishing the digestive organs, it is time to work on the arms, beginning with the patient's left arm. This is done by taking both hands, as if about to grasp the patient's arm and running your hands down the arm, from the arm-pit to the hands and fingers. Now, you are not really touching the arm itself, although you may accidentally come in contact with it. The gesture involved is almost as if you are trying to rip off the person's sleeve, coming to an end at the fingers with a 'throwing off' action, like you are casting away what you are removing from the arm. This is done three times, each time you will repeat the *"Dei Fuss"* charm. Afterwards, you seal the arm with the three crosses, usually along the outer side above the elbow. You will then do the same with the right arm.

6) <u>Sweep of the solar plexus/abdominal area</u>

This title is sort of a misnomer, as the actual work is done at hip-level. Start with having both hands along the sides of the patient's hips. You are not actually touching the hips; your hands are only held alongside in the air near them. The gesture looks almost like you are going to pick the person up by the hips from your kneeling position. Once your hands are situated, move both hands simultaneously to the middle of the upper abdominal area. When the hands come to the middle, and then push them outward, as if parting a veil, pushing the ill energies away. This is done three times while saying the *"Dei Fuss"* charm. Seal the area of the solar plexus with the three crosses.

7) <u>Sweep of the kidneys</u>

The following passes are made for the kidneys and the rest of the urinary tract. Reach around to the patient's back to where the kidneys are with both hands. Bring your hands down and around from the back, through the lower abdomen, over the uro-genital area, down between the legs -- all the while you are 'pushing' the 'illness energies' away from these areas and downward. Remember that you are not making any physical contact with the patient, especially in no-go areas like these. Repeat this motion twice more for three in all. The *"Dei Fuss"* chant is repeated during the motions. Seal the area with the three crosses.

8) Sweep of the legs

As you can see, you are to gradually make your way downward. The idea is to both symbolically and in actuality move the 'bad' energies down and away from the patient. The legs are done in much the same way as the arms. Start with the patient's left leg. You will again make use of the *"Dei Fuss"* for this. Take both hands and begin at the thigh area. In the same manner of the arms, you are to make the gesture as if getting ready to pull on the leg. Go over and down the leg in a smooth, single gesture from the thigh to the toes. Once at the toes, push the energy away. Do this three times. Seal the area with the three crosses. Repeat this procedure for the right leg.

Reminder: shake your hands after making these sweeps and circuits -- do this as if shaking excess water from them. This will refresh your hands, increasing their circulation; it will also shake off any energetic contagion from the patient. Wipe both your arms down as well, from the elbow downward.

III) The Specialized Brauche Circuit

First part of the circuit
In all of the above steps, you were in the kneeling position. It is now time to stand up. Remove your kneeling pillow and place it out of the way. Unless there is further work to be done after the General circuits, you will not need it again.

1) Working the head
A) Movement 1
Stand at the person's *left side*. That is, face the patient's left. Take your left hand and place it on the patient's forehead. This third circuit is just about the only time you will actually make physical contact with the patient. In this position,

your right side will be towards the patient's back (see figure). Take your right hand and place it at the back of the head, without touching it. Make counterclockwise circles toward you with that hand. While you make these circles, done three times, you will also be chanting. Since you are now working again above the collar bone, use the *"Dei Hand"* chant. Seal the *left side* of the head with the three crosses.

B) <u>Movement 2</u>

Next, stand immediately in back of the patient. Place the left hand upon the head above the ear. Using the right hand, make counterclockwise circles three times on the right side of the head -- again, these circles will be towards yourself. (See figure) Use the *"Dei Hand"* chant. Seal the *back* of the head with the three crosses.

The head is often the seat of many problems: vision and eye problems, sinusitis, earaches, etc. If your patient has any of these ailments, there are specific things that can be done for them. This style of Brauche, although intricate, is very accommodating to special work needing to be done. After this introduction to the General Brauche, more techniques for specific ailments are provided that can be incorporated into the second and third "circuits".

2) <u>Working the lungs</u>

This is the trickiest of all the Brauche movements to describe, as well as to perform. Please examine the figures provided closely. Stand at the patient's left side again, and place the left hand upon the breast plate. Place the right hand on the 'bump' at the back below the neck. (See figure). With the right hand make repeated counterclockwise circles in series of threes while moving the hands around to the person's right side. Bring the hands around, as if you are hugging the patient from the side. When the hands meet, let the separate so you can bring the around (that is, the left hand will begin gliding over just above the solar plexus area, and the right hand will be crossing the patient's back over the back of the lungs area. Both hands, therefore, are working their way towards the patient's left. Once both hands are at the far left side, make a pushing/dragging motion to sweep away the ill energies. Note that with all of these circuit sweeps and motions, the energies are usually *swept away via counterclockwise and leftward movements.*

As mentioned above, this really is once of the hardest movements to do. It can be a source of much clumsiness and embarrassment. For those who may be concerned about "no-go" areas such as the breasts (especially for a male Braucher working with a female patient), actual physical contact can be avoided. However, it is traditional for the hand to make physical contact with the breast plate. A female practitioner (Braucherin) will probably not have any difficulties with this. Also, despite the hug-like position, you are not actually hugging the person.

When you employ this movement for the first few times, it will be rather difficult for you to keep count of your hand motions *and* chant at the same time -- a little like trying to rub your head and pat your tummy simultaneously while standing on one foot! Since this portion of the body is below the collar bone, use the *"Dei Fuss"* chant. Remember to seal the patient at the left side with the customary three crosses.

Second part of the circuit
Throughout all of the above circuits, the patient has been comfortably seated with the Brauche Bible in the lap. During this phase of the Brauche, the patient will now stand. Upon standing, remove the chair so it does not get in your way.

1) A sealing of the shoulders
The person is now standing. Go behind, facing the back, and proceed to squeeze the shoulder tendons -- left hand on the left side, right hand on the right. Squeeze tightly, but not so tightly as to inflict pain. Once you have a good grip on the tendons, bring the hands upward. Do this like you are trying to pluck the tendons off the shoulders. Do this three times. Chant the *"Dei Hand"*. Seal

the top of the back with three crosses.

2) <u>A sealing of the back, first pass</u>
The patient remains standing. Stay at the back. Take the right hand and move it down the back in counterclockwise circles, in threes, from above the shoulder blades (but below the neck) down to the area above the tail bone. This is done three times while saying the *"Dei Fuss"*. Seal the back with three crosses.

3) <u>A sealing of the back, second pass</u>
Now, make a second pass down the back with both hands. Your hands will be side-by-side moving simultaneously in counterclockwise circles in sets of threes from the top of the back down to above the tail bone. And, of course, this is performed three times while repeating the *"Dei Fuss"*. Seal the patient's back for the last time with three large crosses in the three highest names.

<u>Third part of the circuit</u>
Previously, you have been working *on* the back. This part of the third circuit is a concentration upon and sealing of the front. The front part of the body, in this style of Brauche, is said to encompass the liver, spleen, and heart.

1) <u>The sealing of the front</u>
   A) <u>From behind</u>
   For this, you are still standing behind the patient. Reach around with both hands to the abdominal area, then bring the hands back to the "love handles" and then push the energy away from the person's sides in a single 'whooshing' motion. Do this three times while saying the *"Dei Fuss"*. *Do not make the customary crosses just yet.*
   B) <u>From the front</u>
   Go around to the patient's *right side*, and bless the right side of the abdominal area with the sealing of the three crosses in the three highest names.

2) <u>The sealing of the legs</u>
To finish the third circuit, you finish with the legs. This sweep of the legs is a little different from the first time going over them. It has been the custom to begin at the left side of the body, but this is reversed for the closing of the General Brauche.

Kneel (with or without the pillow) at the person's right side, which may be either sitting or standing at this point. Place the left hand at the back of the leg just under buttocks, with right at the front where the main artery begins. Move the hands down the leg simultaneously, with the right hand making counterclockwise circles in sets of three. Do this in a smooth motion down to the feet, pushing the energy away when at the floor. As always, you are chanting while sweeping; in this case you are still using the *"Dei Fuss"*. Now do a sealing -- but there is a twist here. Remember, when you are making the crosses, your hand is always in the fist-form with the thumb sticking out. After 'pushing' the energy away from the leg, seal the leg by making the sign of the Brauche cross **on the floor** in front of the foot. This is a sign that you are earthing and fixing the Brauche. Do this action twice more for three in all.

Finish up by kneeling at the patient's left side and working the left leg in the same manner, ending it with the earthing Brauche cross. Remember to always do this in threes.

<u>To finish it all up</u>
To conclude the General Brauche, do a final sealing of the patient with a three large Brauche crosses, in the three highest names. You may also wish to cleanse yourself after brauching to minimize contagion. If you are Catholic, you can rinse your hands with holy water. Otherwise, rinsing the hands under brisk tap water will do; rinsing in salt water is another possibility.

An Important Note: It is standard to repeat this general Brauche procedure twice more. Traditionally, the patient would visit the Braucher on two more occasions, making three consecutive visits.

However, circumstances have sometimes precluded this. In such an event, the patient might return twice more, but a day or so later -- or, to give the visits more uniformity, the same day a week later. There are certain times that are more conducive to healing work than others; the time chosen will depend upon the type of illness or situation. We will look at these timing considerations more closely in the following chapter.

After being gone over, a patient ought to pray in thanksgiving. The Lord's Prayer and the Apostles' Creed is sufficient.

<u>Some final notes for the General Brauche</u>
1) Remote Pow-Wowing
2) Pow-Wowing yourself
3) Pow-Wowing animals

All three of these are possible. Yet not everyone will be successful. Common sense dictates that if you are successful trying for another person, then trying for yourself or for an animal ought to not be a problem. Unfortunately, the forces that move Braucherei have their own logic, and what might appear to be common sense does not always hold up when it comes to practice. Once you get started you may find that you are only good when working on animals, for instance.

Regarding remote Pow-Wowing – that is, trying for someone at a distance: when using the General Brauche this is no different that when using it in person. The patient and the Braucher will agree on a time when the work is to be done. When the hour comes, the patient will sit facing east holding a Bible. The patient is to remain seated for at least a half hour; if the work is more intensive, then an hour might need to be scheduled. The Braucher will then face the empty treatment chair on his or her end and go through the entire series of Circuits as if the individual were physically present. This process will be followed three times as usual. The spacing of these three full Circuits can be as little as 10 to 15 minutes apart. More usually the intervals can be up to a half hour.

Pow-Wowing yourself: this can be a tricky thing. It is quite easy to charm yourself by way of the use of single prayers and charms. The use of the General Brauche is a bit different, as you need to go over yourself with the hand motions. However, from what you learned of these complex hand movements, it is not possible to do them all – such as Pow-Wowing yourself from behind, etc. There are two ways you can try for yourself: 1) procure a full-length mirror and go over your own image. Of course, as pointed out, there are limits to this; 2) sit in a chair facing east and do the Circuits over yourself while in this position. In both instances the Bible will be present. In either case, do as many of the Circuits as completely as possible.

Pow-Wowing for animals: trying for an animal is tricky too as they like to move around, unless they are very ill. Cats and dogs especially can be challenging as they will find the process strange and may run away, or they may think that you are trying to play with them. In the latter cases, your efforts to do the full set of Brauche circuits could be limited. For a seriously ill animal, they will be stationary and the full set can be completed. **Do not hesitate to seek professional veterinary care** in addition to trying for animals. Even though animals are shaped differently than people, the manner in which you start will differ very little from the usual method outlined above.

The principles of using the *"Dei Hand"* and *"Dei Fuss"* chants are the same too: from the animal's head down to its collar bone is the *"Dei Hand"*, and everything else below the collar bone is the *"Dei Fuss."* The animal's back is treated the same as the human's. The only addition is the tail. If the animal is standing, such as a horse, the initial sweep is done from head to the tail. If the horse is especially large, this may require that you find a sturdy stool to stand on. The *"Es Wasser"* chant will start at the animal's head with sweeps to the forelegs. The *"Datt so grosse"* chant will commence with standing at the animal's side and sweeping from the head to the hindquarters and tail. The size and type of animal will determine how you need to modify the Circuits in order to make the process work. House pets are much simpler, but are more 'jumpy.' A dog or cat lying on its side is done the same way, from head to hindquarters and tail. If they will allow it, move them from their right or left side as needed, otherwise you will have to work with what limitation that you have.

Old Augustus Lutheran Church in Trappe, PA -- completed on October 6, 1745. Architecture is of the "meeting house" variety. Immediately next door is the "new" church build in 1853. Old Trappe Church is still in use for Sunday services during the months of July and August. This is the oldest unchanged Lutheran church in North America.

7: The Details of Pow-Wowing
Timing and Sympathetic Alignments for Healing Work

For those of you already familiar with magical practices, none of what follows here will be a surprise. There are two dimensions to consider when timing the practice of Braucherei: the mundane and the planetary (astrological). The former consideration is pretty simple: can you *try* when your personal energy is low, when you are busy working a regular job, or the kids are in need of attention, etc.? Braucherei, with the exception of a few full-time Pow-Wow doctors and "hexenmeisters", is and was the pursuit of everyday (otherwise 'normal') people who have a gift for healing: people with responsibilities, needs and necessities. It is assumed that should you decide to pursue this art and craft, you will also fall into this category.

It has been said before by others, but it is worth repeating: **Pow-Wow is no way to make a living**. At the end of our praxis section, a separate chapter addresses the ethics and morals of Pow-Wow practice more specifically. However, let it suffice for now that trying to place a roof over your head and food in your belly by the practice is *a bad thing*. That statement is not written that lightly.

Pow-Wow as you need to. If there is an emergency and regular medical attention is not immediately possible: 1) call for help, 2) apply first aid as you can, then 3) *try* for the injury/ailment until further help can be secured. As far as having others schedule visits with you, take into consideration your own needs. You will not be able to concentrate on your Brauche if you are distracted with too much else. Most importantly, pay attention to your personal energies and cycles. Pay attention to when you feel most energetic or 'powerful'. Trying for a person when you are feeling under the weather or at an energetic ebb is not a good thing. Some past practitioners have found that they were more useful or powerful during certain phases of the moon, specific days, or times of the year. Many such folks would only then Pow-Wow, and at no other time. This leads us to the consideration of planetary or astrological timing.

As a possibly beneficial exercise, pay attention to the lunar phases and begin to make a few light notes on how you are feeling at that time. This needn't be an extensive diary or journal -- a daily planner will do fine. After some time has past, you may begin to see a pattern of energetic ebbs and flows. You may find that you are more intuitive during one phase, and less on others, and so on.

Astrological timing can get very complex. Before going further let it be known that the author is not an astrologer. In truth, the most important heavenly body you will need to pay attention to is the moon. And, specifically, there are only two overall phases you will want to note: the waxing moon, and the waning moon. The moon actually has eight phases: New Moon, Waxing Crescent, First Quarter, Waxing Gibbous, Full Moon, Waning Gibbous, Last Quarter, and Waning Crescent. We say that the moon is "waxing" from Waxing Crescent to Full, and "waning" from the time of the Full Moon's end to New Moon. In order to keep a close eye on the exact times of these phases, you will need to consult with an almanac. If the night sky is clear, you can go 'by eye', but you will not know the exact moment of the phase changes.

Some, but not all, of the charms in this book will have specific lunar phases noted for their performance. Provided here is a figure that is sometimes known as "the Zodiac Man". This term has been applied to a male figure with various astrological sun-sign symbols draw upon or surrounding him. I have also seen a few "Zodiac Women" as well. The gender, however, is unimportant. All twelve Sun Signs have a specific rulership over the various parts of the human body -- both male and female. This is pretty useful knowledge for those who wish to get a razor like precision and focus for any given ailment. Below there is a table with some of the most pertinent data for those interested. It is my opinion, though, that too much of this sort of thing can get distracting and limit your opportunities to do Brauche work more frequently. The tedium to which this sort of categorization can descend is enormous: specific planets and signs for each and every bone in the body considered in aspect to the overall planet or sign of the general body zone in which that bone is located! Only a true medical astrologer would need this sort of minutia.

Also, before presenting the table of correspondences, there is one major reminder: it is truly *the Power of God* that does the healing. When we take astrological and lunar tides into consideration, it is only in regard to the efficacy that such a tide can bring in the application to a healing. This is not to imply that God's Power is constrained by the planets! Everything created by the Deity is, as we have seen in the section on magical theory, interconnected. "Magic" is natural and works best when we are laboring harmoniously with Nature's tides and cycles. God works through Nature. As we, too, are a part of Nature and heir to the spark of divinity, God works through us as well. Keep Divine immanence forefront in your prayers and thoughts when brauching.

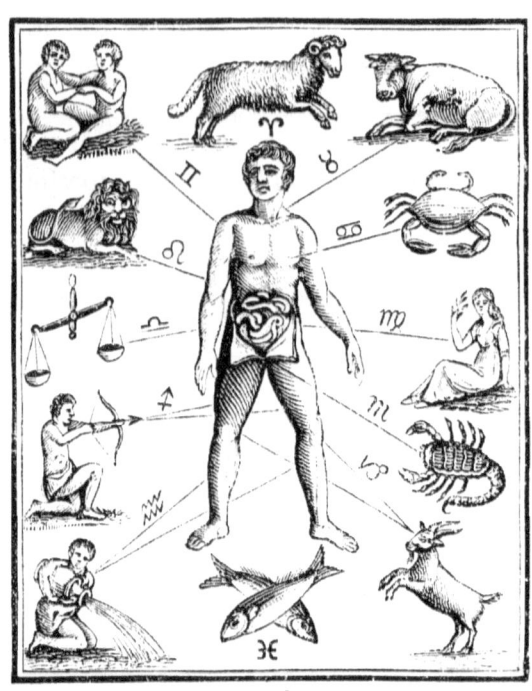

General Lunar Influences

Lunar Phase	Best areas to work on
New Moon	The waxing phases are good, in general, for all manner of healing that encourages the body to restore
Waxing Crescent	itself. All wounds, sprains, breaks, are best done during this time. Also, after banishing or exorcising
First Quarter	depressions, obsessions, or malevolent spiritual forces and entities during the waning phases, the waxing
Waxing Gibbous	phases are especially helpful to restore and mend the patient after a rigorous "cleansing".
Full Moon	Any healing can be accomplished at this time. However, banishing unwanted growths is best done during waning.
Waning Gibbous	The waning phases of the moon are useful for making a decrease in any ailment or problem: tumors,
Last Quarter	warts, swellings, the elimination of addictions, all blockages, some types of inflammation and rash.
Waning Gibbous	Stress and the induction of relaxation. Also, exorcisms and banishing of spirits and thought forms.

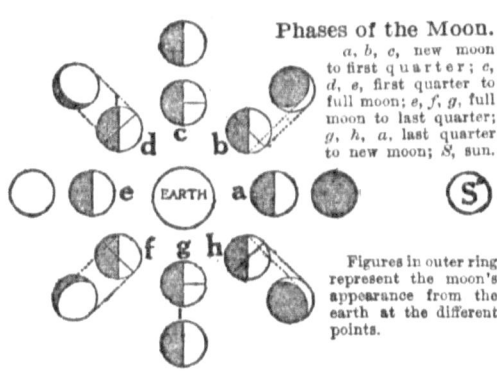

[Need better figure of lunar phases]

General Planetary Influences

Planet	Day of the Week	Rulership or Influence
Sun	Sunday	Vital energy, increasing one's energies; use of tonics, warming and drying out of wounds and inflammation; relates to the heart and its functions
Moon	Monday	Cleansing and clearing afflictions; cooling inflammations, fevers, and rashes; encourages moistness, and is good for working against "dry" conditions.
Mercury	Wednesday	Relates to the nervous system and all its conditions: mental disease and aberrations; also shingles can be treated under this influence as this is a "nervous" affliction. Mercury's influence can be considered brauching for stuttering, etc.
Venus	Friday	Relaxing and soothing influence. Relates to the lymphatic system, and also the bowels -- hence it rules over nutrient absorption and elimination. Venus is also 'moist'.
Mars	Tuesday	Relates to inflammations and eruptions; its energies can be used to encourage warming, as well as the vitalization of the sexual drive, and instances of impotence/frigidity.
Jupiter	Thursday	Relates to the metabolism, the liver, the blood and the circulatory system; this is a very nourishing energy, which encourages growth : good for treating the weak and underweight ('slow' metabolism).
Saturn	Saturday	Relates to restrictions and constrictions. This is used to advantage in order to 'bind' or slow the growth of any disease or condition.

General Zodiac Influences

Zodiac Sign	Name of God	Planet	Archangel and Angel	Body Area
Aries	YHVH	Mars	Malchidiel/Sharhiel	Front of body, upper jaw, eyes
Taurus	YHHV	Venus	Asmodel/Arziel	Neck, throat, ears, pharynx, upper esophagus, palate, thyroid gland, vocal chords, lower jaw,
Gemini	YVHH	Mercury	Ambriel/Sarayel	Sympathetic nervous system, lungs, bronchi, trachea
Cancer	HVHY	Moon	Muriel/Pakiel	Breasts, chest, stomach, pancreas, esophagus, left side of body, thoracic duct, gallbladder
Leo	HYVH	Sun	Verchiel/Sharatiel	Back of body, thymus gland, heart, spinal chord & marrow, spleen, & upper back
Virgo	HHYV	Mercury	Hameliel/Shelathiel	Bowels, abdomen, solar plexus, duodenum, parasympathetic nervous system,
Libra	VHYH	Venus	Zuriel/Chedquiel	Adrenal glands, lumbar region, loins, ureters, ovaries, skin, filtration organs
Scorpio	VHHY	Mars/Pluto	Barkiel/Saitziel	Reproductive organs, testes, bladder, prostate gland, ovaries (see Libra)
Sagittarius	VYHH	Jupiter	Adnachiel/Samequiel	Sacrum, sciatic nerve, hips, thighs, liver (see Libra)
Capricorn	HYHV	Saturn	Hanael/Saritiel	Right side of body, joints, knees, hair, teeth, parathyroid, nails, skeleton (all), skin (see Libra)
Aquarius	HYVH	Uranus	Gambiel/Tzakmiqiel	Coccyx, calves & ankles, cones & rods of eyes
Pisces	HHVY	Neptune	Amnitziel/Barchiel	Feet, toes, soles of feet, lymphatic system; all extremities; duodenum (see Virgo) & caecum

Bones	Muscles	Arteries & Veins	Diseases/Disorders Governed
Skull, face (but not nasal bones)	Used in eating & talking	Temporal & internal Carotids; cephalic: coming from the right	Pimples, ringworm, headaches, migraine, encephalitis, smallpox, harelip
Cervical vertebrae in neck	In front & back of neck	External Carotids & basilar artery; jugulars in the neck & veins of the thyroid gland	Sore throat, glandular swellings in neck, croup, mumps, goiter, abscess, suffocation, apoplexy, piles, fistulas
Upper ribs, collar bones, shoulder blades, bones in upper arms, forearms,	Those of the arms and shoulders	Those coming and going from the shoulders, arms, lungs, & rib cage	Asthma, bronchitis, pleurisy, pneumonia, all ailments and breaks in the ribs, arms, and shoulders
Breast bone, ribs nearest to the stomach, womb	Intercostals (between ribs) and diaphragm	Diaphragmatic, those in the stomach; mammary, gastric	Hypochondria, colds and chills; also, gallbladder disorders, and those of the sinuses -- sinusitis; stomach disorders.
Dorsal vertebrae	Back and around shoulder blades	Vena cava, aorta (anterior/posterior), coronaries	Heart disorders, palpitations, fevers, spinal meningitis, heat exhaustion, sunstroke, pestilence, inflammation
	Rectal & abdominal	Those serving the digestive system and intestines	Bowel disorders, constipation, peritonitis, IBS, diarrhea; this sign governs some nervous disorders in conjunction with Cancer & Taurus
Lumbar vertebrae, & below ribs	Lower back & top of pelvic bone	Those coming to and from kidneys; also those of the lower back	Brights disease, nephritis, suppression of urine, neuralgia of kidneys, weak lower back; venereal disease
Pelvic and pubic	Those of the bladder, rectum, & urethra	Those serving the pelvic region and reproductive organs	Ruptures, fistulas, piles (see Taurus), afflictions with the genitals; groin injuries, venereal disease (see Libra)
Sacrum & tibia	Thighs & buttocks	Those serving the thighs & buttocks	Felons, abscesses, suppuration, septic inflammations, enteric disorders, rheumatism, gout, hip dislocation, wounds (general)
Whole skeleton (generally), knees (specifically)	Those of the knees	Those serving the knees	Epidermis, skin diseases, impetigo, pruritis, falls, bruises, dislocations (general), rheumatism (see Sagittarius)
Coccyx, lower leg bones & shins	Calf muscles, & those in ankles/shins	Those of the lower legs	Circulatory disorders (generally), but especially of the lower legs -- e.g. clots, etc.; mental disorders
Feet/toe bones	Those of the fingers and toes	Those that serve the feet, toes, and all extremities	Deformities of feet/toes: bunions, gout (see Sagittarius), corns warts; discharges, dropsy, glandular softening, lung trouble, bowel disorders (see Virgo); contagious diseases, & drug inducted illness, addictions

Please take careful note of the various crossovers in governance. Some signs will "share" body parts, illnesses and disorders. The correspondences listed here are by no means exhaustive. In general, when considering the use of this sort of data in practice, you can simply note the afflicted area of the body and then consider applying a sympathetic treatment without consideration to 'sub-rulerships' by other signs. For example, Capricorn governs the whole skeleton. In brauching for a broken bone, you cannot go wrong with Capricornian influence. If the break is, for example, in one of the toe bones, you may consider calling upon the Piscean energies via its Angel or Archangel, etc. In practical application, you are working with the lunar phases in these signs. That is, when the moon is waxing in Capricorn, this would be a great time for brauching for calcium deficiencies or bone fractures. Another example: you can Brauche for warts any time the moon is waning; however, it would be more advantageous to Brauche for them during a waning moon in Pisces, and so on. The use of the Names of God, which are actually just permutations of the letters of the Tetragrammaton (YHVH), are more for use in written talismans. For verbal charming, there are ten Names that correspond to the Sephiroth of the Tree of Life. These are listed with their corresponding applications below.

Adam Kadmon -- the Universal Man

Before going further with this, please note that Braucherei is not Kabbalah. It is true to say that some aspects of Braucherei have been strongly influenced by Kabbalistic thought by way of German ceremonial magicians, but it is in no way dependent upon it. For those who are true adepts of Kabbalah, basic Braucherei can be magnified a thousand times over through that paradigm. Kabbalah is a very convenient pigeon-holing system by which a practitioner can classify and magnify various bits of minutia. As we've seen above, you can take your magical timing for your work from the seasonal, lunar, stellar, or planetary cycles. Each of these, alone or in combination can assist you in focusing upon very specific ailments and body parts. By way of Kabbalah, this sort of focus can help a practitioner to classify that ailment, and apply the appropriate Name of Power or planetary force to the disease. In short, Kabbalah in terms of Braucherei is just a means to an end --it is a tool-- and not the end in itself. This is aside from whether or not the Braucher is also a Kabbalist.

The Sephiroth of the Tree of Life

This is just a very elementary description of each Sephira ("Sephiroth" is the plural). For those of you well versed in Kabbalah, this will be very basic indeed. For those who are completely unfamiliar, this will give some idea what I am going on about.

The Tree of Life has 10 Sephiroth (sometimes described as being "jars" or spheres):

Name	Description	Part of Human Self/Body	Name of God
Kether	The crown, I AM-ness, emanating from the transcendent Godhead Ein Soph	Spirit	EHEIE
Chokhmah	Wisdom, masculine emanation of God	Brain (or only right hemisphere)*	Y O D YEHOVAH
Binah	Understanding, feminine emanation of God	Spleen (or left brain hemisphere)*	YEHOVAH ELOHIM
Hesed	Love/Mercy, the emanation of Divine expansiveness; the imparting of creative grace: a sort of "Jupiterian" expansion.	Liver (also the left arm)*	EL
Din / Geburah/ Gevurah	Severity, the halting of God's emanation of grace: a sort of Saturnine restriction of creative energies	Gall (also the right arm)*	ELOHIM GIBOR
Tiphareth	Splendor: this is the heart of the Tree and balances both Mercy and Severity	Heart	ELOHA
Netzach	Victory: Mediator of grace from Hesed	Kidneys	YEHOVAH SABAOTH
Hod	Majesty: Mediator of grace from Din	Lungs	ELOHIM SABAOTH

Yesod	Foundation: generation and propagation in the lower worlds	Genitals	SHADDAI
Malkuth	The Kingdom: God in physical creation; divine immanence	Feet/entire physical self	ADONAI MELECH

*These assignments are potentially contentious.

Each of these spheres is described as an "emanation" of God, an outpouring of Divine grace and creativity. These emanations of grace can be compared to what Eastern Orthodoxy calls God's "Creative Energies". The various emanations are the way in which the Divine manifests creation, with increasing 'densities' until it finally brings into being physical reality (being Malkuth). All of the 10 ultimately proceed from the transcendent, unmanifest Godhead, Ein Soph: the Divine which Is and Is Not.

Adam Kadmon is the "Universal Man", a sort of personification or anthropomorphic projection upon the Kabbalistic Tree of Life. This is an over simplification, but the gist of it is really all we need here: that various points or sections of the human body correspond to related points on the Tree. Examine the figure on the next page.

The middle column of the Tree is the vertical axis of the body. This comprises the Sephiroth Kether, Tiphareth, Yesod, and Malkuth. Easy enough. Next are the Supernal Triad of Kether, Binah, and Chokhmah. Here's where it gets contentious. If we superimpose the form of the human body upon the Tree, with the body facing forward (as in the above figure), then the right side of the body is under Binah, whereas the left is under Chokhmah. When superimposing the body upon the Tree, the Supernal Triad of Kether, Binah, and Chokhmah surround the head. Binah and Chokhmah then becomes representative of the right and left sides of the brain (as I understand it). There are some who speculate that Chokhmah governs the right hemisphere of the brain, while Binah governs the left. BUT, then there is the consideration of

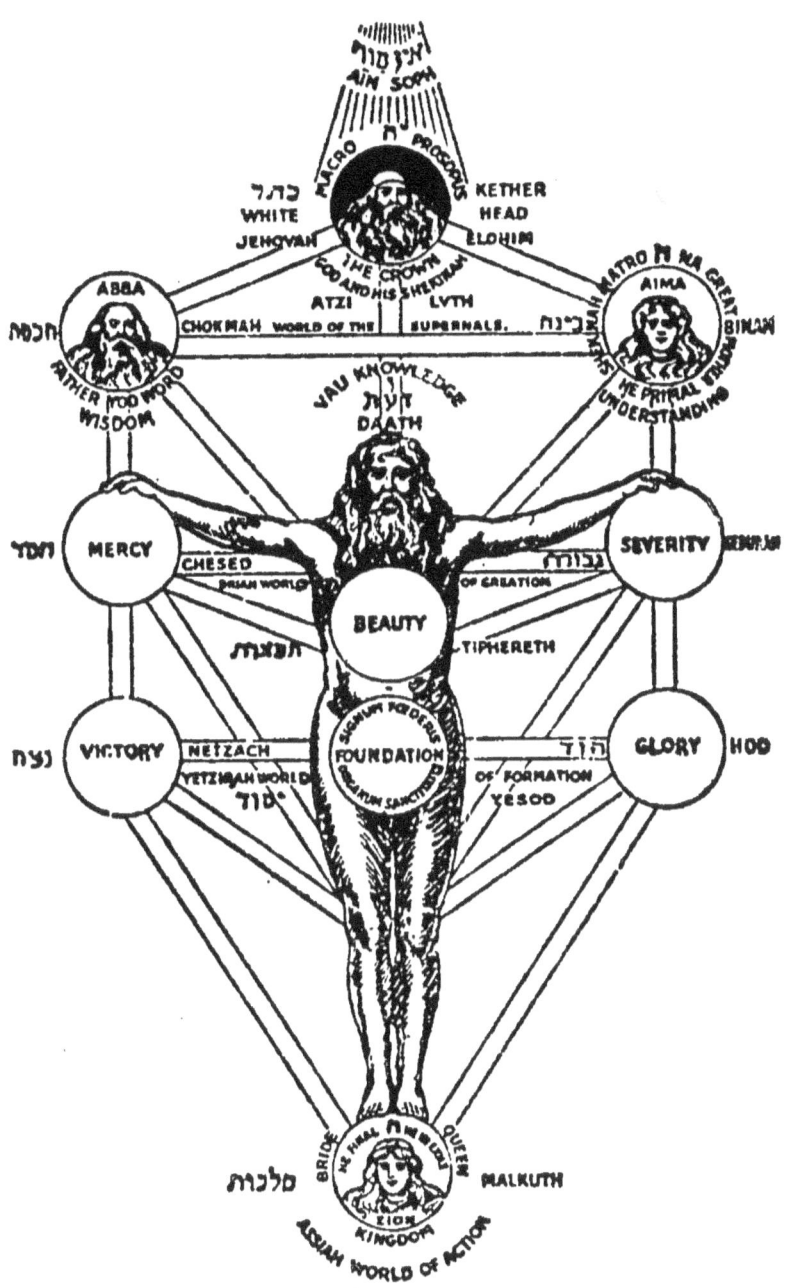

modern neurology: that the left side of the brain governs the right side of the body, and the right governs the left. Altogether, this can be far too complicated if you get overly analytical with it, especially within the confines of Braucherei. If you do wish to use any of this Kabbalistic information, you may do so. It can be rather useful to bless 'out' a stubborn infection by use of an appropriate Name of God when trying for a patient. However, it is the author's opinion that too much minutia and ritualization, far from helping a practitioner to focus, may actually have the opposite effect.

When the author was taught to Pow-Wow, Daisy always instructed to go over the patient with the General Brauche, regardless of whatever was ailing them. Even if a specialized sort of work is needed, "the General" is done. The reason for this is presented in counterpoint to what is written above regarding the use of Kabbalistic pigeon-holing: the whole person needs treatment because a disease/illness/disorder brings about disharmony and imbalances throughout.

Additional Names with explanations
To round out this little section on Kabbalah in Braucherei, here is a further list of the Names of God, which you may plug into various prayers and charms to follow.

TETRAGRAMMATON -- this is not actually a name *per se*. It is a stand-in for the Hebrew letters YHVH (i.e., Yod Heh Vau Heh). Written Hebrew has no vowels; therefore, the original pronunciation of this name is lost. In Judaism pronouncing the name of God was/is taboo. To this day, God (sometimes spelled "G-d") will be referred to indirectly as 'The Lord' (Adonai), or at one time as *Adoshem* (which means something like "The Lord-Name" -- being a combination of the word *Adonai* (Lord) and *Ha Shem* (the name).

From what I understand, this latter practice has been abandoned. The letters YHVH have been phoneticized to be pronounced as either Yahweh, or Jehovah (or Iehovah/Yehovah). The actual word Tetragrammaton is more something that you will write on talismans than actual use in prayer (although I've seen it used that way too).

ADONAI -- As noted above, this means 'Lord'. Grammatically, in Hebrew, this is a plural word. I take this to be like the use of the "royal" We in English. Therefore, this does not connote more than one Lord. The same grammatical condition exists with the word:

ELOHIM -- This can be translated as being equivalent to the English word 'God' or Latin 'Deus'. Please understand that the word 'God' in English (or in any other language) is not a name -- it is a title. As I mentioned, the actual *Name* of God amongst the Hebrews was lost with the fall of the Temple. What we now call "Names" of God are no such thing, they are merely titles or job descriptions, if you will. Elohim appears to be in the plural (denoted by the *im* ending). It is true that this word can be used to refer to the many gods of various polytheistic systems, but in this matter, it is treated as a singular. From what I have found in my research, there are a few singular nouns in Hebrew that appear to have plural case endings.

EHYEH-ASHER-EHYEH -- This is a Hebrew phrase that denotes God's timeless, eternal, immanent Power: I AM THAT I AM. Some have translated this also as: *I will be what I will be*; *I shall be what I shall be*; or even *I will be because I will be*.

EL -- *God*, or when referring to polytheistic systems: 'a god'. It is a word that although plainly singular can be a plural when referring to the aforementioned non-Hebrew deities. El is related to the Akkadian *ilu* having the same meaning. It is also found in names such as 'Micha*el*', 'Salathi*el*', etc.

ELYON -- "The Most High". Elyon (Elion) is often found as a companion to other Names: El, YHVH, or Elohim.

SHADDAI -- Sometimes translated as "Almighty". There are various streams of thought on this word however. Some have theorized that the name derives from the Hebrew word 'shadad', meaning 'to destroy'. Others hypothesize that it stems from an antique Semitic word meaning 'mountain'. Yet another theory holds that the word is connected to shadayim, meaning 'breasts' -- emphasizing God's fruitful, mother-like nature.

SHALOM -- Peace.

SHEKINAH -- Dwelling Place. Shekinah is the manifestation of God's presence that dwells among human beings. This is a term that was used by rabbis when referring to God's presence in the Tabernacle. Since there is a feminine feel to this word, a few today have taken this as a sign of the Divine Feminine within Judaism. Author Raphael Patai has done extensive work on this subject (see the bibliography), but it is wrought with controversy.

YAH -- Yah, sometimes spelled 'Jah', is the first two letters of the Tetragrammaton (YH). It can be found in names such as 'Hezek*iah*', etc.

YHVH SABAOTH -- God of Hosts (a host being an army). Sometimes this name/title is seen as just 'Sabaoth'. In closer spelling to the Hebrew pronunciation, this word is sometimes seen as 'Tzevaot'.

YHShVH -- Yehoshua. In Christian Kabbalah (or spelled Cabala when referring to the Christian practice) this is a variant of the Tetragrammaton, which refers to Christ. It is composed of five Hebrew letters (the 'Sh' standing in for the letter 'Shin') that are associated with the five points of the pentagram. In Braucherei practice this 'star' is called the hexenfoos, or Witch's foot (more on this latter). In relation to Christ, the five points of the pentagram are the five wounds that were suffered on the cross.

MESHIACH -- Messiah; anointed one. The Greek equivalent of this Hebrew word is *Christos* -- Christ. In charms, prayers, and invocations, you may use any combination of these words along with:

SOTER -- This Greek word specifically means 'Savior' and not just 'anointed' (Christos). Therefore an invocation can run thusly: *"Fever, I conjure you by the Five Holy Wounds suffered by Our Lord and Savior Jesus Christ. Diminish and be gone by the Power of God: Adonai Shamayyim, Shaddai El Chai, El Elyon, Messias, Soter, Emmanuel, Sabaoth, Adonai. Diminish in the name of God the Father, God the Son, and God the Holy Spirit. Amen"* In this invocation the word Meshiach appears in a Greek or Latinate-type spelling 'Messias'. Emmanuel is Jesus' name at birth meaning "God is with us". 'Adonai Shamayyim' can be translated as "Lord of the Heavens".

Chanted or spoken with feeling, these Names can lend great power to any Pow-Wow, in conjunction with the usual chants and charms that you have learned thus far.

Lastly, in regard to timing, there are 'special' times of the year that are considered to be more favorable for certain types of work than others. The earth has cycles and phases. Those of us in temperate climates know the four seasons. Each season has an 'energy' or quality. Some of these observed times were, formerly, heathen holidays. The most popular days today, due to the rise in Neo-pagan practice, are largely Celtic festivals, such as Halloween (Samhain).

Neo-pagan practitioners, such as Wiccans, will talk of a "Wheel of the Year." This terminology is not used in Braucherei. If and when it is, the person doing so has borrowed the term and not because it is native to the practice. These special days, and many others, are what are now called "liminal" points in time. That is to say, they are neither "here nor there," but signify a time when the boundaries between this world and the spirit world are most blurred. ***Braucherei is not a religion***, and therefore it does not have 'holidays.'

With that said, old-time practitioners did recognize power cycles. The waning moon, as seen above, is only good for getting rid of certain illnesses and conditions – such as warts and other growths; the "waning" year also works similarly. The spring, being of the 'waxing' cycle, encourages a momentum in the healing process. Animals are best treated during the Ember Days (see Glossary entry).

Among Germanic peoples the solstices (*Sonnenwende*) were important times of the year, being the waxing and waning of the Sun's power: the Summer and Winter Solstices. Around the actual solstice (being the 21st or 22nd of June) St. John's Eve (June 24th) was, and in some parts still is, a popular observance among Europeans. This was the time to build bonfires for purification, symbolic of Christ's Light. On the feast day itself, St. John's Wort was collected for healing and the warding off of evil (see Glossary entry for ST. JOHN'S EVE). The Eve of St. John is a superior time for healings, and ought to be taken advantage of. While it may seem appropriate to heal on days like Christmas and Easter, major holidays ought to be avoided, unless there is an emergency. *Do not heal on Good Friday.*

8: The Cyclopedia of Working Braucherei
The Prayers, Charms and Formulae

As mentioned in the introduction to this section, the prayers, charms and formulae for Braucher use have been arranged in a somewhat general, but alphabetic manner for easier consultation. These categories are not exhaustive and, in fact, each one could be subdivided quite easily. No use would be served by such detail, but to make the categories too broad would place us back in the domain of the old Pow-Wow books where everything is jumbled together.

To keep things neat and orderly, under each heading you will find 1) the verbal Brauche(s), followed by 2) sympathetic, non-verbal remedies, 3) Psalm(s), 4) Sigils or talismans, and 5) herbal remedies. The first variety will always be present. The second, third, fourth, and fifth may or may not be. Now, if any of these last four are absent, it does not mean that such do not exist. A word about the Psalms: their inclusion here depends upon their size. This means that you will find 'small' Psalms or psalmic verses included in the instructions. However, beyond this you will need to have your Bible handy to look up the others.

Before going further, please note that these charms and formulae can stand alone, without use in the "General Brauche". As mentioned previously, not all Brauchers practiced in the same way. The "modality" which was covered previously would not be familiar to all practitioners. That technique, indeed, has enough backbone to stand all by itself without the foregoing remedies. However, it would be remiss not to point out a personal observation. After having learned Daisy's method of brauching, it seems to us that (perhaps) many of the old Braucher manuals may have had deliberately missing steps or operations. Of course, that is just opinion and not a fact. If you wish to incorporate these prayers and invocations into the "General", they may easily be done so during the circuit that concentrates upon the affected body part. Or, they may be used for extra 'power' after the General's circuits are finished.

As always, remember that Braucherei operations are done in three's, unless you are otherwise instructed. When in doubt, do it in three's anyway. Always finish a Brauche by blessing in the "Three Highest Names" of Father, Son, and Holy Ghost (Spirit), sealed by three crosses made with fist and thumb gesture. DO NOT OMITT THESE STEPS. If the Brauche is to be finish in another way, instruction will be given.

When undertaking these charms on someone other than yourself, make certain to wear your cross, hexenfoos, holy medals (if Catholic), etc. Also make sure that the Bible is present. Work no Braucherei without your Bible at hand. It is ironic that so many practitioners of the occult arts these days poo-poo this one book when it happens to be the largest *magical grammary* in print. If the Bible were known for what it actually *is*, it would have been banned a long time ago.

A Note on Sources: Please observe that the source of the charms below are identified and noted. However, many of these, especially in regard to the instructions for their usage, have been rewritten. Some of the old directions and wording are less than clear. Any charms created by the author shall be noted as such.

The Verbal Healing Charms

ABSCESSES, BOILS, SORES, AND ULCERATIONS
(*SCHWAER, GSCHWAER, SCHLIER, VERSCHINNE*)

Brauche Remedy

For A Swelling Wound:
Pass the hand over the swelling three times and speaks the charm each time:
"Swelling, thou shalt disappear, ye pains, drive off. Thus we are one body in Jesus Christ, but members of one another. Swelling, thou shalt disappear, ye pains, drive off in the name of Jesus of Nazareth. Thou shalt be helped as true as it is that the three Wise Men from the Levant worshipped Jesus first." + + +

Another for the healing of a wound:
This one is a combination of Brauche charm and sympathetic remedy:
On a morning before sunrise during the waxing moon, take a sharp knife, pruning clippers, or saw and sever a young, thin branch from an ash tree pointing in the direction of where the sun rises (in lieu of that, any tree that bears fruit or flowers will do). It needs only be nine inches in length. This must be done in ONE stroke or clipping. Don't mangle and hack the thing. The energy won't be as good if you do. Take the switch into the house and clip it into three three-inch pieces.

When you are ready take the sticks to your patient, holding them in your right hand. Begin using the first stick closest to the right side of your body.

Take each stick individually and put it gently into the wound (or at least on top of the lesion). Say at each time:

*"With this switch and Christ's dear blood,
I banish your pain and do you good."* + + +

Take the remaining two sticks and repeat the procedure, one at a time. After the first stick, let a half hour go before repeating with the second stick. After the second, allow an entire night to pass, and then repeat with the third stick in the morning. As you collect the sticks, keep them wrapped in clean, white paper and stored in a safe, warm, dry place until the wound heals. Afterward, they may be destroyed in fire.

Sympathetic Remedy

Other uses of wood and stone:
A "rukschtee" or "rest stone" can be used to absorb pain from wounds and other skin eruptions. To obtain a *rukschtee*, go to the area of a border (traditionally this would be a farm fence) and find a small round stone that is above ground (visible) and close by the fence. Once you find that stone, that's your *rukschtee*.

To use: place this stone underneath the patient's pillow. This will absorb the pain and deliver a more restful sleep.

After each use of the *rukschtee*, bathe it in salt water and sunlight for a day, or alternately, bury it in a patch of ground over night. If the latter, place a marker near it so you can find it again.

These stones are related to "thunderstones" (*gwidder schtee* or *dunner schtee*): **black**, round or jagged stones used to ward off lightening. They were thought to be produced from lightening strikes. As a result, these special black stones may be used for the pain of electrical burns.

When employing this, or any other "sympathy" that comes without a Brauche charm, you may utilize a prayer of your own when about to put the sympathy to use. It isn't necessary, but it would only give it extra force. Here's a detail not in the old charm books: when you find this stone, <u>tell</u> it what you want it to do. You are NOT praying to the stone. You are <u>TALKING</u> to it. When using objects like the *rukschtee* over and over for the same purpose, it will gain a "memory" of what it is supposed to <u>do</u>. You will not need to talk to it every time. Here's something else to remember: just like with the "General", there is no need to visualize anything. When talking to stones, trees, plants, or so-called inanimate objects, the necessary requirement is that you simply state your desire or purpose. If this feels 'silly', that's alright. You'll get over it. Just *know* that the recipient of your instructions has *absorbed* them. Here is a formal type of 'conjuration' or ritual way of talking to a stone:

"***Stone, creature of God, by our Lord and Savior Jesus Christ, who shall come again in glory to judge the quick and the dead and the world by fire, I call upon you to observe your duty to the God of your Creation, the Lord of Heaven and Earth, to be a tool of healing for both man and beast unto His Glory.***" + + +

At some point in an address of this type, you can mention specifically what you want the stone to do. Or, you can save that for your next, less formal address to the stone.

"Wound Wood":
Wound Wood is said to heal all wounds. This is very similar to the Brauche charm above. To get Wound Wood: Find an ash tree. On Good Friday, prior to sunrise, cut off a branch that is a little larger than a finger's width in diameter. The branch need not be longer than a foot. Here's the trick: the branch must be cut off in <u>three strokes</u>. If the wood does not sever completely and fall to the ground on the third stroke, IT IS USELESS. Let the branch lie upon the ground until the rays of the rising sun are on it. Then, cut the wood up into little sections and preserve these pieces in a dry place for future use. This, then, is Wound Wood.

To use Wound Wood:
Lay the wood upon a wound until the whole piece is warm. This is said to prevent infection.

If treating a swollen wound, lay the wood upon it and then make the three blessing crosses in the three Highest Names. + + +

When the wound is pussy or bleeding, allow the wood to become soaked with the liquid, using it like a bandage. Since ash is a hard wood, it won't really soak up a lot, as much as it will just get wet and messy. The use of wood in sympathetic treatment is good when puss (*dreck*) is present in an inflamed wound (*rodlaefich*). When finished, destroy the used pieces by fire.

BLOOD, AND BLEEDING (*BLUT SCHTILLE*) -- "*For the blood is the life...*" Deuteronomy 12:23

Brauche Remedy

Bleeding wound I:
Put the left thumb with pressure on the wound and say:
"***Christ Wunde***
War noch nicht verbunda" + + +
("*Christ's wound; was never bound*" + + +)
Bless with the right thumb. This is done three times. Remember to say the patient's name first. That is, "*N.N., Christ Wunde...*", etc.

Bleeding wound II:
Say over the wound:
"***Jesus Christ, dearest blood, who stops the pain and stops the blood; in this help you*** (person's name here)." + + +

Bleeding wound III:
Speak the name of the patient then say nine times:

"*Christ has suffered for us, tired Himself struggling and bled to death on the cross, which is good for all bleeding. In the name of Christ it shall stand, not run, nor go further, remain at the proper place, not flow nor float; the bleeding be healed, divided rightly.*" + + +

Bleeding wound IV:
This is the charm I used the most. In fact, I prefer this one to all others. It comes from the Bible: Ezekiel 16:6.
"***When I passed by thee*** [insert person's name here] ***I saw thee polluted in thine own blood, I said unto thee*** [insert person's name here] ***when thou wast in thy blood live! Yea! I said unto thee*** [insert person's name here] ***when thou wast in thy blood, live!***" + + +

Here it is again in Luther's German, should you desire to use it:
„***Ich aber ging vor dir über*** [insert person's name here] ***und sah dich in deinen Blut liegen und sprach zu dir*** [insert person's name here]***, da du so in deinem Blut lagest: Du sollst leben! Ja, zu dir sprach ich*** [insert person's name here]***, da du so in deinem Blut lagest: Du sollst leben!***" + + +

Bleeding wound V:
A miscellaneous wound/blood/illness blessing:

This is not an old charm or prayer, but one that I have made to suit any occasion for healing – especially in the case of wounds. Despite its newness, it is based upon the Catholic devotions to the Wounds of Christ. Therefore, its style and symbolism are consistent with old-time Braucherei. Each wound corresponds to a point on the Hexenfoos (pentagram), as this symbol in Christian tradition is synonymous with the Five Wounds of Christ. Unlike what some paranoid alarmists would have folks believe, the pentagram is not a diabolical device, but an abstract symbol of the crucifixion. See the glossary entry for "Hexenfoos".

To employ this prayer, it is only necessary for you to place your hands over the ill or wounded spot. As with all Braucherei charms, this is to be done three times. If necessary, it can be done nine times. The repetition of charms and related prayers are best done in odd numbers: 3, 5, 7 & 9.

German:

Durch seine Wunden wir geheilt...

Durch das Blut seiner rechten Hand

--Wunde Christi heilt alle.

Durch das Blut seiner linken Hand

--Wunde Christi heilt alle

Durch das Blut seines rechten Fusses

--Wunde Christi heilt alle

Durch das Blut seines linken Fusses

--Wunde Christi heilt alle

Durch das Blut und das Wasser seiner Seite

--Wunde Christi heilt alle

English:

Through His wounds we are healed...

Through the Blood of His right hand

--The Wounds of Christ heal all.

Through the Blood of His left hand

--The Wounds of Christ heal all.

Through the Blood of His right foot

--The Wounds of Christ heal all.

Through the Blood of His left foot

--The Wounds of Christ heal all.

Through the Blood and Water of His side

--The Wounds of Christ heal all.

While Brauchers tend not to work in groups but individually, the above prayer/charm can be used in a group setting where a healing is being prayed for by more than one person – hence its litany-like call-and-response style.

Bleeding wound VI & VII:
These Brauche charms call specifically on the Blessed Mother. There are, in fact, many such charms recorded, even among largely Protestant Brauchers.

"Maria ging über den Kamp
Hatte zwei Krüge in der Hand:
In eins Blut,
In eins Wasser. –
Blut steh,
Wasser geh."[1]

"Mary goes through the land
She has two pitchers in her hand:
In one is blood,
In one is water.—

---

[1]   Jahn, *Hexenwesen*, pp. 72 - 73

Blood stay,
Water go."

Say this three times and bless the wound in the Three Highest Names.

Another similar charm:

"Mutter Maria ging über den Kampf*
Sie trug zwei Becher in ihrer rechten Hand:
Den einen voll Blut,
Den andern voll Wasser.—
Blut steh!
Wasser geh!"

Muss dreimal gesprochen und beim dritten Mal Amen gesagt werden.

"Mother Mary goes over the land
She has two mugs in her right hand:
The one is full of blood,
The other is full of water.—
Blood stay!
Water go!"[2]

Must be spoken 3x and at the third time say "Amen".

Sympathetic Remedy

The Bloodstone (*blutschtee*):
A Bloodstone[3] is collected in a similar manner to the *rukschtee*.

---

2   *Ibid.* *The word *"kampf"* ought to be *"kamp"* – translated by the author as "land."

3   This can be the jeweler's stone due to its 'sympathetic' coloring; however, this is really just an ordinary roundish, smooth, small stone. Some would find a reddish colored ordinary rock (the color of which would signify the presence of iron – and, of course, the blood contains a good deal of iron) for this purpose. Yet, from repeated usage such a stone would acquire a dark patina anyway.

The best place to find these stones is in liminal areas: places that are transitional -- from one property to another, an out lying spot, an unusual place, or appearing in "fairy rings", the boundaries of a field onto a forest, etc. These Brauche stones may also come to the practitioner in an uncanny manner when they are genuinely needed. Some times such objects will just appear, apparently 'out of nowhere'. The stones used in Braucherei are usually round and solid, not holed. Naturally holed stones have another use. The Bloodstone can be of any color, but two favorites are white or reddish. Again, talk to this stone after you find it.

To use a Bloodstone:
hold this stone tightly onto the bleeding wound, like a bandage. If the stone is good for this use, the bleeding will stop in moments.

For Nosebleed I:
Press a *silver coin* on the one of following places: on the back of the neck, against the upper lip, or against the upper gum. I have also been told that it can go underneath the tongue. Make sure the coin is clean before putting it into the mouth. The coin you will need for this is one of the old **Mercury Dimes**. Get a bunch of these, as there are many opportunities to use them in Braucherei. They are relatively inexpensive. The reason for employing this dime is its genuine *silver* content.[4]

For Nosebleed II:
Tie a red string around the little finger. Choose either the left or right hand depending upon the nostril bleeding. Tie between the tip and the first knuckle.

For Nosebleed III:
Take an egg and let the dripping blood fall upon the eggshell. Throw the egg into a fire.

---

4   A variation on this technique is the use of a large key (the old fashioned sort). Run the key under cold water for a few moments, and then apply it at the back of the neck, or above the lip.

Nosebleed IV:
Take an egg and make a small hole in the big end of it. Drain out some of the contents. Make sure the hole is large enough to allow the blood to flow into it. Allow the blood to drain into the egg until it is quite full. If you have an active fireplace, woodstove, or burning pit, place the egg into some very warm ashes with the hole-side up. As the egg and blood cook and harden, the bleeding subsides.

Nosebleed V:
With the blood of the patient, write on his/her forehead: **It is finished**. Or, write **DO:I:P It will soon cease**.

Bleeding (general):
Make small wedges of wood, the best being ash, and wet them with the blood. Hammer the wedges into the crack of some dry piece of wood. Or, take some of the blood and write this on the forehead: **O, I, P, U, L, U.**

Herbal Remedy

Blood purifying remedies (*blutreiningungsmittel*):
Roots are very traditional blood purifiers. Herbalists reading this will already be acquainted with many of these remedies. Modern allopathic doctors cringe when hearing archaic terms such as "blood purifier". However, I believe it is safe to speak of *detoxification*. There is no doubt in my mind that modern life, much like old age, doesn't come alone. This means that we absorb the toxins of our environment and that in our food stuffs (pesticides, hormones, antibiotics). Thankfully, our bodies do eliminate many of these poisons (otherwise we would be dead). Detoxifying herbals, when not taken to extremes, help the body do what it does best.

The life of a plant is in its roots. Five traditional blood purifiers are: sassafras (*Sassafras officinale*), sarsaparilla (*Aralia nudicaulis*), burdock (*Arctium lappa*), devil's bit (*Aletris farinosa*), and red beets (which I count as a root).

Recipe:
Take half a cup of burdock root and half a cup of pepperwood (*Angelica Tree -- Aralia espinosa*) and boil in three quarts of water. Boil this down to a half its volume. Take a teacupful every morning.

Another tea:
Take half a cup of sassafras root, sarsaparilla root, and burdock root to three quarts of water. Same as above recipe. This is best taken at the end of winter and throughout the spring.

Herbal for Nosebleed:
Put elecampane root (*Inula Helenium*) under the tongue, or have the patient hold pennyroyal (*Mentha Pulegium*) in the hand until it absorbs his/her body warmth -- this could really be categorized as a sympathetic remedy.

A tea of shepherd's purse (*Capsella bursa-pastoris*; German: *hirtentasche*): use the standard herbal tea formula of one heaping teaspoon full of dried herb to one cup of boiling water. The usual dosage of most herbal teas is the sipping of one cup over a period of an hour or so. It is said that this herb is best used in this capacity when harvested on St. Jacob's Day (July 25th).

COLDS, AND ILLNESSES OF THE THROAT, LUNGS, EARS, AND MOUTH

Brauche Remedy

For mouth sores, diphtheria, mouth infections:
"Johannes Hannes hast du ein weh Maul
Hast du die Mund Fauling oder die Breining
Bloss ich mein Adem in dein Maul [insert person's name here]*.
+ + + (in German, "Im Namen Gottes...")

In English:
"John Hannes, hast thou a sore mouth,
Hast thou scurvy or quinsy?
I blow my breath into thy mouth [insert person's name here]*.
+ + +

*Right after saying the person's name, blow into the mouth. Repeat this procedure three times.

For sore throats, tonsillitis, assorted throat infections and discomforts:
Job zog über Land, der hatt' den Stab in seiner Hand; du begegnete ihr Gott der Herr, und Sprach zu ihm: Job, warum trauerst du so sehr. Er sprach: ich Gott, warum sollt'ich nicht trauern? Mein Schlund und mein Mund will mir abfaulen. Da sprach Gott zu Job: Dort in seinem Thal, du fliesst ein Brunn, der heilet dir *[insert the person's name here] *dein Mund.* + + + (*"Im Namen Gottes des Vaters, des Sohnes und des Heiligen Geistes."*) 5

In English:
"Job went through the land, holding his staff close in the hand, when God the Lord did meet him, and said to him: Job, what art thou grieved at? Job said: Oh God, why should I not be sad? My throat and my mouth are rotting away. Then said the Lord to Job: In yonder valley there is a well which will cure thee * [insert person's name here], *and thy mouth, and thy throat.* + + + ("*In the name of God the Father, ...*" etc.)

*Just <u>before</u> speaking the person's name, blow into the mouth.

I have found that this Brauche charm does a nice job at ridding the *pain* of a sore throat. But, in my experience, that's just about all it does.6

5   From *Der Sympathetischer Haus Freund*; Beissel pp. 148-149
6   Dieffenbach (*Pennsylvania Folklife*, Winter 1975-76, p. 33) records an instance of an old

For earache:
"[insert person's name here] *He touched his ear, and it healed at that hour. The ear hears the wonder-works of heaven; pain, diminish in the name of Jesus Christ, and be sunk into the deep sea in the names of the Twelve Apostles.*"

This Brauche is to be said *seven times* while simultaneously rubbing the outside of the sore ear with two forefingers. Don't forget to bless at the end of each of the seven 'rounds' with the
+ + +.

Sympathetic Remedy

For mouth blisters:
Take three small ash sticks, or alternately, birch twigs approximately three inches long. Place the stick into the mouth, touching all of the blisters. Do this with one stick a day for three days. Bury the used sticks in a pile of compost or manure as you use them.

For earache:
Get an old smoking pipe and fill it with tobacco. Place the stem into the patient's sore ear; blow upon the lit bowl. Do this in the three Highest Names.

Psalm Remedy

For ear troubles (besides deafness), use Psalm 119, the Resh and Tau divisions.

Resh ø Depending upon the Bible you are using this set of verses will either begin at verse 152 or 153. This section is for pains and infections of the *right ear*. Speak these verses over a little onion juice. Place both of your hands over the receptacle holding the juice, or hold it in both hands while praying the Psalm slowly.

Braucherin (a female Pow-Wower) by the name of "Ketty" taking away his mother's mumps induced sore throat via this method of blowing into the mouth.

"Consider mine affliction, and deliver me: for I do not forget thy law.| Plead my cause, and deliver me: quicken me according to thy word. | Salvation is very far from the wicked: for they seek not thy statutes. | Great are thy tender mercies. O LORD: quicken me according to thy judgments. | Many are my persecutors and mine enemies; yet do I not decline from thy testimonies. | I beheld the transgressors, and was grieved; because they kept mot thy word. | Consider how I love thy precepts: quicken me O LORD, according to thy loving kindness. | Thy word is true from the beginning: and every one of thy righteous judgments endureth forever."

<u>Tau ú</u> This usually begins at verse 169. Tau is used for the same purpose, but only for the *left ear*. Pray over the onion juice the same way.

"Let my cry come near before thee, O LORD: give me understanding according to thy word. | Let my supplication come before thee: deliver me according to thy word. | My lips shall utter praise, when thou hast taught me thy statutes. | My tongue shall speak of thy word: for all thy commandments are righteousness. | Let thine hand help me; for I have chosen thy precepts. | I have longed for thy salvation, O LORD; and thy law is my delight. | Let my soul live, and it shall praise thee; and let thy judgments help me. | I have gone astray like a lost sheep; seek thy servant; for I do not forget thy commandments."

After praying either set of verses over the juice (depending upon the ear affected), get an eyedropper and place <u>one drop</u> in the ill ear.

Herbal Remedies

Elecampane for congestion:
Take elecampane *Inula Helenium*, called *Aland* or *Alantwurzel*, also known as Elf Dock or Elf Wort for breathing difficulties such as

congestion or asthma. Make an electuary of the dried root powder. Add 1 ½ oz of the dried root to ½ lb honey, which you first boil then skim. Stir the mixture until it thickens. Take a ½ tsp of the preparation three to four times a day.

COLIC, AND "THE LIVERGROWN" (*AAGEWACHSE*)

Livergrown is considered to be a "folk illness" peculiar to the Pennsylvania Germans. It means "grow together," referring to a sticking of muscular tissues of the lower chest seemingly to inner parts, such as the liver. This condition leaves the lower ribs more defined and prominent than normal, along with the abdomen being raised. The sensations of Livergrown are cramping, a feeling of restriction in the lower chest and upper abdominal areas, accompanied by difficult breathing, sometimes referred to as *hazschpann* (*or haerzgschpaerr*). In the past this condition was associated with "rickets." Another name for aagewachse is "cardiology," which has nothing to do with the modern use of this word. The labored breathing and 'attached' sensations can also be accounted for by pleurisy. Colic also comes underneath the category of aagewachse, and both conditions are treated identically in children. "Straining" and gas pains also account for some cases of aagewachse.

Brauche Remedy

<u>General Brauche Circuit remedy for colic and aagewachse</u>:
1) Perform the entire General Brauche Circuit on the patient
2) Use a sparing amount of extra virgin olive oil rubbed onto the tips of the first two fingers of both hands
3) Run the fingers of both hands side-by-side down the breast bone, trailing underneath the ribs. Both hands will separate from each other at the end of the sternum when about to go beneath the ribs; the fingers, following the contour of the ribcage, will meet together in the back

4) While doing this motion, recite the inflammation charm that starts out *"Ich bin dei gebruchman..."*
5) The motions and the chant are done three times.
6) Repeat all of the above twice more, 15 to 30 minutes apart the first time, then an hour afterwards the third time. The actual time interval between treatments can vary due to severity of the case.

A shorter brauching for colic:
Lay your hand lightly upon the child's mouth; speak its baptismal name before each repetition of the charm; do this three times.

"O beloved Lord Jesus Christ, Thou who hast died on the cross; in Thy name, help this child at this hour quickly. Jesus helps all children, so shalt thou be helped in His name, Jesus Christ of Nazareth." + + +[7]

A new Brauche for colic and aagewachse:
A short preface is needed to explain this technique. Over a series of months, a few years ago, I had recurring lucid dreams of receiving and treating patients. In these dreams were people that were unknown to me – strangers.

The most vivid of these was the time an infant came to me. It was suffering from a bad case of colic. The baby was lying in front of me with its head at my left, and feet at my right. A crucifix without a stand was lying on the table near the crown of its head. My left hand was on the baby's forehead, and my right was on its abdomen.

In this position I prayed for him (it was a baby boy). Then, with my left hand still on the child's forehead, I took my right hand, reached for the crucifix, and blessed the infant in The Three Highest Names; I made the sign of the cross with the object itself, blessing the tummy area.

[7] Beissel p. 43

Please feel free to use this, and if it works well for you, pass it along. Do this Brauche in odd numbers; three is standard, but others can be used depending upon the condition.[8]

Another Brauche for aagewachse:
Lay the child on its back. Place some spittle on the tip of your index finger and run it down in a line from the sternum to the abdomen. Turn the child over on the stomach and repeat, drawing the finger down from between the shoulder blades to the end of the spine. While doing these two motions be sure to say the following, prefacing it with the child's baptismal name.[9]

"Adhesion and heart-span go out of my child's rib; as Christ the Lord went out of His crib. God the Father, God the Son, and God the Holy Ghost."

Herbal Remedy

A remedy for infant colic:
Mix ½ teaspoon of mineral oil with four to five drops of anise extract; add 1 teaspoon of sugar. Place this mixture in a cloth formed by tying into the shape of a nipple. Dampen the 'nipple' with chamomile tea. Massage the baby's stomach while it is suckling on the cloth nipple.[10]

A healing prayer by Ruth Weil Kusler for use with this mixture, or on any other occasion:

---

[8] Since this is a book that attempts to capture traditional methods, I have kept adding this sort of material to a minimum. However, in cases such as this, where the technique is compatible with tradition, it is felt that its presentation will be of benefit.

[9] Brendle and Unger p. 198

[10] This recipe appears on p. 32 of *Tender Hands*, by Ruth Weil Kusler. This is a small but lovely book that demonstrates a variety of Brauche used by the Germans from Russia. It is a style closely related to massage accompanied by much herbal use. A variation of this recipe is to use Knorr's Genuine Hein Fong Essence (Green Drops). Ruth used Green Drops for stomach ailments; chamomile tea for sores and burns, and Dr. Forni's Alpen-Kraeuter "for nearly everything." Ruth's prayer can be found on p. 23 of her book.

"Dear Lord, I demand that all ailments will leave this body that is ailing, in Jesus' name. Jesus, you are the provider and have the power to heal. I ask it in Jesus' name." + + +

ATROPHY (*ABNEMMES*)
Abnemmes, like aagewachse, is classed by anthropologists as a "folk illness". As with all such ailments, the symptoms will usually be recognized as belonging to another sort of disorder by medical science. More or less, abnemmes is atrophy. Also known as "the take off" or "the wasting away", it was a condition primarily found in children as a result of malnutrition. It was also considered to be a result of bewitchment or an infection of worms living deep down in the flesh and bones. The symptoms of abnemmes include: shrinking flesh, loss of appetite, emaciation, and muscular atrophy.

Brauche Remedy

There are several Brauche charms for this illness. However, due to the serious nature of the illness, the General Brauche Circuit is highly recommended.

Sympathetic Remedy

There are two well-known sympathetic folk remedies for abnemmes in children. The first is the taking of the child's measure. Taking a person's measure is an all-purpose sort of operation that can be applied to any number of afflictions.

To take the measure:
Get a length of red yarn, enough to measure the child. Use the yarn like a measuring tape, and take one end as a starting point and wrap the yarn around the head until the yarn comes full circle about the head's circumference. Where the yarn meets the end, make a knot. Use that first knot as the beginning place for the second measure around the chest, then make a second knot. With this last knot as

the starting point, measure the right arm, make a knot; and then measure the left, and make a knot. Repeat this procedure twice more with each leg around the thighs.

There are different ways to make measures, but this is a simple method. What also differs is what people do with the string afterward. Depending upon what the condition is being treated will determine how the string is treated. For abnemmes, the string is usually just hung up. The "magic" behind this measure is that the child will out grow it – in the same way as when a child's growth is measured by making notches or pencil marks in a doorframe. This latter activity has also been used for childhood illnesses. Another method of 'disposal' is to take the string and hang it somewhere there is a lot of activity and traffic, such as on a gate that will wear it out quickly. The wearing out will break sympathetically wear out the illness – i.e., the illness' energetic signature is theoretically in the string linking back to the patient.

Table legs:
This is perhaps the best know of the abnemmes folk cures for children. To do this, take the child and weave it in and out between the legs of a kitchen table, with all four legs. One circuit is enough, although three altogether can be made. Another related sympathy is to pass the child through a horse's collar three times. The use of a horse's collar indicates the archaic nature of all these treatments. Similar sympathetic remedies exist in Cornwall, where children are passed through naturally hole bearing large stones (a 'holey' stone). See the Glossary for information on the "shaving" treatment for abnemmes.

EYE TROUBLES

Brauche Remedy

An adjuration for a thing caught in the eye:
The following is a so-called "narrative charm." It begins by citing a popular legend regarding a saint, then goes into the charm proper (the "adjuration"). It is not necessary to recite the "legend." Only the charm itself is necessary.

The Legend:
> Saint Nicosius, the holy martyr of God, had a speck in his eye, and besought that God would relieve him of it, and the Lord cured him. He prayed [again] to the Lord that whoever bore his name upon his person would be cured of all specks, and the Lord heard him.

The Charm:
> Thus I adjure you, O speck, by the living God and the holy God, to disappear from the eyes of the servant of God N. [insert person's name here], whether you are black, red, or white. May Christ make you go away. Amen. + + + Amen.[11]

The charm will be done 3x. "Narrative" charms have a similar function to the stories contain in the himmelsbriefe.

A Brauche remedy for an eye blister:
Do this Brauche near the house's front door. Speak the sufferer's Christian name, and then blow into the eye 9x, saying each time:

"Jesus asked: 'What doest thou want that I may do unto thee?' And the sufferer said to Jesus, 'Lord, may I see!' And Christ answered, 'Be it so! See!'
In the name of Jesus Christ, thine eyes shall grow light, bright, clean, clear, are the moon and stars of the firmament of heaven."
+ + +[12]

---

[11] Kieckhefer, p. 3, from the *Wolfsthurn* handbook.
[12] Beissel pp. 37-38; this charm has been greatly modified from the original, the wording

A Brauche-psalm remedy for the eyes:
1) Go over the patient with the General Brauche Circuit, the proceed to finish up with the eyes – that is, go back to the eyes after the usual circuit is done
2) When going over the eye, cup the eye with your right hand (or which ever one is dominant)
3) Read Psalm 6 six times while cupping the eye
4) Perform the circuit twice more, so that the Psalm will be read 3x that day
5) This procedure is done two more days in consecutively, making three
6) Be sure this is done at the waning moon

Herbal Remedy

An herbal remedy for sties:
In a shallow pan of water boil a handful of juniper berries (*juniper virginiana*). Allow the steam from the berry water to bath the affected eye.

FEVERS (*FIEWER, KALTFIEWER, HITZ*)
Under the heading of "fevers" are also "hay fever" (*kaltfiewer*) and other similar chills symptomatic of allergies. Illnesses such as scarlatina (*Roten Schaden*), pleurisy (*bruschtfiewer*) and pneumonia (*lungefiewer*) are covered under "fevers." It is best to charm for fevers on uneven days (such as the 3rd, 5th, 7th, or 9th of the month, etc.).

Blutreinigungsmitteln have been used to great extent in the treatment of fevers prior to the advent of antibiotics. Of course, our ancestors also employed blood-letting and cupping as well as keeping patients extra warm and snug in order to treat fevers. These latter procedures probably killed more people than we will ever know.

---

of which was obscure.

Fevers can kill. Unless the sufferer's body temperature can be brought down, there is the likelihood of brain and other organ damage. The foregoing charms can be applied to fever sufferers in an effort of help break it, in conjunction with regular therapies, such as antibiotics. Fevers called "agues" in the old hausmitteln usually refer to malaria: quotidian, tertian, quartan, and quintan agues are malarial fevers that cycle between cold and hot spells every so many hours or days.

The 'spells' involve muscle spasms, loss of blood to extremities such as finger tips, and then cycle into raging heat – first starting from within, and then giving the sensation of working outward. The 'hot' phase of the malarial fever leaves the patient dehydrated and the skin dry until that phase ends and the profuse sweating begins. Usually, after the sweats, the fever will start anew with another cold phase. Some cycles will go 24 hours (a quotidian ague), and others may have long respites in between and not commence for another 72 hours (a quartan ague).

Brauche Remedy

For fever:
Say the patient's name before speaking the charm below. Do this three times.

"Heaven and earth are created, and all was good, all that is made by God is good; only the fever is a vexation, therefore, avert [name of patient]*, leave* [name]*, and disappear before* [name]. *Thou shalt flee upon high mountains; thou shalt move into the abyss – go out from* [name] *in the name of John, the Holy Apostle, and Jesus Christ, the Son of God."* + + +[13]

Another remedy for fever:
This charm must be started early on a Thursday morning before the sun rises, and then continued for the next two days. Each day the

---

13   Beissel p. 41

charm is recited, the name of the day needs to be changed in the charm. No one is to speak to another before the sun rises. Besides the pronouncing of the charm, there must be complete silence. The sufferer is to avoid pork, milk, and must not cross running water for nine days. On each morning, speak the charm three times, as usual.[14]

"Good morning, dear Thursday! Take away from [name] **the 77 fold fevers. Oh! Thou dear Lord Jesus Chris, take them away from** [name]*!"* + + +

Sympathetic Remedy

To dissipate a high fever:
Write the following on a piece of clean paper, and then sew it into a muslin bag with a cord so it can be placed around the neck of the sufferer.[15]

    AbaxaCatabax
    AbaxaCataba
    AbaxaCatab
    AbaxaCata
    AbaxaCat
    AbaxaCa
    AbaxaC
    Abaxa
    Abax
    Aba
    Ab
    A

Another similar talisman to dissipate a long fever:
Write the following on a piece of clean paper, and then sew it into a red pouch. Pierce the the cloth pouch and the paper inside three

14   Hohman pp. 11-12
15   Hohman pp. 16-17 Note: the SATOR square can be used in the same manner.

times (so as to make three holes). Draw a red woolen string through these holes in order to make a cord for suspending around the sufferer's neck. When drawing the cord through the holes, do it in the Three Highest Names. Hang the letter around the patient's neck on a Friday, which then must be worn for 11 days consecutively. On the 11th day, take off the pouch and the burn it to ashes before the hour is out.[16]

```
H B R H C H T H B R H
H B R H C H T H B R
H B R H C H T H B
H B R H C H T H
H B R H C H T
H B R H C H
H B R H C
H B R H
H B R
H B
H
```

Herbal Remedy

Teas for fevers:
These herbs and plants have been used in Pennsylvania Dutch folk medicine for the treatment of fevers. The technical term for them is a "febrifuge." In addition, they are diuretics and diaphoretics. These actions are great for clearing out the body of toxins. The danger is dehydration. A modern suggestion for hydration is Gatorade, in addition to potassium vitamins.

Sassafras (*Sassafras albidum*); also known as ague tree, or *fiewerbaam*: some people use the blossoms, but the best part is the root. Use one teaspoon bark to one cup of water. Take one cup per day. The tincture can be taken at 15 - 30 drops.

---

16   Albertus p. 44

To make a potent herbal whiskey, place one teaspoon* each the following roots into 3 – 4 cups of whiskey:
Sanicle (*Sanicula marilandica*)
Pipsissewa (*Chimaphila umbellata*)
Virginia Snakeroot (*Aristolochia serpentaria*) – *CAUTION this root is traditional to a recipe such as this, but in large doses Virginia Snakeroot can cause respiratory paralysis. Use only a ½ teaspoon, if at all.
Dandelion (*Taraxacum officinale*) – the root

Let these sit in the whiskey, the longer the better. Give it two weeks before straining out the root matter. Take it by the teaspoon.

These plants can be used as teas from their roots or herb. For Sanicle: 1 tsp rootstock to 1 cup water; take 1 cup per day. Take tincture at 15 – 30 drops. For Pipisissewa: 1 tsp leaves to ½ cup of water. This is to be sipped over the course of a day. For Virginia Snakeroot (see caution note): 1 tsp dried root to 1 cup of water; take at tablespoon 3 – 6 times per day, or 1 – 20 drops of tincture to a glass of water. For dandelion: take 2 tsp of the root and infuse in one cup of water; take at 1 cup per day.

Parsley (*Petroselinum sativum*): 1 tablespoon of leaves to one cup of water; let sit for 15 – 20 minutes. CAUTION: if there is kidney disease present, do not take large doses of parsley.

Elderberry (*Sambuca Canadensis*) blossom tea: One large handful of blossoms to one pint of boiling water. Do this in a Pyrex vessel, as it will need to go into the oven on its lowest setting for a half hour. Strain and drink while bundled (if the illness is a cold or influenza). A handful of peppermint can be added when preparing this tea, which will increase the sweating.

Mugwort (*Artemisia vulgaris*): One ounce herb and rootstock to one pint boiling water. Take in frequent doses of 1 to ½ tsp through the course of the day. CAUTION: do not use mugwort *excessively*, as it can lead to poisoning.

Feverfew (*Chrysanthemum Parthenium*): One ounce herb to one pint boiling water. Take in frequent doses of 1 to ½ tsp through the course of the day.

Wormwood (*Artemisia absinthium*): Two tsp dried leaves to one cup boiling water; one half cup per day by the teaspoon. CAUTION: wormwood is a cardiac stimulant.

Blackberry (*Rubus villosus*): 2 tsp leaves, and 2 tsp of Shepherd's Purse (*Capsella bursa-pastoris*) to 1 ½ cups of boiling water. This tea is good for fever accompanied by diarrhea.

Psalm Remedy

Psalms 105, 106, & 107: for fevers – 105 is used for a fever of three days; 106 for a fever of four days; and 107 for a daily fever. The Holy Name associated with these three Psalms is JAH. The Name can be intoned following the word LORD in the first verse of each Psalm.

HEADACHE (*KOPPSCHMAERZE, KOPPWEH*)

Brauche Remedy

A remedy for headache:
Place your hands upon the sufferer's head, wherever the pain in the head is. While doing this, say the patient's full baptismal name 7x; after speaking the name, say the charm.[17]

"Jesus bent His head and died on the cross. He was patient as a

[17]   Beissel p. 39; this is actual a modification of the charm that appears in Bill Beissel's "Secrets of Sympathy" in *Powwow Power*. In addition to shortening the beginning of the prayer, the names of the traditional four ministering angelic powers are listed. The original wording of the charm does not specify the "Holy Guardian Angels."

lamb. He shed His blood for us; that is good for head and nerves. In the name of the Holy Guardian Angels: Uriel, Raphael, Gabriel, and Michael."* + + +

Another remedy for headache:

"I implore thee, by the living God that thou may draw the headache from [name]*, and hurt him (her) as little as it did hurt the Lord Jesus to be crucified; by these names I command you: God the Father, God the Son, and God the Holy Ghost. Amen."* Do 3x.[18]

Hohman's headache remedy:
Say the charm below three times. All three repetitions are to be done within three minutes: one repetition per minute.

"Tame thou flesh and bone, like Christ in Paradise; and who will assist thee, this I tell thee [name] *for your repentance sake."* + + +[19]

Sympathetic Remedy

To prevent a headache from sunstroke:
Carry underneath your hat some plantain leaves (*Plantago lanceolata* or *major*), and burdock leaves (*Arctium lappa*) while you are outside in the sun.[20]

---

18   Albertus p. 56; this is a modification of the original charm appearing in *Egyptian Secrets*. Christ's pain during crucifixion is a common formula in a great many of these old charms. It may seem odd for us today to consider that the crucifixion did not hurt Jesus – it did; He suffered. It was awful. The sadistic Roman-style flogging alone would have eventually killed Him. However, the logic behind the crucifixion statements in these charms is that Christ bore His pain and endured for a greater purpose and eventually triumphed in Resurrection.

19   Hohman p.20

20   Brendle and Unger, pp. 98 - 101

Herbal Remedy

A vinegar remedy for headache:
Take a cloth and soak it in vinegar; wring out the cloth and place it on the forehead, or wrap it around the head. When the cloth dries out, wet it again and repeat.

Ground Ivy (*Nepeta hederacea*) snuff:
Gather up a handful of fresh herb and mash it up until the juice is extracted. Gather up as much juice as will come out, and then snuff it up the nose. It is good for swollen membranes and headache.

Psalm Remedy

Psalm 3: Good for headache and backache
Pray the prayer below with the Holy Name, followed by the Psalm. Pray these first over a small amount of olive oil. Then proceed to anoint the sufferer's head with this oil while praying the prayer then the Psalm. This is done three times. During the first set, make the sign of the cross with the oil on the forehead, on the crown, and on the back of the head near the base of the skull. During the second set, make the sign of the cross in oil first on the forehead between the eyes; next on the right ear, then on the left one. During the third set, make the sign of the cross with the oil on both eyes and then on the lips. Only a very small amount of oil is needed. [21]

The prayer:
"ADONAI of the world may it please thee to be [name's] ***physician and helper. Heal him (her) and relieve him (her) from his (her) severe headache and backache, because we can find help only with Thee, and only with Thee is counsel and action to be found. Amen! Selah."***

---

21   This procedure is a modification of the one suggested on p. 146 of the *Sixth & Seventh Books of Moses*' "Use of the Psalms" appendix.

Psalm 3:
"LORD, how are they increased that trouble me! Many are they that rise up against me. Many there be which say of my soul, there is no help for him in God. Selah. But thou, O LORD, art a shield for me; my glory, and the lifter up of mine head. I cried unto the LORD with my voice, and he heard me out of his holy hill. Selah. I laid me down and slept; I awakened; for the LORD sustained me. I will not be afraid of ten thousands of people, but have set themselves against me round about. Arise, O LORD; save me, O my God: for thou hast smitten all mine enemies upon the cheek bone; thou hast broken the teeth of the ungodly. Salvation belongeth unto the LORD: thy blessing is upon thy people. Selah."

Psalm 2: For a raging headache
Write the first eight verses of this Psalm followed by the prayer below with its Name of God on a clean piece of paper. Fold the paper into a triangular form (see the directions in the section on Zauberzetteln), or roll it into a tight scroll secured by red string. Place this into a muslin bag with a cord. Suspend this bag around the neck of the sufferer then place your hands upon the person's head. Pray the prayer and Psalm while doing this. This operation is done three times.

The Prayer:
"Let it be, Oh, SHADDAI Thy holy will, that the raging headache of [name] *and the roaring of its agony may cease, and that the pounding waves of pain may be stilled. Lead him (her), oh, all merciful Father, to a place of succor and good health, for only with Thee is power and might. Thou alone canst help, and Thou wilt surely help to the honor and glory of Thy name. Amen! Selah!"*

Psalm 2:
"Why do the heathen rage, and the people imagine a vain thing?
¹ | The kings of the earth set themselves, and the rules take counsel

together, against the LORD, and against his anointed, **saying,** [2] | *Let us break their bands asunder, and cast away their cords from us.* [3] | *He that sitteth in the heavens shall laugh: the Lord shall have them in derision.*[4] | *Then shall he speak unto them in his wrath, and vex them in his sore displeasure.*[5] | *Yet have I set my king upon my holy hill of Zion.*[6] | *I will declare the decree: the LORD hath said unto me, Thou* art *my Son; this day have I begotten thee.*[7] | *Ask of me, and I shall give* thee *the heathen* for *thine inheritance, and the uttermost parts of the earth* for *you possession.*[8] | *Thou shalt break them with a rod of iron; thou shalt dash them in pieces like a potter's vessel.* | *Be wise now therefore, O ye kings; be instructed, ye judges of the earth.* | *Serve the LORD with fear, and rejoice with trembling.* | *Kiss the Son, lest he be angry, and ye perish* from *the way, when his wrath is kindled but a little. Blessed are all they that put their trust in him."*

HEART TROUBLES (*HAERZSCHLAEK*), APOPLEXIA, and CONVULSIONS

The three conditions treated in this section are rather broad. "Heart troubles" by itself covers a wide array of illnesses. Apoplexia is the old-fashioned term denoting any manner of stroke or paralysis, regardless of their origin; the same can be said for "convulsions" which can have a multitude of causes, not the least of which is epilepsy. In the ancient world (and in some cases, the not so ancient world), convulsions were considered to be the torments imposed by one possessed by an unclean spirit.

While the likelihood of one suffering convulsions due to genuine spirit possession are slim, they do happen. The Brauche treatments are the same regardless of the ultimate cause, because a child of God is being tormented and is in an unbalanced state. The purpose of the brauching is to bring the sufferer's energies back into line and restoring health. In the case of an unwelcome spiritual force, the

Brauche, if successful, will expel the spirit in the name of Christ. All of these conditions have one superficial thing in common: when they strike they give their sufferers "fits." Therefore, another possible title for this section is "Brauche Remedies for Fits."

Brauche Remedy

Lengthy Brauche remedy for heart problems:
Go over the patient with the General Brauche Circuit, and then work the area of the heart with the *"Dei Fuss"* charm. This procedure is to be done three times. Note: when finishing up each 'round' with the crosses in the Three Highest Names, make the first sign on the area over the patient's heart, then another on the palm of the left hand, and the final one on the back of the left hand.

A remedy for angina pain:
Speak the patient's Christian name and say the charm below. While reciting the charm, take your two thumbs and cross them over each other. Hold this gesture over the area of the patient's heart while charming.[22]

"Three lilies are growing upon thy heart: the first one is named God the Father, the other God the Son, and the third is God's Will. I command the heart pain to stand still. In the name of God the Father, God the Son, and God the Holy Ghost be still. Amen"

A new Brauche charm for convulsions:
The charm below is brand new and composed by this author for the purpose of settling convulsions. While first aid is being applied to the person convulsing (so s/he will not choke on the tongue) and waiting for an ambulance, this charm can be spoken. As with most of the charms in this book, it is done three times. It is also necessary to have the person's full name ready if known, otherwise simply change the pronoun in the prayer from "him" to "her" as necessary.

22   Albertus p. 178; this charm has been modified from its original form.

These lines are based upon **Mark 9:20-25**.

"Straight away the spirit tare him; and he fell on the ground, and wallowed foaming. It hath cast him into the fire, and into the waters, to destroy him. Lord Jesus Christ help thou our unbelief! By He who shall come again in glory to judge the quick and the dead and the world by fire: dumb, deaf spirit, I charge thee, come out of him, and enter him no more!" + + +

Sympathetic Remedy

A sympathetic remedy for apoplexy and epilepsy:
Dig the root of the peony plant (*Paeonia officinalis*) when the sun is in the sign of Leo during a new moon on a Sunday morning just before sunrise. Gather the root with gloves on. Do not directly handle the root with bare hands. Take the root carefully back to the house and lay out to air dry. Once the root is dry, wrap the root in gold foil (which can be found in arts & crafts stores). Make a cord and suspend the gold pack around the neck with it, or place the pack into a muslin bag for suspension around the neck.[23]

Herbal Remedy

An herbal remedy for numbness in the limbs:
To restore some feeling in numb limbs, take stinging nettle plants (*Urtica dioica*) and strike them upon the numb areas. This is also a good remedy for rheumatic joints.

Psalm Remedy

The ultimate Psalm remedy:
The foregoing is what might be called the "ultimate remedy" among the medicinal uses of the Psalms, being Psalm 91. The suggested usage of this Psalm is Rabbinical in origin and quite tedious, but the results are said to be well worth the effort. The Holy Name

---

[23] Brendle and Unger, p. 107; this formula has been slightly modified from the original.

associated with this Psalm is EL. Together with the last verse of Psalm 90 the Holy Name is EL SHADDAI (or as spelled in the original text of the *Sepher Schimmusch Tehillim*, EEL SCHADDEI, using the German spelling for Hebrew). The final verse of 90 and the whole (or some say, the final verse) of 91 compose the *Vihi Noam* prayer. As translated by Selig, the directions are to recite the final verse of the 90th and the whole of the 91st to make up the *Vihi Noam*. Therefore, this prayer, as presented in the Sepher has several parts: 1) the final verse of Psalm 90, 2) the whole of Psalm 91; 3) the introductory prayer to the Psalm with the Holy Name; and 4) an additional prayer that is prayed at the 14th verse of Psalm 91. The entire prayer is prayed 99 times in one day, which is to be done for two more days consecutively. This prayer is said to be excellent for asking God's help during dire, incurable illness or extreme danger. Therefore, this prayer can be used for any illness or danger, not just for heart troubles, etc.

Note:
- During these cycles of prayer, should you attempt it, always keep in mind the Holy Name of EL SHADDAI, especially during the beginning prayer, and the middle one at the 14th verse.
- It is also suggested that you fast before doing this prayer, unless for medical reasons you need to eat (regardless of whether you are praying this for yourself or another).
- If doing this prayer for another, you will need their full baptismal name, along with the names of their parents. The original usage here only needs the father's name, but both can be included.
- In order to keep an accurate count of these prayers, make a cord of 99 knots – a sort of Rosary—so you will not loose your place.
- Where the text uses the masculine pronoun, substitute the feminine as needed.

Introductory prayer:

"Let it be thy holy pleasure, oh my God, to take from [name], *son of* [name] *the evil spirit by which he is tormented, for the sake of thy great, mighty and holy name EL SHADDAI. Wilt thou presently send him health and let him be perfectly restored. Hear his prayer as thou once did that of thy servant Moses when he prayed this Psalm. Let his prayer penetrate to thee as once the holy incense arose to thee on high. Amen. Selah!"*

Psalm 91, the *Vihi Noam*:
Verse 17, Psalm 90:
"And let the beauty of the LORD our God be upon us: and establish thou the work of our hands upon us; yea, the work of our hands establish thou it."

Psalm 91:
"He that dwelleth in the secret place of the most High shall abide under the shadow of the Almighty. I will say of the LORD, He is my refuge and my fortress: my god; in him will I trust. Surely he shall deliver thee from the snare of the fowler, and from the noisome pestilence. He shall cover thee with his feathers, and under his wings shalt thou trust: his truth shall be thy shield and buckler. Thou shalt not be afraid for the terror by night; nor for the arrow that flieth by day; Nor for the pestilence that walketh in darkness; nor for the destruction that wasteth at noonday. A thousand shall fall at thy side, and ten thousand at thy right hand; but it shall not come nigh thee. Only with thine eyes shalt thou behold and see the reward of the wicked. Because thou hast made the LORD, which is my refuge, even the most High, thy habitation; there shall no evil befall thee, neither shall any plague come nigh thy dwelling. For he shall give his angels charge over thee, to keep thee in all thy ways. They shall bear thee up in their hands, lest thou dash thy foot against a stone. Thou shalt tread upon the lion and adder: the young lion and the dragon shalt thou trample under feet. *<u>Because he hath set his love upon me, therefore will I deliver him: I will set him</u>

<u>on high, because he hath known my name</u>. He shall call upon me, and I will answer him: I will be with him in trouble; I will deliver him, and honor him. With long life will I satisfy him, and shew him my salvation."

*14th verse middle prayer:
"Thou art the most holy, king over all that is revealed and hidden, exalted above all that is high, sanctify and glorify thy adorable name in this world, so that all the nations of the earth may know that thine is the glory and power, and that thou hast secured me form all distress, but especially out of the painful emergency [state here the emergency or illness], **which has overcome me** [or name of other], **son of** [name]. **And I herewith promise and vow that I will now and ever after this, as long as I shall live upon the earth, and until I return to dust from which I was taken** [here make your promise to God]. **Praised be JEHOVAH, my Rock and my Salvation.** *Thou wilt be my representative and intercessor, and wilt help me, for thou helpest thy poor, feeble and humble creature, and in time of need releasest from fear and danger, and dealest mercifully with thy people; merciful and forgiving, thou hearest the prayer of everyone. Praised are thou, JEHOVAH, thou who hearest my prayer."*

Before tackling this prayer, think carefully upon the nature of what you are asking for, framing it as concisely as possible. Think even more carefully upon the vow. Make certain that you can fulfill your end of the 'deal,' making no promises that you know cannot be kept. Prayers such as these, truly any prayers at all, are not to be 'dabbled' with. Unless you really mean it, do not do it.

SNAKE BITE, AND OTHER ANIMAL BITES

There are remedies here for mainly two types of bites: from insects and from rabid animals. When approaching these remedies, or any other alternative treatments, please use common sense. If bitten by an animal that you suspect might be rabid, go to the hospital *immediately*. Apply Braucherei and first aid until you can get to the emergency room. Use Braucherei treatment afterwards too in supplement to these methods below. It is my belief that Daisy's "General" method is the best for treating these situations *after the fact* of orthodox medical treatment. Also in addition to Pow-Wowing bites, get a good first aide manual that gives instructions on how to work with things such as snake bites. As for insect stings or spider bites, the above applies too – especially if you are highly allergic (such as to bee stings); spider bites are nasty and nothing to fool with: these sometimes lead to blood poisoning.

Brauche Remedy

For snake bite:
Recite the following charm, and then take your right hand in the usual in the Pow-Wow gesture of blessing making the three crosses over the bite while saying "tsing" each time. Follow it up with blessing in the Three Highest Names ("In the name of God the Father, etc."). This charm, in the German below, is recorded as having come from "Northern Lehigh County" by Brendle and Unger. However, it is quite a 'universal' PA Dutch charm as it appears almost identical in the English translation of Hohman's *The Long Lost Friend*, p24.

Gott hot al'les arshaf'fa, und al'les war gut:
Als du al'le shlang, bisht ferflucht[24]
+ + +
Tsing. Tsing. Tsing.

English:
God created everything, and it was good; except thou alone, snake, art cursed, cursed shalt thou be and thy poison.[25]
+ + +

Tsing. Tsing. Tsing.
Two charms for wasps not to sting[26]:
If a wasp is hovering around you closely, without drawing breath speak the following words "on" the wasp:

Wish'bli, wesh'bli, schtech mich nicht
Bis der Dai'w'l di Sega schricht
English:
Wasp, wasp, sting me not; until the devil recites the creed.

Or

Wespi, wespi, wespi, ich Beschwere Euch bey Gottes kraft das ihr mich nicht stechen sollet Ihr sollet nicht so wenig dass ein Falscher Ketzer in dass Himmel Reuch kommt. + + +

English:
Wasp, wasp, wasp, I conjure you by the power of God that you sting me not as little as a false heretic may get into heaven. + + +

---

24   Brendle and Unger 1935, p 202. See the glossary appendix of *The Red Church* for a discussion of the word "tsing" under the entry for THE BRAZEN SERPENT. Note the spelling used in the charm cited above. Pennsylvania German has several spelling conventions. See Appendix II for more information regarding PG spelling and pronunciation.

25   Genesis 3:14.

26   Brendle and Unger 1935, p 207.

Sympathetic Remedy

For a beast or human suffering from a bite (anti-rabies talisman)[27]: Write the following on a small, clean piece of paper:

X haga XX maga XXX paga X

The bite victim is to eat the paper, which is why it needs to be small. It is not unusual for some sympathetic 'papers' to be ingested or drank. For this purpose, use an edible dye such as food coloring for an ink. It won't look very nice, but you won't poison your patient. This paper needs to be eaten *before* the person sleeps after having received the bite. Also, after eating it, one *cannot* sleep 12 hrs after ingesting the paper. Another written sympathetic charm for the same is:

BAS or	**BAS**	**BAS**
MAS	**MAS**	**MAS**
EMAS	**EMAS**	**EMAS**

For snake bite:
Just as with the charm above for a rabid bite, prepare the charm below for snake bite. This too is to be eaten: 3x in the evening and 3x in the morning for 3 days:

XXX bego XXX mego XXX ebego
This particular charm may also be efficacious for other "venomous bites" such as those of bugs and spiders.

---

27   Brendle and Unger make mention of a special "madstone" for use against hydrophobia (rabies), but this author has found little more about such a stone. Any Brauche stone may be able to function in this way, especially one 'charged' to specifically heal wounds. However, doubtless there are some very special stones for this purpose or rabies alone. In *The Book of Secrets of Albertus Magnus* (entry No. 44, p47) recommends the use of "orites" stone as a carried amulet (*sideritis* or *magnetite*) to avoid being bitten in the first place. For a brief discussion of hydrophobia, see glossary under DOG. The editor of *Pennsylvania Folklife* (Winter 1975-1976) comments in Victor Dieffenbach's article "Powwowing Among the Pennsylvania Germans" that "mad stones" is a widespread practice in folk medicine. However, this author believes that the editor has conflated the stones specifically meant for hydrophobia with all other stones in sympathetic use.

Herbal Remedy

To avoid mosquito bite:
Carry a sprig of pennyroyal in a muslin bag and wear cord around the ankle. Also, a few drops of pennyroyal essential oil added to a 'carrier' such as almond or grape seed oil may work well to keep off the bugs. Mosquitoes can also be driven away with tobacco smoke. The itch of a mosquito bite can also be eased by rinsing the site with salt water.

For bee stings:
Gather a little clean soil and add some fresh water to make a mud plaster. Apply the mud to the area of the sting.

SORES: TETTER, HERPES (*GSCHWAER, SCHLIER*)

Brauche Remedy

A new general charm for all sores:

"Sore, I command thee by the power of God to cease; sore, for the sake of Christ's blood decrease; sore, by the prayers of God's Mother cease. By God the Father + and God the Son + and God the Holy Ghost + decrease and cease."[28]

Repeat this three times. If it is done for another, make the triple sign of the cross over the wound.

Herbal remedy

For Tetter (herpes sores):
Ground Ivy (*Glechoma hederacea*) – the best time to pick ground ivy is in the spring. Pick a large handful of the plant, the whole herb (roots too). Clean it off in cool water then pat it dry. Take the herb and rub it between the hands so it is bruised and releasing

---

28   Charm created by the author.

its essential oils. Next, heat a cup of vegetable oil in a pan. Fry the herb in the hot oil. This plant is stringy and shrinks like spinach. It will brown very quickly. Make sure to take the pan off of the heat before this happens. With a wooden spoon (don't use any aluminum utensils) fish out the plant matter, and allow this to cool a little. Strain the herbed oil through cheesecloth onto a pewter platter or bowl. Take approximately a tablespoon or more of powdered sulfur and mix this into the oil until a thicker salve forms. Smear the sores with this. According to Mrs. M. Grieve, ground ivy is an astringent; sulfur has also been used for centuries in doctoring in order to dry out various types of wounds. Lee Gandee in his book *Strange Experience* tells readers how he healed a third degree burn he received by dusting it with alum and sulfur.[29]

A remedy for ulcers and boils:
A sympathetic remedy is to take the root of iron weed (*Centaurea scabiosa*) and bind it into a string from which it can be hung from around the neck. This is said to cure running ulcers (the author has not tried this out). According to Mrs. Grieve on p. 456 of her book, she states that iron weed is also good for catarrh, and is also very healing when made into a decoction or ointment for wounds, bruises, and sores. While this author values sympathetic remedies, it seems that the sympathetic root charm/necklace, along with the herbal unguent would be the most efficacious use of iron weed. A decoction of iron weed can be made by boiling the roots (about a half ounce of root matter to a cup of water, and two tablespoons of honey – increase measures as needed) for 10 minutes or longer. It is this decoction that is good for soothing catarrh.[30]

A remedy for piles:
Chickweed (*Stellaria media*) according to the researches of both William Woys Weaver and Mrs. M. Grieve can be made into a good

---

[29] Brendle and Unger, 1935, p 59.

[30] It is also said of iron weed that if it is planted among fruit trees and grapevines that they promote their growth. Children who carry iron weed as an amulet are said to be educated easily.

unguent for sore piles due to its demulcent properties. To make this ointment take the fresh chickweed, which is best gathered between May and July, and boil/fry it in a pan of oil. In days gone by, this would have been lard. Perhaps a cleaner choice would be vegetable oil, or almond oil. The resulting greenish oil can then be thickened with small amounts of beeswax. The pure liquid tea of chickweed is also a good wash for sores and external abscesses.[31]

SPRAINS (*VERRENKDER*) AND RHEUMATISM
Note: it is best to work on sprains during a full moon. If you should take to massaging a sprain, do so in a downward direction. According to one of Brendle and Unger's sources[32], it is best to work on sprains the first Friday of the full moon.

Brauche Remedy

Christus ist ans Kreuz gehengt
Und dein Bein ist verrenkt
Schadet ihm sein Henken nichts.
So schadet dir dein verrenken nichts.
+ + +

Christ hung on the cross in pain,
And thy leg has got sprain.
As His hanging hurt him not,
So thy sprain will not hurt thee.[33]
+ + +

This is spoken three times while gently massaging the sprain downwards. If using Daisy's General Brauche modality, go over the patient with the General and after each circuit, concentrate your massage on the sprain. Keep your hands hot: when massaging a

---

31   A decoction of chickweed is a great laxative – so is chickweed salad, as this author found out accidentally.
32   Brendle and Unger, 1935, p 55
33   Ibid. pp 55-56

sore muscle or sprain, make your hands 'hot' by briskly rubbing them together, gently kneading in the 'heat' from your hands.[34]

Another Brauche technique for sprains as documented by Brendle and Unger:
Stroke the sore part of the limb three times while charming thusly,

Christus machte Lahme gehen,
Todte machte er auferstehen;
So heile denn dein verrenken
In die Tiefe soll es versenken.
Jesus allein heilet Kranke,
Ihm allein soll man danken.
+ + +
Christ maketh walk the lame,
The dead He raiseth up again.
So thy lameness cured be,
Sunk into the deepest sea.
Jesus only heals the ailing,
To Him along give thanks unfailing.[35]

For a twisted limb:
Pass your right hand over the twisted arm or leg making an "X" pattern (a cross) and say the charm below three times:

---

34   This is a technique that I discovered to be useful from going over people. As far as my research has carried me, I have not seen this specific direction given for Brauche massage.

35   Brendle and Unger, 1935, p 56. Throughout *The Red Church* I have taken many Brauche formulae straight as I found them from my sources. However, I have also occasionally made some minor adjustments to these texts. Please note the rhyming patters of the charms. Many charms when translated into English seldom have the original rhyme intact; when the rhyming is preserved, often the translator has to take some liberties in the translation. Victorian antiquarian and folklorist Charles Godfrey Leland did this quite often with the charms and incantations that he collected from the 19th century Italian countryside (and sometimes the English translation left a lot to be desired as a result). This particular charm has its counterparts in other Pow-Wow texts such as Bill Beissel's *Secrets of Sympathy*, 1938; charm No. 1-B p 34 of *Powwow Power*, 1998.

Be it exorcised[36] and sent away! It shall harm nothing and lade nothing! It shall heal and abide not! The wind shall blow it away. It shall be blown away like dust. It shall sink into the deep sea. Abate, heal, go, pass away, pain! In the name of the seven guardian angels![37]

For sweeny or lameness:
Do this Brauche at the waning moon. If the moon goes out of this phase, you cannot proceed further. During the early morning, go out side while speaking to no one. Do not attract attention to yourself. Look for a bone on the ground; any piece of bone you find is fine. Remember the exact location of where you have found this. Go to the lame animal. Stroke the lame limb with the bone, working your way from the top to the bottom. Do this three times while saying quietly each time:

Sweeny, I bid you to depart from the marrow into the bone, from the bone into the flesh, from the flesh into the skin, from the skin into the hair, and from the hair into the wild wood.[38]
Perform this Brauche two more mornings in a row. After the third time, go back to the place where you had found the bone and then put it back exactly as you found it.

---

36   The original has the word "exercised" when "exorcised" is meant. Also, the next sentence has the word "lade", which is an archaic variation on the word "laden".

37   Beissel, 1998, charm No. 2, p 34. This charm mentions "seven guardian angels". This is quite interesting: in *Revelation* 8:2 John writes of "seven angels who stand before God". *The Book of Enoch I* lists these angels as: Uriel, Raguel, Michael, Seraqael, Gabriel, Haniel, and Raphael. Alternately, Gustav Davidson on p51 of his *A Dictionary of Angels* lists the seven as: Barachiel, Jehudiel, Sealtiel, Oriphiel, Zadkiel, and Anael. For Cornelius Agrippa, "the Seven Regents of the World" are Orphiel, Zechariel, Samael, Michael, Anael, Raphael, and Gabriel. According to the Sixth and Seventh Books of Moses the angels are: Zaphiel, Zadkiel, Camael, Raphael, Haniel, Michael, and Gabriel. These angels preside over the seven classical planets: Sun, Moon, Mercury, Venus, Mars, Jupiter, and Saturn. In some works on magic, these planetary angels are said to be the masters of seven planetary demonic spirits. They are guardian angels because they keep these seven forces of chaos at bay and in control. This is the same relationship that is seen between the 72 angels of the Shemhamphorash who master the 72 demonic spirits of the Goetia.

38   Dieffenbach p 31, *Pennsylvania Folklife*, Winter 1975-1976.

A Brauche remedy for rheumatism:
Like fevers, there are said to be 77 different types of rheumatism. The danger of rheumatism, in the old view, is that if it is not treated, it can "set to the heart."[39] If disease is not treated, it goes deeper into the body. In Braucherei treatment, the patient is often an active participant in the remedy. This usually consists of saying regular prayers after the treatment.

In the case of rheumatism (arthritis), after the general treatment, the patient will need to 'go over' him or herself. Every day the patient needs to recite the Lord's Prayer and the Apostles' Creed. The number of times repeated will always be in multiples of three. The more extensive the disease, the more recitations: 3, 6, and 9 being the most usual. This cycle of prayer in threes is to be done for each affected limb. The patient will need to start from the upper most affected part of the body downward. Always Pow-Wow from top to bottom, sweeping the rheumatism down and away from the heart.

STOMACH AND BOWELS

Brauche Remedy

For stomach ache and intestinal cramping:
In the place where this charm uses the word "me" can be replaced with another person's full baptismal name.
"Stomach ache and bowel ache, I adjure thee by the holy Gospel: pain break! Draw not up, drawn not down, subside within me now. For Jesus Christ's side did run with water and with blood, which is for stomach ache and bowel ache good." + + +[40]

---

39   Snellenburg, p. 41
40   Brauche charm composed by the author.

Sympathetic Remedy

For painful intestinal cramps:
On a clean strip of paper write the following, and then place the paper on the stomach for an hour. Afterward, bury the paper underneath the eaves of the house; under a gutter spout is best.[41]

Ninte. tis. qi. om. neq. odinos. inte. inve. vad et in secemtur.
    DOLOR
    DOLO
    DOL
    DO
    D

Herbal Remedy

Quince for stomach ache, queasiness, etc.:
Make syrup from quince (*Cydonia oblonga or vulgaris*, German *Quitten*). Do this by taking enough quinces to make two cups, cleaned, skinned, cored and diced. Boil these until they are soft. Mash the soften fruit with a masher or fork in the water. Use only enough water to boil these and make a mash. Strain the mash through a damp jelly bag or four layers of cheesecloth. Allow it to drain into a pan without squeezing. After the juice is all drained away, combine it with the following: 2 cups of sugar, ¼ cup of corn syrup. Bring the mixture to a rolling boil and boil for one minute. Take the pan off of the heat and skim off the foam. In order to store this syrup for any length of time, you will need to can it properly.

Quince is very good for settling upset stomachs, queasiness, nausea, and diarrhea. The juice can be made into a liqueur, which is called *Gwittegortschel*[42] in Pennsylvania German.

---

41   Sympathetic zettel composed by the author.
42   See comments by William Woys Weaver on p 253 of *Sauer's Herbal Cures*.

A remedy for children's stomach aches:
If a child has a stomach ache accompanied by vomiting or diarrhea, the recipe below may be of some help.

Take a small handful of each fresh herb: wormwood (*Artemisia absinthium*; German, *Wermuth*), rue (*Ruta graveolens*; German, *Raute*), centaury (*Centarium Erythraea*; German *Tausenguldenkraut*), and spearmint (*Mentha spicata*; German, *Balsam, Müntze*). In an iron pan melt a few tablespoons of butter and place these herbs into the sauce. Make sure that the heat is low enough so that the herbs and the butter do not burn. Leave them in until they are very soft. Strain this mixture and rub it over the child's stomach during the waning moon. Do this three times per day. Apply the grease as warm as possible without causing a burn or blister.

SWELLINGS (*GEWECKS, HEISCH*), TUMORS, AND ERYSIPELAS (*ROTLAUF*); Also BURNS

Under this section the inflammation called *"rotlauf"* (*rotlaufe* – literally, "red-walk") takes precedence. Also called wildfire (*wildfeier*), St. Anthony's fire, and erysipelas, among many other things, refers to any spreading inflammation of skin or wounds. This would also include measles, or any burning rashes that develop out of fevers. Allergic rashes, dermatitis, generally called *"flug"* come under the heading of rotlauf. Some Brauche charms equate rotlauf with *drach* – that is, a dragon.

The name of this book is taken from a phrase used in the relieving of rotlauf. The color red is used extensively in Braucherei, having many associations and meanings. Within this context, it is the sympathetic color of inflammation. Therefore, the charms and prayers will be full of 'hot' and 'red' symbolism: red forests, red churches, red dragons, etc. The "fire" must be removed from the affected area, so that it does not "set" or go deeper into the body. Inflammation is "fire" and fire is "corruption" of the tissues.[43]

Brauche Remedy

A thorough Brauche treatment for rotlauf:
1) Do the General Brauche Circuit on the patient
2) After going over the patient, charm the inflamed area: *"Ich bin dei gebruchman." – "I saw a Red Wald; I went into the Red Wald and saw a Red Church; I went in the Red Church and saw a Red Altar; and on the Red Altar I saw a Red Book; and on the Red Book I saw a knife. I pick up the knife and cut out the inflammation."* + + + [At the spot mentioning the knife, make a gesture as if picking up a knife and using it to cut out the inflammation.]
3) Steps 1 and 2 are done three times.

Another related remedy:
I strolled through a red forest, and in the red forest there was a red church, and in the red church stood a red altar, and upon the red altar lay a red knife and cut red bread. [44] + + +

Another version of the same:
"Rotlauf, ich gehe durch en rodi wald; in dere rode wald is en rode Kirche; in dere rode Kirche schteht en rode aldor; auf dem rode aldor liegt en rode messer; mit dem rode messer schneid ich des Jesu brode." [45] + + + *"Amen."*

"Red-walk, I go through a red woodland; in the red woodland there is a red church; in the red church there is there is a red altar; on the red altar there is a red knife; with the red knife I cut the bread of Jesus." + + + *"Amen".*

---

43   Dluge, p.41
44   *Egyptian Secrets*, p.8
45   Brendle & Unger, p.86

Brauching for rotlauf with red string[46]:
1) Take a length of red string or wool yarn and hold the ends – one in the right hand and one in the left. Stretch the string wide.
2) Your patient will be in a sitting position. With the string or yarn stretched between your hands, make sure it is wider than the patient so your hands have room to pass over the person.
3) Start from the head and work your way down towards the feet. Go over the patient both front and back with the string in this manner. Do this three times. With each passing of the string, say: *"Rotlauf, move out of the body of* [insert baptismal name of patient], *as the red string chases you: Go! Go! Go!"* After all the passes are made (three in front, three in back) make a gesture with your arms as if throwing the string away from yourself and the patient.
4) Take the string and pass it through the smoke of a smoldering stick.
5) If you have a fireplace that is active, hang up the string where the smoke will get at it, otherwise 'smudge' it in smoke over a period of three days consecutively. If you do Step 4, allow the string to fall down by itself. Once it does, destroy it in the fireplace. If otherwise, on the third day destroy it in fire.

A different Brauche charm for rotlauf:
Blow over the inflammation 9x and say each time:
"Three men from the Levant went in search for the 'Rothlaufstein'; they search, they find, they come, they go, they run, [and] *they jump. Rotlauf, go away and come back never* [again]. *Fly out into the deep sea. Become a stone forever. In the name of Jesus it shall be."*

---

46   This method is a variation created by the author on a brauching technique used by Sophia Bailer. "Aunt Sophie" would tell her rotlauf patients to stay away from salted meat until the inflammation went away. This may have applied to all salty things.

When doing this for a woman, change the wording of "three men" to "three women."[47]

A Brauche charm for burns:
This charm from *Egyptian Secrets*[48] is quite straight forward. It is to be done 3x in the Three Highest Names. The burn can be blown upon after the charm is said, at the end during the blessing, punctuating each divine Name with a blow of air for three in all.

"Away burns, unto the band; if cold or warm, cease the hand. God save thee [baptismal name of person]*; thy flesh, thy blood, thy marrow, thy bone, and all thy veins: they all shall be saved,*

for warm and cold brands reign." + + +

Another charm for burns:
The following charm uses the 'story' or 'narrative' devise of a traveling spirit, saint, or other holy person. In this case, it is the Virgin Mary. It very similar in intent and wording to the charm found in Hohman for relief from fever; that is: "Our dear Sarah went through out the land, holding a fiery-hot brand in her hand…" This charm illustrates the notion that if burns and inflammation are not treated promptly (or well) that they 'set' deeper into the body.

"The blessed Virgin went over the land; what does she carry in her hand? -- A fire-brand. Eat not in, thee. Eat not further around."[49] + + +

A lengthier, but more efficacious Brauche treatment for burns:
Go over the patient with the General Brauche Circuit. At the end of the 'circuit' blow 3x on the burn and use the *"Dei hand"* or the *"Dei fuss"* charm, depending upon which zone of the body the burn

47 Beissel pp 40-41 "Rothlaufstein" – red-walk stone.
48 Albertus, p.9
49 Brendle & Unger p.82

is located upon. Remember to do the circuit and this final phase twice more, 15 minutes to a half-hour apart.

A general note for the treatment of burns:
Unlike when treating some forms of inflammation that call for greasing, **never grease a burn**. Grease will just drive the burn deeper. There are some folk remedies that call for putting butter on a burn. Do not do this!

Treating heisch in animals:
"*Three maidens went helter-skelter, hurry, click, over mountains and hillocks, mighty quick. The first spoke: The filly[50] has the heisch. The other said: It has it not. The third said: It has it.*" +
+ +

A charm for non-hot swellings:
Pass your dominant hand over the swelling. Say the patient's name [full baptismal name, if possible], then speak the charm. Do this Brauche 3x.[51]

"*Swelling, thou shalt disappear, ye pains drive off. So we are one body in Christ, but severally members of one of another. Swelling, thou shalt disappear, ye pains, drive off, in the name of Jesus of Nazareth. Thou shalt be helped as true as it is that the three wise men from Levant worshipped Jesus first.*"

Sympathetic Remedy

A sympathetic remedy for rotlauf:
Take a red string and measure the patient's head, chest, and limbs. That is, hold the string around the circumference of each body part. When the end meets up with the other half, tie a knot there.

50   Albertus p.9; the word "filly" can be substituted with the name of any other animal.
51   Beissel p. 42

Do this for each part mentioned. This is what is called "taking the measure." This action alone is said to be good for shifting the rotlauf from the body to the string. No charm needs to be recited (although one could be if desired). Without the charm or prayer, this becomes a purely sympathetic act.

A sympathetic remedy for breasts with rotlauf:
When a woman's breasts have rotlauf, take a fresh hen's egg and write the following characters on it (this can be done with an indelible marker):

+ K a o r KSSO r E z o n r h
a r KOC tz tz a h u r o x K a o tz a
Ea ES x i i x a r o ttt o x

Take the egg and rub downward along the contour of the breast. Afterward, take the contaminated egg and place it into a pre-dug hole in the ground. Once in the hole, crack the egg with a stick or tool. Cover it up. Turn your back on the buried egg and do not look back. Before burying the egg, make certain that the egg is well broken. Do not bury the egg whole. This will only incubate the rotlauf.

A sympathetic remedy for infected or tubercular glands:
Take nine different types of grease (natural ones, lard). Grease yourself from the navel up to the neck. Say the Lord's Prayer three times while doing this. Do this for nine nights consecutively.[52]

A remedy for felons:
Write this on a clean slip of paper, and then place it upon the felon directly.[53]

---

52   Snellenburg p.43; along with the greasing the Braucher told her patient that if the infected gland did not get better by the end of that period of time that she [the Braucher] would have to lance it with "a golden needle." This author does not recommend lancing without professional consultation.

53   Albertus p. 104

+ Rabhq + Hasba + EbnLH
a + Kackaabula + KasHaS
+ a + ao + b + o + + + o +

For a felon on the finger, this slip can be affixed to the finger by wrapping the zettel around the sore (like a bandage) and lightly tying it with some red string. This can be worn over night. Alternately, you can use some tape. If this is being used on an animal, keep it on the creature as long as it will allow you. It is best to do this during the waning moon.

TEETH, TOOTHACHE (*ZAEWEH, ZAESCHMERZE*)

Brauche Remedy

A Brauche remedy for toothache:
Say the Christian name of the individual before saying the charm; do this three times.

"On the grave of our dear Lord Jesus grow three roses. The first is called youth; the second is called virtue; and the third is called His divine Will – toothache be still." + + +[54]

Sympathetic Remedy

A zettel for toothache:
Write the following on a slip of clean paper. Place it in a muslin bag with a chestnut and an animal's tooth (if such can be found). Hang this around the neck of the toothache sufferer.

Quosum sinioba ze mitan tus lect ferri

Tree sympathies for toothache:
   1) Take a splinter from a tree, especially one that has been struck by lightning. Use this sliver to draw a small amount

---

[54] Brendle and Unger p. 119

of blood from around the gums of the sore tooth. Then take the bloody sliver back to the tree from which you got it; place it back into the spot from which it was removed. Or…

2) Go to an Elder tree on a Friday morning before the sun rises; make a slit in the bark on the side of the tree that will receive the sunrise; cut out a small sliver of wood. Follow the same procedure as with the first sympathy. Once the sliver is replaced back into the tree, back away from the tree in three steps. On the first step say *"ubi"*; on the second step say *"ropy"*, and on the third step say *"porpy"* – then turn around counterclockwise and go home without speaking.[55]

A sympathy from the *Wolfsthurn* manual:
Write the following sympathetic words on the cheek of the toothache sufferer, on the side with the aching tooth. Use a writing utensil that has a washable medium, such as an eyebrow pencil.

rex, pax, nax, in Christo filio suo

Another similar sympathy:
Find a cross roads and with a horseshoe nail write these words on each road:

Kex, Par, Mox, ppo, in folio

After this is done, take the nail home and drive it into a beam (in the house, garage, barn, etc.). Leave the nail there.[56]

55　These sympathies can be found in Brendle and Unger, p.117
56　Albertus p.94

URINARY

Brauche Remedy

A Brauche remedy for painful urine retention:
"In yonder valley lie three wells: they are called Brimming, Streaming, and Flowing into the Jordan where Holy Saint John dwells, to baptize by running water going. Lord Jesus Christ, unbind the devil's knot." + + +[57]

Sympathetic Remedy

Sympathetic Remedy for blocked urine:
If the origin of the blockage is witchery, the try this remedy: urinate in a pot, dip one of your shirts into it (it needn't be soaked). Stick the shirt with seven pins in the Three Highest Names + + + If you know the Witch's name, speak it, and then lock the shirt in a chest. [Note: the witched urine has a connection to the Witch by virtue of the curse. Sticking the pins into the shirt is to stick pins into the Witch. Locking the item into a chest locks up the Witch's power from acting again.

A sympathetic remedy for all urinary illnesses:
The following is a remedy that is found among the sympathetic cures of Paracelsus. Brendle and Unger mention it also, but as a cure for abnemmes.

Take a new pot and a good measure of the urine from the patient. Place an egg into the urine and cook the egg in it until it is hardboiled. While there is still some liquid left in the pot, take a gimlet or other thin, sharp object and bore holes into the egg. Place the egg back into the urine until the liquid is all boiled away. Afterward, take the egg to an ant hill and bury it so the ants will eat it. The eating away of the egg will sympathetically remove the infection or inflammation.

[57] This is a new Brauche charm composed by the author.

Herbal Remedy

An old herbal diuretic:
Slightly crush the berries of *juniper virginiana* or *juniper communis*, 1oz berries to one pint of red wine. The alcohol of the wine will help to extract the oil of the berries. It is the oil that is the diuretic. Allow this mixture to stand for an hour or two. Another way of taking juniper is to steep 1 tsp of the crushed berries in a half-cup of water for five to 10 minutes. Take the former at a half-cup per day; the latter at a half-cup to a cup. Juniper is a wonderful diuretic, antiseptic, carminative, stomachic, and tonic. It is useful for helping to pass "gravel".[58]

Horsetail (*Equisetum arvense*) and corn silk are very good for treating urinary tract infections and difficulties passing urine. Bearberry (*uva ursi*) is another good diuretic and healer, but the leaves must first be soaked in brandy before making it into a tea; it is easier to use as a tincture.

WARTS, CORNS (*GEWECKS, GEWEX, WARZ*)

Brauche Remedy

A whole body Brauche treatment to get rid of warts:
This is the method of treating warts that utilizes the General Brauche Circuit. Going over the patient first realigns his or her energies, clearing out any spiritual or energetic imbalances that may be the root of the infection (warts are caused by a virus). Next the warts themselves are treated. Most of the other wart cures are quite simple as they only treat the warts; whereas this method tried to eliminate any root causes first.
Note: As with **all** wart removal charms, this operation needs to be done *during a waning moon*.

---

[58] William Woys Weaver comments on the use of juniper in *Sauer's Herbal Cures*.

1) Go over the patient with the General Brauche Circuit.
2) The person being treated must have a penny and give it to you.
3) You will use either the *"Dei fuss,"* or *"Dei hand"* charms depending upon what area of the body the warts are located at. As a reminder, the *"Dei fuss"* is used for all areas of the body below the collar bone; the *"Dei hand"* is for everything above the collar bone. You will use either of these charms while working on the wart with the penny.
4) Take the penny and rub the wart with it 3x counter-clockwise.
5) Place the penny in the opposite hand so it will be free to squeeze the wart: squeeze the wart between the index finger, middle finger and the thumb as if pulling it off.
6) After the squeezing gesture, follow through by keeping these fingers together, like a three pronged claw, as if the wart were actually free and caught between those fingers. Now place the "wart" underneath *something made of metal*. If the chair that the patient is sitting on is made of metal, place "it" under the chair.
7) Replace the penny back into the grabbing hand (which will be *your dominant hand*: right if you are right-handed, left if you are a 'lefty'); once again rub the wart with the penny 3x counterclockwise, and the repeat Step 6.
8) Take the penny once more, and then rub the wart 3x **clockwise**.
9) Repeat Step 6.
10) Next bless the warts in the Three Highest Names.
11) Finish off with the Inflammation Charm: *"Ich bin dei gebruchman."* – *"I saw a Red Wald; I went into the Red Wald and saw a Red Church; I went in the Red Church and saw a Red Altar; and on the Red Altar I saw a Red Book; and on the Red Book I saw a knife. I pick up the knife and cut out the inflammation."* + + + [At the spot mentioning the knife, make a gesture as if picking up a knife and using it to cut out the wart.]

12) If there is more than one wart, skip Step 11 and proceed with Steps 4 through 10 for each wart. After all the warts are done, proceed to Step 11.
13) Once all of the warts are done, and then do everything all over again twice more for three times in all. Each treatment can be spaced 15 to 30 minutes apart.

Final Note: After the three treatments are administered, the patient needs to take back the penny and has to *spend* in as soon as possible. S/he cannot keep the penny. You cannot keep the penny either, unless you want the warts for yourself!

Another Brauche remedy:
To remove warts using the moon: instruct the patient to go somewhere s/he can observe the moon. This is one of the *very few* wart charms that utilize the waxing moon. Once the moon is in sight, the afflicted will say:

"Was ich raib, nem ab; was ich sen, nem tsu."[59]

English,
"What I rub, decrease; what I see, increase."

The Brauche is done three nights in a row. This is begun two nights prior to the moon being full. You will need an almanac to see when this will be. There are a multitude of Brauche formulae that rely upon this use of the moon: the wart is charmed to decrease and the moon increases. The only difference between them all is a slight variation on the wording of the charms. Some employ the use of sticks or twigs that are then touched to the warts, one stick per wart. The charm is recited upon touching the stick to the wart, and then all of the sticks are buried as *per* the sympathetic remedies below.

---

59   Brendle and Unger p. 67

Sympathetic Remedy:

A cluster of traditional sympathetic remedies for warts:
As you will see, these are rather old fashioned remedies. They involve the use of things related to the dead, which would have been common at one time due to pre-funeral home wake practices; the other 'ingredients' involve an animal part that would have been common enough on a farm.[60]

- Rub the wart with a cloth that was used to wash a corpse. The patient is to take this cloth and bury it underneath the eaves of his house. Or,
- Take a nail from a coffin and scratch the wart until it bleeds.
- Rub the wart with the head of a recently killed cock, and then have the patient bury this underneath the eaves of her home.
- Smear the wart with the blood from the head of a freshly killed eel and then have the head buried in a secret place.
- Rub the wart with roasted chicken's feet and have the feet buried underneath the eaves.
- Rub the wart with pebbles and then have them thrown into an open grave.
- Rub the wart with a dead apple tree twig then have it buried in a furrow that is to be plowed closed.

This paragraph here is presented for historical purposes only: stolen objects are said to be good for treating warts. This is an instance where secrecy is the key ingredient in the treatment. Rubbing warts with a dishcloth obtained in this manner and buried under the eaves has been recommended. Raw beef used the same way would be buried at a crossroads. Onion halves or raw potato halves can also be used and then buried under the eaves.

A few of these remedies are distasteful by present-day standards

---

60   These remedies can be found on p. 65 of Unger and Brendle.

and sensitivities. Therefore, the first method given in this section is the highly recommended one. There are simpler, less disgusting methods to be sure. The use of a raw potato, not necessarily stolen (!) can be employed. In fact, anything that is currently fresh, but can *rot* is acceptable. This object will then be buried. Burying under the eaves of a person's home is a protective act. In pre-Christian Teutonic times the eaves were the outermost border of the home, providing a boundary between the safe realm inside, and the dangerous one outside. The eaves at that point in time were quite overhanging. The best that can be managed today is the burial of the object near the foundation of the house, preferably underneath a drain spout. The water will help to decompose and wash way the sympathetic link or contagion target.

Another sympathetic remedy:
Take a red string and tie knots into it. Tie as many knots are there are warts. Rub each knot on each wart, 3x counterclockwise. Do this three times. Bury the string underneath the eaves.

Corns can be treated in the same way as warts. If corns are being actually cut out, only do this during a waning moon. Another recommendation is to also do this corn cutting, or wart removal, when the moon is in the sign of Libra (again, an almanac will be needed to determine this). According to Brendle and Unger, 1935, another good time to do these removals and charming is on July 30th, called *Abdansdaek* (or *Abdansdaag* – St. Abdan's Day).

WOMEN'S AILMENTS

For ailments or imbalances in the reproductive organs, it is best to go over the patient with the "General" first. Afterwards, you can apply the following Brauche as an extra boost. For women especially, please note the phase of the moon. Stopping blood for an excessive or heavy period[61] is most successful when done during the period

---
61 Menses was referred to as "ihre zeit".

of the waning moon. Unfortunately, these ailments do not always fall into the most auspicious of astrological times. Therefore, you will need to just work with what you have. The moon during its fullness may indicate that you will need to work your Pow-Wow a little more intensely – possibly having to decrease the waiting period between each set of three treatments. The normal amount of time between each 'going over' is fifteen minutes to a half hour (sometimes longer: an hour after the second treatment). Also, instead of your patient coming back for the next set of three a week later, she ought to come back the very next day; then also the day after that to make three whole treatments.

Brauche Remedy

For excessive menstrual bleeding:
Speak the name of the patient 3x and then say the following after it:
And the flow of blood ceased and He healed her from that hour; now then cease to flow in the name of Jesus Christ. As truly as Jesus made wine out of water so shall the flux leave off in proper time. The Lord made all things well, and of man thought well. + + +

For *"Mutterweh"* or womb pains:
Say this charm for menstrual or womb pains. It is generally advisable to always mention the full baptismal name of the individual when brauching. You can do this here by saying something along the lines of the following prior to the charm below: *"In the Name of God the Father, God the Son, and God the Holy Ghost, bless this your child N.N. in her hour of need for your healing."* From there you can proceed to the charm.

"Mutterweh heckte mutterweh legte
Leg dich an die selbig Wand
Wo dich Gott hat hingesetzt.

In Namen Gottes des Vaters, Gottes des Sohnes, und Gottes des heiligen Geistes"[62]

English:
*"Womb confine thyself, womb lay thyself,
Lay thyself down at the very wall where God placed thee.
In the name of God the Father, God the Son, and God the Holy Ghost."*

For irregular or spotty menstrual flow:
Say the woman's baptismal name 3x and then say this charm after each repetition of the name. Do this for three days consecutively.

"And she touched His garment and was healed. Thus I command thee, blood, by the precious blood of Jesus Christ, take thy regular course. I command thee, constipated blood, by Christ's flowing wounds, take thy regular course. As true as Paul was bound, this sickness shall be overcome." + + +[63]

For a copious menstrual flow:
As usual say the baptismal name 3x, then after each time say the following:

"And the flow of blood ceased and he healed her from that hour, now then cease to flow in the name of Jesus Christ. As truly as Jesus made wine out of water so shall the flux leave off in proper time. The Lord made all things well, and of man thought well."
+ + +

---

62   Brendle and Unger p. 221

63   Beissel p. 45 This charm uses a reference to **Mark 5:27**. Interestingly that passage describes a woman *who could not stop bleeding*, whereas this charm calls upon a remembrance of this gospel scene in order to *promote* bleeding. The next charm takes this into account.

Sympathetic Remedy

For labor pains:
Write the following on a single line upon a clear paper, 4" X 4" will do.

Ahbz POb L 9 h b m g n † Subratum nome nex gr.

Next write the patient's full baptismal name beneath this. After this also write in a single row:

+ Ecgitar + Circabato + Bessiabato + Argon + Vigaro Tanet

Place this paper into a small leather bag with a cord attached for suspending it. Sew the bag up on its right side. When sewing the bag's side closed make sure not to make any knots in the thread or band. Hang this amulet up near the patient in an uneven hour.[64]

For menstrual pains and complications:
On a piece of paper write the words -- **By Him, with Him, and in Him**. Place this paper on the woman's head.[65]

Herbal Remedy

An old herbal tonic for menstruating women:
Take a quarter ounce of horseradish and a quarter ounce of burdock root (*Arctium lappa*; German, *Kletten*, or greater burdock). Pulverize these, and add them to a quart of Rye whisky. Drink in small doses several times per day. Horseradish and burdock are great blood purifiers (*blutreiningungsmitteln*). Horseradish breaks up phlegm and "purifies the womb" according to Sauer; and burdock is both a diaphoretic and diuretic. Combining these with whisky is sure to

---

[64] Albertus p. 74

[65] Kieckhefer p3 from the *Wolfsthurn*. These are the words that are recited during Catholic Mass after the consecration: *"Per ipsum, et cum ipso, et in ipso"* ("Through Him, and with Him, and in Him").

make one sweat and produce urine. Alternate to use exclusive to women, this is a great mixture for sweating out a cold or flu.

Psalm Remedy

Psalm 128 for the protection of a pregnant woman:
Write this Psalm out full on a clean strip of paper, place it in a muslin bag, and then hang it around her neck. This will safeguard the woman and child during pregnancy, labor, and after the birth.

It is good for the mother to pray this Psalm in the morning and evening.

Psalms 102 and 103 for female infertility:
Either of these Psalms may be prayed in order to conceive. For Psalm 102, the Holy Name is JAH, and can be intoned after the word LORD: "Hear my prayer, O LORD…" For Psalm 103 it is AHA: "Bless the LORD…"

Psalm 1 against premature delivery:
The use of Psalm 1 is a bit involved. When a premature delivery is feared, the first three verses of this Psalm should be written on deerskin parchment, along with the Holy Name (**Eel Chad**) and the accompanying prayer. A new bag needs to be sewn together to house the parchment. The fabric ought to be natural, preferably uncolored.

Roll the parchment strip into a little scroll and tie with a thread of natural fiber. Sew a cord of the same fiber onto the bag; make the cord long enough so when it is hung around the neck, it will make contact with the raised stomach. When the scroll is inside the pouch, sew it up in order to seal it. The bag is not to be opened. The zettel needs to be worn underneath the mother's clothing, so it comes in contact with her flesh.

Blessed is the man that walketh not in the counsel of the ungodly, nor standeth in the way of sinners, nor sitteth in the seat of the scornful. But his delight is in the law of the LORD; and in his law doth he meditate day and night. And he shall be like a tree planted by the rivers of water, that bringeth forth his fruit in his season; his leaf also shall not wither; and whatsoever he doeth shall prosper.

May it please thee, O Eel Chad, to grant unto this woman, N.N., daughter of R.R., that she may not at this time, or at any other time, have a premature confinement; much more grant unto her a truly fortunate delivery, and keep her and the fruit of her body in good health. Amen! Selah!

WORMS

"Worms" (German *warm*) can mean many things depending upon the illness and its context. Generally, when speaking of "worms" the usual meaning designates the infestation of intestinal worms. Older herbals are filled with recipes to flush out these parasites, called *vermifuges*. However, "worm" has also broadly referred to any sort of footless or crawling parasite (real or imagined) as the cause of disease. These creatures have ranged from the common earthworm to "dragons" (*drache* in German, or *wyrm* in archaic English) otherwise called "serpents". Lice, maggots, and other creatures came under the heading of "worm".

A good many diseases that we would not think of as being parasite related also were blamed on worm-infestation, such as heartburn or indigestion. Skin ailments such as blackheads and pimples were blamed on worms. As we know today, there are, indeed, parasitic worms that can be found in the intestines, lungs, or heart – mostly these are found only animals. Before improved food preservation techniques and sanitary measures were implemented, parasites were a genuine source of concern. Lethargy, fatigue, and sundry aches and pains nowadays can be chalked up to inadequate nutrients in the food supply, along with its many additives, preservatives, hormones, and antibiotics. In days gone by, feeling sickly, crampy, bloated, and full of fatigue were symptoms of parasite infestation. Many of the "worms" of yesterday are now recognized as being viral, fungal ("ringworm"), or bacterial infections.

Brauche Remedy

A benediction against worms:[66]
"Peter and Jesus went out upon the fields; they ploughed three furrows, and ploughed up three worms. The one was white, the other was black, and the third was red. Now all the worms are dead." + + +[67]

Sympathetic Remedy

For ringworm on the finger:[68]
On a piece of paper the size of a band-aid, write the following, and then tie it around the infected finger:
Afriass, aesteias, Srus, Srus, Sras, Atestoos, Xaa ja + se do + da da + Abia Am bies + Greem Er A. ran + C y y + Um + + +

Herbal Remedy

An herbal remedy recorded by Brendle and Unger for expelling worms is the constant eating of garlic until the worms pass into the stool. Many of the herbs listed in the "Pharmacopeia" have vermifuge properties. Teas and decoctions can be made of the following to expel intestinal worms: elecampane, devil's bit, agrimony, angelica, camphor[69], gentian, ground ivy, and masterwort. Of course, there

---

66   Hohman, p. 49
67   A version of this is also found in Brendle and Unger, p. 183 where the tilling is done by Jesus alone in a cemetery: *"Unser Herr Gott fahret zu Acker, auf einem Gottes-Acker…"*
68   *Egyptian Secrets*, p. 69 (Empire Publishing Co. edition)
69   Camphor can be poisonous, which accounts for its ability to kill intestinal parasites.

are a great deal more than these, but the preceding eight are listed in greater length later on.

MISCELLANEOUS

A blessing for an unknown ailment:
Say the full baptismal name of the afflicted person 3x, and after each repetition say:

"Hast thou recovered health and God so will I lead thee again to God the Father, God the Son, and God the Holy Ghost. I do not know what has happened to thee or what ails thee; therefore, so help thee Father, Son, and Holy Ghost. Our Lord Jesus Christ readily cometh, and shalt thou be blessed, even as the cup of wine and the holy bread which Our Lord offered up on the night of Holy Thursday." + + +

A blessing to take away pain:
Say the full baptismal name of the person in pain 5x. With each repetition follow it with this blessing:

"Pain, I banish you back. Let these limbs enjoy rest and peace; be exiled upon the highest mountain and sunk into the deepest sea! The Blessed Virgin Mary had pains in her labor, but Christ Jesus was born. Through it all, these pains are forever forlorn, in the name of the Guardian Angels!"[70]

---

70   The guardian angels referred to here are most likely Michael, Raphael, Gabriel, and Uriel.

Verbal Charms for Protection, Exorcism, and Allied Needs

Various Charms of Protection and Defense

The old books are full of charms and prayers such as are provided below. Some of these may seem archaic, but they are of just as much use today as yesterday (or 200 years previous). Of course, in the process of using these charms it is quite possible to add or subtract as the need arises. The world in which most of these charms were written was a very violent place. Death could be 'caught' as easily as the common cold. The Old World from which the Germans escaped was bleeding profusely from unending cycles of political strife and religious warfare. The American frontier was equally as dangerous, but for perhaps a few different reasons. For those of us who live in Western countries, we are truly blessed to live in the relative peace and safety that we do. *This is not the norm for most of the world.* Give thanks to God for your wellbeing and pray that our quality of life is sustained in the midst of such a dangerous place as this planet is; and, of course, pray for those who are less fortunate that their native corners of Mother Earth will someday see the peace and plenty that we also enjoy.

Yet we do not live in Eden. The *Lilienzeit* or the true age of the Holy Ghost is still a long way off as far as any of us can know. So, for that reason these prayers, charms, and blessings for protection are very good to have recourse to. Praying charms such as these are best in conjunction with praying the Psalms. The Psalms are spiritual shields for the protection of body and soul. If a Braucher wishes to stay strictly Biblical (that is, using no other prayer devices other than the Bible), then the Psalms are the way to go.

A prayer for a safe journey:
This is a protective morning prayer to be spoken before going out of the home. It is a preventative against misfortunate during the

outing.

"*I* [here speak your name] *will go on a journey today; I will walk upon God's way, and walk where God Himself did walk, and our dear Lord Jesus Christ, and our dearest Virgin with her dear little babe, with her seven rings and her true things. Oh, Thou! My dear Lord Jesus Christ. I am thine own, that no dog may bite me, no wolf bite me, and no murderer secretly approach me; save me, Oh my God, from sudden death! I am in God's hands, and there I will bind myself. In God's hands I am by our Lord Jesus' five wounds, that any gun or other arms may not do me any more harm than the virginity of our Holy Virgin Mary was injured by the favor of her beloved Jesus.*"

After this prayer say the Lord's Prayer three times, a Hail Mary, and the Creed.[1]

A charm against violent injury:
"*I* [your name] *conjure thee, sword or knife, as well as all other weapons, by that spear which pierced Jesus' side, and opened it to the gushing out of blood and water, that he keep me from injury as one of the servants of God. + + + Amen.*"

Another charm against violent injury:
"*The peace of our Lord Jesus Christ be with me* [your name]. *Oh shot, stand still! In the name of the mighty prophets Agtion and Elias, and do not kill me! Oh shot, stop short. I conjure you by heaven and earth, and by the Last Judgment, that you do no harm unto me, a child of God.*" + + +[2]

A blessing against all misfortune:
"The blessing which came from heaven, from God the Father, when the true living Son was born, be with me at all times; the blessing which God spoke over the whole human race, be with me always.

1   Hohman pp37-38.
2   Both this charm and the one preceding are also from Hohman, p57.

The holy cross of God, as long and as broad as the one upon which God suffered his blessed, bitter tortures, bless me today and forever. The three holy nails which were driven through the holy hands and feet of Jesus Christ shall bless me today and forever. The bitter crown of thorns which was forced upon the holy head of Christ, shall bless me today and forever. The spear by which the holy side of Jesus was opened, shall bless me today and forever. The rosy blood, protect me from all my enemies, and from everything which might be injurious to my body or soul, or my worldly goods. Bless me, oh ye five holy wounds ✴, in order that all my enemies may be driven away and bound, while God has encompassed all Christendom. In this shall assist me God the Father, the Son and the Holy Ghost. Amen. This must I [your name] be blessed as well and as valid as the cup and the wine, and the true, living bread which Jesus gave his disciples on the evening of Maundy Thursday. All those that hate you must be silent before me; their hearts are dead in regard to me; and their tongues are mute, so that they are not at all able to inflict the least injury upon me, or my house, or my premises: And likewise, all those who intend attacking and wounding me with their arms and weapons shall be defenseless, weak and conquered before me. In this shall assist me the holy power of God, which can make all arms and weapons of no avail. All this in the name of God the Father, the Son, and the Holy Ghost. Amen.

A charm to use if a person or animal is being attacked by evil spirits of malignant Witchcraft:
"Thou arch-sorcerer, thou hast attacked N.N.; let that Witchcraft recede from him [or her] into thy marrow and into thy bone, let it be returned unto thee. I exorcise thee for the sake of the five wounds of Jesus ✴, thou evil spirit, and conjure thee for the five wounds of five wounds of Jesus ✴ of this flesh, marrow and bone; I exorcise thee for the sake of the five wounds of Jesus ✴, at this very hour restore to health again N.N/, in the name of God the Father, God the Son, and of God the Holy Ghost."

Say this three times in the Three Highest Names.³

A charm to enchant an herb for your protection:
First find a protective herb such as Artemisia or St. John's Wort (or other of your choice). To use current jargon, the below conjuration is a way of 'programming' the herb to do a specific task. In this case it is for protection. The wording that follows comes in two phases, the original as recorded in Thorndike's *History of Magic*, and the second is a more contemporary rewording done by this author.

> In the name of Christ, amen. I conjure you, O herb, that I may conquer by Lord Peter...by the moon and the stars... and may you conquer all my enemies, pontiffs and priests and all laymen and all women and all lawyers who are working against me.⁴

In the name of Jesus Christ, I conjure you [insert name of the herb] *that I may conquer by St. Peter, who holds the Keys, and by the moon and the stars, that you aid me to conquer all of my enemies, both seen and unseen, known and unknown; both spirit and human, male and female, and all the powers that are working against me. + + +*

Charms and Prayers for Exorcism

A primary brauching for general exorcism:
After going over the patient with the Brauche "General Circuit," if the she or he needs extra help due to spiritually induced illness, or

---

3 Albertus: this is the very first charm in *Egyptian Secrets*, although the pagination depends upon the edition. The charm is an interesting piece of sympathy. Unlike other charms that draw out disease and evil from the depths of a body to its most topical regions the out of the body altogether, the process here is reversed. This is the procedure that would be used when cursing. However, in this instance a curse is not being made, but being conjured so as to reabsorb into the *hexe* who sent it.

4 History of Magic, vol. I p. 598 cited by Kieckhefer p. 84. The charm is obviously antiquated, written in a time when the clergy held enormous power. To be excommunicated in those days was a veritable death sentence: loss of livelihood, legal status, and protection. An excommicant was "dead" to the community. Heresy was not just a religious crime, but it was also considered treason.

obsession/possession, do the following:

1) Have the patient sit down. Stand in front of him and place your hands firmly (and with pressure) on the shoulders. Your left hand will then be on the person's right shoulder, and your right hand will be on his left. While doing this say **"SAINTS!"**
2) Take the right hand and move it over the head to the opposite (right) shoulder. The left hand should remain on the shoulder where it is.
3) Take the right hand and tap that shoulder (the right) area saying: **"Matthew"** –
4) Then move the right hand to the other shoulder (the left) saying: **"Mark"** –
5) Now diagonally move your right hand down to the area of the patient's opposite "love handle" (patient's right) saying: **"Luke"** –
6) Then move your hand over across the solar plexus/stomach area to the opposite side (patient's left) saying: **"John"**
7) Finish up with this prayer:
"Bless this blessed body, mind, and soul; free it from all hindering thoughts, sin, and depression. Enlighten it with forces harmonious to Thy divine Law." + + +

An old charm of exorcism from the *Wolfsthurn*[5] manual:
For possession, speak the following into the ear of the patient:

"Amara Tonta Tyra post hos firabis ficaliri Elypolis starras poly polyque lique linarras buccabor vel barton vel Titram celi massis Metumbor o priczoni Jordan ciriacus Valentinus"[6]

---

5   The *Wolfsthurn* handbook is a German 15th century ancestor to all future "land and house" manuals. It contains the sorts of recipes that would be useful in the everyday life of that time period, such as making soap, preparing leather, etc. It also contains many sympathetic formulae and herbal remedies for common ailments.

6   As with most of these hoary charms, it is anyone's guess what these words mean (if anything); however, it appears that they are a mish-mosh of Latin and Greek, or trying to look like

A charm to banish evil powers and people.
This is the second charm that appears in Egyptian Secrets. It is more of an exorcism that a defensive charm, hence its inclusion in this section. The original lengthier name for this is *"If a man or beast is attached by wicked people and how to banish them forever from the house so that they may never be able to do any harm."* The "bedgoblin" in the first verse is a household spirit that can produce poltergeist-like phenomena (see the Glossary entry for BEDGOBLIN for more details).

"Bedgoblin and all ye evil spirits, I forbid you my bedstead, my couch; I forbid you, in the name of God, my house and home; I forbid you in the name of the Holy Trinity, my blood and flesh, my body and soul, I forbid you all nail holes in my house and home, till you have counted all the leaflets of the trees, and counted all the starlets in the sky, until that beloved day arrives when the Mother of God will bring forth her second Son." + + +[7]

Speak this charm three times. If this is being recited on behalf of another, be sure to substitute the word "my" with the afflicted person's baptismal name. Using the exact baptismal name in traditional Braucherei is of utmost importance.

A charm to 'fix' a thief:
One of the abilities credited to the hex doctors of yore was the ability to be able to 'fix' a thief; that is to say, they were able to make a thief 'freeze' where he stood when in the act of stealing, so as being unable to escape. The charm comes in two parts. The first is to 'bewitch' or 'enchant' the area to be protected (sort of

---

these. Some old charms were, in fact, composed of 'nonsense' words *via* a sort of glossolalia. Many Brauchers **will not** use these charms, no matter how old or traditional. They prefer to keep to the strictly Biblical verses. Considering the dubious origins of some of these devices, that policy may be best. All manner of these devices are presented here in order to give a good overview of the history and practice of Braucherei.

[7] No one knows the exact manner in which Christ will return, although the Bible does not indicate that He will come again the second time as He did the first. The wording of this charm is then theologically mistaken, unless it is taken in a wholly esoteric sense.

like a supernatural booby-trap); and the second is to resolve the enchantment (when the Braucher finds the thief he or she will be able to release him). In order to accomplish this task, go to the area that you want to protect. Muster as much faith as intent as you are able while intoning the following charm.

"Mary walked with her dear child, when two thieves came by, and quickly took it away from her. But Mary spake to St. Peter: St. Peter, St. Peter bind. St. Peter said: I have bound him with Jesus' bands.[8] With His five holy wounds ✶ my good have bound. Whoever steals from me, shall stand like a stick, and look around like a buck. If he can count more than all the stars which stand on the sky, can count all leaves, all blades of grass, all drops of rain, all flakes of snow, he may depart with his stolen goods. If he cannot do this, he stands on this place for a ransom, until I may be able to view him with my own eyes, and my own mouth bid him to go thither."

To resolve the enchantment say: ***"Depart in the name of the Holy Trinity."***[9]

---

[8] **Matthew 16:18-19**: "And I also say to you that you are Peter, and on this rock I will build My church, and the gates of Hades shall not prevail against it. And I will give you the keys of the kingdom of heaven, and whatever you bind on earth will be bound in heave, and whatever you loose on earth will be loosed in heaven." Lee Gandee referred to these passages as a Biblical statement of the Hermetic Axiom, "As Above, thus Below." It was Gandee's belief that Matthew 16:18-19 applies to all believers, and it is the Christ given authority that lends the Braucher the power to bind spirits, diseases, and natural forces.

[9] Albertus p. 88

Unlike some of the more well preserved, newer specimens, this colonial era grave marker displays a carved heart flanked by two six-pointed stars.

9: The Talismantia of Working Braucherei: The Talismans, Briefe, and Written Charms

Up until this point you have been walked through the processes of verbal Pow-Wowing. Braucherei is very much a verbal and physical practice: the various charms and prayers, the *besprechen*, and the oft-times complex hand movements to accompany the verbal work. Yet, there is also the work of the written brauching. Written prayers (sometimes called talismans) will sometimes be used in supplement to a healing, blessing, or exorcism. The manner in which these can be employed is only limited to the imagination of the Braucher; the same can be said of the forms these talismans may take. Below are some examples of old Braucherei talismans, along with a few newly made ones by the author, designed in a traditional manner (that is to say, designed by way of traditional ideas, aesthetics, etc.).

Anyone who is familiar with books such as *The Long Lost Friend* will already be acquainted with a few of these. In fact, most of these talismans (zauberzetteln/annängseln) are taken directly from the Hohman book, Agrippa, Paracelsus, and Albertus Magnus. A few also come from the infamous *The Sixth and Seventh Books of Moses*, which has gotten more than its share of a bad reputation.

As with every part of *The Red Church*, it is not my goal to confound you with too much of a good thing, a literary sensory overload of Pow-Wowing. However, it is my hope that there is enough material included in all sections to give the Braucher to-be (or interested parties) ample examples and demonstrations in order to find his or her niche to Pow-Wow competently (if not expertly).

The Annängsel and the Zauberzettel

The annängsel and the zauberzettel (annängseln and zauberzetteln in the plural) are more or less the same thing. The former specifically refers to a written prayer or talisman placed upon the person of the patient; whereas, the latter is a more general term denoting all forms of written brauching. Translated into English, "zauberzettel" means a 'charm slip' – as in a 'slip' of paper. These 'papers' as they are sometimes called act as batteries. They carry a charge or blessing that will work over an extended period of time for the one to whom it is given. Quite often these papers are bundled into the form of a Brauche bag, the subject of which will be covered in more detail below. Another term cognate with 'papers' is the German *briefe* (literally, 'letters' – as in a written letter or note). In the final section of this chapter is covered the topic of the *himmelsbrief*, or 'letter from heaven'. The himmelsbrief, as you will see, is a more articulate and extended form of a zauberzettel or annängsel. Some minor forms of written charm usage have already been encountered in the former catalogue of verbal charming (such as the charm for blutschtille named "Nosebleed V"). This section will take that form of praxis much further.

The above figure is a contemporary reworking of an annängsel or zauberzettel to be used against plagues and fires by this author.

Reviving the art of the Zauberzettel

Even a slight perusing of the old charm books will lead to the casual observation of the occasional odd strings of letters meant for employment in written charms (zauberzetteln). Unless one has a key for the decipherment of these letter charms, there is no way to know what is being "said" by the letter-strings -- at least none that this author knows of[1].

When making use of these old zauberzettel letter-strings, their mysterious quality may be all that's needed to trigger a response in the Braucher, making him or her more open to God's working through the so-called subconscious mind.

Presented below is a method that I have devised in order to create your own symbolic, meaningful letter-strings. This method is founded upon the observation that some of these old charms may have been formed from certain phrases and sentences from Scripture. The most likely candidate for this sort of charm-creation would be the Bible in its Latin translation (called *Textus Vulgatus* – or the *Vulgate*).

While this might not have been exactly how some of the Brauchers created these letter-string/charm-line talismans, the present method offers you a manner in which you can create brand-new zauberzetteln in accordance with your needs. Doing your talismans in this way can make this style of Brauche praxis accessible as a revived and *living* piece of traditional Braucherei art.

The following are some examples of how this process can be done. By selecting a passage of Scripture, in this case the Latin Vulgate, for a need (such as a hemorrhage), begin by reducing the phrase or sentence(s) to each word's first letter. When done this way, you

---

[1] Another possibility is that the words contained in some of the original charms might be the product of a sort of written "glossolalia", which we might call 'writing in tongues.' Words of this caliber make up the cyclopedia of so-called "barbarous" words or names. See the glossary for the entry on *Barbarous Intonality*.

will arrive at something that looks like Example 1. To make this sentence more abstract, and thereby aid in its sublimation, a more 'esoteric' reworking can be done by taking these first letters and restringing them by forming new 'nonsense' words, as in Example 2.

Example three offers an even further 'estericized' variation on Example 1 by way of inserting extra letters (such as using a few of the second letters of chosen words from the text), along with the addition of crosses. These crosses can be used to 'punctuate' the new letter string where important words or intervals are to be marked. Such an instance would be wherever the name of God is used; or in the example of Ezekiel 16:6 below, where the Latin word "te" (thee) occurs, for it is here where the Braucher will insert the Christian name of the individual being Pow-Wowed during the spoken charm.

Written charm for blood stopping based on Ezekiel 16:6, Vulgate:

> *Transiens autem per te vidi te conculcari in sanguine tuo ex dixi tibi cum esses in sanguine tuo vive dixi inquam tibi in sanguine tuo vive.*

When done in 'notarikon' fashion it looks like this:

Example 1

T.A.P.T.V.T.C.I.S. T.E.D. T.C.E.I.S. T.V.D.I. T.I.S. T.V.

Example 2

ta. p. t. v. t. cisted. t. ceist. v. ditis. t.v.

Example 3

ta. ap. tev + t. ciste. dx. t. + ceist. v. dx. itis. + tuv. +++

The cross also indicates a blessing. The three crosses at the end, of course, indicate the concluding blessing in the three Highest Names. As an example: if the person's name is "Jacob Yoder" this can be abbreviated as initials (J.Y.) or appear as JY, or Jy – hence:

ta. ap. tev + t. JY ciste. dx. t. JY + ceist. v. dx. itis. + JY tuv. +++

Numbers, astrological signs, planetary signs, as well as other mystic figures (e.g. the hexefoos) can also be worked into these charm-lines. In the case of a blood stopping charm, harmonious planetary alignments for the sympathetic stopping of blood may be worked in. In the latter case, Saturn is a planet of constriction, which is what one wants for hemorrhaging blood vessels. Mercury could stand for a quick coagulation. Other numbers to be considered: the number 7 for blessing; number 8 for Saturn; number 5 for Christ's Wounds. Hence:

𝔇𝔲𝔯𝔠𝔥 𝔚𝔲𝔫𝔡𝔢𝔫 ℭ𝔥𝔯𝔦𝔰𝔱𝔦 𝔰𝔢𝔤𝔫𝔢𝔫

Einz und 8 ta. ap. tev ✷ *7* † *t. JY ciste. dx. t.* ✷ † *JY ceist. v. dx. itis. 7* † *JY tuv.* †††

The line begins with One or "Einz" as all health proceeds from the One. From there the hexefoos is doubled (i.e., 5 x 2 = 10), plus the Saturnine 8, and double blessed 7 = 33, Christ's age at crucifixion (i.e., 1+10+8+7+7). This way, the charm line is tweaked in a magical manner, but also in a religious way as well in order to work in more scriptural allusions and sympathies.

A Written Charm of Exorcism

Below is a charm paper entitled "Against Evil Spirits and Witchcrafts." This charm was given to me by "Daisy". With the exception of a few minor details, it is exactly like the one that appears in Hohman's *The Long Lost Friend* (p43).² Daisy and Julius received

2   The title of Hohman's charm on page 43 of the English edition of *The Long Lost Friend* reads: "Against Evil Spirits and all Manner of Witchcraft"; also, the end note reads: "All this be guarded here in time, and there in eternity. Amen." In the charm reproduction here, the charm

this charm from Ruth Strickland-Frey. Due to the slight variations from Hohman, Ruth herself probably received this charm verbally from her own teacher, rather than directly from Hohman. However, at some point further back, someone had to have consulted with *The Long Lost Friend* (due to the tight similarities).

Against Evil Spirits and Witchcrafts

I.

N I. R

I.

SANCTUS   SPIRITUS

I.

N I. R

I.

All this regarded here in time and there in Eternity. Amen. †††

Hohman's instructions for this charm are as follows: *"You must write all the above on a piece of white paper and carry it about you. The characters or letters above signify: "God bless me here in time, and there eternally."* (p44). Daisy's instructions are a bit different and diverge from Hohman in this manner: when the charm is written out on a 2" X 2" square of paper, it needs to be folded in three's, thereby making a triangular paper charm. That is to say, you fold it 1) horizontally in the middle, then 2) vertically in the middle.

At step 3, the paper will now look like a rectangle or square (depending upon the paper's original dimensions). At this point, the paper gets folded twice more by folding crossways (diagonally)

---

features the six "I." that appear in Hohman, but on Daisy's charm paper appear as simple 'pipe' like vertical dashes. "Sanctus Spiritus" in proper Latin ought to read Spiritus Sanctus," meaning the "Holy Ghost".

so that the charm looks like a small triangle. This charm can be then used to either protect a dwelling or other building, or can be carried. When it is used to seal a house, garage, barn, etc., please observe the following rules:

1) Count up the number of windows, doors, and other openings the dwelling has (including unlikely things, like dryer vents, attic vents, old cellar coal chutes, etc.). Make as many of these charms are there are openings.

2) Each paper will be hidden or fixed above each opening. However, please note that NO METAL is to be used in affixing these papers, such as thumbtacks, pins, nails, etc. Flatten the charm as well as possible, and then squeeze it behind the window or door's wood. Wooden 'pins' or slivers can be used to secure the paper.

3) If the charm is to be carried, the triangle form will not keep well unless it is being perpetually squeezed in something like a wallet – otherwise, this charm can be bound up in red string in order to remain triangular.

4) When placing the charms begin in the very top of the house (attic) or the very bottom (cellar), working your way either up or down, ending with one or the other. Do not begin in the middle. Work your way around the rooms counterclockwise. Regardless of whether you begin in the attic or the cellar; start in the **east-most** point of the room.

5) This operation is not just a sealing, but an exorcism as well. Therefore, have a Bible in hand (containing both the Old and New Testaments). As you enter each room pray continuously. The Lord's Prayer is good enough for this purpose.

6) It's best to do exorcisms at a waning moon, if only for the fact that all things tend to ebb at this time; thereby, the Braucher works with the tides of nature. However, (and this may sound a bit sarcastic or tongue-in-cheek) *Jesus Christ is not affected by the moon*. God, the Creator of All, is **not** subject to His creations. Therefore, if someone is spiritually oppressed, he or she can go directly to God regardless of times, seasons, etc. Working with the tides of nature is always smart, but this sort of knowledge cannot ever be allowed to degenerate into elemental worship. For Christians and Jews, this is just basic knowledge: Commandment #1.

Fire and Pestilence Charms

Towards the beginning of this section is a contemporary charm paper designed for warding off illness and out breaks of fire. You will recognize in its form many of the foregoing techniques described here. Zauberzetteln and briefe designed for exorcism or sealing against illness and fires make up a large part of the corpus of written charming. A building's destruction by fire was more of a deep concern in the days prior to electric lighting, but this calamity is unfortunately still with us. What applies to "fire" can generically apply to any other disaster – if you wish to work with only the old charms. The nice thing about knowing how to make your own charms and talismans is the ability to tweak the old charms to meet new or expanded needs, or to make brand-new briefe altogether. There are many books on the market that show how to make talismans, but with the exception of a very few these are all written from a wholly non-Christian perspective. This is simply this author's opinion, but my advice is for you to stick to creating charms with the aid of Scripture, and Judeo-Christian symbolism. If you wish to go deeper into this form of study, consult with works on Jewish and Christian Kabbalah. To go outside of this symbolism is to go outside of traditional Braucherei.

Analysis of the charm:
The fire and pestilence zauberzettel above invokes Scripture, being "The Song of Azariah and the Three Holy Children" recorded in the *Book of Daniel* 3:88 of Latin Vulgate – Douay-Rheims. The actual passage (from the Latin) has been sublimated into "barbarous" words, accompanied by copious amounts of religious symbolism. The three crosses signify the Three Highest Names, and also recall the three crosses at Golgotha. The letters I.N.R.I., of course, stand in for the notice on Christ's titulus board: "*Jesus Nazarenus Rex Judaeorum*" (Jesus of Nazareth, King of the Jews). Also included are the letters "CMB" which stand for the Three Kings, or Wise Men (Magi) who visited Christ: Caspar, Melchior, and Balthazar. The charm incorporates the old SATOR formula (see below) written vertically, plus three hexefoos (pentagrams) signifying the Christ's wounds, and the Trinity.

The author has seen very primitive versions of this sort of symbolism where the repetition of the above formulae "CMB", "SATOR" and "I.N.R.I" (and other related letters-strings) appear almost like the old Futhark bind-runes. Early on, this is what this author thought they were until setting to research them much more closely. It is not out of the question that a vestige of rune-work might have been retained via this manner of talisman-making, but it is unlikely. When an untrained eye looks at a few of these old briefe that have been discovered hidden inside walls, lintels, wooden joists, and opened Brauche bags, the jostled and cramped writing can be misinterpreted as "runic". This is especially so when the abbreviations are printed instead of written in longhand. [3]

---

[3] These talismanic abbreviations and letter-strings do take some rather abstract forms. Often letters were reversed, which can be possibly accounted for by a practitioner being (semi) illiterate. Letters were combined together to make symbolic figures. This is reminiscent of Austin O. Spare's talisman-making praxis and his "Alphabet of Desire". Old-time PA Dutch Brauchers were not "rune" magicians, at least not in any recognizable sense as now seen in revival runic heathen praxis. However, there may be some support for the Christian use of runic forms in Scandinavia.

Use of this particular charm:
As with the anti-evil spirits and Witchcrafts zauberzettel above, this paper against sickness and calamity can be hidden inside non-metallic nooks, such as a hole drilled or carved into a joist. Unlike the anti-Witchcraft charm, this can be simply rolled into a tight, little scroll and stuck into the crevice or hole. If it is a self-made hole, a plug of wood will be retained to seal up the cavity once the paper is placed. Should the paper be carried by someone, the paper can be folded in the triangular manner, or just folded enough to be compact for a purse, wallet, or pocket. A truly traditional way in which to carry such zauberzetteln (and other talismans) is to hide them inside the hems of pants, coats, and skirts.

If you might be worrying about the need for cleverness or artistic ability in order to make really good briefe, you can set your mind at ease. A quick look at the old charms will reveal absolutely horrible handwriting and "art" work. But, of course, these briefe were never (and are never) meant to be works of art. They are entirely functional. If you are concerned about the need to physically modify Scriptural passages into symbolic chunks -- as is done above -- that is not necessary either. In fact, you can simply take a chosen passage straight out of the Bible and write it down as-is in Latin, English, or German supplemented with a few basic Christian symbols. The triple crosses (+++) are highly recommended.

Here is a similar charm recorded by Hohman on page 61 of the English version of *The Long Lost Friend* also uses "The Song of Azariah and the Three Holy Children":

> A Charm to be Carried about the Person
> English
> Carry these words about you, and nothing can hit you: Ananiah, Azariah, and Misael, blessed be the Lord, for he has redeemed us from hell, and has saved us from death, and he has redeemed us out of the fiery furnace, and has

preserved us even in the midst of the fire; in the same manner may it please him the Lord that there be no fire.

I.

N I. R

I.

German
Trage diese Worte bei dir, so kann man Dich nicht treffen: Annania, Azaria, und Misael lobet den Herrn, denn er hat uns erlöset aus der Höllen, und hat uns geholsen von dem Er, der Herr, kein Feuer geben lassen.[4] [The figure above goes with the German as well.]

Another variation on this charm is a two-sided 'paper,' the front of which reads:

> [This is] an amulet to carry on your person. Carry these words with you and no one will be able to assail you. Agania, Azaria, Misael. Praise ye the Lord for He has kept us from Hell and rescued us from death and preserved us in the fire. Therefore, may the Lord present the fire against us from adversities. N.R. Prince of Peace and all manner of contention power his protection for all who carry this blessing with them.

The back side:

> They will possess a Grand Secret, which no other being understood. Christ is in the midst, of Peace went His disciples abroad St. Matthew, St. Mark, St. Luke, St. John. The Four Evangelists protect me [name of person carrying

---

4   *Romanusbuch*: Besprechen 41

the paper], the ever-praised majesty and Unity of God. J.J.J. Amen.[5]

For further fire and pestilence letters, see the section below on the Himmelsbriefe.

The SATOR Square

```
SATOR
AREPO
TENET
OPERA
ROTAS
```

The above assemblage of letters is perhaps the most ubiquitous and popular magical square palindrome in existence. It is truly an all-purpose piece of Braucherei and is not restricted to one especial use, although its application is primarily protective. As with so many things of great antiquity and unknown origin, the history of the Sator Square is rife with controversy. For whatever reason, it seems that everyone wants to own this puzzle. In fact, that's what some folks refer to it as being, perhaps being nothing more than an antique word game that has become surrounded by "superstition" (as some researchers of the Sator formula call it).

Some opine that the "formula" is mostly of early Christian origin as a unique devise for encoding the faith in cunning symbols. Others are of the opinion that its beginning can be found in the 1st century mystery religion of Mithras, or other forms of paganism; yet a few more claim that its roots are Jewish. Because the Sator formula has been used quite extensively in European Christian folk magic and medicine, the overview here will center on its Christian associations with brief mentions of other ideas in order to round

---

[5]   This is a Brauche amulet that was handed down to esoteric author Mark Stavish by one of his Pow-Wower uncles. Only the spelling was corrected by this author. Note the wording. At the very end of the paper on the reverse side is a final sentence that is noted by Stavish to be unintelligible: "...*with me at all distances. Amen.*" Letter details via personal correspondence with author.

out the subject.

Below is one of the many corruptions or variations on the Sator formula. This particular one is more elaborate than the plain square of letters. The words TESET and ARETO are corruptions or substitutions for the usual words TENET and AREPO.

```
O++ * X * X * X * ++O
      S A T O R
      A R E T O
      T E S E T
      O T E R A
      R O T A S
            O
        O /I\ O
            I
```

No one really knows what these words mean; that they are Latin derivation is of little doubt. *Sator* means "sower" (as in one who sows seeds); *Arepo* is a complete mystery – some think it might be a personal name, but that doesn't seem likely. *Tenet* is Latin for "he (or she) holds"; meanwhile, *Rotas* means "wheels". If taken literally, a sentence to this affect can be made, but not from the very best Latin: *"The sower Arepo holds the works the wheels"*. Truly no one has any clue.

From the original words it is possible to extract the Latin phrase *Pater Noster*: "Our Father." Father Felix Grosser came to this conclusion back in the 1920's. Around the same time, as synchronicity would have it, two other scholars stumbled upon this breakthrough too.[6] The Pater Noster solution absorbs almost all letters in the square with the exceptions of two couples of A and O, which have been taken to stand for the Greek letters *Alpha* and *Omega*. In *Revelations*

6   "Ein neuer Vorschlag zur Deutung der Sator-Formel," Archiv fur Religionswissenschaft 24 (1926), 165-169. The other two parties were Sigurd Agrell, and Christian Frank.

Christ is revealed as the Beginning and the End. Duncan Fishwick[7] sees in this not a Christian formula, but a Jewish one where he focuses upon the word TENET and sees the "T" as a Latinate stand-in for the Hebrew letter *Tav*, which symbolically functions in the same manner as the Greek letter *Omega*.

```
                    P
    A               A               O
                    T
                    E
                    R
        P A T E R   N O S T E R
                    O
                    S
                    T
    O               E               A
                    R
```

As you can see from the figure above, the Latin phrase "Our Father" plus the two couples of A/O neatly account for the Sator formula. In archeological studies, Sator was found carved into the plaster of a home in Pompeii prior to the town's demise in 79 A.D. It has been argued that this date and prior was too early for a Christian presence; yet as early as 60 A.D. St. Paul had found Christians in the town of Puteoli (a port city in Campania, Italy, now called Pazzuoli) not far from Pompeii.

Since the sign of the cross became a known Christian symbol at a later date, skeptics say that the Pater Noster cross could not be a solution to the Sator square. This is just an opinion, but it appears that there are quite a few who wish to expunge the presence of Christianity from as many things as possible by nay-saying and discrediting every point both large and fine to make it disappear;

---

7   Duncan Fishwick, M.A. "An Early Christian Cryptogram?," CCHA, *Report*, 26 (1959), 29-41. The Jewish derivation of the Sator formula has been largely dismissed in the excellent research article "The Sator rebus: An unsolved cryptogram?" by Professor Rose Mary Sheldon, which was available at the time of this writing at: http://findarticles.com/p/articles/mi_qa3926/is_200307/ai_n9291635/print?tag=artBody;col1

that includes battles over a curious little word square such as this one. Regardless of its origins, Sator can be put to very good use.

SATOR to extinguish a fire without water, or in order to prevent a fire:
Draw the Sator in its square-block pattern upon a dinner plate. The plate can then be used to extinguish the fire by tossing it into the flames; or, it can be used to prevent fires by placing the same plate in a hidden space in the dwelling – preferably in an attic space between the joists.

SATOR to break curses and spells:
Write out the letters in their square format or in their form of the Pater Noster cross. Use a small, clean piece of paper (standard size is around 2" X 2"). Use a dark food coloring or edible berry juice for the ink. Make nine of these and *eat* one three times per day for three days.

SATOR to prevent contagion and the entrenchment of curses and 'bad luck' in the house or out buildings:
Carve the square or the cross into one of the beams or lintels of the home, barn or other out building.

SATOR to banish high fevers:
Write out the square on a clean piece of paper, and then fold it into the shape of a triangle. To do this, follow the directions for folding under the heading above *A Written Charm of Exorcism* ("Against Evil Spirits and Witchcrafts"). Secure the triangle with some red thread so it does not unfold. Make a small bag of red cloth to house the talisman. Once it is in this bag, sew it closed. Attach a red cord to the bag so it can be hung around the person's neck. The red color of the bag will act as a sympathetic sponge to attract the heat of the fever out of the sufferer.[8]

---

8   There are more talismans for fevers that are constructed in this manner. See the section on *Fevers* above.

Written Charms of Protection

A Charm to be carried for protection:
In nomine Patris, et Filii, et Spiritus Sancti. By the power of the Lord, may the cross + and passion of Christ + be a medicine for me. May the five wounds of the Lord be my medicine +. May the Virgin Mary aid and defend me from every malign demon and from every malign spirit. Amen. +A+G+L+A + Tetragrammation +Alpha + Omega[9]

A Prayer for the machine:
This is a written prayer that is used for protecting cars and other vehicles.[10] It can be simply folded and placed in the glovebox.

Our Heavenly Father, we ask this day a particular blessing. As we take the wheel of our car, grant us safe passage through all the perils of trouble. Shelter those who accompany us and provide us from harm by Thy mercy. Steady our hands and quicken our eyes that we may never take another's life. Guide us to our destination safely, confident in the knowledge that Thy blessing be with us through darkness and light, sunshine and showers, forever and ever. Amen.

Anti-Theft Amulets

To prevent personal goods from being stolen[11]:
Write the following on a small, clean piece of paper. The writing

---

9   *Popular Antiquities of Great Britain*, 1870, p 73. This is one of the very few charms in this book that is not from a Continental or Pennsylvania German source. It is English and a product of Braucherei's English sister practice called "Cunning Work". It is a very workable amulet and directly in sympathy with standard Braucherei charms and talismans. In fact, many of the operative devices of Braucherei are shared by other European traditions of folk magic and medicine, such as English cunning work – a good example of this overlapping is the ubiquitous SATOR square. AGLA is a notarikon. It is Hebrew: *Ata Gibor Leolam Adonai* – meaning *"Thou art mighty forever, O Lord."*

10   This is one of only two written 'charms' (amulets) given to the author by Daisy Dietrich.

11   *Egyptian Secrets of Albertus Magnus*, p69.

can be in either red or black ink. Talismans such as this these can be outlined on their edges (like a square or rectangular box) in red ink in order to 'boost' their martial effect.

+ Z. + D. + I. A. + B. + Z. + S. A. B. Z. + H. V. W. F. + B. E. R. S. + + +

The Brauche Bag

Aside from charming and the writing of zauberzetteln, the making of a Brauche bag is an elementary feature of Braucherei practice. That's not to say that everyone who practices makes these, but they are traditional and very simple to make. The bags themselves range in size from tiny 2" X 2" bags to small purse-sized sacks. The material is often very 'neutral': unbleached muslin, sometimes canvas; other bags are made of red colored wool, felt, or cotton.

The function the Brauche bag serves is to hold a zauberzettel with, perhaps, the addition of "Mercury Dimes" and on the odd occasion bits of root or herb. Unlike the much more famous "mojo" bags made by practitioners of hoodoo or root-work, a Brauche bag does not contain a whole lot of different 'ingredients'. More often than not, it will only contain a zauberzettel (a written charm). The more intricate bags have multiple pouches sewn *within* the larger bag in order to contain individual charm slips.

Completed bags are then placed within a dwelling, or worn upon a person. In the former, the bag will be placed within walls, between joists, or within holes bored into lintels and beams. In the latter, the bag may be laid on the wound or area of illness directly, worn around the neck, pinned to undergarments, or sewn within the clothing (between the cloth and the lining, within the seam).

If you find that you create many Brauche bags and zauberzetteln for others, you may want to acquire a few things:
- Pre-made muslin bags, such as can be found in health food stores for herbal teas – these work very well for use as Brauche bags; or;
- Large squares of muslin, cotton, felt, or wool material to make bags; choose between unbleached material or a good, strong red colored cloth – make certain that the cloth is natural, no man-made fibers.
- Squares of clean, blank paper or parchment: generally 2" X 2", or 4" X 4".
- An assortment of inks; black is all-purpose, and red is good to have; other colors can be employed, but it's best to keep simple with basic-black. The zauberzetteln really do not need fancy inks; in a pinch ball-points can be used. What matters most is the intention.
- A selection of drilling or boring tools and various sized wooden pegs to stopper up the holes made; these are for creating holes in wooden beams and sealing them up. Have a rubber mallet handy for hammering in the pegs; the pegs ought to be just slightly smaller in diameter than the hole. The sealing up can be done with plaster; do not affix Brauche bags with metal; do not use metal in any part of the bag with the exception of the Mercury Dimes.
- If Roman Catholic or Orthodox, have tiny sealable vials that can contain holy water; these can go into the bags, or otherwise can be sealed up in holes by themselves.
- A selection of thread for sewing the bags: white, unbleached, or red; sew by hand, don't use a machine.

Creating a Brauche bag can be as simple or involved a process as desired, but the suggestion is to stay simple. As with creating himmelsbriefe, there really is no set form. It is suggested that you incorporate frequent prayer when making the bags. Prayer ought to also accompany the placing or affixing of the charms.

Some bags incorporated vials of liquid mercury; since this metal is poisonous, some have used actual bits of solid silver. Between 1916 and 1945 the dime called the "Winged Liberty Head" or better known as the "Mercury Headed Dime" was produced and contains 90% silver; the bust depicted on the coin is that of Liberty wearing a Phrygian cap (which as been interpreted as being a figure of the classical deity Mercury). These coins have been used in place of the liquid mercury. Although the metal mercury has its own positive esoteric properties, the metal silver is an excellent replacement.

To create bags with multiple compartments or pockets, sew the pocket patches onto the inside before sewing the bag together. *These bags will always be sewn shut.* When you create them for others, make sure that they understand that *the bags are never to be opened.* Opening them spoils the charm and they will cease to work. This includes opening up the holes where the bags or zauberzetteln are sealed. If that occurs, then the bags will need to be remade.

Brauche bags with bits of root matter or herbs are not the norm, but they are not unheard of. There are many remedies in *The Red Church* that do, in fact, direct the creation of bags with herbs. Usually, it will be a single herb or root. As with all other matters in Braucherei, pay attention to the lunar phases as well as the day of the week. Unless you are making a bag that is designed to *diminish* something, always make them during the waxing to full phases. Once the moon is full, it soon begins to wane, therefore do not wait until the "full moon" to make these. When making the final stitches in the bag, or hammering in the pegs (and so on), always finish up in the Three Highest Names: The Father, the Son, and the Holy Ghost.

Should you decide to sew a bag or a zettel into a piece of clothing, be sure it is not an article that will get washed frequently, as the zettel inside will deteriorate. To combat this, the zettel can be written upon a separate piece of cloth instead of a paper, and employ indelible ink.

Below is an example of a Brauche bag that includes an herb, a zettel, and the creation of which demands a particular day and lunar phase.

A bag to protect against 'shot' or bullets:
Take the usual bag and place within it mouse ear herb, being hawkweed (*Hieracium Pilosella*), gathered on a Friday during a half or full moon. Get a small slip of paper and write the following upon it: **Light, Better, Clotental, Sabaoth, Adonai, Alboa, Florat**. Fold this slip into the usual triangular shape and place within the bag. Suspend the bag from around the neck.[12]

The Petschaft

The tool called a "petschaft" is not often spoken of or written about. In fact, the only place this author has seen it mentioned in connection with Braucherei is in the writing of Lee Gandee. However, the use of this device is not unknown outside of the wider scope of "magical" practice. A petschaft is just a stamper, such as is used to impress insignia on wax seals. The petschaft will have an appropriate symbol on its face, and a stem used to hold it when preparing it to make the impression. This tool is probably the most difficult to acquire or make, unless you're handy, or find a metallic or ceramic symbol that can easily be converted by way of attaching a handle.

Since heat is involved, the petschaft will be made of metal or heat-durable ceramic. The symbol can be as simple as a cross, or as complex as a Kabbalistic seal reproduced from *The Sixth and Seventh Books of Moses*, for example. Esoteric and magical supply houses carry a wide variety of these seals in the form of rings and pendants; these can be converted for stamper use by attaching the handle (which is just a shaft that need not be longer than a few inches). For those with metalworking skills, the most traditional

---

12 A modification of a bag described in Albertus, p58.

method of creating these tools (and many others) is to use the proper virgin ore, and to melt it down and to cast it in the proper planetary hour. The best most of us can do these days is to either employ someone who does have these skills, or to make do with piecing together such tools. Assuming you will be piecing these together, observe the proper planetary hours when doing so. As an example, a petschaft of a "Martial" nature will be made of iron ore and cast on a Tuesday during the hour of Mars.

The petschaft is used to impress the symbol upon the body of the patient, usually around the area where the illness lies. The mark it leaves is not from heat (branding) or ink, but soot. The soot is produced by holding the tool over the flame of a specially prepared candle. The tool is allowed to cool and the mark is made in the desired area.

The candle is made of beeswax and will include various herbs, roots, and blessed oil if desired. Today high quality essential oils are quite easy to come by and may be incorporated into the candle with the herbs. The candle must be hand-made.

To make the candle: acquire a pound or more of beeswax -- (the more raw the better). If the wax is in a thoroughly raw state, you will need to melt it down and strain out the larger impurities, such as dead bees. Do the melting in a double boiler. A stocky column-type candle will be the easiest to make. Craft shops will carry column molds and wicks; cardboard cylinders from toilet paper and paper towels can be used instead. Only melt down as much wax as you will need to make one candle. Retain the remainder of the wax for other projects.

Once in liquid form, add the desired herbs and oils to the wax, and then pour into the mold. Observe the correct planetary hours when doing this. The hours used will depend upon the nature of the candle, as dictated by the purpose of the petschaft. Along with the herb or herbs, metal ore can be incorporated into the candle.

If such is desired, before filling the mold entirely, pour a little wax into the bottom and allow it to firm slightly. Drop in the ore, and then pour in the rest of the wax. The metallic ore will impart its sympathetic virtues into the candle, which will conversely be imparted to the soot that forms on the petschaft.

An example of a petschaft:
Here is an example of a petschaft that can be made. All diseases and ailments have their unique "signatures." In sympathetic medicine the disease is treated by knowing that signature and what elements 'vibrate' in sympathy or antipathy to the signature. The signature is planetary, qualitative, and elemental. A disorder such as a sinusitis comes under the archaic heading of "rheum".[13] Rheums then come under the quality heading of "moisture" or wetness. The head is ruled by the sign of Aries and the planet Mars. Sinusitis is inflammatory, which makes it "hot"; therefore a full-blown sinus infection is a wet/hot condition.

Paracelsus gives a talismanic remedy for all "catarrhs" and phlegm in the head. This is his seal of Aries, and it is made of an alloy of iron, gold, silver, and copper. These conditions can be met by the Braucher, who is not a metalworker, by adding these ores to the candle. Ideally, the petschaft for this purpose would be made of this alloy. The tool would be made on Tuesday during the hours of the Sun (purifying fire), Mars (head/Aries), or Venus (coolness; glands, filtration). The sign of Aries, in this case, would not signify "fire" so much as creating sympathy with the head. A true medical astrologer would figure in a patient's natal chart when creating tools and devices such as these. The candle would be made on another Tuesday, as there would not be enough time during one day to make all of the components. The moon in its waxing phase is needed as well.

The herb mix employed in the candle can have the same planetary configuration as the alloy:

13   A rheum is a watery "flux" or congestion, such as mucous.

- Angelic, chamomile, and St. John's Wort (Sun)
- Coltsfoot feverfew (Venus)
- Ginger, horseradish, masterwort (Mars)

The following figure is in place of Paracelsus' seal of Aries, which is double-sided. It is presented here to give you an idea of what a petschaft seal *can* look like.

The example above is quite detailed, and this degree of detail can only be attained by someone skilled in making jewelry-sized metal or ceramic work. The petschaft stamp is an inch in diameter at the most. Therefore, if you make your own designs, keep to basic symbols such as the cross, pentagram, hexagram (or six-lobed star), elemental signs (such as the triangle of fire in the figure above), one or two Hebrew letters, and so on. However, if you should utilize modified esoteric jewelry, then the restrictions will not be as great. On that note, it must be said that tools such as these made entirely from scratch are the best. Craft shops often carry an assortment of wax-seal stampers in their calligraphy sections, which may be of use.

To use the petschaft:

There are no set prayers or incantations. These may be made up as the need requires. If the sigil of the petschaft is 'tuned' to a certain planetary energy, then it is necessary that the tool is utilized during the proper day and hour. In the case of the example above, the day would be Tuesday, in the hour of Mars.

To make the impression, the tool is held immediately above the candle flame until a layer of soot builds up on the seal. Once the seal has cooled, the impression or stamp can be made upon the appropriate area of the patient's body. The patient will then allow the design to wear off naturally.

Divination and Miscellaneous Operations

Procedures against Thievery and Witchcrafts

A divinatory technique for locating goods, thieves, or Witches:

The authoress Ann Hark once met a Braucher known locally in her area of Dutch Country as "Grandpappy" back in the mid to late 1930's. Ann and her "chauffeur" visited the old fellow under the guise of being a married couple with various 'problems' as they were curious about Pow-Wow and wanted a pretext for visiting. When they enquired as to how one can find out if he or she is *verhext*, Grandpappy gave the following advice.

> Sharp on the stroke of eleven at night, you go to a lonely crossroads. A "genuine" right-angle crossroads, mind you, our instructor insisted. With you, you take a "glass," or mirror, and on its face you write, in solemn silence, certain secret magic words. Still silently, you bury the mirror in the ground and go back to your home. Three days later, at eleven o'clock, you return to the crossroads. Without speaking a word, you dig up the mirror, taking care not to uncover its surface, and carry it home with you. Once there, you brush away the earth and offer it to a cat or dog. When the animal

has seen its reflection, you yourself are free to peer into its depths and there discover what you crave to know. If something has been lost or stolen the glass will tell you where it is and who's the thief; if someone *verhext* you, the face of the Witch will be shown.[14]

Obviously, this operation is missing a few details. Here is what "Grandpappy" (or Ann Hark) omitted. The "secret magic words," in truth, could be just about anything. However, there are some educated guesses that can be made. Firstly, magic mirrors are just ordinary mirrors that are used for magical operations. Do not use a mirror for magic that is also for everyday use. Secondly, throughout European magic the names of the four main Archangels are pretty standard for talismanic writing on these mirrors: MICHAEL, GABRIEL, RAPHAEL, and URIEL.

A variation on these spirits is found in the beginning of *The Sixth and Seventh Books of Moses*: SALATHEEL, MICHAEL, RAPHAEL, and URIEL. Also sometimes found on the mirrors and their accoutrements: TETRAGRAMMATON, EMANUEL, ADONAI (ADONAY), AGLA, ELOHIM, SADAI (SHADAI/SADAY), and ELOHE (ELOHA). The writing can be accomplished with black enamel paint and a thin brush. This option will ensure that the writing will not come off when buried. Grease pens and eyeliner pencils may also work.

To further add to these instructions, do this operation during a waxing moon, with the first night being a Wednesday and the third night being a Friday. When performing this according to actual planetary hours (see Appendix IV) the 11th hour will be the hour of the Moon; and the 11th hour on Friday night will be the hour of Venus. Wednesday is the day of Mercury, or the god Woden in the Teutonic heathen pantheon. Both are 'airy' spirits or deities of arcane knowledge, swiftness, and insight. Friday is the day of

[14]   *Hex Marks The Spot*, Chapter 3 "Witch Stuff", pp 62-63.

Venus. Aside from the usual associations of 'love,' the planet Venus (as the ancient Roman Light Bringer) is stimulates secret Wisdom. The crossroads itself is a liminal place and has both chthonic as well as Mercurial properties.

The hazards of mirrors:
Grandpappy's advice to **not** be the first to look into the mirror is worth remembering. *This is something you may not want to show your pets*; here is why: as with many old style magical operations, animals were (and are) used as buffers between the magician and an enchanted object. For example, the harvesting of a mandrake root is to be carefully done within a circle drawn around the plant, and it is a dog harnessed to the plant that is to pull it out of the ground. For the magician to do the extirpating himself is said to be a death wish. The same applies to these mirrors. Once the mirror is 'witched' it may contain a 'zap' that will be absorbed by the first living thing that looks into it. After that, the mirror can be safely looked into by the interested parties.

A mental note for all Brauchers-to-be: do not ever look into a mirror that is received as a gift from a questionable person. Brauchers or hex doctors will sometimes draw the attentions of other magically adept folks who do not appreciate their spell-breaking. This is not written to make anyone paranoid, but on rare occasions it does happen. Mirrors can be like batteries and will store a 'charge' or intention that's been placed within it by those who know how. Unfortunately, mirrors are not the only objects that can be witched and used as innocent looking presents.

Second mental note: working in utter silence and secrecy is a must. This is not because you are doing anything "bad" (although some may beg to differ), but because 1) a secret contains power. A wish or desire vocalized prior to its manifestation is to stop it in its tracks. It won't happen. 2) Tell no one what you are doing, unless they are involved too – but these things are best done alone. 3) Prepare the mirror in silence; leave your home in silence, bury the mirror in silence; return home in silence and tell no one what you have done. If you want to conjure the mirror, very quietly recite whatever prayers you want. There is an angelic conjuration below provided as an example. 4) Take care to find a truly lonely crossroads out in the countryside. Examine the site by day and plan where you will deposit the mirror. Have an unobtrusive marker ready so you can readily find the mirror again on the third evening. 5) *Do not be seen* on either night while working there. The shame of it is, as rural areas are being quickly built up and paved over by unthinking, greedy "developers" and local governments, choices for such ideal loci are dwindling fast.

Here is an angelic conjuration of the mirror that can be recited during its preparation with the angelic names. This example is a modified version of a prayer that is located in *The Sixth and Seventh Books of Moses*.

Salatheel, Michael, Raphael, and Uriel: oh ye aforesaid angels, ye that execute the commands of the Creator; be willing to be present with me in the work which I have undertaken at this time, and help me to finish it, and be ye attentive hearers and assistants, that the honor of God and my own welfare may be promoted. Amen.

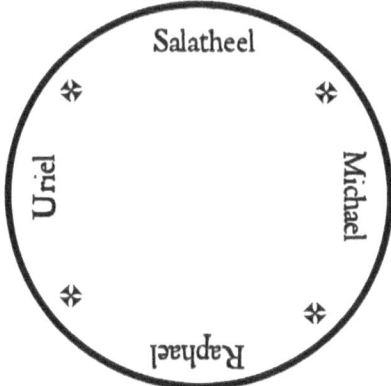

The magic mirror: one possibility for its design.

A divination to find iron, ore, or water:
This device is basically a dowsing rod. These are instructions given in *Egyptian Secrets* (slightly modified).

On the first night of Christmas, between 11 and 12 o'clock, break off from any tree a young twig of one year's growth, in the Three Highest Names, at the same time facing east. Whenever you apply this wand in searching for anything, apply it three times. The twig must be forked, and each end of the fork must be held in one hand, so that the third and thickest part of it stands up, but do not hold it too tightly. Strike the ground with the thickest end, and that which you desire will appear immediately, if there is any in the ground where you strike. The words to be spoken when the wand is thus applied are as follows:

"Archangel Gabriel, I conjure thee in the name of God the Almighty, to tell me, is there any water [or whatever] **here. Tell me!"**

The instructions seem to imply that if the substance is in the ground where you are searching that the wand will make it pop up out of nowhere. That's not the case. You strike the ground with the wand where you think the substance is and then use the forked wand just like any other water Witching rod. To do this, hold the forked ends very gently – one fork in each hand. Let the forks rest lightly between the thumbs and ring fingers. The "thickest end" is then outstretched over the area where you are dowsing. If the substance is there, the wand will bend downward. The more and better the substance there, the more insistent the pull on the wand will be.

A serious method of punishing thieves:
This is a device for the punishing of thieves recorded by Adolph Spamer in his *Romanusbüchlein: Historisch-philogischer Kommentar zu einem deutschen Zauberbuch* (1958), from the grimoire *Magia de Furto*.

Spricht ferner:

"Ich beschwere euch teufel durch den Vater, durch den Sohn, und durch den Heilige Geist und durch die ☉ und den ☽ und Sterne, und durch die 7 Lichte die da stehen vor den Herrn, und durch die Gewalt der Apostel, und durch die Heilige Jungfrau Maria, und durch den der dich regiret ohne Ende, daß ihr hier erscheint machet den Deib welcher gestohlet hat N. daß N habe einen."

Nagel setze den aufs Auge, und einen neuen eisernen Hammer ehe du aber schaegst liess folgendes.

"Ich beschwere euch Teufel Beelzebub, Satanas, Asterott, und alle euer Geselschaft durch Gott den Vater, Sohn und Heilige Geist ich beschwere euch durch die Gewalt, da durch ihr verstoßen seid aus den Himmel zu der Tiefe der Hölle, ich beschwere eich durch das Blut unseres Heiland Jesus Christ, ich beschwere euch durch die Jungfrau Maria der Mutter Jesu Christi ich beschwere euch durch die Patriachen und Propheten durch die heiligen Märter durch das gewaltige Geboth Gottes, ich beschwere eich und heiße euch teufel daß ihr ☉° rast und Ruhe empfahet, so lange biß erfuellet werde das werck dieses Diebstahls. Hier schlage den 1, 2, und 5 Schlag hinein so ist es geschehen."

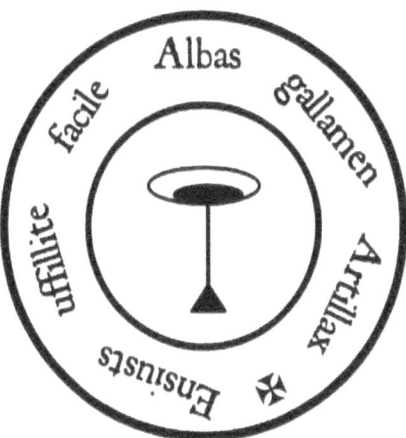

The above conjuration of a thief is reproduced here with a few minor changes. The German spelling has been modernized, along with the elimination of abbreviations of various words, such as *u.* for *und* and *H.G.* for *Heilige Geist*, etc. What follows is my own translation of the text.

Say the following:

"I press thee, devil, by the Father, by the Son, and by the Holy Ghost; and by the sun, and by the moon and stars; and by the seven lights[15] that stand before the Lord, and by the authority of the Apostles, and by the holy Virgin Mary; by He who rules over you without end; I press thee that you make appear the thief who stole N, that NN[16] may have it back.

[With a new iron hammer thou drivest the nail that sits upon the eye.] *I press the devil Beelzebub, Satan, Asteroth, and all you companions through God the Father, Son, and Holy Ghost; I press you all by the power that cast you off from the heights of Heaven to the depths of Hell; I press you all by the blood of our Savior Jesus Christ; I press you by the Patriarchs and the Prophets, by the holy Martyrs, and by the powerful commandment of God; I press you and command you devil, that you receive rest and peace only if you comply to resolve this theft. Here I strike 1, 2, and 5 strokes; thus is it to be."*

This device demands a good amount of explanation. In the chapter on hexerei it is noted that not all operations that conjure devils are evil magic *per se*. Here in this spell is the calling upon various devils by the power and authority of God, the sole purpose of which is to force the devils to hand over 'one of their own' for justice. In this case that would be the thief who violated **Exodus 20:15**, *"Thou shalt not steal."* This is the work's *only* purpose. It is not a thing of devil worship, but a compelling of devils. The idea behind spells

---

15   The "seven lights" – that is, the seven classical planets.

16   The double NN indicates that this 'spell' is designed for being worked on behalf of others – the name of the wronged party would go in this space. The single N is where the stolen goods would be specified.

like these is that the Devil inspires the sin and governs the sinner, the tempter. Therefore, it is he who is compelled to hand over the "temptee."

The diagram above shows an abstract eye with a nail in it. The drawing of the nail is just an illustration of what one is to do with the figure. Since the identity of the thief is largely unknown, the use of a drawing such as this is used to create a sympathetic link with the thief *in lieu* of an actual possession of his. When the wording at the end indicates the strikes of the nail, this is when an actual nail is driven through the 'eye' of the figure. The hammering upon the eye is both a torment to the devils as much as it is to the thief. Such is the theory behind this sort of device.

It is quite understandable that many will be rather squeamish at the thought of using such a work. They will not want to risk trafficking with any demonic forces, even if it is to coerce or punish them in some way.

There are other devices that can accomplish the same thing, but **the above is a rather old working and is presented here for that reason.** A hex doctor of previous times would not have worried over using such a tool because he (or she) is an exorcist and "master" of devils – that is, a "master" as a tamer and punisher: hence the title of the hex doctor is sometimes that of *hexenmeister* (see the Glossary for HEX DOCTOR).

For compelling a thief to return stolen goods:
Before sunrise take three coffin nails or three horseshoe nails (unused) to a pear tree. Face east, and as the sun begins to rise take the nails into your right hand and hold them with points outward, arm outstretched towards the sun. While doing this speak the charm below.

"Oh, thief, I bind you by the first nail, which I drive into thy skull and thy brain, to return the goods thou hast stolen to their

former place; thou shalt feel as sick and as anxious to see men, and to see the place you stole from, as felt the disciple Judas after betraying Jesus. I bind thee by the other nail, which I drive into your lungs and liver, to return the stolen goods to their former place; thou shall feel as sick and as anxious to see men, and to see the place you have stolen from, as did Pilate in the fires of hell. The third nail I shall drive into thy foot, oh thief, in order that thou shalt return the stolen goods to the very same place from which thou hast stolen them. Oh, thief, I bind thee and compel thee, by the three holy nails which were driven through the hands and feet of Jesus Christ, to return the stolen goods to the very same place from which thou has stolen them." + + +[17]

Another way of protecting against thievery:
Old time Brauchers were not all full-blow ceremonial magicians. However, many of them knew enough in order to utilize basic devices such as the infamous "magic circle." Ned Heindel, on pages 24 and 25 in his book on the Hexenkopf Mountain in Williams Twp., describes Braucher Dr. Peter Saylor this way:

> When drawn on the ground as circles – with or without the star or petaled flower – these modified hexenfuss are widely known among Brauchers as a way to "call down power." Peter Saylor occasionally drew charmed circles or stood within them to increase his own powers and, on one occasion, to catch a thief who had come to steal Saylor's freshly butchered pig.

This sort of charmed circle can be accomplished simply by drawing a circle around the object to be protected. Inside a home this can be done with a stick of chalk or a ring of salt. Outside it can be done with salt, flour, or simply inscribed into the dirt with a regular

---

17   Hohman, p. 47. Before the days of "fluffy bunny" politically correct "magick," a charm such as this one would have never raised an eyebrow. It must be made clear that this sort of spell is not a curse, *per se*. By way of the nails the operator is attempting to prick the conscience of the thief so that he (or she) will have no rest until they undo the theft. There is nothing morally wrong with this. There is no "karmic" backlash from an operation such as this. Something was stolen and you want it returned. A curse in the truest sense is an unprovoked, unmerited, spiritual attack upon an innocent person. It is a species of violence and violation no different from getting mugged, beaten, or murdered.

stick. The circle will be made clockwise. The ideal charm to use with a circle such as this can be found above under the heading *"A charm to 'fix' a thief."*

To strike at a Witch who has cursed you.
Take a cup or so of butter and melt it down in an *iron* pan until it begins to boil. Add to the boiling butter ivy and wintergreen, frying them. As these are frying, place three coffin nails (or unused horseshoe nails) into the sauce. Once this is done, take the pan and its contents outside and leave in a place that will not be touched by the direct light of sun or moon. Do this operation on a moonless evening, preferably during a waning moon cycle. It is said that the afflicting sorcerer will be "sick" for "half a year".[18]

Various Exorcisms and Wardings

An herbal exorcism:
Take three sprigs of juniper (*juniper communis* or *juniper virginiana*) and boil these in red wine for about five to 10 minutes. Afterward, take the sprigs and place them on the possessed person's head, but it must be when he or she is asleep and unaware of this procedure taking place.

An herb to ward off sorcery:
To ward off sorcery carry a sprig of Artemisia (*Artemisia absinthium*), wormwood – in German, *Wermuth*. A combination of wormwood and salt fed to barnyard animals is said to stave off contagion. *Please note:* **do not** *take wormwood internally, no matter how traditional some usage may be. It is a poison. The above farm use is for historical illustration only.*

Elmwood to ward off sorcery:
Go to an elmwood (*Ulmus campestris* or *americana*) on Good Friday before the sunrises. Cut off chips of this wood that are an inch or two in length (you are making slivers). When cutting be

18   Albertus p. 56

sure to make each cut in the Three Highest Names. Make three crosses upon each sliver with your knife. These slivers are amulets. Wherever they are places, the power of sorcery is destroyed. These chips can be wedged into lintels, cracks, holes, and other places where they will be inconspicuous (and especially around openings to the outside where 'things' can enter the home or barn.[19]

To unWitch farm animals:
On the St. Mary's Eve, September 7th, being the evening before the Nativity of Mary on September 8th, do the following operation.[20] Gather as many quinces (*Cydonia oblong or vulgaris*) as you have animals to treat. Core the fruit and give the cores to the animals to eat.[21]

To find something that is lost:
Should something be lost or stolen, carve or scratch these words over the door of your home (on the inside): **+ Chamacha, + Amacha, + Amschala, + Waystou, + Alam. + Elast Lamach**.[22]

To secure justice for you when in court:
Write these words upon a slip of paper: **Jesus Nazarenus Rex Judeorum**. After this, speak the charm:
"I [your name] *appear before the house of the Judge. Three dead men look out of the window; one having no tongue, the other having no lungs, and the third was sick, blind and dumb."*

This charm can only be used when you are truly in the right and it looks as if you will not get a fair hearing. While on your way to

---

19 Ibid. p.55

20 As a side note: it was the Synod of Salzburg that determined and fixed the days of Mary's 'cult' in the Western Church being: The Purification (February 2nd), The Annunciation (March 25th), The Assumption (August 15th), and The Nativity of Mary – The Feast of the Nativity of the Blessed Virgin Mary (September 8th).

21 Albertus p163

22 Ibid. p.76

court, repeat the charm quietly to yourself. Have the slip of paper on your person.[23]

If someone comes to your house to cause trouble:
If you know that someone is coming to your house that might cause trouble, scatter salt on the floor where this person is likely to walk. Should this person step upon the salt, their power against you will be gone.[24] Salt is like a sponge that absorbs "malignant" energies – or to be blunt, it absorbs the 'energy' of evil. After the person goes away, be sure to sweep up all of the salt.

A divination with the Bible:
This operation is technically a work of "biblionomancy" – literally, divination by way of a book. Biblionomancy has been practiced for thousands of years in many different cultures. This version uses the Bible itself. Some forms of this manner of divination are performed by randomly opening the book and taking as an omen the first words, sentences, or paragraphs seen. However, what is being done here is a little different.

You will need an old key, some twine (or rubber bands, string, or even a hair tie – anything that can be used to bind the Bible shut), and a small to medium-sized Bible.

Take the key and place it into the Bible. Some traditional places to put it are the *Book of Ruth* (Chapter 1), the *Gospel of John* (any of the Four Gospels, really), and the *Epistle of James*. The top of the key needs to stick out of the Bible and be sandwiched in, so that it looks like it is inserted into a lock. Take the string, or whatever you have, and bind the book shut so the key will not come out.

To use this, hold the Bible by the key and ask a question. The questions need to be simple, preferably of the 'yes' or 'no' type. An answer is indicated when the Bible gives the sensation of wiggling

23   Hohman, pp 49-50
24   Snellenburg, p44.

or vibrating; there may even be a light thumping or rapping sound too.

An Important Note on Conjury

It is important to note that a Pow-Wow doctor is not necessarily a conjuror of spirits, although hex doctors have fulfilled that role from time-to-time. There are many entries in *The Red Church* that the author himself *does not* practice, but are given here in order to round out some of the historical record on many Braucherei-related operations.

Theological and moral considerations aside, Witchcraft at its most elemental is simply the conjuring of spirits and making alliances with them for the working of sorcery. *Having* a familiar spirit is the hallmark of Witchcraft. Yet, not everyone who has a "familiar" spirit is a Witch. There are, indeed, Brauchers who have had protective or guiding spirit helpers. The important difference is that these spirits were not conjured, they were *given*. It is equally true that both inheritors of Pow-Wow and hexerei can inherit these spirits from their predecessors, although this is more of a phenomenon of Witchcraft than Braucherei. However, for the most part, these guides or guardian angels are given by God. It is common New Age belief that everyone has at least one of these beings; however that might be, not everyone is allowed to know them directly.

Among the Kabbalistic rabbis, few of them actually practiced magic of any sort. When they did do so, it was only under extreme circumstances that called for it. This is quite a difference from the spell-a-day recommendations of some popular authors on the subject.

For those who are interested in hard-core spirit conjuration, Joseph Lisiewski's book *Ceremonial Magic & the Power of Evocation* is highly recommended. After carefully reading Lisiewski's book, it will make a person think twice before embarking on the path of evocation. Personal experience has validated much of what Lisiewski has written. Conjury is **not** necessary in order to practice Pow-Wow.

Here is this author's sincerest recommendation to future Brauchers:
- Study Scripture
- Regularly attend a church of your choice; it's not good to be totally alone
- Practice healing others through straight-up Pow-Wow, such as with the aforementioned "General Brauche" technique
- Study herbalism: although not Pow-Wow *per se*, it is a great (and traditional) adjunct
- Study astrology: get to understand lunar phases and planetary influences on herbs, as well as on the Pow-Wowing process

These points will make you a well-rounded Braucher. And, what they boil down to is this: 1) the study of God and 2) the study of Creation (Nature). This becomes the Braucher's foundation in Natural Magic. Paracelsus, for example, denounced conjury in the strongest of terms; yet, he was the most enthusiastic advocate of the highest octave of Natural Magic, being the Royal Art of alchemy.

The problem with conjury is that the practitioner **does not** have 100% control over the process, no matter how good he or she thinks they are. Lisiewski gives details on how to avoid the worst consequences of an out of control operation. But, what needs to be pointed out here is that the act of conjuration opens a gate or doorway. The operator (magician) does not have total control over whom or what passes through. Even if only "one" spirit is being called, *no spirit ever comes by itself.* It is always a "them" situation. This is where being "read fast" comes in.

> Then He asked him, "What *is* your name?" And he answered, saying, "My name *is* Legion; for we are many." **Mark 5:9 NKJV**

Further regarding spirit guides, if you want them (and are meant to have one or more in your work), pray for them to be sent. The most likely way you will meet them is in dream-time, or during a trance-state (such as "day dreaming"). Some gifted clairvoyants can see them quite plainly.

While on the subject of spirits and hexerei, please take note that curses can be anchored into material objects. A common way to pass along a curse is through a "gift" of some sort. If you suspect that the source of a gift is dubious, do not accept it. Material gifts are an open-sesame for psychic vampires; they leave a person feeling indebted, while planting the seed of the actual curse or energy-drain. This subject has been briefly covered in the previous discussion on magic mirrors.

The Himmelsbriefe

Himmelsbrief is a "heaven's letter." All himmelsbriefe are variations of one another. The **Koenigsberg Fire Brief, 1714,** and **The Magdeburg Himmelsbrief, 1783** provided below are excellent examples of these letters whose function it is to protect the bearer (or place where it is ensconced) from all dangers and evils. By their nature they are generic, being the ancestors of our present-day "chain letters" according to Professor Bill Ellis (see bibliography). In the case of **The Letter of Protection** given in William Wilson Beissel's *Secrets of Sympathy*, it is claimed that *"This letter fell from Heaven, and was found at Holstein's in 1724. It was written in gold letters, and moved over the baptism of Madaginery, and when they tried to seize it, it disappeared until 1791, that everybody may copy it and communicate it to the world..."*

Beissel's brief is not unique to him, but is a copy of a copy. The past creators of the himmelsbriefe founded the power of their letters by establishing their authority in their purported mystical and exotic origins. The message of the brief is very clear: obey the Laws of God and He will look after your needs. All of the rigmarole of Gypsy kings and miraculous origins might be described as 'pious fictions' in order to work its wonders. In modern psychology, we have the concept of the subconscious mind.

From that area, the suggestions made by the briefe will 'sink' to that level and modify an individual's behavior. From another contemporary perspective, parapsychologists (people involved in "Psi" studies), will say that these beliefs that have worked themselves into the subconscious may find a 'vent' in the physical world. Therefore, these letters can act as catalysts for the desired effect (i.e., protection). On the nasty side, if the contents of these letters do sink that deeply and one does not live up to his or her end of the bargain, then there will be a 'negative sanction' for violating any one of the admonitions, such as breaking the Sabbath, for example.

Now, prior to modern psychology, none of the foregoing was even a consideration, at least not in that terminology. Either one obeys God's commandments and adheres to the Covenant, or one does not. Not obeying has a price, and it has nothing to do with any aspect of our 'minds' – except, perhaps, for that portion that likes to rebel and disobey causing the problem in the first place.

New Age teachings often state that we create our own reality, but that leaves a rather unpleasant tickle in the back of the throat. If a person jumps off of a ten-foot ladder, he's going to land 10 feet down, and not fly an extra 10 feet up like Peter Pan. The 'laws' of physics are God's physical laws when He created the universe. Rules such as the Decalogue ("The Ten Commandments") are His moral laws. Violating either has its results, some of them not always immediate.

The most important feature of the himmelsbrief is the legend that it was written by God Himself; the original usually having been lettered in gold and having disappeared after being copied by a mortal hand. These injunctions are just basic Biblical morality, although many today might feel 'oppressed' by such tenets. In an era where this morality is not "in keeping with the times" the realization that some things are timeless and eternal is a hard pill to swallow.

Closely related to the himmelsbrief is the "fire and pestilence letter", some of which are purported to be the "invention" of a "Gypsy King of Egypt". The story usually tells of an old, condemned Gypsy man who is released from prison in order to quench a raging fire. After successfully quenching the conflagration, the Gypsy is freed, and the 'letter' is allegedly endorsed by a provincial official, such as the "Superintendent General at Koenigsberg" (as found reproduced in the *Albertus Magus*).

The creation of a himmelsbrief is a variable thing. How involved it gets depends upon the person making it. Sometimes this will be a letter passed down through generations within a family – a treasured family heirloom. Then circumstances will arise that the letter needs duplication. Today's remedy for that is the photocopy machine. Down in PA Dutch country there are numerous outlets that have kitschy Dutch trinkets for sale, and sometimes photocopies of the briefe will be available. When Arthur H. Lewis' book about the York 'hex' murders was published, the first edition sold in Pennsylvania came with a himmelsbrief in each copy. This was a marketing enticement for the PA Dutch audience to buy the book.

Far superior to photocopying is creating a brief from scratch. It can be as artistic as can be managed, or as plain and utilitarian as talents and time will allow. The creation of these letters is one of a few things that a Braucher can legitimately charge a fee for. A fee for such an item is no different than paying an artist for doing a sketch or painting. These take time and resources, especially if the Braucher is also a fraktur artist or calligrapher. A quality letter will have a quality price. The text itself can be done in German or in English. Hexefoos and other symbols or art work may or may not accompany the text, such as can be seen with traditional taufscheine (baptismal certificates) and geburtscheine (birth certificates).

Tips on creating the himmelsbrief:
- As always, use clean paper with no marks upon it.
- This is an important document; use the best paper you can afford.
- If you have a modicum of talent for calligraphy or fraktur work, use it or learn it. You needn't worry if it isn't 'good'. The point is, if someone needs a brief, make it as best as you are able.
- When writing each letter concentrate on what it is you are writing and its purpose. Pray for the person for whom this is intended. **This is important: do not forget to pray!** Simply photocopying without thought or conviction is just

a sign of superstition, or not caring enough.[1] There are no set prayers for making a brief. The act must be sincere.

- As with the paper, use quality inks. It is ideal if the paper, inks, and pens/quills are used for no other purpose than creating these letters.
- There is another way to produce a quality himmelsbrief that is somewhere between "by-hand" and by copy machine. If you have a good word processor and a fraktur font, you can reproduce a German himmelsbrief to good effect. However, the catch is that you still have to concentrate on each word as you are typing it and getting it ready. The concentration involved in this non-traditional "modern" way of crafting a brief is the same and allows you a few more creative options for design if you are not good in penmanship or drawing. An example of this is given below in the Holstein brief at the very end of this section.
- Once the brief is completed, give the receiver instructions on its care. If it is small and meant to be carried, it ought to be neatly folded and put in a place such as a wallet where it will not get dirty or torn. For the larger brief for the home it can be framed and placed above the front door (or anywhere else). Keep them clean and treat them with respect for what they represent.
- Catholic practitioners may use holy water to bless the paper and other utensils before creating a brief. If this is the case, give the paper time for the water droplets to fully dry. Holy water made on the Feast of the Magi (so-called "Three Kings Water") is great for these operations.
- If one has an open-minded priest or pastor, see if he will give a blessing for your brief tools.
- If you are an astrologer, you may look for the most harmonious times to prepare a brief. Never make one of these during a waning moon. Make them during a waxing phase a few days before full. Doing them on a full moon

---

[1] It needs to be noted here that in times past generic himmelsbriefe were mass-printed in the same manner as taufscheine and geburtscheine – see Don Yoder's *Pennsylvania Broadsides*.

is fine, but it can be a little tricky. Once the moon is truly full, it begins to wane. Thursdays are best; the next best is Sunday. Fridays are alright. Avoid Saturday, as it is governed by Saturn. The forces of Saturn can be protective, but are constrictive and confining (unless that's the effect you really want).
- The briefe below are some well know traditional ones; however, using the basic ideas contained in these, you can easily make your own customized ones.

The Koenigsberg Fire Brief, 1714
Welcome, thou fiery fiend! Do not extend further than thou already ready hast. This I count unto thee as a repentant act, in the name of God the Father, the Son, and the Holy Ghost.

I command unto thee, fire, by the power of God, which createth and worketh everything, that thou now do cease, and not extend any further as certainly as Christ was standing on the Jordan's stormy banks, being baptized by John the holy man.

This I count unto thee as a repentant act in the name of the holy Trinity.

I command unto thee, fire, by the power of God, now to abate thy flames; as certainly as Mary retained her virginity before all ladies who retained theirs, so chaste and pure; therefore, fire, cease thy wrath.
This I count unto thee as a repentant act in the name of the holy Trinity.

I command unto thee, fire, to abate thy heat, by the precious blood of Jesus Christ, which he has shed for us, and our sins and transgressions.

This I count unto thee, fire, as a repentant act, in the name of God the Father, the Son, and the Holy Ghost.

Jesus of Nazareth, a king of the Jews, help [us] from this dangerous fire, and guard this land and its bounds from all epidemic and disease and pestilence.

The Magdeburg Himmelsbrief, 1783

He who labors upon Sunday is damned; therefore, I command you not to labor upon the Sunday, but go regularly to church, but do not ornament yourselves; you shall not wear false hair and not follow pride; of your riches you shall give unto the poor; share abundantly with them and believe that this letter was written by my own hand, and was published by Christ Himself; and that you do not like unto unreasoning beasts; you have six days wherein to do all your work, but the seventh you shall keep holy; if you do not then I will send war, hunger, pestilence and sorrow among you and shall punish you with many plagues.

Also, I command you every one, whether he be young or old, small or great, that you never work late on Saturday; rather that you repent of your sins that they may be forgiven; lay up neither silver or gold; follow not after the lusts of the flesh and of matter; remember that I have made you and can destroy you, rejoice not that your neighbor is poor, have the more patience -- or charity -- with him that it may be well with you; you children honor father and mother, so that it may be well with you on earth; he who does not believe this and keep it, is damned and lost; I, Jesus, have written this with my own hand; he who denies it and ridicules it, that same person shall have no help to expect from me; whoever has this letter and does not publish it, he is accursed from the Christian church; and if your sins were as large again, if you repent and are sorry they shall be forgiven you; whoever does not believe it shall die and be punished in hell; also, I shall ask about your sins at the judgment day, where you then must answer; and that same person who carries this letter with him, or has it in his house, he shall not be harmed by thunder storms, he shall be safe from fire and water and whoever publishes it to the children of mankind, he shall have his reward and shall have a happy departure from out of this world; keep my command that I have sent you by my angel. I truly God, of Heaven's Throne, God's and Mary's Son. Amen.²

Letter of Protection (William Wilson Beissel)
From *Powwow Power* pp 48-49

IN THE NAME of God the Father, the Son, and the Holy Ghost. As Christ stopped at the Mount of Olives, all guns shall stop. Whoever carries this letter with him, he shall not be damaged through the enemy's guns or weapons. God will give him strength that he may not fear robbers and murderers, nor guns, pistols, swords; muskets shall not hurt him, through the command of the angel Michael, in the name of the Father, the Son, and Holy Ghost. God [is] with me.

Whoever carries this letter with him, he shall be protected against all danger and he who does not believe in it may copy it and tie it tight to the neck of a dog and shoot at him, and he will see that it is true.

Whoever has this letter; he shall not be taken prisoner, nor wounded by the enemy. Amen. As true as it is that Jesus Christ died and ascended to heaven, and suffered on earth, he shall not be shot, but shall stand unhurt, and adjure all guns and weapons on earth, by the living God the Father, the Son and Holy Ghost. I pray in the name of Christ's blood that no ball shall hit me, be it of gold or silver [or any other substance], but that God in Heaven may deliver me of all sins, in the name of the Father, the Son, and Holy Ghost.

This letter fell from Heaven, and was found at Holstein's in 1724. It was written in gold letters, and moved over the baptism of

---

2   Below is a more 'artistic' version of the Magdeburg Brief in German. This version is the author's rendition of an older-style brief.

Madaginery, and when they tried to seize it, it disappeared until 1791, that everybody may copy it and communicate it to the world. There was further written in it: "Whosoever works on Sunday, he shall be condemned. You shall not work on Sunday but go to Church, and give the poor of your wealth, for you shall not be like the unreasoning animals. I command you six days you shall listen to the word of God; if you do not do so, I will punish you with hard times, epidemics, and war. I command you that you shall not work too late on Saturdays. Be you rich or poor, you shall pray for your sins, that they may be forgiven. Do not swear by His name; do not fear the intrigues of men; sure as fast as I created you, so fast I can crush you. Also, be not false with your tongue; respect father and mother; do not bear false testimony against your neighbor, and I will give you health and peace. But he who does not do so, or does not believe in this shall be left by me, and shall not have happiness or blessing. If you do not convert yourself, you certainly will be punished at the Day of Judgment for what you cannot account for your sins. Whoever has this letter in his house, no lightning shall strike it. All women who carry this letter with them shall bring forth living fruit. Keep my commandments which I sent to you through my angel in the name of Jesus. Amen.

†

† Ein Brief †

So von Gott selbsten geschrieben und zu Magdeburg
niedergelassen worden ist.

Er war mit Goldenen Buschtaben geschrieben, und von GOTT durch einen Engel gesant worden; wer ihn abschreiben will dem soll man ihm geben, wer ihn verachtet, von dem weicht

der Herr.

Wer am Sontag arbeitet der is verflucht. Demnach verbiete ich, dasz ich am Sontag nicht abeitet, sondern andechtig in die Kirche geht; aber euer Augesicht; nicht schmueket ihr sollt nicht fremdes Haar tragen und nicht Hoffart treiben; von eurem Reichthum sollt ihr den Armen geben, reichlich mittheilen, und glauben, dasz dieszer Brief mit meiner eigenen Hand geschrieben, und von Christo selbsten ausgesandt sey und das ihr nicht thut, wie das unvernuestige Vieh: ihr habt Sechs Tage in der Woche, darin sollt ihr eure Arbeit verichten, aber den 7benden (nemlich den Sontag) sollt ihr heiligen: werdet ihr das nicht tun, so will ich Krieg, Hunger, Pestilenz und Theuring under euch schicken, und euch mit vielen Plagen strafen. Auch gebiet ich euch, einem Jeden, es sey were es wolle, Jung oder Alt, Klein oder Grosz, dasz ihr am Samstag nicht spaet arbeitet, sondern ihr sollt eure Suenden bereuen, auf dasz sie euch moegen vergeben werden. Begehret auch nicht Silber oder Gold, treibet nicht Bosheit: meidet des Fleisches Lust und Begierden; dankt dasz ich euch gemacht habe under wieder zereheitern kan Freuet euch nicht wann euer Nachbar arm ist, habe vielmehr mitleiden mit ihm, so wirds euch wohl gehen. Ihr Kinder ehret Vater und Mutter, so wirds euch wohl gehen auf Erden. Wer dieses nicht glaubt noch haelt, der ist verdammt und verloren. In Jesus habe die es selbsten mit meiner eigenen Hand geschrieben, wer es widerspricht und mich laestert, derselbe Mensch soll keine Huelfe von mir zu gewarten haben; wer den Brief hat und ihn nicht offenbaret, der ist verflucht von der christenlichen Kirche, und meiner Allmacht: sondern man soll ihn jedermann geben der der ihn begehret. Und wenn euer Suenden noch so grosz waeren, sollen sie euch, wo ihr herzlich Reu und leid habt, doch vergeben werden. Wer es nicht glaubet der soll sterben und in der Hoelle gepeiniget werden, und ich werde euch am Jungsten Tage fragen um eurer Suenden willen, da ihr mir dann antworten muesset. Und derjenige Mensch so diesen Brief bey sich traegt, oder in seinem Hause hat dem kein Donnerwetter Schaden zufuegen, er wird fuer Feuer und Wasser sicher sein; und wer ihn offenbaret vor den Menschenkindern, der wird seinen Lohn haben, und froehliche Abscheiden aus dieser Welt empfange.

Haltet meinen Befehl den ich euch durch meinen Engel gesand habe. Ich wahrer GOTT vom Himmels-Thron, GOTTES und Marien Sohn. Amen.

Dieses ist geschehen zu Magdeburg, im Jahr 1783.

What about "Hex Signs"?

When it comes to "foreign cultures" (and to some extent Pennsylvania German culture falls into this category), there is a level of assumption that conflates a handful of popular images and makes them fit the whole. Today this phenomenon is usually called "stereotyping". The 1950's marked the beginning of tapping into Pennsylvania Dutch culture as a tourist industry. Barn stars (i.e., "hex" signs), Amish and Old Order Mennonites, shoo-fly pie, the Moravian Star, etc., and really atrocious "ferhooled" English somehow get squashed into the same "Dutchy" mold. Find an old dinner mat from a tourist-trap restaurant of that era, and you will see it decorated with bizarre cartoon images of grinning, gnome-like Amishmen along side of barns and hex signs (among other things). On a personal level, this author finds those images to be as offensive as some people do the old postcards depicting equally cartoony little black children on fence rails happily munching down on slabs of watermelon. Of course, all of these things are in the eyes of the beholder, and perhaps some of us just need to develop a sense of humor. Those popular images haven't changed very much.

The Hex Grex

THE PROBLEM OF THE BARN STAR: when it comes to Braucherei, here's the problem with these designs – they have *nothing* to do with it. A more diplomatic phrasing would have been "*almost* nothing," but that would be fudging the truth. The reason *why* any of this is problematic is because there are a good many who *want* this folk art to be something "witchy" or occultish. To deny that sort of meaning or purpose to the barn star is something of a killjoy for those hankering for such meanings. Because these designs are abstract and geometrical it would seem that they *ought* to have an esoteric purpose. The thought that they really do mean nothing in themselves is a deeply frustrating notion for some. Popular occultism and the Witchcraft (Wicca) subculture have latched onto the barn star and have been instrumental in pushing the 'hex'-sign-as-talisman agenda in recent years. By calling these figures "barn stars" we remove a huge level of misinformation straight off the top, as the word "hex" is an unbelievably loaded term.

On page 28 of Wallace Nutting's *Pennsylvania Beautiful* is the following sentence:

> Candor compels the admission that these cabalistic marks on barns were a simpler and more humane measure against Witches than those which were adopted in New England.

Nutting has been credited as having coined the term "hexefoos" in relation to the barn star. It was from there that the conflation of "cabalistic marks" with the folk art may have had their origin. For those familiar with real Kabbalah, these designs are anything but. Of course, when it comes to stereotyping, any "star" shape fits that bill.

Don Yoder and Tom Graves' work *Hex Signs: Pennsylvania Dutch Barn Symbols and Their Meaning* is just about the last word on this subject. After having interviewed many barn sign painters and done a thorough analysis of the literature, Yoder and Graves condense their analysis of the barn star question in the chapter "Do Hex Signs Have Deeper Meaning?" Directly after having dismissed the notion that farmers painted these signs as talismans they observe:

> That is not to say that these farmers did nothing to keep Witches away or to protect themselves and their horses and cattle from disease or evil influence. These protective measures were done in private, however, and were not visible. Some of the same geometric designs were used, but the context was completely different.
>
> What gives meaning to the motifs was not the design itself, but the context in which it is used. It is the context of being used in a ritualistic way and placed in prescribed locations that gives a magical meaning to a certain geometric pattern. And it is the context of publically displaying geometric

designs for all to see that gives these designs meaning as ethnic symbolism. Meaning is something that can only be imparted through context and use. So, are hex signs actually *hex* signs? Yes, but not on barns.[1]

As signs of ethnicity, the barn stars are unparalleled. Yoder and Graves refer to barn stars within *this context* as "ethnicity markers." They cite folk art scholar John Joseph Stoudt (1911 – 1981) who did believe that the designs have meaning, but that meaning is wholly outside of the realm of Witchcraft, an interpretation that he found "slanderous."

> Stoudt felt that if the designs were really "hex" marks, then why should they appear on Bible covers, tombstones, and other "potent" religious artifacts that certainly needed no protection against Witches? He found in the signs not a pagan meaning, but rather a Christian one. Though his symbolist theory has been attacked as forced – certainly not every hex sign can possibly represent his "divine lily" of the "Age of the Holy Spirit" – Stoudt was not entirely alone in his thinking.[2]

The Christian meaning of the most ubiquitous of signs, being the six lobed (or pointed) 'star', is explored by Craig Benner in his pamphlet the *Low Dutch Morning Star*. Here he traces the history of this figure through drawings and photographs of churches, crypts, and ossuaries. In the foreword he states that

> The design is very old, but the interpretation as a monogram of Christ started about 1,900 years ago.
>
> The Coptic or Egyptian Christians first used the design to symbolize the resurrection of Christ. In ancient Egypt resurrection in the afterlife was associated with Osiris. Several Morning Star designs can be found at the Temple of Osiris in Egypt. The Coptic Christians regarded the Morning Star as

---

1   Yoder & Graves, p. 69
2   Yoder & Graves, p.13

the monogram of Christ, much like the Chi-Rho design.³

Christianity's parent religion is Judaism. It is utterly astounding how "Dutchy" 1ˢᵗ century Jewish stone ossuaries are. These mini-coffins for the bones of the deceased display amazing similarities to boxes and dower chests painted by Pennsylvania Germans centuries later. If the six lobed 'star' is drawn out point for point, we get the *Magan David*. Benner rightly complains,

> The Morning Star design has been called a "Hex Sign" and "Flower of Life" by new age mystics and those who failed to recognize its connection to Christendom. To some the design appears to be a flower, but gravestones are engraved with both the Morning Star and flowers. Clearly, the Morning Star is a unique design. The Morning Star is the monogram of Christ.⁴

The pseudonymous Karl Herr in *Hex and Spellwork* devotes some space to the barn stars and describes a method of using these paintings within a Braucherei context. This sort of usage as described by Herr is something of a compromise on his end in order to appeal to a wider audience.⁵ The fact is a Braucher can bless *anything*. It doesn't matter what it is: houses, cars, chicken coops, barns, or even barn stars, etc. However, just because a Braucher, for whatever reason, *can* charm or bless someone's barn sign *does not mean* that the said sign is a device of Braucherei. If we take the road of the symbolist, such as Stoudt does, a case can be made for an esoteric meaning of *some* signs (the best case can be made for the six lobed Morning Stars) within certain contexts, but this meaning (if any) would be outside of the magical or prophylactic usage. This author has come across some who refer to these designs as "painted prayers" which would nuzzle them into the symbolist approach.

---

3   Benner p. 2

4   Ibid.

5   Lee Gandee does something similar in his Strange Experience, using barn star-like symbols to introduce each chapter; he also ascribes meanings mystical and prophylactic meaning to the symbols.

Preston Barba, a follower of the symbolist interpretation, took issue with the signs as being *"yuscht fer schee"* ("just for nice").

> Today we have little understanding of such things, and yet we should hold the old signs in honor because our forefathers honored them and viewed them with respect as holy signs. No, they were not yuscht fer schee. These signs were necessary to them, growing out of their hearts. And it would not hurt if we too would today view those old signs for what they were once in earlier times – signs of that mighty power that slumbers in winter, awakens in springtime, and brings new life to nature, ripens the grain and the fruit in summer – and then goes to sleep again in the winter, in an everlasting circle or ring which is again the most beautiful evidence in nature of our Lord God. And whoever does view them in this way must agree that the painted stars on our barns are pure prayers. But HEX-FEET? No! – No! – Phooey on that idea! That we can let other and more stupid people believe.[6]

These sentiments are well and lovely, but they are not easy to prove, at least not in every case. The damned word "all" usually sneaks into the picture where it is "all" or nothing. Either *all* of the symbols mean something *all* of the time, or *all* of them never do.

A barn star painter who wishes to remain anonymous informed the author that among his many professional contacts in the folk-art, *not a single one of them* either know of or assign meaning to these signs (witchy, mystical, religious, or otherwise).[7] Lester Breininger will not call them "hex signs" and neither would Milton Hill (back in the 1950's) – for them they were always "just for so," despite the remonstrations of symbolists such as Barba. Who would know better than the very artists themselves? There is a level of intellectual conceit, which suggests that such artists are either lying about the

---

6   Yoder and Graves pp 17-18

7   Of course, that's not to say that they are unaware of the popular "meanings" assigned to these designs by those catering to tourists.

signs or are misinformed.[8]

The history of these designs on buildings can be traced back to Europe only sparingly. There is some evidence that what we now call "barn stars" are much larger versions of smaller designs that appear on structures in Switzerland, Westphalia and Hessia, and also in Silesia. However, these designs are so few and scattered that it is hard to make a case for them as a wide-spread folk art. Taking these elementary figures and painting them onto the sides of barns and other farmyard out buildings seems to be an innovation of the Pennsylvania Germans. According to Yoder and Graves the barn signs appear for the first time on record around the mid 19th century. Prior to this practice, these figures were only found in miniature form on pieces of furniture and on documents such as *taufscheine* and *geburtscheine*.[9] My anonymous artist acquaintance makes the analogy of the fore-bay of the Pennsylvania German barn as being a larger version of the dower chest. Much like the dower chests, which were decorated beautifully with these folk-designs and contained a bride's bounty, so too does the fore-bay contain the treasures and bounty of the farm.[10] These immense spaces on the barns almost 'beg' for something artistic, hence the farmer's painting of the fore-bay.

The symbolists argue their point from the perspective of a sort of mystic Natural Theology, some of which we have taken a glance at in early chapters regarding the ideas of German Christian theosophists such as Jacob Boehme. *If* we extend the arguments of the symbolists into the realm of God's imminent divine energies, especially as they work through the act of Pow-Wowing *and* how

---

8   The inference being that such lying would be out of embarrassment of their culture, or superstitious protection of "inside" secrets. To ascribe misinformation to these artists is just a left-handed way of calling them unlearned bumpkins.

9   Baptismal and birth certificates

10   Private communication with the author – my source wishes to be anonymous as he is disgusted by the close associate of his folk-art with occultism. He objected to being named here as he did not want to perpetuate the association, even though this work exists to refute many misconceptions and misappropriated practices.

that Pow-Wowing is not separate from ourselves and God's creation, *then* another sort of argument can be made to link these barn stars with Braucherei. **But**, *that is a huge stretch*. The boring fact remains that the barn stars *in themselves* have nothing to do with the practice of the Braucherei.

To be a genuine barn sign painter takes a good deal of talent and technical know how. It is a folk artistic discipline all by itself, with an interesting history and pedigree in its own right. It does not need to be weighted down and burdened with the extra baggage of Pow-Wowing. Conversely, Braucherei is deep and complex enough without adding to the mix.

10: A Braucher's Pharmacopeia

The title of this chapter is a bit of a misnomer. The practice of Braucherei is not really bound up with herbalism *per se*. In times past, there was sometimes very little to distinguish the Pow-Wow doctor from the allopathic practitioner. A few country MDs and homeopaths in Dutch country were also Brauchers. Prior to the advent of antibiotics and the regulation of pharmaceuticals, there were "patent medicines." It is from the latter that we get the pejorative term "snake oil" for ineffectual remedies. Before these over the counter cure-alls came into being our ancestors had access to herbs, the only real medicines that existed. Therefore, it is not odd at all that a Braucher, at that time, would have prescribed herbal remedies for various ailments in conjunction with brauching for the illness too (they also prescribed the aforementioned patent medicines). After the strict regulation of medical practice and the production medicines, unlicensed practitioners had to curb some of their activities.

Earlier in *The Red Church* there is the admonishment that should you wish to practice Braucherei, **you make neither diagnoses nor prescriptions**. To do so is to find yourself in a world of hurt if you are caught. This has especially been the case ever since "The Hex Murder" in York, PA, back in 1929. Brauchers have found themselves on the short end of the stick ever since then, and have had to modify their activities in more ways than one. Today there are still some practitioners who will *suggest* a few herbal remedies. A few practitioners are known who sell herbs, vitamins, and various alternative health products. The latter activity is legal as they are not prescribing anything. The charges for these products are completely separate from their Braucherei practice, which has *no charge* attached. If you do happen to be a licensed medical practitioner, then of course, the above does not apply to you.

It is the object of this book to provide as much information as possible regarding the practice of traditional Braucherei in its most important phases along with 'side' disciplines such as herbalism. Herbs have been used as both remedies and amulets. The herbs listed below are a few associated with Braucherei, and can be found in most of the old Pow-Wow manuals, farming almanacs, and *hausmittel* (home remedy) books. Since most of these are very rare and long out of print, it is hoped that this compendium, such as *The Red Church* is, will be able to adequately satisfy the needs of those wishing to practice.

A further note about the herbs involved:
Through out the research to cull this sort of data, there were remedies and herbal 'prescriptions' that this author has found dangerous. Some of the ingredients in the old remedies combine herbs along with agents that we now know are poisonous. These have been omitted altogether.[1] Nothing is served by presenting them. As for the herbs that are present, please treat all herbs with respect. While they are not medicines in the currently accepted sense, they are medicinal in their action. **Consult with your physician before engaging an herbal regimen**. This is especially the case if you have a 'patient' who asks for herbal advice in addition to Brauche treatment. They need to talk with their doctors before and after seeing you. Some herbs stimulate the immune system, for example. In the case of a person with an auto-immune disorder such as Lupus, treating him or her with such herbs would be a major mistake. Other herbs have *abortifacient* action and should never be given to a woman in any stage of pregnancy. ***A thorough knowledge of an herb and all of its properties is a must before engaging its use***. Should anyone desire to employ an herb listed below, take the time to further research the plant; do not rely solely upon the information provided here. For the sake of space any enumeration of an herb's properties here is minimal.

---

1 An exception to this is the mention of herbs such as stramonium, which are presented from a historical perspective due to their importance in past use and folklore.

A second note on non-herbs in this chapter:
Within the list below you will find substances that are either not herbs or are naturally derived products, such as camphor oil and scorpion oil. Such things are included here, as they have been listed among ingredients of various remedies combined with herbs. Fruits and vegetables also make an appearance here. The Glossary in Appendix I contains any and all of the non-organic or partially organic remedies that would not be proper in a list of mostly herbs.

The herbal here is organized alphabetically by the herb's name, in the same way as the information presented in the Glossary contained in Appendix I.

One final acknowledgement:
I am highly indebted to the work of the Reverend Thomas R. Brendle. His works with Claude Unger and D.E. Lick have been invaluable. So much of this material is disappearing from common knowledge, and works such as these are usually rare and hard to get. If a person wants them badly enough, he either has to pay exhorbitant prices for copies, or go through long library hunts and multiple book loans to get this knowledge. My hope for *The Red Church* is that I have pulled together enough quality, scholarly sources that this information no longer remains obscure – so that you, the seeker, will have a large amount of this footwork already done for you within these pages. For those who wish to go further, please do yourselves a great favor and get these old books on loan. They will be well worth the effort. Hopefully one day these older sources will be reprinted and easily available to all who want them. Good hunting!

AGRIMONY (*Agrimonia eupatoria*): *Kleiner Odermennig*, (German), *Otermenig* (German: Albertus), *Oderminnich* (dialect). Agrimony is virtually an all purpose herb in German folk medicine. It is a hepatic, diuretic, expectorant, alterative, astringent, tonic, vulnerary, vermifuge, and febrifuge. It has been used for gallstones, dog bites (hydrophobia or rabies), intestinal worms, skin disease (rotlaufe), inflammation, bed wetting, and diarrhea. An unguent of agrimony is good for gout and varicose veins. As an expectorant is helps clear the lungs and is useful during influenza. For the latter use, it is best to seek out agrimony as homeopathic remedy. Odermennig, therefore, also makes an excellent ingredient in any *blutreiningungsmittel* (blood purifier). As a strong tea frequently taken, it is good for dissolving blockages in the kidneys and liver. One of its other virtues is that it makes a good amulet against hexerei and Witch-induced hauntings.

ANGELICA (*Angelica archangelica*; *Angelica officinalis*): *Angelika* (Sauer). Parts used: mainly the roots, leaves, and seeds. The root is best dug up in the fall where as the whole herb is best harvested in June. Angelica has the following properties: expectorant, carminative, stimulant, diaphoretic, stomachic, tonic, and vermifuge. Angelica is also an emmenagogue. It has been used for colds, coughs, pleurisy, gas ("wind"), colic, rheumatism, and diseases of the urinary organs. *Diabetics should not take Angelica.* Sauer suggests that the root ought to be extirpated when the sun is in Gemini and the moon is passing into the sign of Cancer. During seasons of infectious disease (such as influenza), Sauer advises that one carries the root in his mouth and chews on it while in public places in order to stave off infection. As a deterrent to the forces of Witchcraft Sauer gives the following formulation (pp 40-41): take a handful of angelica leaves, devil's bit, the top sprigs of St. John's Wort, periwinkle, sanicle, Venus's goldilocks (*polytrichum juniperum*), and mugwort. Chop all of the ingredients finely and place into a pewter flask with 2 quarts of spring water and a quart of white wine. Bring to a boil via double-boiler (the flask in a pot). When the elixir is cool, open the flask and strain. Administer to the bewitched six tablespoons per dose once in the morning and once in the evening.

BEETS (White and Red): Turnip, White Beet (*Brassica Rapa*), *Rübe* (German), *Rieb* (dialect); Red Beet (*Beta vulgaris*) *Rotrieb* (dialect). **Turnips**: Sauer does not recommend eating raw turnips as they will "chill" a "feeble stomach." A decoction of turnip can be used for cough – Sauer directs that rock candy can be added. For hemorrhoids: decoct chopped turnips in milk until the pieces are soft enough to spread. Spread the mass on a thin cloth in order to make a plaster for the piles. Oil of the seed is supposed to be good for pains after child birth. For a kidney cleanser: drink warm several cups of the decoction throughout the day. **Red beets**: Culpepper indicates that red beets are effective in combating headache. However, beets find their greatest use in blutreinigungsmittel formulae; the juice all by itself is sufficient as a blood purifier. Sauer writes that the fresh leaves of the beet, when pressed against the cheeks can relieve facial neuralgia. The juice can be used as a snuff for sinus problems and tinnitus.

BIRCH (*Betula*): *Birke* (German), *Barricke* (dialect). There are two varieties of birch, the European and the American. Both are antilithic in their action and are good for removing "gravel" in the kidneys and bladder. Sauer recommends birch wine for kidney gravel, gout, and rheumatism. A decoction of the leaves and bark is good vulnerary for external lesions and sores. Oil of birch, according to Mrs. M. Grieve is useful in treating eczema. This author thinks that *birch soap* would be very healthful for such skin conditions. The sap of birch induces urine production (diuretic); while the inner bark is astringent and is very good for intermittent fevers or malarial agues.

BLESSED THISTLE (*Cnicus Benedictus*): *Benedikt* (German), *Gordebenedikt* ("Garden Benedict:" dialect); also called Holy Thistle, and *Carbenia benedicta*. The whole herb is used in the making of medicinal; the flowering tops are collected in July. According to

Culpepper's astrological sympathies, Blessed Thistle is ruled by Mars under Aries, making this a plant of "heat" and dryness, especially good for "rheums" and congestion in the head. Its properties and actions: tonic, stimulant, diaphoretic, emetic, and emmenagogue. Mrs. Grieve gives a formulation of 1 oz dried herb to 1 pint boiling water, taken in wineglass doses for intermittent fever. Blessed Thistle has also been used for vertigo, dizziness, tetters, ringworm, boils, itch, sores, and dropsy. For all of the above, a decoction would suffice. As used in the German hausmitteln, Blessed Thistle is listed among blood purifiers or blutreinigungsmitteln; it is also a vermifuge to expel intestinal worms. A salve of the herb is good for sores. The distilled water of Blessed Thistle is good for headache and "putrid" fevers.

BURDOCK (*Arctium minus*): *Klette* ("Burs:" German), *Gleddegraut* (Bur herb: dialect), *Kletten* (Sauer). According to Sauer burdock is a diuretic, diaphoretic, and facilitates breathing and gives relief from coughing in farm animals. The chopped up roots are a good vulnerary and can cleans sores and wounds. A salve of the roots can be made for the treatment of burns. When decocted in red wine, burdock can be administered for quartan ague (see FIEWER). For Mrs. Grieve burdock is a blood purifier and alterative, being in the seed and the root (in addition to the other properties cited by Sauer). When used with yellow dock and sarsaparilla, it can be used in the treatment of eczema. The tea from the leaves is good for indigestion. The bruised leaves are used as a wrap for wounds and sores, making the herb a vulnerary. The candied root of burdock has been used for generations in the pleasant treatment for cough. In its more sympathetic uses, it is said that to wear the leaves in a hat can cure a headache, while wearing pieces of the root strung together as a necklace can cure various ailments. A blutreinigungsmitteln formula cited by Lick and Unger:

> Take one quart of ale, put into it nine pieces of burdock root and nine pieces of plantain root, and after dark bury the vessel under the eaves of the house. Take it up next morning and drink.

A decoction of burdock is useful for boils, rheumatism, and scurvy. As a stomachic, use an infusion of the seeds; while a tincture of the seeds is useful for skin conditions.

CHAMOMILE (*Anthemis nobilis*): *Kamille* (German, same in dialect). There are two varieties of chamomile: the German (*Matricaria chamomilla*) and the Roman or "common" (*Anthemis nobilis*). The properties of chamomile make it useful for treatment of mild nervous conditions, and as an antispasmodic and anodyne. The herb is usually administered in the form of a tea of its flowers. Chamomile has also found use as a carminative and vulnerary. Oil of chamomile is good for baby colic when rubbed on the stomach. Sauer recommends the oil for treatment of ague. The following is his formulation for oil of chamomile:

> A find oil of chamomile can be prepared when one takes olive oil and adds chamomile flowers; the more flowers, the stronger it becomes. After it stood four to six weeks in the sun, strain it through a clean cloth, press it well and store away…

Other German names for chamomile are *ackerhundskamille* and *deutscherkamille* (being *Matricaria*).

CAMPHOR OIL (*Cinnamonum camphora*): *Campher* (Sauer). The use of camphor was rather popular at one time. Modern products such as "Vicks" are largely based upon a camphor formulation. *It has abortifacient properties and ought not to be used by pregnant women.* It is a strong vermifuge, but can also be poisonous. Sauer recommends camphor brandy as a liniment for sprains and wounds. His formula for this is simply dissolving as much camphor into double distilled brandy as the liquid will hold. The liquor can be applied directly to the sprain, or a compress made. Its other uses include treatments for nervousness, rheumatism, inflammation, and bronchitis.

CELANDINE (*Chelidonium majus*): *Schellegraut* (dialect). There are two varieties of celandine: the Greater (*Chelidonium majus*) and the Minor (*Ranunculus ficaria*). The minor celandine can be made into a salve for hemorrhoids. The juice of the greater celandine when mixed with wine and vinegar is a good treatment for eczema and poison ivy. A distilled water of celandine is used to treat open sores and cancers; while equally healing is a salve made from the fried stalks for boils and sores. The greater celandine has alterative, diuretic, and purgative properties, and has found use in the treatment of jaundice, and scrofula. The juice is said to also be efficacious in the removal of warts; and when used as a hepatic an infusion of 1 oz dried herb to one pint of boiling water is administered.

CHICKWEED (*Stellaria media*): *Vogelmiere* (German), *Hinkeldarem* ("Chicken bowels:" dialect). The whole herb of chickweed is used; it is best collected in the months of May, June, and July. According Culpepper, chickweed is under the dominion of the Moon, and its nature is cold and moist. Chickweed is a demulcent, refrigerant, laxative, and vulnerary. Decocted chickweed when placed in a muslin bag is a poultice for external abscesses; the water from the decoction is a good wash for the wound. If the plant is chopped and then fried in lard or Crisco, it makes a soothing, cool unguent for hemorrhoids and sores. Chickweed is a tasty addition to salads; over indulgence in the plant can trigger its laxative properties (as this author found out by accident). Distilled chickweed water has been used to treat agues as well as tuberculosis; the tea or water of chickweed has been employed in dieting to loose weight. Sauer says that fresh chickweed laid upon lactating breasts will draw out unwanted milk.

CLOVES (*Dianthus caryophyllata*, also: *Syzygium aromatic*, and *Eugenia caryophyllata*): *Gewürznelke* (German), *Negelin*, *Gwaersnegelin* ("Little nails," "spicy little nails:" dialect)
At one time cloves were used in the same way smelling salts are today. The most useful property of cloves tends to be its stomachic action, making it good for nausea and diarrhea. The oil has also

been used for dizziness, palpitations, and as an antidepressive (of sorts).

COLTSFOOT (*Tussilago farfara*): *Huflattuich* (German), *Hutschefuss* (dialect); it is also known by the English name "coughwort". Coltsfoot has long been known for its demulcent and expectorant properties. It was smoked in the same manner as tobacco, often mixed with horehound herb as a remedy for asthma. A strong decoction of coltsfoot is a good remedy for asthma, bronchitis, and other breathing problems. Take 1 oz of leaves to one quart of water and reduce to 1 pint. The decoction can be sweetened with honey, or made into a more syrupy texture by stirring in white rock candy into the hot liquid until it thickens. A tea will have the same properties, but perhaps in a lesser way than a decoction.

COMFREY (*Symphytum officinale*): *Wallwurtz* (Sauer), Wallwort. The roots of comfrey are used medicinally. Comfrey is used as a demulcent, astringent, expectorant, and vulnerary. Hemorrhages, ruptures, and wounds have all been treated with decoctions of comfrey. The decoction has also been used for treating women with heavy periods. The distilled oil of comfrey treats syphilitic sores, while the distilled water of the same will treat internal and external injuries. The water can be employed as a compress for wounds, abscesses, cracked skin, etc. The leaves also have medicinal properties and are used as a vulnerary. The root can be decocted in either water or wine: 2 teaspoons root to 1 cup water or wine; take a teacupful one to two times per day.

CORIANDER (*Coriander sativum*): *Koriander* (German), *Kariander* (dialect). Coriander is best used as a carminative. It has also been used as a stomachic and a stimulant. Candied coriander and coriander vinegar have been used to these ends.

COXCOMB (*Rhinanthus Crista-galli*): Cocks Comb, also known as Yellow Rattle. Coxcomb (the spelling used by English edition of *Egyptian Secrets*) is a semi-parasitic plant that has astringent and tonic properties. It has been used to treat coughs as well as "dim" eyesight. An eyebath can be made by taking 1 oz of the herb to 1 pint of boiling water.

DANDELION (*Taraxacum officinale*): *Kulblume* (German), *Bedseecher* or *Pissbett* ("bed pisser:" dialect), *Bitterselaat* (bitter salad: dialect). The folk name for dandelion comes from the belief that if children smell the flowers they will wet the bed in their sleep that evening. Dandelion is an excellent springtime tonic and forms part of many traditional blutreinigungsmittel formulae. It has hepatic action and works to clean the blood through the cleaning of that organ. It is also is used as a tonic. A decoction of 2 oz of the herb/root to 1 quart of water reduced to a pint: this is a treatment for scurvy, scrofula, eczema, and pimples. For these conditions a ½ cup is taken every three hours. A tea of dandelion root is good for all hepatic concerns; the tea is also said to be good for fever. Dandelion combines nicely with horseradish for the treatment of jaundice. The leaves are best in the spring before the flowering begins. It is traditional for dandelion to be gathered on "Green Thursday" (Maundy Thursday). A wine made from the flowers is a good liver tonic.

DEVIL'S BIT (*Scabiosa succisa*): *Abbiss* (Sauer); *Deifelbiss* or *Deifelsabbisswarzel* (dialect). It is said that this herb got its name from the shape of its root, which looks as if a bit was taken from it; accordingly, it was the devil himself who was said to have taken the bite in a fit of anger. According to William Woys Weaver in his commentary on devil's bit:

> It has been speculated that one of the reasons the Pennsylvania Germans had such a low rate of heart attack years ago was their frequent use of devil's bit in herbal teas, as devil's bit is extremely active in dissolving clots in the blood.

Devil's bit it a blood purifier, diaphoretic, demulcent, vermifuge, and febrifuge. M. Grieve indicates that the whole herb is best collected and dried in September. The leaves have been used to treat epilepsy ("falling evil") and can be used as a vulnerary in treating puncture and stab wounds. The distilled water of devil's bit is more specifically used for epilepsy, as well as being used for congestion, coughing, and pleurisy. Sauer gives a recipe for preparing devil's bit as a preventative medicinal when contagious disease is about: 1 whole plant of devil's bit (root also) chopped fine; 2 handfuls of scabious leaves (*Knautia arvensis*), and a handful of the leaves and root of tormentil and blessed thistle. All of these are dried and ground to powder. Add to this a handful of coarsely ground juniper berries and 1 oz of ground masterwort. Place all in a glass jar large enough to hold the mix in addition to the brandy that will cover the whole mass. Seal the jar and let it stand in sunlight. Sauer's dosage is 1 tablespoon every morning. William Woys Weaver indicates that the extract needed here is the clear liquid that forms on top of the mix.

DRAGON'S BLOOD: is a product of the Mediterranean tree *Dracaena Draco*. A red resin is exuded from the leaves and bark when cut. It is used in the making of varnish, dye, and incense. Dragon's Blood is also useful in medicine, where it can be used in a wash for wounds or other lesions. Internally it has been used to stop hemorrhaging, and for angina.

ELDER [BERRY] (*Sambucus*): *Holunder* (German), *Hollerbeera* (dialect); also *Schwartsholler* (American Elder: *Sambucus canadensis*). The elder tree or bush has a long history of use and 'superstition' surrounding itself. Many of the latter are genuinely old in a pagan sense and account for the names of this plant being *Hylde Moer* (Danish: Elder Mother), Dame Elder, and Dame Holle. It was (and still is) believed in many places that to cut down an elder without the tree's permission invited disaster. It was the tree of fairies, and as such was a gate to their world. The lore of "fairies" is complicated by the varying streams of mythology that conflate different types of spirits under the heading of "fairy." Some of these spirits are simply nature elementals; others are the spirits of the dead, the ancestors themselves. The Elder Mother is seen by some heathen reconstructionists as a deity of the otherworld and perhaps even the Witch Queen (or at least *a* Witch queen). Sauer suggests that the young sprouts of elder, which look like asparagus, be cooked with spinach, making a cooked salad good as a laxative and emetic. Elderberry vinegar is good for cutting phlegm, and has diaphoretic action making it useful in the treatment of fevers. Elder blossom water and camphor brandy when laid on the joints treats rheumatism and St. Anthony's fire. A tea of the blossoms (*hollerblummatee*) is a diaphoretic. The inner bark juice when collected in the fall will cut phlegm.

An electuary of the berries is good against "all poisons, swellings, dropsies" (Sauer, p130). A Tyrol sympathetic use of the green branches is to place them into coffins with the newly dead in order to protect the corpses from being possessed by evil spirits, according to M. Grieve. The bark of elder is a powerful purgative. Elderberry wine is an excellent treatment for many ailments. When heated up and drank it is good for sore throats and catarrh, colds and asthma. A rob of the juice/berries thickened with sugar creates a cordial for colds and coughs being: five pounds of crushed berries to 1 lb of sugar cooked down to a syrup. The dose is 1 – 2 tablespoons mixed into a glass of hot water. When the green inner bark is fried in lard, it makes a salve for skin diseases.

ELECAMPANE (*Inula helenium*): *Alant* (German), *Aland wurzel* (German: Sauer) *Olandswartzel* (Holland root: dialect); also called "elf dock" or "elf wort". The parts used are the rootstock and the roots. Elecampane is a diuretic, tonic, diaphoretic, expectorant, alterative, antiseptic, astringent, and stimulant. A decoction of the root is good for animals with skin diseases. It is also used in the treatment of coughs and bronchitis. Syrup made from the powdered root treats "wind"; where as a decoction of the root in wine is a vermifuge and also used for cramps, gout, sciatica, rheumatism and other joint pain. This drink was also believed to protect one from contagious diseases such as influenza. The root preserved in sugar was used as an expectorant and to easy breathing. Lick and Unger give the following formula for tuberculosis:

> One handful each of elecampane, dogwood bark, wild cherry bark, and hops, added to two quarts of water and boiled down to one quart. Add one pound of sugar and boil down to a pint. Take several teaspoons every day.

FENNEL (*Foeniculum vulgare*): *Fenchel* (German), *Fenichel* (dialect). The seeds are used in the treatment of colic. Fennel tea is a carminative and stomachic, while eating the seeds (especially when roasted) will have the same effect. Distilled fennel water can be used as an eye-wash. Sauer suggests that this water is mixed with white vitriol (this author does not recommend that). A decoction of fennel leaves is a good stomachic and also useful for the kidneys. If fennel seed and sage are boiled in milk with added sugar, it makes a good morning time drink for sore throat (Sauer).

FERNS (*Polypodiaceae*): *Farn* (German), *Wilde farns* (dialect). The roots of ferns are best harvested in October and November. Fern is an alterative, tonic, expectorant, demulcent, cholagogue, purgative and a mild laxative. A decoction of the rootstock is good for intestinal complaints. Boil the rootstock until it becomes syrupy. Take 2 – 8 tablespoons three to four times per day. Be careful if wild crafting: the fern *Dryopteris filixmas* can cause blindness and death.

GARLIC (*Allium sativum*): *Knoblauch* (German), *Gnowwelloch* (dialect). The benefits and uses of garlic are so well known today that it seems almost redundant to repeat these attributes. There are, perhaps, a few unknown preparations and uses that here. Among these is the alterative of eating garlic to get its healthful benefits: it was the practice of some to place garlic in their shoes in order to absorb garlic's beneficial properties through the soles of their feet. If two wild garlic bulbs are dissolved into ½ pint of boiling honey, it makes good syrup for coughs and bronchitis (Grieve). Another way of doing this is to boil 1 lb of sliced fresh garlic in 1 quart of water; let this stand overnight and then add sugar until syrup forms. Vinegar and honey can be added to the syrup. A poultice of garlic mixed with bran or oatmeal and laid upon the abdomen for bowel inflammation (Sauer).

GENTIAN (*Gentianaceae*): *Enzian* (German – used by Albertus); *Entzian-Wurtzel* (Sauer); parts used: rhizome and roots. Gentian's uses: stomachic, vermifuge, hepatic, diuretic, bitter-tonic, febrifuge, emmenagogue, and anthelmintic. Mrs. Grieve suggests that equal parts of gentian and tormentil are mixed for treatment of intermittent fever.

GINGER, Wild (*Asarum canadense*): *Haselwurz* (German), *Hasselwatzel*, or *Hasselwortsel* (dialect). Ginger is good for a "cold stomachic" according to Sauer. Ginger tea is most excellent in treating nausea and indigestion. Ginger candy makes a tasty stomachic. A slight variation on a recipe for this candy (due to the archaic weight measures in the original): 3 tablespoons of powdered ginger, powdered lemon rinds, ½ tablespoon of cinnamon and nutmeg, ½ teaspoon of cloves and mace, 2 lbs of sugar. Mix the sugar with rosewater until it is moist, and then heat it over a slow flame. As the sugar liquefies, mix in the powders.

GROUND IVY: (Nepeta Hederacea): *Grunderman* (German), *Grundelreewe* ("Poison vine:" dialect). The whole herb is used. Ground ivy is a diuretic, astringent, vermifuge, hepatic, tonic, and stimulant. May is the optimal month for harvesting ground ivy. The powdered leave can be used as a snuff for catarrh, also the freshly expressed juice too. The hot steam of a decoction of ground ivy funneled into the ear is a remedy for tinnitus. When the plant is decocted in wine "it provoketh a powerful piss" as some of the old-timers liked to phrase it.

HOREHOUND (*Marrubium vulgare*): *Andorn* (German), *Aadorn*, *Eedann* (dialect). There are two varieties of horehound being the white and the black. The former is *Marrubium vulgare*, and the latter is *Marrubium nigrum*. One of its German names is *Lungenkraut* (lung herb) which is also used for the herb *pulmonaria officinale*. Horehound is a well known remedy for coughs and congestions. The herb can be administered as a tea, syrup, or candy. To make syrup, make as a decoction and add sugar until the liquid thickens. A candy would cook longer than syrup, with more sugar added, and then it would be poured out into a pan to cool.

HORSERADISH (*Radicula armoracia* or *Cochlearia armoracia*): *Meerrettich* (German), *Mehrreddich* (dialect). Horseradish is a stimulant, aperient, rubefacient, diuretic, antiseptic, and an antilithic. Horseradish is good in helping to remove stones and "gravel" in the kidneys and bladder. Because of its diuretic properties is can be used to treat dropsy. Horseradish vinegar is very good for coughs, and a poultice of horseradish can be applied to rheumatic joints. Mehrreddich is often a component in the old blutreinigungsmittel formulae.

HORSETAIL (*Equisetum arvense*): *Schaftheu* ("Sheep tea:" German), *Schof tee* (dialect)
Geilsschwanzgraut ("Horse tail herb:" dialect); also known as shave grass. A tea of horsetail can be used for wounds, lesions, or sores in the mouth and throat. The tea can also be used for urinary tract illnesses: 2 teaspoons herb to ½ cup of water; take one cup daily. Horsetail ought to not be used in excess as it can lead to poisoning. Sauer recommends the distilled water of horsetail for "blood-spitting" and for healing "injured intestines, liver, kidneys, and bladder."

JUNIPER [BERRY] (*Juniperus communis*): *Wacholder* (German, same in dialect); fruit is *wacholderbeera*. During times when contagious disease would be making the rounds, fumigations (incense) of juniper berries and wood would be used to cleanse the atmosphere of the home. Oil of juniper is used as a diuretic, stomachic, and carminative. It is used in kidney and bladder complaints, dropsy, and is powerful in breaking up phlegm. For colic a salve of juniper oil, nutmeg oil, wormwood oil, butter, and beeswax is recommended by Sauer. For a more powerful diuretic effect, juniper oil is added to the juice of violets, and has the benefit of removing "gravel," making it an antilithic as well.

LUNGWORT (*Pulmonaria officinalis*): *Lungenkraut* (German), *Lungegraut* (dialect)
Lungwort has been used primarily in the treatment of tuberculosis. It is best gathered in July. Lungwort has a dry and cool nature, according to the old reckoning. It is designated as a vulnerary due to its use to treat wounds and lesions of the lungs. It also has a hepatic action and is able to remove "blockages" of the liver. Sauer gives a recipe for the treatment of the "chest, lungs, and viscera": 2 handfuls of lungwort decocted in 2 quarts of wine with an equal amount of water in a covered vessel; this is boiled down to 1 pint and strained. The dosage Sauer gives is 2 tablespoons (½ gill) morning and evening for tuberculosis. Syrup of lungwort has also been employed in the treatment of consumption. Mrs. Grieve suggests a tea of lungwort for lung inflammations: 1 teaspoon of the dried herb to 1 cup of boiling water; several cups of this tea can be consumed many times throughout the day.

MAGIC BALSAM: Mention of the "magic balsam" occurs in Egyptian Secrets. This author assumes it to be Balsam of Gilead (*Commiphora Opobalsammum*), which is native to neither Europe nor America. "Albertus" includes a few ingredients in Egyptian Secrets that would have been exotic to the common folk (or, at the very least, not easily secured). Balsam of Gilead has expectorant and stimulant properties, with specific use for urinary complaints.

MARIGOLD (*Calendula officinalis*): *Samtblume* (German), *Schtinckros* ("Stink rose:" dialect). Per Culpepper's astrological sympathies, marigold is ruled by the Sun under the sign of Leo. Its sunny nature makes it very useful as a stimulant. It is also an antispasmodic, aperient, cholagogue, diaphoretic, and vulnerary. A decoction of the leaves and flowers can loosen phlegm in the chest.

As a salve, marigold is soothing and healing for wounds, bites, stings, and varicose veins. The salve can be prepared by taking a teaspoon of the fresh juice and mixing it into 1 oz of melted lard or Crisco.

MASTERWORT (*Imperatoria ostruthium*): *Meisterwurz* (German), *Meeschderwarzel* (dialect)
The medicinal value of masterwort is held in the root, which is a stimulant, antispasmodic, diaphoretic, vermifuge, vulnerary, emmenagogue, febrifuge, and carminative. It has been used for asthma relief, menstrual complaints, dyspepsia, dropsy, and gout. A decoction of the root in wine is used for congestion. Masterwort has a sharp, hot, bitter taste. Culpepper suggests that a distilled water of masterwort is a more palatable way to take the herb. According to William Woys Weaver's commentary on masterwort in *Sauer's Herbal Cures*, masterwort is a "sexual elixir" for barren and impotent people. Sauer writes that it is useful against contagion, and that the distilled water of masterwort is good for female cramping when taken in tablespoons at a time. When made into a salve, it is a treatment for ringworm. The tincture has been used to treat quartan ague.

MOSS (*Polytrichaceae* and *Bryaceae*): *Moos* (German), *Buschmoos*, *Buschwawsem* (woodland moss: dialect). There are many different kinds of mosses. Sauer writes on Oak Moss or *Everinia prunastri*, also called *baummoss*. When this moss is boiled in water or red wine, it is a remedy for diarrhea or "bloody flux" as Sauer calls it. The decoction of moss is also a preventative against premature birth. When the moss is decocted in white wine it is used in strengthening the teeth and for rinsing swollen gums or an inflamed uvula. The American club moss called *Lycopodium* is used as a diuretic for dropsy, and also for diarrhea and dysentery (as with Oak Moss).

MOUSE EAR (*Hieracium Pilosella*): Hawkweed. Mouse ear has been used in the treatment of asthma and tuberculosis. It is a diaphoretic, tonic, and expectorant. For Culpepper, the juice of mouse ear mixed with wine was good for jaundice; where as the bruised herb is a vulnerary and can be bound to cuts and wounds. The best time to collect mouse ear is May and June. Sauer believes that mouse ear has hepatic action and can clear "blockages of the liver." His formula for this treatment is: 1 handful of mouse ear and wild strawberry leaves in 2 quarts of white wine; these are decocted. A dose of four tablespoons morning and evening is suggested.

MUGWORT (*Artemisia vulgaris*): *Beifuss* (German), *Aldifraa* (old woman: dialect); also known as the "girdle of St. John." The leaves are collected in August, and the roots are dug up in the fall. A tea of mugwort leaves has been used for female problems and is an emmenagogue. Mugwort is also a stimulant, tonic, nervine, diuretic, and diaphoretic. For a more efficacious emmenagogue M. Grieve suggests mixing the leaves of mugwort with pennyroyal and southernwood; Sauer's formulation is simpler being a decoction of the leaves in wine. Regarding some of the folklore surrounding mugwort, M. Grieve notes that

> There were many superstitions connected with it: it was believed to preserve the wayfarer from evil spirits generally: a crown made from its sprays was worn on St. John's Eve to gain security from evil possession, and in Holland and Germany one of its names is St. John's Plant, because of the belief, that if gathered on St. John's Eve it gave protection against diseases and misfortunes.

MULLEIN (*Verbascum Thapsus*): *Königswollenkraut* (King's woolen weed: German), *Keenichslichter, Wollengraut, Wolleschtengel* (Wooly herb, wooly stalk: dialect). Mullein is a demulcent, emollient, astringent, and is also a slight sedative and narcotic. A decoction of mullein can be used externally for dropsy as a compress. Lick and Unger note that it has been used to treat horses for nausea and jaundice. M. Grieve gives a recipe for mullein tea:

> The homely but valuable Mullein Tea, a remedy of greatest antiquity for coughs and colds, and must indeed always be

strained through a fine muslin to remove any hairs that may be floating in the hot water that has been poured over the flowers, or leaves, for otherwise they cause intolerable itching in the mouth.

MUSTARD SEED (*Brassica*): *Senf* also *"mostart"* (German), *Mostard* (dialect). There are two types of mustard: black and white (*alba* and *nigra*). Mustard plasters are well known as useful for congested chests, but they are also good for stomach aches and indigestion. Care must be taken with these plasters as they can burn the skin. Vaseline or calendula ointment can be used to cover the patch of bare skin where the plaster will be laid. The mustard paste is spread out on a square of thin cloth with an identical second cloth covering this to make a "sandwich". This way, the mustard does not make direct contact with the skin. An infusion of the seed is used to relieve chronic bronchitis (Grieve). Mustard, aside from being an irritant, is also a stimulant, diuretic, and emetic. If the dose of mustard is high enough, it will induce vomiting. Mustard baths are good for foot circulation, as the mustard draws the blood to the surface of the flesh. Sauer indicates that mustard is a febrifuge and a glass of wine containing a dram of mustard is good for the quotidian and quartan agues prior to their on set.

NETTLE (*Urtica dioica*): *Grosse nessel* (Great nettle: German) or *Brennessel* (Burning nettle: dialect). Nettle is one of this author's favorite herbs. It is an excellent food, more healthful than spinach (and cooks the same); and nettle tea in regular use is good for a great many illnesses and disorders. The fresh leaves can be used in an effective (but painful) treatment for rheumatism: take the fresh leave and smartly whack it against the arthritic joints. This will sting smartly, but it will relieve the pain and swelling of the disease itself. The juice of the roots is good for asthma, and snuffing the juice of the plant will stop a bloody nose. The decocted root will break up phlegm. Nettle is a common ingredient in past blutreinigungsmittel formulae – it is a very good herb for the liver. A cup of nettle tea on a daily basis is a good habit to acquire.

PIPSISSEWA (*Chimaphila umbellata*): *Wintergrie* (Wintergreen: dialect), *Grundbein* (Ground pine: dialect). Pipsissewa is a diuretic, astringent, tonic, alterative, and antilithic. A decoction of pipsissewa is used in the treatment of gonorrhea and also "catarrh" of the bladder. As a treatment for rheumatism Lick and Unger write:

> A favorite rheumatic remedy was a quart of rum and a mug measure of leaves allowed to stand a fortnight when a swig was taken three times daily.

PRICKLY ASH (*Xanthoxylum Americanum*): *Zahnwehgelbholz* (German), *Bruckelesch* or *Schpickliesche* (dialect), toothache tree. The root-bark and the berries are used medicinally. Prickly Ash is a stimulant, stomachic, tonic, carminative, antispasmodic, and an emmenagogue. It has been used for treatment of chronic rheumatism, and as an ingredient in springtime blood purification tonics.

PUMPKIN (*Cucurbita*): *Kürbis* (German), *Karbs*, *Seikarrebs* (Pumpkin, "hog pumpkin:" dialect). The seeds of pumpkins are said to have vermifuge properties. Among the American Indians they were used for urinary complaints; today, raw pumpkin seeds are consumed as a remedy for prostate infection and as a tonic for that gland. According to folk-astrology, if the seeds are planted in the sign of Virgo, the vine will flower but not produce fruit. Pumpkin or squash leaves laid upon lactating breasts will relieve a woman of unwanted milk. Oil of pumpkin is used for inflamed kidneys; Sauer directs that the oil is rubbed into the pit of the stomach for this purpose.

SANICLE (*Sanicula marilandica*, *canadensis*, and *Europa*): *Heilnecke* (German), *Gleene* or *Grosse Sanickel* (Little Sanicle and Greater Sanicle: dialect). *Canadensis* is called the "greater" or gosser sanickel; *marilandica* is the "lesser" or gleener sanickel. Sauer in his herbal writes about the Europa variety. Sanicle is used for inflammations, hemorrhage, blood purification (blutreinigungsmittel), diarrhea and dysentery. The root of sanicle in brandy is a stomach tonic;

the root in whiskey is for tuberculosis – being useful for the hemorrhaging of the lungs, and also for the same in the bowels and other organs. Culpepper gives decocted sanicle as a remedy for quinsy and sore throat; where as a strong decoction is good for bleeding hemorrhoids. The decoction can also be used as a wash for rashes: one handful of herb to 2 quarts water boiled for 10 minutes. Tincture of sanicle has the same virtues as the decoction.

SARSAPARILLA-ROOT (*Aralia nudicaulis* – "*False Sarsaparilla*"): *Wildisassefrillwatzel* (dialect). The rootstock is medicinal; it is an alterative, blood purifier, diaphoretic, pectoral, carminative, vulnerary, and an antisyphilitic. It is an ingredient in many spring tonics, and was used in the past to combat the symptoms of syphilis. It can be used as a wash for shingles, ulcerations, tetters, as well as ringworm. Internally, it has been used for gout, and paralysis. A tea used as a purifier is 1 teaspoon of the rootstock decocted in 1 cup of water. Dosage is one to two cups per day. It can also be taken as a tincture.

SASSAFRAS (*Sassafras officinale*): *Sassafrasbaam* (*baam* = tree: dialect). The bark-root is medicinal. Sassafras is a stimulant, antiseptic, diaphoretic, alterative, and a diuretic. It is often combined with sarsaparilla root in older spring tonic formulae. The oil of sassafras is potentially poisonous, and it can cause death by organ degeneration. However, the oil has been used to quell the pain of menstrual obstructions, as well as the pain associated with gonorrhea. A decoction of sassafras has been used to treat syphilis, and skin diseases. American Indians used it as a febrifuge.

SCORPION OIL: Much like earthworm oil (see RAIN-WORM OIL), scorpion oil is the oil that is baked (among other methods of extraction) out of the animal itself. This oil has a long history of use in the Middle East. Scorpion oil is another of Albertus Magnus' more exotic remedies, which he prescribes for "gripping pains" (intestinal cramping), associated with diarrhea and Dysentery (*Egyptian Secrets*, p 144).

SNAKEROOT (*Aristolochia serpentaria*): *Schlangewurtzel* (dialect). Snakeroot is a tonic, diaphoretic, and a stimulant. An infusion of snakeroot makes a gargle for sore throat. High doses of snakeroot have emetic action, and can cause cramping; in small doses, it is an aperient. Mrs. Grieve writes that it is good for gout as it increases "arterial action, diaphoresis" but that prolonged use in high doses is poisonous.

SPEEDWELL (*Veronica officinalis*): *Ehrenpreis* ("honor and praise:" German; dialect same as the German), also *Fimffingergraut* ("honor and praise," also "five finger herb;" dialect) [Note: Cinquefoil is also called "Fimffingergraut"]. Speedwell is an alterative, diaphoretic, diuretic, tonic, and expectorant. It has been used for chest, and kidney ailments, and also for skin diseases and hemorrhages. Sauer gives the following recipe for "pain in the chest and lungs": take a handful of scabious leaves, speedwell, ½ tablespoon of licorice root; 2 – 3 chopped figs; chop all of these together. Boil the mix in one gallon of water for 10 minutes; strain and add 6 tablespoons of rock candy. A tea of speedwell is best made before the plant flowers, which is good for congestion, coughs, and has the added benefit of cleansing the kidneys; the tea also makes a good gargle for sore throat.

ST. JOHN'S WORT: (*hypericum perforatum*); called *Johanneskraut* in German; also *Jesu Blut, Christi kreuzblut, Teufelsflucht,* and *Hexekraut*. At the present time St. John's Wort is well known, thanks to the upsurge in the popularity of herbal remedies. The most common use for this plant nowadays is for the treating of depression. This herb is so aptly named. St. John the Baptist was a herald to the Light of Christ. Strong solar associations abound.

Hypericum is cleansing, antibacterial, antimicrobial, and anti-depressive. It is also an astringent and analgesic. This herb is truly a gift from God. But, as with any such gifts, it needs to be used wisely. People who are already on antidepressants, or other medications such as anticoagulants or medications for high blood pressure need to consult with their doctors before taking hypericum; like wise pregnant women ought to avoid its use. Some of the side effects include stomach upset, photosensitivity, and a rise in blood pressure; dermatitis has also been reported for those who demonstrate sensitivity to the herb.

Bundles of dried St. John's Wort, harvested during the Feast of St. John, can be hung over doors and windows to keep out evil influences. The tea and tincture of the herb is the most common means of ingesting hypericum. Two teaspoons of dried herb are added to one cup of boiling water and allowed to steep for 15 minutes. The usual dosage is one cup three times per day. The tincture is made from the flowers creating "St. John's Blood" as a result of its bright red color. Take about three ounces of the dried flowers and place in a large mason jar. Add 100 proof Vodka to near full. Close the lid and shake once daily. Do this for two weeks, and then strain the liquid. It is best if the tincture is distributed to smaller eye-dropper bottles for easier use. Amber-tinted bottles are best, as direct sunlight damages these tinctures.

RADISH (*Raphanus sativus*): *Rettich* (German, same in dialect). Radish is a diuretic and antilithic. It is also good for ridding phlegm, and is possibly a vermifuge. All herbals seem to agree that radish juice is a most excellent food for dissolving kidney and bladder stones. Taken in too high a dosage, the juice can also be an emetic. According to Sauer, eating too many radishes is "not good for the eyes", but he does not explain why. The ground seed of radish taken in wine is a diuretic. Much as with turnip and red beet, Sauer recommends taking these juices with rock candy, but this author has his doubts as to how much tastier that would make these drinks – in fact, sweeteners sometime make difficult tasting herbs and vegetables much worse. Corns on the feet can be treated with radish juice *during a waning moon*: cut down the corn after soaking in warm water, then treat with the juice.

RAIN-WORM OIL: is a product derived from the common earthworm (German: *regenwurm*), or rainworm, *lumbricus terrestris*. The product is literally oil which is baked out of earthworms and put to medicinal use. Medicinal use of earthworm is common to Chinese medicine, and found in older European usage. Albertus Magnus, on page 128 of his *Egyptian Secrets*, mentions rain-worm oil as being a beneficial topical-use pain reliever for neuralgia and arthritis.

RHUBARB (*Rheum rhaponticum*): *Rhabarber* (German), *Barberaa* (dialect), *Boischtuck* (pie plant: dialect) Dr. Santee's "Rhubicac". The root of rhubarb is a laxative, and is best dug up in October. The leaves are poisonous as they contain oxalic acid. Excessive use of rhubarb is said to cause constipation. Rhubarb is an aperient, astringent, purgative, and tonic. Lick and Unger write:
> At one time rhubarb root and golden tincture were the main remedies in many households. The rhubarb root was ground and made into little pills. (p. 75)

To employ rhubarb rootstock as a laxative, take one teaspoon of the powdered or chopped rootstock and decoct in ½ cup of water. To have the reverse effect, alter the recipe to ¼ root matter to ½ cup of water. Either of these are only taken one time per day.

THORNAPPLE (*Datura stramonium*): *Stechapfel* ("Stinky apple:" German), *Hexekimmel* (Witches' cumin: dialect), *Hexagraut* (Witches' herb: dialect). CAUTION: HIGHLY POISONOUS. Despite how poisonous thornapple can be, it does have medicinal virtue, but only in the right hands. It is an antispasmodic, anodyne, and narcotic. According to Mrs. Grieve, it has the same action as belladonna, but without the side effect of constipation. A salve of thornapple was used for swellings, and was known among American Indians as the "White Man's Plant" as it was introduced to the colonies through Jamestown. The lore surrounding thornapple is ample, as the folk names of "Witches' cumin" and "hexagraut" attest. It has been listed as an ingredient in the Witches' infamous "flying ointment". Müller-Ebeling, Rätsch, and Storl go into greater depth regarding these sorts of herbs in their book *Witchcraft Medicine*.

TORMENTIL [WORT] (*Potentilla tormentilla*): *Tormentill* (Sauer). Tormentil is an astringent that is primarily used in treating diarrhea and dysentery. A strong decoction of tormentil is used as a wash for hemorrhoids. In addition to these uses, tormentil is also an antiseptic, vulnerary, and vermifuge. The strong decoction can also be used for swellings in the mouth; the diluted solution makes a gargle for sore throat. Sauer writes that tormentil is good for chest wounds and sore lungs; it is also recommended for head troubles, such as dizziness. A decoction of the rootstock can be made this way: 1 tablespoon of the rootstock to 1 cup of water; for an infusion: the same as the decoction but allow it to steep for a half hour. A tincture of the rootstock can be used in place of the tea at 20 – 30 drops two to three times per day.

TURPENTINE: is the distilled resin of pine (among a few other things). It has been used for centuries, indeed, since antiquity in medicine. Few today can stomach the thought of taking turpentine orally, but the oil was used widely as a vermifuge to expel intestinal worms. Turpentine was also applied externally as a vapor rub for congestion and as an external antiseptic, and to destroy lice. It also has diuretic action. Turpentine is a solvent and can cause the following: renal failure, vapor burns to the eyes and lungs, as well as poisoning to the central nervous system. In former times, turpentine was made more 'palatable' by sweetening it with honey, molasses, or sugar. Turpentine-based remedies can be found throughout the hausmittel books and almanacs of the past. They are examples of traditional remedies that are best left alone.

VERVAIN (*Verbena hastata, officinalis*): also called Iron Herb (*Eisegraut*: dialect), *Eisenkraut* (German); also called Iron Weed (Albertus). According the M. Grieve, the lore surrounding vervain bolsters its reputation as a healing herb. Vervain was believed to have been at the foot of the Cross and was used to staunch Christ's wounds. Both Sauer and Grieve cite the old custom of wearing the bruised leaves of vervain around the neck as a remedy for headache. Vervain is a diuretic, diaphoretic, astringent, febrifuge, and antispasmodic. A poultice of the herb can be used for hemorrhoids, neuralgia, rheumatism, and headache. Distilled vervain water makes a good eye-wash for burning eyes.

Conclusion

It is prayed that you who now possess this book will seek to make good use of its operative contents, and that the theories, history, and ideas put forth will give you food for thought.

Were *The Red Church* written only 50 years ago, it would not have been necessary to emphasize and magnify the various cultural and religious aspects in a book such as this. Those things would have been just understood and taken for granted.

No single book can ever capture the totality of a subject such as Braucherei. Since the practice exists within the matrix of traditional Pennsylvania Dutch culture, it is imperative that everyone who is interested in pursuing Braucherei further does so by as much immersion into the culture as possible.

When practicing Pow-Wow, always remember that the Power is not your own – it is a gift given to you for the service of others to the glory of the Highest. *In Namen Gottes des Vaters und des Sohnes und des Heiligen Geistes.* Amen. J.J.J.

A Chapter of Dedication and Remembrance
Dr. Frederick LaMotte Santee, and Edna (Janie) Kishbaugh-Williams -- A Ship called "Fredna"

Fred

URBAN LEGENDS are powerful things. The history of Braucherei and hexerei reads like a catalogue of these spooky tales that everyone enjoys hearing over a good cup of coffee on a dark night. They also create a lot of problems for innocent people, and are more trouble than the trills are worth. To this day, there are people who still snoop around old Nelson Rehmeyer's homestead hoping to see…? What? Maybe they think they'll get a peek at the restless soul of the "Witch of Rehmeyer's Hollow," or maybe of Old Nick himself? It's hard to say. 'Hunting expeditions' such as these, when undertaken by more than two teenagers, usually devolve into spooky beer parties or back-pack Ouija sessions (with beer, etc. of course). During the life times of those who are the loci of these legends, innumerable annoyances and out-right crimes are endured by them. Dr. Frederick Santee was no different.

Considering the strong belief in witching throughout the previous eras of the Pennsylvania Dutch communities, it really is a miracle that more people were not killed. Dr. Santee's home village of Wapwallopen, Pennsylvania, is small – small enough even today that it can be missed if driving too quickly past it. Port Clinton, PA, makes it look large by comparison. Everyone knew Dr. Fred, needless to say. Four generations of Santees made little Wapwallopen their home. The village lies on the very outskirts of the PA Dutch cultural area, only a little north of Berwick but on the same side of the Susquehanna River as Nescopeck. A bit further south and then there is Bloomsburg, Catawissa, Elysburg in one direction; and in another there is Tamaqua, Jim Thorpe (old Mauch Chunk) and Port Clinton, and so on. From there, we go into "Dutch Country" proper.

Dr. Frederick LaMotte Santee was born on September 17th, 1906 to Charles LaMotte and Verna (nee Lloyd) Santee. Four generations of the family resided in Wapwallopen, every generation having at least one physician. Fred's grandfather was a Civil War surgeon, and his father too was a doctor whose little country practice Fred inherited – whether he liked it or not. He really didn't like it, and later in his life often lamented that he did not spend his earlier adulthood concentrating on making money. He usually referred to himself as being "a poor country doctor." That was mainly true. At the time of his death on April 11th, 1980, his *entire* estate was worth only a little over $221,000, which included a very used 1971 Dodge Demon. All of this is unusual, so one would think, for a man who was a real-life "Doogie Houser."

Dr. Fred was a prodigy. He was could read both English and German by the age of six, and learned Latin from his grandfather's grammar books by the age of eight, at which time he tried his hand at translating Caesar's *Gallic Wars* from Latin into English (just for the fun of it). He began his early schooling in the village, but attended high school in Wilkes-Barre, Pennsylvania. Soon after racing through high school, he attended Harvard at the age of 14; shortly thereafter he attended Oxford. It was around this time that he "went abroad" with his mother. He received his B.A. in 1926 and his M.A. in 1928. By 1938 he had his medical degree from John's Hopkins.

> Frederick Santee, 13, Wapwallopen, son of Dr. and Mrs. Santee has matriculated for the regular course in Harvard University. He is youngest ever to enter as candidate for degree. The boy has been unusual since his first day in school, and has been able to read foreign languages almost without study ever since he was six years old.[1]

---

1   From the *Scranton Times*, Saturday, September 11, 1920: http://www.rootsweb.ancestry.com/~palackaw/news/1920misc.html

Dr. Fred was always torn between his first love of classical literature, and medicine, which he practiced out of expediency. He managed to get various teaching jobs: Harvard, Temple, Kenyon, and John's Hopkins. Due to his political beliefs, he unfortunately never got tenure at any of the named institutions. Fred liked to describe himself as a "pre-New Deal Democrat." His opposition to the United State's entry into WWII also placed him in the socio-political box of suspicion.

Among the other pieces of his unique career, he practiced homeopathic medicine in Berlin and left before things got too 'hot' on the world-stage. The doctor made a lot of friends over seas. In England he made the acquaintance of W.B. Yeats, Aleister Crowley, and H.P. Blavatsky. He was a member of the Theosophical Society of England, and attended school also at the University of Berlin.

During his time in Germany, he was introduced to a group of magicians, who it is said were located approximately 30 miles outside of Berlin; the group was headed by a magister by the name of Arnold Reinmann, or Reinmand(t). The Archives of American Art retained some old correspondence of Fred's from 1926 to a Dr. Guerusey regarding his desire to study in Germany:

> I shall be in Rome then, the first of October. My parents want me to come home this summer, but I am trying to convince them I ought to study in Germany. I am thinking of Freiburg or Heidelberg – chiefly, I am afraid, because I like the towns. It is too hot to go to Greece and I shall have other opportunities.[2]

His travels also took him to Egypt where he received either teaching or initiation from a Sufi sheik. Politics aside, Dr. Fred's love of the esoteric was another factor that placed him on the outskirts

2   Fellowship in Classical Studies – Recipients, 1913 – 1941; box reel 19 5780-5781

of his peers – and possibly under the microscope of the Federal Government.

By 1928 he married his first wife Edith Rundle of Allentown, Pennsylvania; and by 1930 his first and only natural child, Ruth, was born (March 18th). Ruth had a short life; by the time of her demise in 1968, she had married three times: W.J. McKnight, Alfred Jenanyen, and Juan Zaragoza – no children. A divorce came in 1942, and Dr. Fred married Betty Addis of Cumberland, Maryland. I

n 1943, despite his objections to the war, Fred was drafted and served in the Navy as a doctor in the South Pacific, later to be stationed in Arkansas. While in his tenure as a military physician, he wrote his first book of poetry *Sawdust and Tomatoes*. He later practiced medicine in Baltimore, Maryland. From his college days until the 1960's and beyond, Dr. Fred was in contact with many luminaries of the literary world, among them being John Colhane, Father James H. Flye (the Roman Catholic Classicist and Latinist), and another Classist, Clyde Pharr, among many others. Below is an example of the sorts of letters Fr. Flye and Dr. Fred shared with one another -- in Latin, of course.

> Fredericus Patri   J.H. Flye   Sal.
> Quem requiris locum de Proverbiis neque tibi excerpere potui neque enim S. Hieronymi opus apud meos libros invenire. Miratus tanti momenti librum abesse memini illum numquam fere librariorum chartis venalem exponi.
> Daeta Wapwallopen   Kal. Feb.[3]

Betty and Fred adopted a German refuge who came to them as a baby, whom they nicknamed "Tao" (pronounced "Tay-oh" – which was a baby pronunciation of the word "tail" in reference to the little

[3] From the Archives of Vanderbilt University, Nashville.

girl's long ponytail). The child's full legal name is still something of a mystery.

At the time of Dr. Fred's death he owned *over* 24,000 volumes, which he housed in a cinder block outbuilding that he called "The Book House." And that was before the fire…which leads back to the topic of urban legends.

When Fred Santee left this world, his estate was indeed not worth a lot. Of course, some of the local "worthies" learned that Dr. Fred had some very old, expensive books (15th century and older). He was also rumored to have possession of several gold ingots that he kept in a safe in the Book House. Combined with the distrust of the village "warlock" and the lure of his hoard of treasure, an unknown number of men broke into the private library, ransacked it, broke into the safe, and then set the whole thing alight. This was around 1978. Even after the fire, the aforementioned number of volumes was left. Many more were damaged and disposed of. It is estimated that he had nearly 50,000 volumes before the fire.

As it happened, Dr. Fred's interest in the occult did manifest in the little village. In the beginning his interests were more "high magic" and along arm-chair speculative lines. It wasn't until the 1960's that his "girls" (nurses) took an interest in the newly emerging Witchcraft movement coming out of Britain. By way of their prodding, he relented and began a study of "the Craft" as it was becoming known, and made contact with Sybil Leek.

Dr. Fred's spin on "Wicca" was always very 'high-brow' and he mixed it with a good portion of his Classical and philosophical studies, and the knowledge he accumulated while being a member of the various European Theosophical societies. His new work became genuinely popular with many of his wide-ranging friends and acquaintances – although one suspects that friends such as Fr. Flye had not an inkling of his activities. In the Harvard Yearbook 25th Anniversary of the Class of 1924 he says this of himself:

In religion, I lean towards Anglo-Catholicism, am a member of no church. In politics, I believe in the decentralization of government and as little government as possible. I am a pre-New Deal Democrat.

Later on in the 50th Anniversary edition of the Harvard Yearbook for the Class of 1924 he included a little poem about himself beginning "If you don't know the poem that served as a model for these verses, you have not done a good job with your grandchildren."

> How pleasant to know the good Doctor
>   Who writes all this horrible stuff;
> Some call him a scoundrel and rotter,
>   But a few think him pleasant enough.
>
> His mind is abstract and fastidious,
>   His nose is remarkable big;
> Were he only a little less hideous,
>   You would say he resembles a pig.
>
> When he changes from far specs to near specs
>   The children are frightened and cry,
> And their mothers shout, 'Hey! Don't you dare hex
>   Poor Sam with your terrible eye!'
>
> He has many friends, layman and clerical,
>   He sleeps every night with his cats,
>
> His body is perfectly spherical,
>   His office girls never wear flats.
>
> His office is unsanitary
>   With pictures of girls on the wall,

> Every week he drinks gallons of sherry,
> > But never gets tipsy at all.
>
> He is silent with people who talk a lot,
> > He won't look at women in slacks,
> His favorite flavor is chocolate,
> > He rails at inflation and tax.
>
> He hides in the depths of the cellar
> > While his patients call down through the flue,
> 'Come out of that cellar, you yeller,
> > You yeller old lazy bones, you!'
>
> He reads, but cannot speak, Spanish,
> > He still prefers women to men;
> Ere the days of your pilgrimage vanish,
> > He hopes you will see him again.

Now, there's a great old-fashioned, unpretentious country doctor – very Rockwellesque, *but* with the addition of high heeled nurses, cats, girly pin-ups, and Witches, among other things Rockwell would not have included in his Americana prints. But this is how it was. From the mid to late 1970's Dr. Fred went to work on his one and only somewhat still available[4] work called *The Devil's Wager: A Faustian Drama of the Second Fall and A Second Redemption*, tagged as "An exciting new version of the struggle between God and Satan for the soul of man."[5]

A rather odd, but certainly not surprising, urban legend wrapped itself around *The Devil's Wager*. During my early college years the following story about Dr. Fred was circulated:

---

[4] The book was out of print almost from the time it was published. Exposition Press went out of business soon after the publication of *The Devil's Wager*. Copies can occasionally be found *via* out of print dealers.

[5] See the reproduction below of the publisher's advertisement flyer; also see the Bibliography for more information.

"You mean that you never heard of Dr. Santee?! He worshipped the devil and wrote this magic book called *The Devil's Wager*. The Devil didn't want him to write it, so evil spirits set his house on fire when he was about to finish it. It started with the curtains. After the book was finished, Satan came back for him and took him to Hell. His funeral was held in a graveyard at midnight, attended by his coven."[6]

This was absolute nonsense. *The Devil's Wager* was Dr. Fred's attempt to rewrite Faust to the late 20th century. However, it would be wrong to say that it was *only* that. The story revolves around the doctor's ideas of beauty (especially female beauty) versus the ugliness of modern post-1960's society; he believed in the transcendental and redemptive qualities of beauty that draw people back into the Divine. For Man, Woman is the ideal who can save the soul.

Such ideas may seem wholly Pagan, which it is supposed they can be in the proper context. Yet, Theosopher Jacob Boehme and his Sophianic Christianity express very similar ideas – that the visage of Beauty awakens the conscience to repentance and draws the soul to perfection and Christ. In Dr. Fred's later life, he explored these issues of beauty and redemption by way of the vehicle of the Wicca his "girls" adopted.

The fire mentioned in the urban legend above is a recollection of the conflagration set by the local thieves to the library outbuilding. Many people stole from Dr. Fred. Not long after his death, someone broke into his house and extracted the stained glass that was there. More books from the library were stolen. As late as the early 1990's, books from his library were still floating around as far north as Wilkes-Barre, and as far south as Orangeville, near Bloomsburg. Eventually, some of his collection found its way into an occult shop

---

[6] This was almost word-for-word what was told to me nearly 20 years ago by a fellow college student.

that existed in Allentown. The bulk of his estate was left to his closest friend Edna Williams, who due to money issues, sold off the vast bulk of his library to William H. Allen booksellers.

Dr. Fred Santee was not a Braucher or hex doctor in any usual sense, except for the fact that he was 1) in the cultural area; 2) his "legend" fits the model of past country hex doctors; 3) he was very independent and extremely intelligent, which are two traits that tend to confound and scare some folks; 3) because of the latter mentioned qualities, he often made some of his own 'concoctions' reminiscent of the old-time "patent remedies" of 60 to 70 years previous – such as his own special formulation of *"Rhubicac"* (Rhubarb and Ipecac, more or less).

Such activities made him a person of occasional interest to the FDA; and 4) he really was a magical practitioner and tended to be rather above-board about it. However it came about, there was an article written about his "coven" in *The Press Enterprise*, a newspaper local to the Berwick-Bloomsburg-Danville area. It was also in this paper that the doctor had his own medical column called "The Country Doctor" which ran for a few years. Along side that, Edna (Janie) Williams wrote her own column called "The Witch's Kettle" – mostly regarding folklore and herbalism that surrounds the subject of Witchcraft.

Edna

Edna or as she was known to her friends: "Janie," was born Edna Kishbaugh to Edgar and Mary Slusser Kishbaugh on April 13, 1921. Janie (or sometimes spelled "Janee") liked to mention that her parents named her "Edna" because it means "rejuvenation." Janie was a good soul and welcomed strangers with open arms, especially when they came to her for teaching. She loved to teach about all things related to spirituality and Wicca. Janie was mostly Pennsylvania Dutch, but had a good amount of Lenne Lennape from her distaff side. When she found herself in an obstinate mood, she'd say that she got it from her mother, and referred to her self jokingly as a "stubborn Injun." Janie's mother Mary was a Braucherin who specialized in stopping blood. When Janie was a girl she recalled that her mother was often in demand with neighbors calling through the screen door "Mrs. Kishbaugh! We need you!" Mary used her Bible to stop blood, which was stained from years of use on bleeding neighbors.

Janie would often tell me of how things were when she was a girl, about how much more wild and woodsy Pennsylvania was only a few decades back. Her father Edgar was employed with the WPA during the Depression and had built many of the walls and bridges that can be found in the Nescopeck-Berwick area (and probably in surround areas as well). There was one bridge that she was fond of, which her father had help build; it was her special place.

Towards the end of her life she tearfully confided that even though she was Wiccan, she would "always have Jesus in her heart." In her personal theology, she chose to see God in terms of feminine symbolism; and Jesus was a Son of the Goddess. When she wanted to relate to the One in masculine symbolism, she would refer to "Father God." However, she was not a true polytheist or even a clear-cut "duotheist" as many Neo-Pagans are today.[7] Janie was always a spiritual person, and saw visions of Dr. Fred and Sybil Leek many years after their deaths. She would also be visited by her late husband, Dale.

She loved Dale. Janie believed in reincarnation and felt that Dale was her brother in a past existence. She carried around a lot of that sort of sisterly feeling for him, yet she was his wife too. In 1956 Janie and Dr. Fred met and they became best friends. The doctor

---

7   There are many different approaches to this subject among Wiccans and Neo-Pagans. Some consider themselves to be monotheistic (such as Sybil Leek, Janie's mentor), others are "soft polytheists" or "hard polytheists" (referring to the belief that there is a Divine Unity or One God expressed as many deities; while the other is the belief that no such One exists and that there is only multiplicity – if a "One" exists, it is only an abstraction). Wiccans have been described as "duotheists" believing in a dual or bi-polar Deity expressed as a God and a Goddess.

was her "soul mate" and their relationship was intense, but chaste. Despite Dr. Fred's appreciation of the female form, there was *no* sexual component to their friendship – at least not in any physical sense. After meeting Sybil, and having convinced the doctor to form a Wiccan coven, Janie became his High Priestess for the new group called The Coven of the Catta: named such because of their mutual love of cats. The group attracted a number of their friends and acquaintances, many of which resided in other states.

The urban legends surrounding Dr. Santee often involve citations of the numerous out-of-state license plates that would be seen lining the street near the doctor's house on "certain days of the years." Being that Wapwallopen is so tiny, this must have been quite a sight, as it spooked just about everyone there. To this day, there are locals who refuse to speak about the doctor and "his girls" as they are afraid that even the mere mention will draw "evil spirits" back to the town.

Quite a few folks that I have spoken with from that area are convinced that Dr. Fred's house was haunted by the spirits he called up. Back in the mid-eighties there was apparently a few local Hare Krishnas who tried to "exorcise" the spirits that were said to roam about the village. Part of the Dr. Santee 'lore-package' surrounds a weird blackened feline silhouette burned into the concrete floor of the library outbuilding where rituals were held. During the fire of 1978 one of the doctor's cats was in the library at the time. The poor creature was cremated on the spot, hence the image.

Fredna
In reality, there was not one scary thing about Dr. Fred, who was a good man and free with his medical services (therefore his poverty). Janie, much like her soul-mate was very much taken advantage of. Due to her association with the doctor, there were people who assumed that she had some of his 'treasures' and was repeatedly robbed herself. Over the years, many of her personal memorabilia of

the doctor began to 'disappear,' and she became protective of what remained. Janie was never really healthy, suffering from a life-long degenerative disorder, which left her an invalid towards the end. After her passing, a family member sold her home, contents and all to a fellow who gutted the building. When he had gone through her many personal effects, he reported to friends of Janie that he found boxes of photographs, and diaries documenting her life with the doctor (including Santee's notebooks). Apparently, from all reports, he unceremoniously tossed it all away, including her "Book of Shadows" into a dumpster, and carried off to a landfill.

The moral of this story: if you know anyone like this, help to preserve history and make sure these things are placed into endowments, or donated to a local university. Doctor Santee was a part of Pennsylvania history, and his life and story are almost lost.

Janie was with Fred when he lay dying; she nursed him through his final illness. He had asked her to promise to write his story, which was also their story. Many times she tried to fulfill this promise, but her health and circumstances often got in the way. It was to be entitled *"A Ship Called Fredna."* Their bond and their adventures together made them a "ship" unto themselves. The combination of their two first names was a symbol of that unity, hence the subtitle of this chapter. Edna, my friend, left this world while in a nursing home on December 5, 2005, taken from her cats and her parent's home (her home) that she dearly wished to die in.

Please say a prayer for the souls of Dr. Fred and for Janie, that they may be happier where they are, than in a world that treated them as freaks and objects of mistrust.

Such is the lot of the hex doctor, who often tried to do the best he (or she) could for his community, and got paid back in spades. There have been shysters among those in "the trade" to be sure; even some practitioners of genuine *hexerei*[8] masquerading as Pow-

---

8   For as much as one may object theologically or philosophically with Wicca, its practitio-

Wows. But on the whole, these were (and are) men and women who try to live out the Great Commission in their own way to the benefit of "Man and beast," as the old Brauche manuals state.

Edna (Janie) Kishbaugh-Williams.

---

ners are neither black magicians nor devil worshippers. If any are practicing such, they have ventured into the realm of what is truly malicious Witchcraft and are only hiding behind the mask of the so-called "white Witch."

Bronze grave marker at the foot of the tomb of Henry Melchior Muhlenberg and his wife Anna. Muhlenberg was the "patriarch" of American Lutheran Christianity, and was responsible for creation of the Ministerium of Pennsylvania in 1748, being the first permanent Lutheran synod in North America.

Appendix J
A Glossary of Braucherei and Related Subjects

Here is a quick reference guide for various terms that you will come upon in your study materials of Braucherei and related subjects, should you go further. Some entries may, at first, seem to have little to do with the subject. However, a perusal of the literature of Braucherei and archaic medical treatments will bring unfamiliar terms swiftly to notice. Albertus Magnus' *Egyptian Secrets* is, unfortunately, one the worst for this sort of thing. The problem of hoary (now recondite) knowledge is that the terminologies involved, once familiar to our ancestors, are difficult to understand without specialized dictionaries and encyclopedias. Hopefully, this appendix will adequately serve that purpose. As always, it is my wish to be as thorough as possible.

AAGEWACHSE: means "grow together" in the Pennsylvania Dutch dialect. It refers to a sticking of muscular tissues of the lower chest seemingly to inner parts, such as the liver. For this reason it is called "Livergrown" in English or "the livergrowed." This condition leaves the lower ribs more defined and prominent than normal, along with the abdomen being raised. The sensations of Livergrown are cramping, a feeling of restriction in the lower chest and upper abdominal areas, accompanied by difficult breathing, sometimes referred to as *hazschpann* or *haerzgschpaerr*. Another name for aagewachse is "cardiology," which has nothing to do with the modern use of this word. The labored breathing and 'attached' sensations can also be accounted for by pleurisy. Colic also comes underneath the category of aagewachse, and both conditions are treated identically in children. "Straining" (constipation) and gas pains also account for some cases of aagewachse, also "rickets."

ABDANSDAK: *Abdansdaag, Abdanstag* – St. Abdan's Day, July 30th. This is the feast day of two obscure martyrs: SS Abdan and

Sennen. It is said that they were Persians who were murdered under the anti-Christian Decius in either 250 or 303 A.D. July 30th is also known as "The Day of Oaths." It is traditional for people to try for the removal of warts and other growths on this day.

ABNEMMES: Also called *opnema*, *abnehmes*, or marasmus: "the take off" or "the wasting away." Abnemmes was a condition primarily found in children; in harder times, abnemmes was a product of malnutrition. "The wasting away" could also be due to Witchcraft or an infection of worms in the spine. Shrinking flesh, loss of appetite, emaciation, and muscular atrophy of the limbs characterized this condition. It was also called *schwinde* or *schwinden*, or at an earlier date *zehrwurm* – "the devouring worm". The term *schwindsucht* while similar to schwinden more precisely referred to the wasting away of "consumption" or tuberculosis.

A remedy for these "worms" in the spine was to rub honey down the child's spine, then face his or her back to a fire or warm stove. The heat and honey was believed to draw out these parasites from the flesh. After an amount of time had passed, the child's back was shaved with a razor. The shaving was believed to cut off the heads of these small parasites as they emerged. A truly folksy treatment for abnemmes in children was to take the child (an infant) and pass it around the legs of the kitchen table in a weaving in-and-out pattern; another was to take the child and pass it through a horse's collar. The Irish, Welsh, and Cornish had a similar custom by passing children through large holed stones.

AGRIPPA von NETTESHEIM, HENRICUS CORENELIUS: Or, simply "Cornelius Agrippa" for short. Agrippa is doubtlessly the fountainhead of all contemporary magical practice. A perusal of any book on "magic" today will betray a good portion of its roots in Agrippa's *Three Books of Occult Philosophy*. Agrippa was born in Cologne, Germany in 1486 to a family of lesser nobility that served in the royal house of Austria. At an early age Agrippa proved himself to be intelligent and astute, having devoured the works of

Albertus Magnus. He graduated from the University of Cologne and possibly had obtained advanced degrees in law and medicine. When he was 20 years old, he studied in Paris. In his non-academic life, he was married three times (he divorced all three wives, and had three children with his second wife). Agrippa was continuously hounded for his theories; his special tormentor was Conrad Colyn of Ulm, the Inquisitor of Cologne.

The Archbishop of Cologne, being one of Agrippa's patrons, shielded him from Colyn's many attacks, allowing him to finally publish the *Three Books of Occult Philosophy*. Because of his well-known activities, "urban legends" grew up around Agrippa. It was believed that one of his favorite pet dogs was actually a "demonic familiar"—such are the ways of ignorance. *The Fourth Book of Occult Philosophy* is attributed to Agrippa, and may well be his work, although this is still a source of controversy. The *Three Books* is a Bible-sized master-work describing the theory and practice of Natural Magic. The *Fourth Book* is quite slim by comparison and is devoted to explaining the basics of Ceremonial Magic. Cornelius Agrippa left this world in 1535, and magicians today own him a debt of gratitude.

ALUM: hydrated aluminum potassium sulfate: $KAI(SO_4)_2 \cdot 12H_2O$; the archaic name for alum is *alumen*. The action of alum is astringent (and possibly antiseptic) and is an ingredient in Victorian shaving powders and styptic pencils. Alum was also used as a mordant for fixing dyes into cloth. Alum is cited on occasion in the remedy books for drying out wounds and sores. Lee Gandee records in his *Strange Experience* that he used alum to heal second and third degree burns he received while working on his property; he combined the alum with sulfur, which he notes in an old colonial era remedy for burns.

ANANIAS (AZARIAS & MISAIL): Also, Hananiah, Azariah, and Mishael (Shadrach, Meshach, and Abednego). These are the youths who were placed into the hot furnace in the Book of Daniel,

Chapter Three, by King Nebuchadnezzar as a punishment for not worshipping the golden idol. These three names are invoked in some Brauche verbal charms and written talismans such as the "fire and pestilence letters" (See HIMMELSBRIEF).

> O Ananias, Azarias, Misael, bless ye the Lord: praise and exalt him above all for ever. For he hath delivered us from hell, and saved us out of the hand of death, and delivered us out of the midst of the burning flame, and saved us out of the midst of the fire. **Daniel 3:88; "The Song of Azariah and the Three Holy Children" (Latin Vulgate – Douay-Rheims)**

ANIMAL PARTS: (See BONE)

ANNÄNGSEL: (See ZAUBERZETTEL)

APOPLEXY: Apoplexy comes from the Greek *apoplexia*. Formerly this word designated any manner of what we now call a "stroke", or the loss of blood circulation to any part of the body resulting in numbness or paralysis.

AQUAFORTIS: HNO_3; nitric acid with water: a solution of nitric acid made from distilling a mixture of alum, vitriol, and saltpeter. The resulting distillate is called *aquafortis* (Latin for "strong water"). Primarily used in alchemy, this solution is used to dissolve or break down various elements for further refining. Some 'house' and Brauche books will occasionally list aquafortis as an ingredient in the preparation certain remedies and sundry household needs.

ASH TREE (*Fraxinus*): *Esche* (German), *Esch* or *Eschebaam* (dialect). Ash tree is sometimes used in Braucherei for the purpose of creating "Wound Wood". Wound Wood is supposed to be a cure-all for wounds, sore, and assorted lesions. The wood is collected on Good Friday, prior to sunrise. The wood is touched to the wound and then disposed of in the proper manner. In pre-Christian Norse lore, the ash is the species for the Yggdraisil, or the World Tree. Between the 'top' of the cosmological tree, down to its roots, all levels of Creation exist. In heathen belief there are Nine Worlds that are represented on the Tree – from a casual glance this is not too different from the Hebrew Tree of Life.

AUSFAUHRES: (See TETTER)

BARBAROUS INTONATION: To understand this practice it is first necessary to understand the concept of "barbarous names" of invocation/evocation. The term "barbarous" comes from the Greek *barbarikos*, meaning something foreign, outlandish or exotic; likewise *barbarophonos* means to speak in a strange voice. Magicians throughout the centuries have relied upon archaic conjurations, which over time became incomprehensible, as languages have changed. Practitioners of magic have been notorious borrowers. It seems that the more exotic or 'unknown' an ingredient was, the better it worked. This is pure psychology.

It is for this reason that some people will prefer the rites of the Latin Tridentine Mass or Divine Liturgy in Old Slavonic over that of a vernacular service. Because these rites are half-understood, combined with the sacred atmosphere, packs an emotion 'wallop'. Any set of words that drives this sort of emotional response (thereby speaking to the subconscious mind) can qualify as "barbarous names". Barbarous intonation is the process of actively working these words during a ritual operation – such as a Brauche session would qualify. For non-Hebrew speaking individuals, the Hebrew Names of God suit this purpose.

Historically, barbarous names have not always been members of proper languages, but seem to have been generated by way of a sort of glossolalia; or otherwise created out of a mish-mash of words from various languages. Medieval magicians were fond of creating "words of power" by combining Hebrew, Greek, and Latin. And, because the practitioner might not be a fluent speaker of any such language, the translations were less than grammatical. As time progresses, such formulae are copied and recopied over the centuries, the result is that some of the oldest spells and charms become nonsensical or utterly incomprehensible – which paradoxically lends such operations some of their force. The working of half-understood/not-understood charms is a double-edged sword. In the hands of a knowledgeable practitioner, the "barbarous" aspect can be used to maximum advantage; however (and unfortunately), these charms usually end up being repeated and used superstitiously. In this instance, the definition of superstition is doing something with no understanding of the why for. Many Braucherei charms have words in them that are no longer understood. Some of these phrases are just worn down Vulgar Latin; or pastiches of equally worn down Greek, or perhaps even Coptic.

BARBAROUS MANIPULATION: By extension of the above entry for barbarous intonation, barbarous manipulation would be the 'mysterious' manipulation of the various objects used in spellwork. This term is one coined by the author in order to describe the methods sometimes used in folk magic and folk medicine. As with the barbarous names, the manipulation of so-called secondary accoutrements to spellwork can be treated with knowledge or with superstition.

Perhaps few have understood why certain rituals need to be done during a certain lunar phase; or why red string is employed instead of a yellow string, for example. Why is bees' wax so much more efficacious than paraffin? Why ought a practitioner to use an egg here, but a set of birch twigs in another place? The use of 'exotic' ingredients or the use of common items within an exotic context can trigger the subconscious mind and add the emotional element that is sometimes needed in this sort of work.

Today's practitioners of the magical arts (Wiccans, Thelemites, etc.) are so much savvier than the homegrown folk magicians of a century ago, since the reasons for why certain things are done or said were lost to many of them. When Braucherei hit its nadir during the last century due to the ugly publicity surrounding the "Hex Murder" in York, PA in 1929, something interesting happened. Practitioners of Pow-Wow purged many of the noticeably "magical" elements of their art and went in for straight faith healing.

This was at once both good and not-so-good. On the good end, it streamlined Pow-Wow practice making it leaner, more easily worked, and more comprehensible – that is to say, it was more comprehensible within the context of Pennsylvania Dutch Christian community. On the unfortunate end of things, what this purging did was to throw out whole swathes of traditional Braucherei practice that are fast becoming lost. In our now secular, largely non-churched society, understanding even the streamlined Pow-Wow of the early to mid-twentieth century is difficult from the outside of what remains of PA Dutch culture.

BARN SIGN (See HEX SIGN)

BEDGOBLIN: This term is found in the second conjuration located in *Albertus Magnus Egyptian Secrets: White and Black Art for Man and Beast, Revealing The Forbidden Knowledge and Mysteries of Ancient Philosophers*. The word "goblin" comes from the Latin *gobelinus*, being a form of the German word *kobold*. A kobold is a household spirit that is mostly helpful and is reputed (at least in the ancient accounts) to help the householders with various chores while they sleep. These spirits are largely invisible, but are shape shifters when they do come to visible form. Some have related these entities to the spirits called amongst the Romans *penates* and *lares*.

In England these same beings have been called boggarts, brownies, or hobgoblins. Knowledge of goblins predates Christianity, where these domestic spirits where considered to be the titular spirits of the home. Everything had its own presiding spirit, including individual houses. If the goblin/kobold was displeased with the family residing in the house, it could be quite mischievous, manifesting poltergeist phenomena. If the spirit was out-rightly angry, it could be quite malevolent, and cause no end of ill luck, sickness, and even death. As a result of the latter, many have tried to quell or exorcise the kobold. Sometimes the exorcism was successful, other times these spirits do no budge. When one kobold goes, another may take its place. When Luther translated the eerie 34th Chapter of **Isaiah** he used the German *kobold* instead of either the term "Lilith" or "shrich owl" in verse 14:

> Da werden unter einander laufen Marder und Geier, und ein Feldteufel wird dem andern begegnen; der Kobold wird auch dafelbst herbergen, und seine Ruhe dafelbst finden.

> The wild beasts of the desert shall also meet with the wild beasts of the island, and the satyr shall cry to his fellow; the shrich owl also shall rest there, and find for herself a place of rest.

BEISSEL, KONRAD: (1691 – 1768) Johann Konrad (Conrad) Beissel was born in Eberbach, Baden (Palatine). In the Old World, he was a baker journeyman who lost his *wanderbuch* due to his religious opinions. As a result, he was no longer legally able to work as a baker. This was a typical move by the powers of that era; religion and politics (far more so than today) were closely entwined. In those days, if one dissented from the religion of his prince, he was guilty of treason. Such agitating was dealt with primarily by destroying livelihoods and/or arrest.

Beissel escaped Germany in much the same manner as Kelpius before him. Before settling in Pennsylvania, Beissel first came to the Colonies through Boston; from there he made his way down to Germantown, where he apprenticed with Peter Becker to learn the trade of weaving. Becker was a founder of the Church of the Brethren, and he had baptized Beissel in 1722. When Beissel came to Pennsylvania it was with the desire to join Kelpius and his "monks" only to find that he was already deceased. "Peaceful, right with God" (or *Friedsam Gottrecht*) was the new name Beissel gave to himself, and lived as a hermit at Mill Creek in Lebanon County. Later on, he withdrew further into the wilderness for greater solitude near the Cocalico Creek near Ephrata.

He was eventually joined by others, and their reputation for charity and holiness became widely known. The cherished solitude did not last long as increasing numbers of seekers made the hermitage more of a 'village'. This was the seed that grew into the Ephrata Cloister of the Seventh Day Baptists. The Cloister was millenarian and Sabbatarian; it was an outgrowth of Radical Pietism, and Christian theosophy.

Beissel was a devoted Behmenist, but did differ from Boehme on a number of points. By 1735 the first monastic house called "Kedar" was erected. Ephrata had one of the best printing presses in the Colonies next to Sauer's. They printed in German the immense *Martyrs' Mirror*, which was the largest book printed in the Colonies. The Cloister enjoyed its peak years between 1745 – 1755; however, after the Revolution, the Cloister declined.

There were several controversies that kept popping up that sapped the community's strength. Due to the compassion and assistance the Cloister rendered to Colonial troops, General Washington honored the Cloister with a gift of three cherry wood communion sets. Fraktur and music were highly developed art forms at Ephrata. Vegetarianism was practiced, at Beissel's insistence, due to the belief that meat eating made the voice less refined for singing.

The Cloister was not "co-ed", but had a Sister House and a Brother House. Celibacy was the norm, except for the lay householders. At its peak, the Cloister was 300 people strong, both lay and celibate. There was a very strong Sophiology at Ephrata, clearly influenced by Jacob Boehme. For Beissel, Sophia was *"the eternal mother, or heavenly femaleness"* (Bach p. 41). The Trinity was a perfect family: God, our Father; Christ, our Brother; and the Holy Ghost, our Mother. It is speculated that there was probably only one real alchemist at Ephrata, being Jacob Martin; yet the imagery and language employed by the Cloister was wholly alchemical due to the influence that art has in Christian theosophy. There is some speculation that Conrad Beissel was a Rosicrucian, but there has never really been any solid evidence to back up the claim.

BESCHPRECHEN: In academic studies this term is often seen in the company of another word: *beschwören*. Literally each term means respectively "to talk to" and "to summon". This is what Pow-Wow doctor or hexenmeister does with a disease. The premise is that disease can be addressed, spoken to, conjured, or exorcised. Often Braucherei charms will speak directly to the disease or injury as if it had personal qualities. Hohman gives and example of how to speak to a tape worm in order to destroy it:

> Worm, I conjure thee by the living God, that thou shalt flee this blood and this flesh, like as God the Lord will shun that judge who judges unjustly, although he might have judged aright. + + +

BEESERGUCK: Pennsylvania German for the "evil eye" (standard High German: *Böser Blick*). See FERHEXT.

BEES' WAX: There is no other wax that is more excellent and conductive to health than *raw*, pure bees' wax. Bees' wax is unrivaled for the creation of candles in Braucherei work (as in the use of the petschaft), or for use in communing with God in good, wholesome prayer. Bees' wax is most appropriate medium for the creation of various talismans due to its organic, living nature.

For this reason also it is the most desirable wax to employ when needing a thickener for herbal unguents. Raw bees' wax is a gift from Mother Nature that should not be written off. Colored, processed waxes do not carry any life or virtue. Raw bees' wax can be a little time consuming to clean, but it is well worth the effort for the finished product.

BLOOD LETTING: This was a medical technique that was popular in use from ancient Greece until the mid- to latter part of the 19th century. Prior to the standardization of medicine, there was little difference between doctors, 'surgeons', barbers, blacksmiths, and Pow-Wow doctors. According to the theories of Galen, blood was one of the four "humors" (the others being black bile, yellow bile, and phlegm – see The FOUR HUMORS).

It was believed that by making cuts into veins and allowing copious amounts of blood to flow (or 'let') would balance the "humors" in one with 'too much' blood, which was believe to be the source of some diseases. In retrospect, bloodletting may have been helpful for hypertension sufferers by decreasing some of the pressure. This author does not subscribe to bloodletting or encourage anyone to its use.

BLOOD MAKING: the "thinning" of blood, and also the "making" of blood. Old country wisdom has it that root vegetables such as red beets are "blood makers"; whereas, sassafras and burdock are two examples of "blood purifiers".

BLOWING FIRE: Otherwise this is also called "blowing for fire" or "trying [using] for fire"; regardless of what it is called this is the Pow-Wowing for all manner of burns. The term "blowing" infers the method of treatment, where the Braucher will use his or her breath to blow away the pain and inflammation of the burn.

Aside from the rationalistic notion that blowing on a burn will merely temporarily cool down the burnt skin, the breath of a practitioner will also carry the healing vitality necessary to stop the damage and pain of the burn.

The old belief held that the *heat* of burns untreated (or treated badly) would actually go "deeper" into the flesh and possibly to the bone as well. This would result in a far more serious condition. Hexenmeister Lee Gandee in his book *Strange Experience* gave an account of his treatment of serious burns. Not all brauching for burns involves actually blowing upon the wounds.

While not seen as a formal part of Braucherei practice, various traditional first aid folk remedies have often accompanied the brauching of burns. Gandee gives an example of using an old remedy of dusting burns with sulfur and alum in order to dry them out and speed natural healing. Meanwhile, he notes that the process of Pow-Wowing for the burns alleviates the pain.

It has been this author's experience that many Braucherei formulae (for burns or other painful conditions) do just this very thing; while they may not always make the condition go away more quickly, they usually keep the pain manageable, if not get rid of it altogether. Another variation on "blowing" is "drawing" where the burn is drawn out either by way of contagion targets or more rarely a symbolic sucking action – as if drawing out a poison.

BLUE VITRIOL: Blue Vitriol is copper sulfate ($CuSO_4$), also called "bluestone". It was used largely as a dye and coloring product. It was also prescribed for various sorts of medicinal baths. In modern use it is said to be an effective fungicide, which may account for some of its archaic use. However, blue vitriol is highly poisonous, and it is most definitely not recommended for any revival folk medicinal usage.

BLUTSCHTILLE: *"Jesus Christ, dearest blood, who stops the pain and stops the blood..."* This is an example of a blutschtille charm or prayer; that is, a prayer the purpose of which is to stop a person from bleeding. The best known of these charms is the Biblical passage Ezekiel 16:6, which begins *"And when I passed by thee and saw thee polluted in thine own blood..."*

Blood stopping charms have often been used to test those who wish to become Brauchers. If the would-be apprentice was able to successfully staunch the flow of blood from a wound, s/he was meant to go further as they were seen to have the ability to Pow-Wow.

BLUTSCHTAERZ: A hemorrhage.

BLUTREINIGUNGSMITTEL: literally, a blood purifying remedy. The lack of refrigeration for our ancestors meant the eating of cured meats and canned or dried foodstuffs during the winter months. This was considered to lead to 'polluted' blood for the absence of fresh vegetables, fruits, and the eating of too much meat. The end of winter meant the cleaning of both one's house and one's self; it is here that we find the origins of "spring tonic" usage.

Today it is considered archaic (and perhaps "bad" or unscientific) usage to speak of "blood purifiers". However, there is much wisdom in the notion of ill health arising from bad diets, lack of exercise, and overall sluggishness resulting from various imbalances. The old fashioned way of speaking of such imbalances was to speak of so-called 'ill humors' (see The FOUR HUMORS).

We needn't speak of the now discredited theory of humors to understand that certain foods will aid one's health, and others will deteriorate the same. There are countless herbal mixtures that act in a detoxifying and purifying way. Personal favorites of the author are Swedish Bitters, and also nettle tea. Blutreinigungsmitteln (the 'n' at the end makes this word plural) being so closely linked with the old notions of humoral medicine, also link to the equally old practices of

BLUTSCHTEE: The bloodstone, or blutschtee, is a device that is sometimes used by Pow-Wowers to help staunch the flow of blood from a wound. This is not necessarily the same stone known by jewelers, being the greenish jasper dotted through with red iron oxide. This latter bloodstone was known as "martyr's stone" which was used by medieval Christians as the medium for carving representations of the Crucifixion and scenes of martyrdom.

Considering the archaic use of the latter, the jeweler's bloodstone would be a fair choice for use in blutschtille. However, a stone chosen for blood-stopping was often a seemingly ordinary rock, stained by the blood of many uses. Such stones are obtained from a natural setting when looking for such. During the search a stone might 'speak' to the Braucher – that is, the Braucher will notice the stone and 'something' about its presence will suggest its use as a bloodstone.

Stones for other types of Brauche work come to the practitioner in this manner. Sometimes these objects 'present' themselves when the Braucher least expects them. For example, this author has two white stones, which are for the use of diminishing pain and swelling. Their use was communicated to the author after picking them up; they need to be used together, simultaneously. Also after retrieving them they left a strong impression of having *personal names*, which the author uses when activating the stones. A person searching for a bloodstone may have a similar experience.

BONE: Bones are useful in Pow-Wow practice as a means of transferring disease (see CONTAGION TARGET). Like eggs, chickens' feet, hooves, hides, etc., bone has the memory of having been a living thing. This also is true for plant materials such as fresh/dried herbs, and pieces of wood. It may be pointed out by some that this can include stones and minerals as well; however, organic materials tend to be the best for the transference and containment of disease.

This is why many sympathetic formulae will direct the operator to take bits of wood contaminated with blood or pus and seal them into holes in posts or trees. Live trees are much better for this sort of activity as they have the strength to absorb the energy of the malady and make it inert and harmless. Victor Dieffenbach gave an example of the Brauche use of a bone for ridding a horse of sweeny in the winter 1975-1976 issue of *Pennsylvania Folklife*.

BRAUCHE BAG: This is a charm bag used in Braucherei. Brauche bags have been traditionally made out of the following materials: sack cloth, bleached linen cloth, and canvas. Some of these bags have also been made of red-dyed material, but have been more often than not made of natural colored or bleached rough fabrics. Generally, the bag will be a single pouch that contains either one or several ingredients and stitched closed.

Usually these contents are folded written charms (see ZAUBERZETTEL), and possibly the inclusion of other materials such as Mercury Dimes (the inclusion of silver), or the actual element of liquid mercury encased in a vial. With the possible exception of perhaps an odd religious item or a piece of talismanic stone or wood, these contents represent the extent of what traditionally makes up a Brauche bag.

Traditionally, more so, the contents are usually limited to a single or assorted mix of zauberzetteln. Some Brauche bags are large enough to accommodate the addition of several smaller pockets or pouches within. These pouches will hold multiple zauberzetteln securely without mixing inside the bag. A comparison to the hoodoo or rootworker charm bags may be made, but to this author's knowledge Brauche bags have not included root matter or herbs.

Brauche bags are sometimes worn upon the person to be helped by the charm; other times, these bags are hidden within crevices or holes in houses, barns, and other outbuildings to be protected with the virtue of these bags' contents. There is etiquette to be observed in the use of these charms, primarily being that they are never to be opened. In the past, it was understood (but the recipient firmly reminded by the Braucher) that to open a Brauche bag was to render it useless.

BRAUCHE STICK: In times past, a few Brauchers had a special cane or staff, the head of which was sometimes carved into the shape of a snake's head. The author has not seen one of these canes or sticks in use for the purpose of Brauche practice. However, it seems that this device was probably used as a 'sign' or emblem of Braucherei practice – such as the mortar and pestle designates a pharmacist, or a red and white striped pole signifies a barber's tonsorial parlor. The Braucher's staff may be related to the blackthorn or whitethorn "blasting rods" traditional to certain English cunning men or Witch masters. The snake-headed Brauche stick may also be symbolic of the rod of Aaron and Moses.

> And the Lord spoke unto Moses and unto Aaron, saying: When Pharaoh shall speak unto you, saying, Shew a miracle for you: then thou shalt say unto Aaron, Take thy rod, and cast it before Pharaoh, and it shall become a serpent. And Moses and Aaron went in unto Pharaoh, and they did so as the Lord had commanded; and Aaron cast down his rod before Pharaoh, and before his servants, and it became a serpent. Then Pharaoh also called the wise men and the sorcerers: now the magicians of Egypt, they also did in like manner with their enchantments. For they cast down every man his rod, and they became serpents: but Aaron's rod swallowed up their rods. **Exodus 7:8-12**

And it was with this very rod that Aaron and Moses initiated each of the plagues upon Egypt.

> And the Lord said unto Moses, Wherefore criest thou unto me? Speak unto the children of Israel, that they go forward: But lift thou up thy rod, and stretch out thine hand over the sea, and divide it: and the children of Israel shall go on dry ground through the midst of the sea. **Exodus 14:15-16**

BRAUCHER: A Braucher is one who practices Braucherei (see BRAUCHEREI below) and who, therefore, "brauchs" or "tries" for an illness in order to cure it or to give the patient some measure of relief. Prior to the onset of the twentieth century, there was little to distinguish a Pow-Wow doctor from that of an allopathic physician (i.e., a medical doctor).

The further back we go in time, the less we can tell the difference between the "scientific" doctor and the so-called "quack". The latter term of abuse arose in use by the practitioners of the then newly formed professional guilds of medicine during the early modern period (circa 1500 – 1700) prior to the Industrial Revolution. This derogatory term then 'stuck' to all who deviated from (or were not a part of) accredited medical training.

At one time, there was very little difference between doctors, butchers, blacksmiths, barbers, faith healers, and surgeons. Midwives also fall into this category. The accredited university trained doctor of ages past was often the cause of as much pain and suffering as the patient's disease itself. Very few individuals were able to afford the services of such a physician, and relied heavily upon the services of herbalists, faith healers, midwives, and the like. If you needed a tooth pulled, you went to a blacksmith; if you needed your "humors" balanced, you consulted a barber or a butcher for bloodletting (see BLOODLETTING).

The Braucher of previous times might also have been a conventional doctor (allopath) and more likely a homeopath, when his Braucherei was combined with more orthodox and accredited training. The old-fashioned archetypal country physician seems to fit this model. Such a doctor was found in the person of Dr. Frederick LaMotte Santee of Wapwallopen, Pennsylvania (see "A Chapter of Dedication and Remembrance").

Today a Braucher is more akin to a faith healer than a doctor in the currently understood sense. Brauchers also treat 'illnesses' that medical doctors will not touch: spirit possession, hauntings, curses, and the like. The local Braucher functioned –and still may function—as a "Witch-finder": that is, one who is able to diagnose a "ferhexed" (cursed) condition and identify the curser (Witch/hexe – see HEXEREI), and remove the curse. An alternative term for the word "Braucher" is "Pow-Wow" or spelled "Powwow" – as in a "Pow-Wow doctor". No one is really sure where this term originated.

Some have opined that it stems from an old Algonquin Indian word (*powan*) related to medicine and magic. Others have hypothesized that it may be a run-down version of the English word "power", as in *power doctor* (Kriebel 2007), a term that was common among the traditional Scots-Irish and German inhabitants of Appalachia, and southern Black root workers ("Hoodoo").

Other names in Appalachia include: Witch doctor, Witch master, goomer doctor, and conjure folk. Gerald C. Milnes book *Signs, Cures, & Witchery* is a treasure trove of information regarding the Germanic influence in Appalachian culture. A *hexenmeister* is sometimes an alternate title for a Pow-Wow practitioner; although some have reserved this as a designation for one who paints hex signs (see HEX SIGN). This latter term has been interpreted to mean one who is skilled at turning back curses: a spell master.

BRAUCHEREI: Also called Pow-Wow. The word "Braucherei" comes from the German *Brauchen* which means "to use", with the word *Brauche* having the meaning of "use" or "custom". Braucherei is the German use of sympathetic remedies for most of the ailments that plague mankind. This author is of the opinion that most (if not all) cultures have their own versions of this manner of folk healing.

Practices that are highly akin to Braucherei, and in many cases identical with it, are practiced throughout Europe, Britain, and their various lands of emigration throughout the West. Among the Pennsylvania Dutch, this practice is commonly known as *Pow-Wow*. There has been some disagreement among the "Dutch" about the correct term to use in reference to the sympathetic healing practice, which in *The Red Church* is called *Braucherei*. For some, the term "Braucherei" very specifically refers to a form of strong massage, which is sometimes accompanied by prayer – such as was practiced by Ruth Weil-Kusler. For others, the term had connotations of black magic, and used only the word "Pow-Wow" to refer to sympathetic healing.

Others still held the term "Pow-Wow" at arms length, as it was believed to be a practice synonymous with black magic, or hexerei. Braucherei has many roots *and is a uniquely Germanic synthesis of these diverse strains*. Much traditional Braucherei practice can be traced to Greek, Roman, Jewish, and Coptic sources, along with the remaining pre-Christian practices of Germanic healers.

Throughout the centuries Brauchers have been influenced by various trends and fads that had passed through Europe, such as Mesmerism. It was quite common centuries back to ascribe magical and sympathetic cures to foreign, exotic influences, such as Jews and Gypsies. *The Romanus Book* (see ROMANUSBUCHLEIN), for instance, was attributed to "Gypsies", hence the word "Romanus", meaning the people called "Rom".

Another charm book, *Albertus Magnus' Egyptian Secrets* has a similar connotation via its use of the word "Egyptian". The Rom people were believed to be of ancient Egyptian stock, and were called "Gypsies" as a result. Also the term "Egyptian" was synonymous with all that was mysterious, magical, and exotic. The above is not to say that there are any genuinely (strong) Rom roots to Brauche practice. As for the American transplantation of Braucherei, some believe that there are American Indian roots to Brauche practices, but this author has not seen evidence of any strong ties to such. Thus are the roots of Braucherei.

BRAZEN SERPENT, The: (Also called the *Nehushtan*)
                   And the Lord sent fiery serpents among the people, and they bit the people; and much people of

> Israel died. Therefore the people came to Moses, and said, We have sinned, for we have spoken against the Lord, and against thee; pray unto the Lord, that he take away the serpents from us. And Moses prayed for the people. And the Lord said unto Moses, Make thee a fiery serpent, and set it upon a pole: and it shall come to pass, that every one that is bitten, when he looketh upon it, shall live. And Moses made a serpent of brass, and put it upon a pole, and it came to pass, that if a serpent had bitten any man, when he beheld the serpent of brass, he lived. **Numbers 21:6-9**

The verbal imagery of this serpent can be called upon in Brauche charms for any manner of snake or insect bite. The serpent of Moses is a perfect example of sympathetic magic, of like curing like. One old Braucherei charm against snake bite is said to invoke what we might call "snakeness" by the supposed non-sense words "*tsing, tsing, tsing*" -- possibly derived from the word *tsingel* which refers to the motion a snake's tongue. The serpent in the book of Numbers is sometimes called the *Nehushtan*, which may be a play on two Hebrew words *nachash* (serpent) and *nahoshet* (brass, bronze).

> And as Moses lifted up the serpent in the wilderness, even so must the Son of Man be lifted up: That whosoever believeth in him should not perish, but have eternal life. **John 3:14-15**

Christ is the ultimate antidote to all of the poisons that ruin humanity, and His power is the strength of the Braucher. In fact, some early sects of Christianity likened Christ to this serpent. The serpent, especially in the early Christian religion, had a dual role: it could represent man's undoing by the devil, or represent Christ's power and wisdom. Indeed, we could speak of a heavenly vs. a satanic serpent – even as the Lamb of Christ (a horned animal) is victorious over the Goat of Satan (another horned animal).

Gnostic Christians of the Ophite sect believed that Christ had already come twice: first as the serpent in the Garden, and then secondly as the man Jesus. In this cosmology, the True God had sent the serpent of wisdom into the Eden in order to liberate humanity from the powers of the demiurge (see The DEVIL). Of course, this explanation is mostly just an interesting digression, as the classical Gnostic cosmology had no direct influence on practitioners of Pow-Wow. Perhaps only the most learned and well-read of hexenmeisters may have come across such notions.

CARDIOLOGY: Or, *cardialgia*. In Pennsylvania German folk medicine this condition was/is related to the "folk illness" of Livergrown or *aagewachse*. In Pennsylvania German "cardiology" has also been termed *haerzgschpaerr* and *hazschpann*. Cardiology has relatively nothing to do with a heart condition, such as the modern scientific use of this term would suggest. Symptoms of cardiology are similar to those of aagewachse. Generally, these symptoms include feelings of cramping and constriction in the lower area of the chest. In fact "cardiology" may be the symptoms of bronchitis or pleurisy.

CHRIST: from the Greek *Christos* meaning "anointed one"; this is the Greek translation of the Hebrew title *Meshiach*, or Messiah. The "savior" is not the meaning of these terms, although that function is implied. In Greek the word for savior is *soter*: *Ihesous Xristos Theou Yios Soter* (ΙΧΘΥΣ) "Jesus Christ God's Son Savior". This phrase spells out in its words' first letters the Greek for "fish" (*ichthys*) and is the reason behind the "Jesus fish" symbol.

The Greek term comes, ultimately, from the Proto Indo European word **ghrei*, which means "to rub". From **ghrei* descends our English words "grisly", "grim", and "grime". In French a related word is "crème". Odd as some of these derivations may seem, even more strangely there is an etymological connection between *christos/*ghrei* and terms used for the Devil in European folklore. (see **The DEVIL**) This latter observation means nothing beyond its curious nature. Theologically there is nothing to it. It might seem a tad redundant to include an entry for Christ, especially for a Christian reader. However, for one to grasp the significance of Braucherei, it might be useful to make a few comments regarding this practice's 'patron' and divine Overseer.

Conventional religion is quickly becoming a spiritless superstition. Priests and ministers have been reduced to being social workers in clerical drag. Theology and spiritual practice have been replaced with soup-kitchens, homeless shelters, and "social justice" (the so-called "social gospel"). There is very little left of the numinous in mainstream Christian religion today, which is why the pews are growing empty and cold. Esoterically speaking, *Christ is the true Light Bringer*: that blessed anointed spirit of supernatural compassion that heals all things at the deepest level. This awesome Power has been demoted to a superhuman Nanny.

The Red Church is written to present what remains of traditional Braucherei practice – at least as this author has experienced it. The orientation of this book is, therefore, from the viewpoints of the mainstream church (and sectarian) folk of the Pennsylvania German Christians. While this is not meant to be an "evangelistic" work, it is this author's hope that it will inspire not just faith *in* Christ, but also the faith *of* Christ. To that end, this book has been left rather open-ended and non-denominational enough that anyone who identifies as being a Christian can put Braucherei to use. Some writers, such as C.S. Lewis, have pointed out a few similarities between the old German deity Balder and Jesus Christ. Dr. Paul Carus writes:

> Christianity to-day is essentially a Teutonic religion. The ethics of Christianity, which formerly was expressed in the sentence "Resist not evil," began, in agreement with the combative spirit of the Teuton race, more and more to emphasize the necessity of struggle. Not only was the figure of Christ conceived after the model of a Teutonic war-

king, the son of the emperor, while his disciples became his faithful vassals... Carus 1996, pp 245-46.

Carus, in the beginning of his study on the conceptions of evil in Northern Europe, briefly outlined the almost Stoic virtues and tribal characteristics of the ancient Germans. Among these being fighters for whom *"life means strife"* and *"their highest ideal was not to shrink from the unavoidable, but to face it squarely and unflinchingly."* (Carus p241)

Mindful of these traits Balder the Beautiful was the healing Christ-like God of Light in heathen times, which would put to flight the powers of darkness and chaos. Much like Jesus, Balder – who was the son of the high-god Woden -- met his end by treachery, but will come again at the end of time (after Ragnarok – the Twilight of the Gods).

While there have been healing modalities prior to Christ, it is only quite logical from a Christian perspective that the Master of all healing arts should be the One who cast out unclean spirits, raised the dead, cured the blind, the deaf, the crippled, and the leprous. Regardless of how one interprets the life of Jesus or interprets what it means to be Christian, without the Paraclete (the Holy Spirit) there is no real healing to be had. If one studies Jesus' miracles in 1st century Palestine, the healings wrought were not only literal (although some deny this) but also allegorical: that if we are healed physically this is a mere trifle to the Work that can be done on our souls, and lastly that if we follow **The Way**, we too can do the same because *"He who believes in Me, the works that I do he will do also; and greater works than these he will do, because I go to My Father."* **John 14-12**. And, of course, His Father is our Father too.

The accounts of the life and ministry of Christ in the Bible are limited to His all-important Work of Salvation. The Gospels are not historical or biographical accounts in our present-day sense.

The ancients had a different way of conceptualizing such things and only wrote of the things most germane to the point they wished to get across. For example, the chronology of the New Testament seems as if the works of Jesus' ministry could be compacted into the time span of a single year; however, we know that is not the case. What vegetables and pastries Jesus might have enjoyed eating while on earth did not concern the writers of the Gospels.

> Even the personality of Jesus, it seems, was not the primary object of interest. The compelling personality which emerges from the Gospels is one and vividly real, but little effort is made to delineate Him fully. We can believe that the atmosphere of mystery in which He appears reflects the atmosphere of His historic presence; those who knew Him and related the anecdotes from which the Gospels were written knew that there were depths in Him which they never comprehended. -- McKenzie, p. 432

Of His miracles, 35 of these are recorded in the Gospels. Doubtless there were more of these. Considering the above, it was perhaps only those miracles illustrative of His ministry's purpose that were recorded. Ryrie, on page 11 in his beautiful book *The Miracles of Our Lord*, enumerates the characteristics of these miracles:

1. They were performed for high purposes. He did not use them for His personal convenience (remember His temptation) but to meet definite needs of others.
2. They were not confined to a single sphere of life, so they could never be considered trickery. They were done on nature (see Luke 5:4-7), on human beings (see Mark 1:29-31, 40-42), and on demons (see Mark 5:12-13).
3. They were done openly in front of spectators and witnesses. When the Gospels were written, there

would have been many persons living who had seen His miracles and who would have know and objected if the Gospel writers had not accurately recorded the stories.
4. They did not always involve the faith of the person healed but sometimes were done in spite of the lack of faith (see John 5:7).

Here is a list of these miracles. The very first recorded is His turning water into wine at the wedding feast at Cana: John 2:1-11. Of the exorcisms (the Gospels actually use the Greek term *exballo* as opposed to *exorkizo*) He performed: Mark 1:21-28, Luke 4:31-37; Matthew 12:22-37, Mark 3:22-30, Luke 11:14-23; Luke 8:26-39, Matthew 8:28-34, Mark 5:1-20.

In the following accounts, Jesus raised the dead: Luke 7:11-16, Luke 8:41-42, 49-56, Mark 5:21-24, 35-43, Matthew 9:18-19, 23-26; John 11:1-44. Of His miracles involving the feeding of others, or otherwise involving a catch of fish: Luke 5:1-11; John 6:1-13, Matthew 14:13-21, Mark 6:31-44, Luke 9:10-17; Mark 8:1-10, Matthew 15:32-39; John 21:1-17. Not included in the foregoing feedings and catches is the catch of the fish with the coin in its mouth: Matthew 17:24-27.

Lastly, here follows all of the healings (of the deaf, blind, mute, leprous, bleeding, injured, and the otherwise ill): John 4:43-54; Matthew 8:5, Luke 7:2; John 5:1-23; Mark 1:29-31, Matthew 8:14-15, Luke 4:38-39; Mark 1:40-45; Matthew 8:2-4, Luke 5:12-16; Luke 5:17-26; Matthew 9:1-8, Mark 2:1-12; Matthew 12:9-14, Mark 3:1-5, Luke 6:6-11; Mark 5:25-34, Matthew 9:20-22, Luke 8:43-48; Matthew 9:27-31; Matthew 9:32-34; Matthew 15:21-28, Mark 7:24-30; Mark 7:31-37; Mark 8:22-26; Mark 9:14-29, Matthew 17:14-21, Luke 9:37-43; John 9:1-41; Luke 13:10-17; Luke 14:1-6; Luke 17:11-19; Luke 18:35-43, Matthew 20:29-34, Mark 10:46-52; Luke 22:49-51, Matthew 26:51-54, Mark 14:46-47, John 18:10-11.

Concerning His control over the forces of nature are these passages: Mark 4:35-41, Matthew 8:23-27, Luke 8:22-25; Matthew 14:22-33, Mark 6:45-52, John 6:14-21; Mark 11:12-14, 20-26, Matthew 21:18-22.

CONTAGION: For the practitioner of sympathetic medicine such as Braucherei, we speak of disease or even spiritual 'evils' as tending to contaminate other beings or objects in order to continue their existence. It is common knowledge (and common sense) that if we share a close proximity with one who has a "cold" that most likely we too will contract the rhinitis. It was also a very common belief that one could not only "catch" a cold, but *buy* one as well – or willfully *give one away* by wishing it to another (a form of cursing).

This is the rationale behind *buying* warts from one afflicted with warts, or *transferring* the same to another creature or object such as a penny, a raw potato, roasted chickens' feet, etc. Evil is mobile and always looking for a place to nest, according to the most archaic strata of this notion of contagion. When Christ cast out the unclean spirits as recorded in **Matthew 8:31-32**, they immediately went from the two men and into a herd of swine, then into the sea. Unclean spirits fear being cast into "the outer darkness" or cast into "dry places", and seem to gather strength from 'wet' environments, such as a human body. They are held well in salt water, which is why this solution is paradoxically both unclean as well as cleansing.

Traditional Catholic holy water is actually a mild salt-water solution. 'Unclean' stagnant waters will hold such spirits well to their own advantage, but they cannot abide by "living water" (being sweet/fresh running water). The latter case is where we get the old notion that ghosts, Witches, vampires and demons cannot cross over running water. The above may seem like nonsense to the modern mind, but there may in fact be an electromagnetic basis to this phenomenon.

The practice of Braucherei often enjoins the removal of disease by varying the levels or depths of contagion. For example, some charms will draw out an illness from the depth of a person's body, such as an organ or bone, to the muscle, then from the muscle, to the skin, and then from the skin to the hair, and then from the hair to the object meant to receive the disease. Such a recipient is called the "contagion target". This is a new technical wording to describe where the disease will go.

CONTAGION TARGET: As written above regarding contagion, the contagion target will be the recipient of the disease or 'curse' (negative energy). A Braucher's ability to transfer maladies from the patient to another creature or object has been a source of distrust on the part of non-practitioners. The reasoning being that what one can remove or take-off can be easily given – that a rogue Braucher could instantaneously become a "Witch" at any moment.

Contagion targets have ranged from animals and animal products (eggs, claws, skulls, leg bones, etc.) to plants (trees, herb bundles, sticks, etc.), to mineral formations (rocks, raw crystals, pebbles, etc.), to geographical features (mountains, hills, caves, holes, lakes, etc.). The Hexenkopf in Williams Township, Pennsylvania, is a good example of a geographical feature used as a target for the Brauchers of that area during the 19th century. Although not as common in Braucherei as in other forms of folk medicine, eggs are an excellent medium for the transfer of disease.

The practitioner himself/ herself is the contagion target, as the Braucher is the one drawing out the disease by divine assistance. Therefore, it is important for the Braucher not to hold onto the contamination. Some will wipe their arms and shake their hands in a gesture of ridding the malady; others will wash with clear, cold running water. Many will transfer the disease to a specific target. Paracelsus referred to a person's *mumia*, or vitality; the Hindus know this as *prana*; in Europe this has also been known as *animal magnetism*, or *vril*. It is this mumia which is transferred from the patient to the Braucher; or from the patient directly to a contagion target other than the Braucher. As an odd point of interest, some old folk medicinal formulae call for "mummy" or "mummy dust".

This is indeed what it sounds like: powdered mummies and it is related to the concepts of mumia, sympathy, and contagion. The parts of corpses were often used to alleviate various ailments. To present day folks, this is a rather morbid notion. Examples of such would be the transfer of disease to the corpse, or using the hand of a corpse to stroke away pain or paralysis. A woman who has miscarried and is lactating might stroke her breasts with the hand of a dead infant to bring the lactation to a conclusion.

COPPERAS: Copperas is iron sulfate $FeSO_4$. In times past this was used as a purgative, as it induced extreme nausea and vomiting. At a time when our ancestors believed that purging our bodies of "ill humors" by way of vomiting, enemas/and induced diarrhea, and blood letting was good for all ailments, an agent such as copperas was used. Needless to say, copperas is very dangerous, and if encountered in any of the old formularies, do not use it. Copperas was also used extensively during the time of George Hohman as a coloring substance: iron gall ink, and as a mordant for wool. A chemical such as this would have been readily available to our Colonial and Victorian ancestors.

CROSS, symbol & sign of the: The cross is the most used 'sign' in Braucherei. The Christian denominations that utilize the gesture of signing oneself with a cross among the Pennsylvania Dutch, would be the Catholics and Lutherans (although not as frequent). During any Pow-Wow session the Braucher will 'seal' the healing with three gestures of the cross in a similar manner to the way a priest or minister makes that gesture in blessing to a congregation. However, the Braucher's crosses are often smaller and localized to the specific place (area of the body) where the charm has been focused. The gesture is also not made with an open hand.

The gesture of the Braucher's cross blessing is made with a closed fist, but with the thumb free and sticking up. The outline of the cross is then made with the thumb. It is also by way of the thumb that unguents are applied to the patient's body (if such are used). The crosses are usually made with the right hand in blessing most ailments or wounds.

The left hand is for 'cursing' various other ailments in order to make them diminish. *Crossing by the right hand is for growth; crossing by the left hand is for diminishing.* The cross' Christian history is well known: it was the instrument of Jesus' execution. Some have criticized the use of the cross as a worn religious symbol as, they argue, wearing a symbol of execution is rather morbid – rather like wearing little replicas of electric chairs. This author understands that criticism, but it is nonetheless a misrepresentation of why a Christian uses this symbol.

In mainstream Christian belief, it was Jesus' death that opened the Gates of Life, atoned for our transgressions, and opened a channel for humanity with God the Father. The cross is therefore a sign of victory. Three crosses are made in blessing (for either growth or diminishment) that echo the Holy Trinity (**see THREE, the number**). The cross, however, was not always the universal symbol of the Christian faith. The early Christians were rather short on symbols and dared not display what they did have openly. Christianity was very much a secretive religion due to the persecutions.

The crucifix, which is the cross plus the corpus, was not seen in use prior to the 7th century. The early Christian crosses took the forms of either the equal-armed "Greek" cross, or the Tau cross (called such as it is shaped like the Greek letter Tau, which looks just like our Latin capital letter 'T'). The early depictions of Jesus never showed the crucifixion, but Jesus as shepherd. The symbol of the cross is very ancient. It was because of its pagan past that early Christians were slow to adopt it use. Almost universally the cross is a solar symbol, often taking the forms of spinning whisks or wheels, such as the fylfot or the now besmirched *swastika* – which prior to Nazism was a sign of good luck.

In the Near East the cross was associated with various deities; and in Europe among the Teutonic peoples it was a symbol of the god Thor. As circumstances would have it, the cross with a "corpus" is not entirely Christian. In pre-Christian Europe the sinister origins of our quaint country scarecrows lay in human sacrifices that were hung upon these instruments in order to promote fertility.

When missionaries came to our ancestral lands, it is little wonder that the folk took to these ways after they were 'dressed up' in a manner that they could understand and absorb. The equal-armed cross that is made by Brauchers can also bring in the symbolism of the Four Directions, the Four Evangelists, the Four Winds, etc. Brauchers would often carve, draw, or etch the sign of the cross into door lintels, joists, door hinges – anywhere or on anything that evil spiritual power could use to enter into a dwelling. It ought to go without saying that the Braucher will always make these crosses in the Three Highest Names: The Father, Son, & Holy Ghost. All Braucherei conjury is done in this fashion.

DEAD, the: Corpses have been utilized in sympathetic medicine as vehicles for the transference of contagion. Warts and other growths have been treated in this manner by way of stroking the dead hand over them. For women whose infants were stillborn, the tiny corpse's hand was stroked down the breasts to relieve them of their unneeded milk. All of this strikes us as quite gruesome today. Our lives are sanitized and the rude facts of life are often quite distant.

Before the days of "funeral parlors" (or as some Pennsylvania old-timers liked to call them "corpse houses") families prepared their own dead and held wakes in the best room of the house; at times that was the bedroom where the person died, but mostly it was the parlor. Our Victorian ancestors took post-mortem photographs (tin types and daguerreotypes) of their deceased loved-ones, along with creating mind-boggling wreaths, jewelry, and other mementos made of the dead person's hair. Conjuration of the spirits of the dead (necromancy) is a practice not engaged in by Brauchers, as such conjury is forbidden in the Old Testament.

Some Brauchers will not even address such spirits, let alone deliberately "call them up." The folksy "Dumb Supper" has been practiced by many different European ethnic groups, which is a meal done wholly backwards in order to attract the spirit of a dead relative. This practice skates a thin line: it is not really conjury as it is merely an *invitation* to the spirit, but it comes pretty close to actual necromancy.

DEVIL, The: As with Hexerei or Witchcraft, the subject of "the Devil" is quite complex. On the surface, this is a rather cut-and-dry affair. For mainstream Pennsylvania German Christians the Devil is simply "Satan" or the spirit of Evil that seeks to challenge and undo God's work. Some have even referred to the Devil as "The Second Highest Name." The "First Highest" being God (in charms invoked as "The Three Highest Names").

Surprisingly the *popular* version of Satan is not strictly Biblical. In the Hebrew Bible (the Old Testament) there is no personality called "Satan", as if that word were a proper name. Much like the so-called Names of God, the names of angelic forces were more-or-less titles or descriptions of actions by those forces. A spiritual being (an "angel" – which only means *messenger* in Greek) sent by God can one moment be a source of healing and good fortune, and then in the next act in an adversarial way, all acts being directed by Providence.

The actual Hebrew word for Satan, in this original context, is *ha shatan* – that is, "the satan," the adversary. In **1 Chronicles 21:1** *ha shatan* incites King David to implement a census contrary to God's will. An angel described as *ha shatan* torments Job to test his virtue. In archaic Hebrew religion *ha shatan*, therefore, is any angelic being sent to test people by inciting *yetzer harah*, or evil inclinations. By no means was this being an adversary of God, although God might have to reel in this angelic power if it were to get too zealous in its work. In **Isaiah 45:7** God declares that *"I form the light, and create darkness; I make peace, and create evil; I the LORD do all these things."*

In the original Hebrew religion there was no dualism. God was responsible for all things. It was not until after the Babylonian captivity those notions of dualism seeped into Hebrew religion *via* contact with the ancient Persian Magian religion. The oft-quoted passage of Isaiah 14:12 thought to describe *ha shatan* as "Lucifer" (*helel ben shahar* – bright star, son of the morning) is a prophetic chastisement of a proud Babylonian king.

All of the foregoing is actually the simple part of the Devil's history. Here is where it gets more complicated. When our ancestors spoke of "the Devil" they were not always referring to the being of *ha shatan* or even the later Satan of early Christianity. The idea of the Devil became mixed in with the lore of many spiritual beings and powers that existed in the old heathen religion. Many of these, but not all, were powers variously known as "giants", "ogres" "woodwoses", "wood sprites", etc. Some of the spirits were the many guises of the most prominent deities themselves: Woden, Thor, and Freya, etc.

During later Christian times the original forms of the spirits were no longer recognized, and were lumped under the title of "the Devil". Our English monikers of the Devil reflect this pre-Christian background: Old Scratch (from *scrat* or *schrat* meaning a hairy wood sprite), and Old Nick (from *hnikkar* meaning "slayer" – a title of Woden). "Grim Reaper" was another of Woden's titles. The word "grim" itself is, oddly enough, related to the word "Christ" *via* their mutual Proto Indo European root word **ghrei* ; also related to this word is another title of Woden's being *Grimr* which means "hooded" or cloaked, covered. It was Woden who was the leader of the Wild Hunt as *Wilde Jaeger* or *Ewigyeager* (the Eternal Hunter), a role later taken on by the Devil in European folklore.

The land spirits and giants who were later lumped together as the Devil were often featured as being dimwitted and easily outsmarted. The tales of Till Eulenspiegel, the mythical medieval peasant trickster, show how "the Devil" and evil can be easily duped and exposed. The Brothers Grimm feature two stories of this sort of non-Christian Devil: "The Devil and His Grandmother" and "The Devil with Three Golden Hairs". In Austria, Switzerland, and Bavaria there is the Devil known as Krampus, who is the dark companion of Father Christmas, or Kris Kringle, which is a corruption of *Krist Kindel* (the Christ Child); his role was to scary little children into being good and to take away the bad ones. Krampus (also called *Belznickel* or *Belschnickel*; or *Schwarze Peter*) is an example of a woodwose or wood sprite.

Father Christmas ("Santa Clause") too, more than simply being a folksy variation on Saint Nicholas, Bishop of Myra, was closely related to old Woden. To this day there are young men who will dress up like Krampus during the first two weeks of December, with especial emphasis on 5 December. With carefully made red wooden masks, black sheep skins and horns, young men take to the streets guising on these nights. Throughout Europe there are bridges, cathedrals, and other architectural wonders that are said to have been built by the Devil.

These structures would be cunningly wrought, but for only one single flaw as the mark of their maker. In Matthew 4:1-11 Jesus is tempted by Satan. Among these temptations Satan said *"All these things I will give You if You will fall down and worship me"*. Here may lay the foundation for the much later notions of selling one's soul. The indigenous spirits of pre-Christian Europe did not demand souls *per se*, but would make deals with individuals. According to folklore human beings could sometimes extricate themselves from these arrangements by varying degrees of cunning, thereby keeping the spoils and leaving the spirit (i.e. the Devil) to gnash his teeth.

In much later Christian times, there has been very little differentiation made between the Biblical (and quasi-Biblical) Satan and these "devils" because many do not realize that there are any differences to make; therefore, "the Devil" exists on a spectrum of varying degrees of evil and uncanny behavior. Students of theology will often speak of one having either a high or low Christology; likewise, we can say that there are those with equally high or low "Satanologies": Satan as a lowly wood sprite or as an exalted but sinister Archangel or Cherub (or Seraph), or in another sense altogether, an anti-God.

The Braucher is the enemy of the Devil. It is the Braucher's purpose to bring healing and harmony; to undo sickness and to break curses – to help undo some of the works of the Devil and his helpers. Despite the history outlined above there is very much something malign and wicked that seems to be at the helm of our planet these days. Call that 'helmsman' what one will; there is **Evil** in the world, which needs to be combated: twisted, dark, perverted things that seek to undo all human joy, security, and spiritual progress.

It is deeply unfortunate (but by no means surprising) that some of this wickedness goes under the guise of religion. There are many philosophies around these days that do not wish to square with this reality, seeing good and evil as "relative." Even some "churches" have veered off into this wayward direction.

Another unfortunate thing regarding the Devil: it is this author's opinion that one of the things that empower the Devil is the *fear* of him. It seems that way too many Christians spend more time worrying about and contemplating the Devil than they do God. Certain folks see Satan under every rock and behind every tree. They give the Devil way too much credit. This can only lead to a life of fear and a rather sour outlook. Please remember that,

The earth is the LORD's, and the fullness thereof; the world, and they that dwell therein. For he hath founded it upon the seas, and established it upon the floods. Who shall ascend into the hill of the LORD? Or who shall stand in his holy place? He that hath clean hands, and a pure heart; who hath not lifted up his soul unto vanity, nor sworn deceitfully. He shall receive the blessing from the LORD, and righteousness from the God of his salvation. This is the generation of them that seek thy face, O Jacob. Selah. Lift up your heads, O ye gates; and be ye lift up, ye everlasting doors; and the King of glory shall come in. Who is the King of glory? The LORD strong and mighty in battle. Lift up your heads, O ye gates even lift them up, ye everlasting doors and the King of glory shall come in. Who is this King of glory? The LORD of hosts, he is the King of glory. Selah.

DOG: Dogs were seen by the Pennsylvania Dutch as being sources of protection from supernatural powers. This may go back to the Mediterranean Pagan notion of dogs being guardians of the underworld. It was quite common to hear a dog being called by the name of "Water" or in German "Wasser". A dog named "Water" was more effective in scaring off paranormal phenomena as live, running water dissolves spectral powers and provides a barrier to such beings.

This was a form of sympathetic naming, imparting the power of living water to a protective animal. It is perhaps that running water creates an electromagnetic interference with paranormal phenomena. Crossing a bridge or fording a stream was a way to dodge any supernatural pursuer.

DRAGON (See WORM)

DROPSY: An old term for edema, sometimes also called "hydropsy," which is the abnormal build up of interstitial fluid causing swelling.

DUNG: animal poop has been employed in medicine for centuries across many different cultures. It has been an ingredient in various philters and drafts to combat fever, and has been employed as an external plaster. Excrement such as from a cat, dog, or bat, would be a sympathetic ingredient for a remedy, and would therefore not be one of the medicinally active ingredients. These mixtures create the archetypal (or stereotypical) "Witch's brew".

Nasty pills and philters aside, Paracelsus made great use of dung as a "magnet" for attracting diseases out of his patients. The desiccated excrement from a patient would be pulverized and placed in a pouch; the pouch was then worn near the diseased area in order to absorb the signature of the ailment. After a time, the pouch's contents would be mixed with dirt and a plant would be grown in the mixture. This plant would then sympathetically absorb the disease through the magnetic excrement. Horse and cow dung give off a steady heat during the decomposition process, which made it ideal for slow 'cooking' medicinal preparations that need a long period of "digestion".

A sealed flask or jar, possibly connected to a reflexive condenser (such as the alchemical 'pelican') would be packed in dung for a set number of days or weeks until the digestion was complete. A direct fire, or even a water bath, may be too hot for working with delicate essences in the preparation of a medicinal. It is said that one method for making oneself into a hexe is to stand on a pile of dung, while swinging a dung hook, and denouncing the Holy Trinity, the Virgin Mary, etc. The Devil would then understand this as a 'pact' and would make one into a Witch.

The author has always found this method of entering Witchdom a bit tongue-in-cheek; it seems to be more of a statement of what it means *to be a hexe* and one's place in life as a result, than an actual method of initiation. However, it would not be terribly surprising if someone actually did this, making himself by his blasphemy the punch-line of a 'dirty' (or smelly) joke.

EMBER DAYS: From the Old English *ymb* (around) and *ren* (running). According to Catholic scholars the term may also come from the phrase *Quator Tempora*, meaning "four times". There may be something to the latter as the German word is *Quatember*, or *Quatemberzeiten* (Quatember Times).

Medieval Germans would have known these days as *Weihfasten*. In Catholicism the Ember Days are four annual sets of three days (Wednesday, Friday, and Saturday) in each set. These are fasting days observed on the first week of March, the second week of June (after "Whitsunday" or Pentecost), the third week of September (following the Exaltation of the Cross), and the week before Christmas (right after St. Lucy's Day).

The observation of these days may have been pre-Christian in origin, but this is not really known for certain. It has been observed that these days tend to fall closely near by recognized holy days on the old Celtic calendars: Candlemass, May Eve, Lammas, and Halloween (All Saints). Just as with the previously mentioned holy days, the Quatemberzeiten were well known for being propitious times for supernatural activity. Such days are sometimes referred to as being "liminal" – they are border areas or middle grounds between this world and the spirit world. Some of the most archaic "shamanistic" strata of Western European peoples can be found in the lore of such sacred times.

The Pennsylvania Germans, being mainly Protestant, would not have observed these days, but during the early days of immigration would have retained memory of them to a lesser or greater extent.

Brauchers and other such practitioners would have been more sentient of these sorts of times, as Braucherei is a pre-Reformation practice and retains elements of Catholic thought. *Here it might be good to note that Braucherei per se does not have "holidays" because it is not a religion.* However, since its practitioners are Christian the holidays are, of course, Christian too. If any phase of the practice occurs at certain 'special' times, it is because of the belief in the quality of the powers or energies available at those times. This is a completely operative thing and does not set up Pow-Wowing as some sort of dubious 'para-religion.'

ERYSIPELAS (See ROTLAUFE)

FALLING SICKENSS: is an antiquated term for epilepsy, convulsions, and other seizures.

FELON: A painful inflammation of the deep tissue of the finger or hand. If the inflammation is underneath a bone, a medical doctor is needed in order to lance it. Should the puss not drain, it can eat away at the bone. Turpentine has been a favorite folk cure for felons, but much care needs to be taken when using such agents. All remedies are designed to draw out the infection. Brauching for a felon is twofold: 1) stop the pain, and 2) draw out the inflammation. The first is the most successful piece; as with Pow-Wowing for a sore throat, the pain is sure to diminish if not go away entirely. If trying for a felon, do not be surprised if the inflammation 'piece' needs going over more than once. Deep inflammation needs lots of work. It is for this reason that Brauchers treat burns quickly, so the "fire" or "heat" does not go deeper and then to the bone.

FERHEXT: Ferhext means being "bewitched" or *berufen*. Most ailments a Braucher treats are not paranormally (supernaturally) induced -- that is to say, illness as a result of a curse. This is more the exception. When a person's ailments can be traced back to the malevolence of another, its root is almost always as a result of petty jealousies, envy, and such. Generally, this condition is what many would call the "evil eye" (*Böser Blick* in German, *beeserguck* in the dialect). It is easily treated by the method of brauching presented in this book. Truly purposeful curses are very rare. Very few have the ability necessary to witch another person with any degree of skill. In fact, if one comes to a Braucher with a psychically induced ailment, it could even be self-induced by way of phobias, limiting beliefs, deeply internalized anger or emotional trauma -- any and all baggage tucked away deeply within the subconscious. It is truly Christ's Fire and Light within the heart that exorcises that darkness.

FIEWER (HITZ): There are several different kinds of fevers that used to be acknowledged in folk medicine. Many of these have disappeared as conventional medicine has made scarlatina or *Roten Schaden* and their like things of the past, at least in the Western hemisphere. Sickness such as pleurisy (*bruschtfiewer*) and pneumonia (*lungefiewer*) have carried the title of "fever."

In English we sometimes still refer to "cold fever" or "hay fever" for allergies. In the dialect the former would be *kaltfiewer*. Fevers can kill. They are the body's response to an infection by heating itself up enough to kill it. Before antibiotics this waiting game was often deadly. If a person was lucky, the immune system would triumph and the fever would 'break.' In the old lore of folk medicine, the breaking of a fever would be sought for on uneven days (such as the 3rd, 5th, 7th, or 9th of the month, etc.).

Aside from herbal remedies such as diaphoretic teas made of strawberry leaves, or blood purifiers such as agrimony and dandelion, charms, Brauche bags, and *zauberzetteln* are employed to break fevers. The archaic term *ague* (French from the Latin *acuta*, English *acute*) comes up quite frequently in the old manuals and herbals – even in contemporary herbals and manuals of homoeopathy. An ague then is an acute fever. Previously, ague more specifically indicated malarial fever. For those unfamiliar, malarial fevers run in cycles. The first 'phase' is the cold stage with muscles spasms (chattering teeth, e.g.), followed by some relief, then an agonizing 'hot' stage and dehydration that remains until the fever breaks in profuse sweating. These cycles could be continuous, which is called a "daily" or "quotidian" ague; the fever that cycle every other day is the "tertian" ague; and a fever-cycle of every third day (or 72 hours) is the "quartan" ague.

It was important to shorten these stages, and to induce frequent urination, sweating, and greatly increase fluid intake. The herbal remedies for these fevers provided for those effects, as well as for their antimicrobial action and astringency to stop any internal hemorrhaging from frequent diarrhea. One of the more unpleasant side effects of malarial ague is the phenomenon of the "ague cake": this is the swelling and hardening of the spleen which presents itself has a hard, raised mass.

Once the fever cycle is broken, the "cake" will diminish and all of the poisons in the liver and spleen will wash out through the urine, leaving a red residue in the pot. The word malaria comes from the Italian *mal* and *aria*, which mean "bad air." Malaria, of course, is caused by a parasite transmitted by the bite of a mosquito. In as much as the mosquitoes are "air born," the air itself is not the problem. However, our ancestors didn't know this; they associated the bad smell of stagnant pools of water, swamps, and sewers as the origin of the fever and not the bugs that live there.

The literal German translation of malaria is *giftigluft* ("poisoned air"). One of the worst things that used to be done for fevers is bundling – swaddling the suffering patient in an abundance of blankets. This practice was only good for trying to induce the *sweating stage* to break the fever; however, many died because instead of cooling off, their fevers shot up and cooked them inside out. The idea of bathing people in snow, ice, or cold spring water was unimaginable as it was though the coldness itself possessed malignant properties.

FIRE & PESTILENCE LETTER (See HIMMELSBRIEF)

FOUR HUMORS, The: *Humorism* is ancient medical theory (or set of theories) that the human body is composed of four "humors" or substances, which when in balance make for health, and when out of balance make for illness. These substances were *blood*, *phlegm*, *yellow bile*, and *black bile*. Various methods were used to diagnose which of the humors was out of balance.

When the imbalance was 'diagnosed', the physician applied varying techniques to place the humor back into balance, such as: bloodletting (see BLOODLETTING), vomiting (emetics), urination (diuretics), and food intake (as certain foods were considered to induce the production of the humors. It is from these ancient ideas that we get some of our folk remedies like "spring tonics" to clean the blood, or that are supposed to "make blood" (see BLUTREINIGUNGS-MITTEL).

The doctors of old believed that these humors were aligned with other substances, times, seasons, and temperaments. The chief exponents of humorism were Galen, Hippocrates, and Avicenna. It was Avicenna who expanded humorism by linking each humor with the qualities of *hot*, *cold*, *moist*, and *dry*. In regard to temperaments, this is where we get our notions of personalities being melancholic (black bile), choleric (yellow bile), sanguine (blood), or phlegmatic (phlegm). For example, too much black bile led one to be melancholic (to suffer *melancholia*), or in today's language "to be depressed" (depression).

Humorism, in some regards, is not unlike theories of pathology, diagnosis, and treatment in medical paradigms found in traditional Ayurvedic (Indian) and Chinese medicine. A few Brauche doctors from times past have used humorism in their diagnosis and treatment of patients. These sorts of Brauchers were professionals who *differed very little* from their allopathic counterparts prior to the twentieth century.

GENERAL BRAUCHE CIRCUIT, the: This is the name that I coined for the method of brauching taught to me by Daisy Dietrich. It is a series of complex hand motions done over a patient that are reminiscent of other practices such as Reiki, and Mesmerism. There is a definite order to the motions and the parts of the body covered, which is done in cycles of three. I call it "general" as this type of brauching is good for all ailments and problems, needing no other forms of charms, prayers, talismans, etc.

It is a modality of Brauche practice that stands alone very well. In fact, Daisy practices no other form of brauching, and she refers to what she does as "Active Prayer". Throughout this book this circuit of hand motions is sometimes simply referred to as "The General", which is how Daisy always refers to it.

GEWECKS: also *Auswachs* or *warz*. Along with warts gewecks is the term used for any sort of outward growths. The previously strong beliefs in contagion and transference made the handling of toads or 'warty' chickens a source of human warts. Also under "gewecks" or *gewex*, are tumors and sebaceous cysts and "heisch" (see **HEISCH**).

GIFTICHE LUFT: "Poisoned air" is something that our ancestors feared most as the source of contagion. Unpleasant odors, such as from open sewers and chamber pots, were considered to be sources of illness. With such an attitude towards potent smells, one would expect that fresh air would have been a top concern. As it turns out, the sick were confined from draughts, where colder air in itself was said to be a source of 'colds.' Night air was especially avoided, more so during full moons.

To that end, windows were shut and shutters and curtains were closed so as to not let in either the air or the moon light. Diseases traveled by air, which we know today that some are truly airborne – but not all. Fetid air, damp or moist air in a home was a source of concern. We know now that a chronically damp room can harbor dangerous mold and cause much sickness. The winds themselves were seen as a source of disease at certain times of the year. Winter winds were dangerous to the elderly and spring winds for children. Perhaps some believed it was the very winds themselves that were a danger; others seem to believe that it is not really the winds that are dangerous, but the 'germs' that they carry.

GOLDEN SUNDAY: Easter Sunday.

GROUNDHOG DAY: February 2nd. If the groundhog does not see its shadow on this morning, it is supposed to leave its burrow, signifying the end of winter; if it does see its shadow, this is a portent of six more weeks of winter weather. This particular holiday was started by the Pennsylvania Germans, and is a variation on similar customs in Europe; however, in Germany the animal is not a groundhog, but a badger. In Pennsylvania there are "Groundhog Lodges" (*grundsow, grundsau*) that celebrate this day with PA Dutch cultural activities, where only the dialect is allowed to be spoken. Should one be caught speaking English, he is 'fined' a few cents and the money goes into a collection.

The first Grundsau Lodge was formed at a private gathering (*fersommling*) on 3 April, 1933, at the Keystone Trail Inn in Allentown, Pennsylvania. The lodge was an attempt to instill ethnic pride and to preserve the Pennsylvania German culture at a time when "German-ness" was looked down upon. The lodge was set to meet every February 2nd.

As of this writing, there are now 17 Grundsau Lodges in Pennsylvania. In 1987, a Grossdaadi Grundsau Lodge was formed as an affiliate of the 17 Lodges in order to plan and carry out programs and activities conducive to furthering the culture. They created a Pennsylvania German flag with the motto *"Liewwer Gott in Himmel Drin, Loss Uns Deitsche was mir sin"* ("Dear God in Heaven, Leave Us Germans What We Are"). Kutztown University has a nice brochure on the Grundsau Lodge available at their website www.kutztown.edu; contact with the Lodges can be made through the website www.padutchculture.com. Regarding the religious elements of this day, it is known as "Lichtmess" or "Lightmass" that celebrates the Feast of the Purification of the Virgin. According to the Celtic calendar, this is one of the four cross quarter days, and Candlemass (*Imbolc* in Gaelic) signifies the first stirrings of spring. In Celtic Christianity, it is also the Feast of St. Brigid (who to a certain extent is merged with the pre-Christian deity *Bride*).

HAND and FOOT, the: in the modality of Braucherei treatment as practiced by "Daisy Dietrich", her husband "Julius" and his teacher Ruth Frey, the symbolism of the hand and the foot play a critical role. Illness and pain are conjured by the Power of God that courses through the Braucher's hands, and the foundation of the Braucher in God. When using this modality, the Braucher will clean and bless everything above the collar bone with the charm/prayer "My hand and your hand is God's hand"; and everything below the collar bone with "My foot and your foot are the same".

By the latter, the Braucher sympathizes (that is, puts him/herself into sympathy) with the patient: 'we are the same'. The latter establishes our sibling hood with each other under the common parenthood of God the Father: God establishes His Kingdom through the work of our hands on this earth, as God works through the patient as well as the healer. The healer is not in a 'superior' position to the patient.

HEART, the: The Heart is a triangle where spiritual power manifests: it is the throne of either Satan or the Holy Ghost. The fire that burns in the Heart is either the Fire of Wrath or the Fire of Love. When the fire of the Holy Ghost is enthroned, Satan cannot enter. There are two serpents, even as there are two fires. The serpent raised by Moses healed the Hebrews of the fiery serpent stings; then Christ was raised on the Cross and took the sting out of the Dragon of death, and at the end of time that dragon shall sink.

O Jesus! My love, if I have but thee, why should I care for heaven or earth! Abide thou in me, and let me be in thee, and then I shall always be a fruitful vine. But without thee I can do nothing: animate my faith more and more that I may embrace thee, Omnipotence, and through thee, to whom all things are possible, gain the victory. May thy love increase within me, and kindle a flame within my whole heart, that I may love thee, the highest beatitude and eternal glory, and without thee find nothing attractive, or inviting, nothing worthy of my love. Grant me the grace of perseverance; it proceedeth alone from thee. Let nothing separate me from thy love. Thy cross, they death, be the nourishment of my love and fidelity to thee. May it unite me inseparably with thee. Grant me through this, what thou hast promised eternal life even here and dwell by faith in my heart. May thy word, which is full of life, awaken, enlighten, comfort, animate and strengthen me daily to strive in all patience and fidelity. May my whole heart, all my inclinations, all my thoughts and desires be devoted to thee. Let me not only subdue some, but all evil desires and passions, covetousness, as well as lust, envy and exultation at others' misfortunes, pride, anger and revenge, as well as indolence and intemperance. Let me pray without ceasing, in order to obtain new power for the victory, and to remain faithful unto the end. Amen. – *The Heart of Man*, pp. 57-58

Our free will determines what fire burns in the Heart; an empty Heart is mistaken for a cold one as it possesses no flame; it's a blocked up vessel that has made no decision and has progressed no further along the Path. The Heart that rages with the fires of Hell is truly cold, as there is no warmth in darkness.

The use of sympathy in the Work of Mercy builds God's Creation, following the Way of Christ; the twisting of sympathy, furthered by Satan's rule in the Heart is the way of damnation and hexerei.

HEIBS: is a PA Dutch pronunciation of the English word 'hives' – see **WIEBELSUCHT**.

HEISCH: sometimes *Haisch*, dialect for Standard High German *heiß* (*heiss* – "hot"), being an inflamed swelling – literally, a hot swelling. Heisch is related to **ROTLAUFE**.

HEX DOCTOR: also *brauchdoktor*. This is often just an alternate title for one whom frequently (professionally) practices Braucherei. According to Don Yoder this is title designates one who has a degree of proficiency and commitment to the practice of Braucherei which goes beyond the level of casual use -- indicating that such a practitioner is stigmatized by the traditional Deitsch community as a potentially dangerous person as a result of that proficiency. Another way of saying it: by Yoder's reckoning a hex doctor, therefore, is a highly skilled Braucher practicing professionally, but is held in suspicion due to their perceived degrees of power. Hex Doctor is also synonymous with another: ***hexenmeister*** (or *hexemeeschder* in the dialect).

This word literally means "Witch Master" –or, alternately, "spell master"-- and is meant to convey that one possessing this title is adept at over-mastering ('defusing' or exorcising) the evil spells of Witches. It is <u>not</u> meant to convey that such a person is *a leader of Witches* -- it is quite the opposite. The role of the hexenmeister is identical to that of the English cunning man and the Mexican curandero who operate as 'Witch Finders' and exorcists. Another meaning to the term hexenmeister is to indicate an artistic person skilled in the production of colorful hex signs (barn signs, barn stars), such as the late Jacob Zook (**See HEX SIGN**).

HEXEN: German for 'Witches'; the singular would be *hex*; in Pennsylvania Deitsch *hexe* would be the plural of *hex*. The hexen of traditional lore and practice are not neo-pagans or Wiccans; they are not even Satanists by contemporary standards (such as we now see with members of the late Anton LaVey's Church of Satan). Pennsylvania German Witches have only one purpose, and that is to 'torment' humanity – *"fa die leid gwele"*. Another Germanic term used to designate 'Witches' is *unholden*, but this is not a term that this author has come across among Pennsylvania German literature.

HEXENFOOS (plural Hexenfiess): Also known as: *hexe marrik* (Witch's mark), *grudafoos* (toad's foot), *drudenfoos* (druid's foot), the endless knot, the Five Wounds Star, and the Three Kings' Star, among many other names. There are basically three symbols in Braucherei practice that come under the heading of the hexenfoos, or "Witch's foot". These are the pentagram (the five pointed star); the hexagram (six pointed star -- *sex standisch Stehen*), and a "three-toed" figure curiously resembling a goose's foot (the symbol has also been known as that too). This resembles a capital letter 'Y' only with the middle line extending slightly above the two upper points – or rather like a "peace sign" minus the circle and facing in the other direction.

Regarding the geometrical figures, the five and six pointed stars are the most common. The so-called hex signs will often feature stars with more points than these. The five and six pointed stars have been used extensively in magic and religion. A few early Christians adopted the use of the pentagram as a symbol of their faith prior to using the cross and even thereafter. Many old churches and cathedrals will have the pentagram design in stone, wood, tile, or in stained glass.

In Christian symbolism the pentagram as the Five Wounds is a powerful sign of redemption, each wound being associated with one of the five points on the star. As the Magi's (Three Kings') star, this has been assumed to be the Star of Bethlehem, or could otherwise represent some aspect of ancient Magian belief. The five points are also the Five Virtues of the Christian knight: generosity, fellowship, purity, courtesy, and mercy. Ascribed to the five points are also the five Hebrew letters that kabbalistically spell out the name of Jesus: hw#hy. YHShVH is, of course, just a variation on the Tetragrammaton (hwhy).

The pentagram is Christ as "the bright and morning star" of *Revelation*. The six pointed star in Judaism is known as the Star of David, or the Shield of David – the *Magan David*. The most popular esoteric 'reading' of this symbol today is as a sort of kabbalistic "Yin/Yang" sign depicting the interpenetration of the male and female forces of the universe.

Among the Pennsylvania Dutch the six pointed star is sometimes called the *Glückstern* or Lucky Star. The five pointed star was the seal of the city of Jerusalem, and shows the *dimensions* of Man (the author uses this term to encompass both sexes), such as we see in the pentagram as drawn by Tycho Brahe (in his *Calendarium Naturale Magicum Perpetuum* of 1582) with a human body in the middle of the geometric figure: the head in the upper-most point, each arm occupying the upper two points, and the legs and feet situated within the lower-most two points. These are the *measure of man*, and as a protective sign project that we are made in God's image.

We, as the *image*, cannot truly therefore be harmed because we bear the divine spark and imprint of our Creator. Christian prophecy speaks of the "new Jerusalem" to descend upon earth at the end of time. At that time, all of humanity will be made new and the 'pentagram' wholly redeemed. Mephistopheles, in Goethe's *Faust* (1808) describes the protective power of the pentagram:

Mephistopheles: *Let me own up! I cannot go away;*
                  A little hindrance bids me stay

>   *The Witch's foot upon your sill I see.*
>
> Faust: *The pentagram? That's in your way?*
> *You son of Hell explain to me,*
> *If that stays you, how came you in today?*
> *And how was such a spirit so betrayed?*
>
> Mephistopheles: *Observe it closely! It is not well made;*
> *One angle, on the outer side of it,*
> *Is just a little open, as you see.*

Mephistopheles can get into a dwelling protected by in imperfect pentagram for the same reason that 'sinful' (imperfect) humanity is subject to the wiles of Satan: the Pentagram of Man is flawed by transgression. Only when the human being is perfected, then the demon can no longer enter.

Among the Jews the five-pointed star was the symbol of Truth, and of the Pentateuch (the Five Books of Moses). The ancient Greeks called this sign the *pentalpha* – that is, the five alphas. For the Pythagoreans it was a symbol of perfection due to its association with the golden ratio. All in all, the five-pointed star is the symbol of Truth, perfection, and protection.

The so-called inverted pentagram, within the above contexts, has very little meaning. The Emperor Constantine adopted an inverse pentagram as his seal, and it is also displayed in and on old churches such as the Marktkirche (the Lutheran "Market Church" of SS Georg and James in Hanover, Germany). The Marktkirche sports a *gigantic* inverse pentagram carved into one of the dormers of its steeple tower.

From another angle, one can also see an equally large hexagram. The "inverted" star is also the Star of Bethlehem, the dipping lower-most fifth ray showing the *incarnation* of Christ. This particular star is also emblematic of the *Transfiguratio Christi*, or the Transfiguration of Christ. It was only much later in history that someone (most probably the French 19th century magician Éliphas Lévi) thought that it would be terribly cleaver to insert a goat's head into the inverse star. There has been no end of mischief and paranoia over this figure ever since then, basically making it unusable for most people.

While the figures of both the five and six pointed stars have definite pre-Christian antecedents, among the three signs mentioned above, none is so blatantly heathen as the "three toed" grudafoos. The grudafoos is none other than the old runic sign called *elhaz*, which has a phonetic value of 'z' or 'r'. The name of this sign means "protection" and the figure was carved into heathen weaponry to ensure victory. This rune is possibly related to the Valkyries who are protective powers. This aside, it must be understood that old-time Brauchers would not have know of these runic associations. It was/is simply a sign of protection and power, *sans* any theological heathenism.

Present day rune workers know of this rune's use as a talismanic bridge between the realms of the Upper, Middle, and Underworlds. The figure may have been associated with the toad due to its traditional connection with the underworld. In pre-Christian times the Underworld was a place of mystery and wisdom, and not necessarily evil. Other researchers have connected this sign with Lady Holda, the old "hag" Goddess and patroness of night-flying Witches, who is the ancestress of our Mother Goose.

HEXENKOPF, the: In Williams Township, Pennsylvania, lies a hill known as "The Witch's Head" – in German, *hexenkopf*. It received this name due to the curious outcropping of rock on one of its peaks that resembles a stereotypical Witch's head: large, hooked nose, heavy brow, etc.

The very last word on the subject of the Hexenkopf is found in Ned D. Heidel's excellently researched book *Hexenkopf: History,*

Healing & Hexerei. Another reason for this rock's name is due to its associations with nocturnal Witch-spirits and its use as a contagion target by local Brauchers. Its associations with evil began not long after settlers came to the area of what was then the Allen and Durham land tracts. The land that the hill occupies was unclaimed land until John Stout made the first claim in 1787, at which time it was known as the "Groggy Rustic."

The area was slow to be claimed because of its poor, rocky, virtually untillable soil. It was then purchased by a Richard Backhouse. The acres in question here had been broken up and sold many times over the coming decades. The land itself was of little use besides grazing for animals and iron ore speculation. Those who came to live upon the Hexenkopf never really stayed very long, many of them meeting with assorted tragedies and strokes of incredibly bad luck.

According to Heindel, it is not certain when the aura of evil and witchery fixed itself to this area, but considering the ill luck of its residents, the thanklessness of its soil, and the fact that moon light reflects off of its rocks' mica giving it an eerie glow during a bright moon-lit night, all contributed to its ominous character. It is hard to tell if the Witch-lore came as a result of these circumstances, or for some other reason.

But the Hexenkopf is very much the American equal to the Witch-haunted peaks in the Old World such as the Brocken in the Harz Mountains. It was on these high places that the Witches were said to gather on certain nights of the year in worship of Satan. The spectral Witches' Sabbath is documented in tales recorded by Heindel up to very recent times (being the early 20th century).

The Braucher, Peter Saylor, used the Hexenkopf as his "contagion target" as a receptacle for the illness that he removed from his patients *via* brauching for them. Today the Hexenkopf is just another part of Pennsylvania's geography with, perhaps, the exception of local lore, dimly remembered and otherwise unknown to the new, non-Dutch populations that have recently moved into Williams Township. Maybe some of that old witchery still flitters around its boulder-strewn summit. But that's simply an indulgent speculation on the part of this author.

HEXEREI: A *hexe* is a 'Witch' and *hexerei* ("hexery") is the practice of a *hexe*. Hexerei is a very complex subject. All treatments of hexerei in *The Red Church* have been only of the briefest sorts, centering on the Pennsylvania Dutch understandings of what hexerei is and who the hexen are. There are currently students of truly archaic strata of hexerei.

Doubtless they will find the concept of the hexen *raison d'être* of *"fa die leid gwele"* ("for to torment the people") to be a massive over simplification, if not an outright prejudice. Unlike the English words "Witch" and "Witchcraft", the continental Germanic usage of the word constellation of "hexe" and "hexerei" give more than a hint to how our remotest ancestors conceived of Witches and their art.

Our modern English word *hag* comes directly from these words, and the meaning is that of a *hedge* or boundary. A Witch is then a *hedge rider*: some one who straddles the boundary between the seen and the unseen; between this world and the otherworld; between the living and the dead. It is from this most ancient stratum of Witch-lore that we have inherited our notions of Witches flying on animals and broomsticks.

These flights indeed happened, but they occurred in what we would now describe as a shamanic trance state. Perhaps, originally, there was no prejudice surrounding the practices of hexerei, but that is doubtful considering human nature such as it is. Where there is power, there is temptation. Any and all technologies (either scientific or spiritual) can be bent in dubious ways. It is therefore not unreasonable that many to this day are of mixed feelings when it comes to healers such as Brauchers or hex doctors. The one who heals can also shift that spiritual vehicle in reverse in order to do harm.

Again maybe the ancestors of these arts drew no divisions between the "healing Witch" and the "cursing Witch" – a Witch, is a Witch, is a Witch. By way of hexerei one can 'journey' to the Underworld to reverse curses, call off or shoo away detrimental powers, and retrieve spiritual powers for healing and blessing for "the people" too.

Despite all of the above, the Pennsylvania Dutch conception of Witchcraft is that the practice is the embodiment of pure malice. *Through this particular cultural lens it is not out of bounds to say that the Pennsylvania Dutch hexen conceive of their art thusly as well.* By way of cultural comparison, the Witches of Mexico share many of the traits of these night-flying hexen. They also share the culturally perceived purpose of being tormentors. The Mexican brujos do not deny this.

In Mexico to this day there is an especially deadly cult of Witches that is called *La Gallina Negra* or *The Black Pullet*. It is the job of the Mexican curandero (the equivalent of the Pennsylvania Dutch Brauchers) to fight with these cursing Witches. As with our own continental ancestors, these fights are just as often physical as they are spiritual. Another cultural comparison would be the Navajo ideas of Witchcraft embodied in the "skinwalker".

It took an exceptional person to be a Braucher. Aside from the dangers associated with fighting spiritual criminals, there was also the ever-present danger of being labeled one as well. If someone came to the Braucher for help and came away in worse condition than he arrived, that Braucher could end up being labeled a "Witch". At the very least such a label would earn one social ostracizing, which in an agrarian society is bad enough; at the very worst it would mean death. As conceived by the old-time Pennsylvania

Dutch Witchcraft is the spiritual means of abusing magical power for purely spiteful and selfish ends; all of this aside from whatever hexerei's remotest practitioners may have actually done.

HEX SIGN: Or, in the Pennsylvania German dialect, *hexezeeche* (hex signs). Some of the most stereotypical images associated with the Pennsylvania Dutch are the lovely barn signs or paintings that adorned the old bank-barns of PA Dutch country. The Dutch themselves have always claimed that these 'signs' were *"yuscht fa schee"*—that is to say, "just for nice" (for decoration).

It has been said that the word "hex" in this context has nothing to do with Witches or spells, but is a misunderstanding of the German *sex standisch Stehen* (meaning "six pointed star"). Dr. Brendan Strasser asserts that this misnomer became popular in the 1920's, prior to which these designs were always referred to as simply "barn signs" – attempts to link these designs to Witchcraft he labels as "balderdash". *It is doubtful if these 'signs' were ever meant to be "good luck" devices, despite the later catering to the tourist trade in PA Dutch country.*

What can be said without fear of contradiction is that the *truly operative anti-Witchcraft devices lay hidden out of sight within the frames of houses, barns, and other out-buildings.* Such hidden charms as Brauche bags (see BRAUCHE BAG) and signs carved out of sight on joists and lintels contained a few geometrical figures that would be recognizable in the larger barn signs (see HEXENFOOS). A cursory examination of some of these designs on the more popular barn signs reveal curious similarities to designs found on 1st century Jewish ossuaries.

The most notable of these designs being the six pointed flower-like sign and various floral motifs. Today there are some who see the "hex signs" as being vehicles for visual "prayers". In fact, this is the function of any and all talismans, being drawn "prayers" or the symbolizing of desires to be manifest. Through the technology of magic these barn signs can, indeed, function this way, but it is doubtful that this was ever their traditional and intended purpose. Karl Herr includes directions in his Pow-Wow book on how such designs can be used in this manner.

As with most stereotypes, various things and people become incorrectly lumped together, such as the barn signs and the Plain People (being the Amish and Mennonites). The Plain People *never* decorate their barns. It has been only among the so-called "Gay Dutch," "Fancy" or "Church Dutch" that these signs have been used. Witchcraft and its antidotes are traditionally secret and hardly ever in the open.

HIDE-BOUND: This is veterinary term for dry skin that clings to subcutaneous tissue due to a lack of fat on emaciated animals, such as cattle.

HIMMELSBRIEF: Himmelsbrief, literally a "heaven's letter" (himmelsbriefe, plural). These are various letters whose function it is to protect the bearer (or place where it is ensconced) from all dangers and evils, especially those arising from a supernatural agency. There are a few 'generic' popular briefe that are well known such as the **Koenigsberg Fire Brief, 1714,** and **The Magdeburg Himmelsbrief, 1783**. All of these old briefe share several curious elements, such as the 'story' that will either precede or be appended to the brief proper.

In the case of **The Letter of Protection** given in William Wilson Beissel's *Secrets of Sympathy*, it is claimed that *"This letter fell from Heaven, and was found at Holstein's in 1724. It was written in gold letters, and moved over the baptism of Madaginery, and when they tried to seize it, it disappeared until 1791, that everybody may copy it and communicate it to the world…"* Beissel's brief is not unique to him, but is a copy of a copy. Related to the himmelsbrief is the "fire and pestilence letter", some of which are purported to be the "invention" of a "Gypsy King of Egypt".

The story usually tells of an old, condemned gypsy man who is released from prison in order to quench a raging fire. After successfully quenching the conflagration, the gypsy is freed, and the 'letter' is allegedly endorsed by a provincial official, such as the "Superintendent General at Koenigsberg" (as found reproduced in the *Albertus Magus*).

Another feature of the himmelsbrief is the legend that it was written by God Himself; the original usually having been lettered in gold and having disappeared after being copied by a mortal hand. A himmelsbrief turns out not to be a 'free lunch' pass for its owner. It is a covenant or sorts, where God promises to continually watch over and protect the household or bearer, *if* the owner of the document obeys the moral precepts outlined.

These injunctions are just basic Biblical morality, although many today might feel 'oppressed' by such tenets. The old-time himmelsbrief may be the ancestral model for our modern 'chain letters'. Much like the present day chain letter, an old fashioned himmelsbrief will outline sever consequences for not obeying its injunctions, and it was an extra blessing to allow others to copy these briefe (so as to 'spread the word').

Bill Ellis in *Lucifer Ascending* covers this concept in much more depth. More examples of himmelsbriefe and fire and pestilence letters, along with their creation and application, can be found in Part III, Chapter 5 of *The Red Church*.

HOHMAN, JOHN GEORGE: Also spelled Johann Georg Hohman (or Homan) -- (b.1778?-d.1845?). Hohman was "essentially a mystery man" according to Don Yoder in his work *The Pennsylvania German Broadside*. Hohman is most famous for his book *Der Lange Verborgene Freund* (The Long Lost Friend – the more complete German title is *Der Lange Verborgene Schatz und Haus-Freund*), a collection of Brauche formulae culled from various Old World sources such as *The Romanus Book* (See The

ROMANUSBUCHLEIN) and *Albertus Magnus Egyptian Secrets*. Ned Heindel indicates that the word "freund" in *Der Lange Verborgene Freund* means less the English word "friend" than it does the word "familiar" (as in a Witch's familiar).

According to Yoder, Hohman arrived with his wife and son on the ship *Tom* on 12 October 1802. He was a talented publisher by trade and came to America in poverty. He and his wife Anne paid off their debt of passage by indentured servitude. After gaining their freedom, John George tried to make a living by way of selling printed birth and baptismal certificates (*geburtscheine, taufscheine*), himmelsbriefe (See HIMMELSBRIEF), etc., eventually producing *The Long Lost Friend* (*TLLF*) in 1819/1820. Hohman states: "*I say: any and every man who knowingly neglects using this book in saving the eye, or the leg, or any other limb of his fellow-man, is guilty of the loss of such limb...*" (Introduction, p 4). And it is upon this moral justification that he printed *TLLF*.

Some have opined, cynically, that Hohman printed *TLLF* in order to doctor-up his meager income. However, Hohman was never wealthy, and *TLLF* was plagiarized remorselessly within his own life time (and afterward). *The Long Lost Friend* has been continuously in print since 1820, testifying to its usefulness. Unlike most of the German folk who came to Pennsylvania, Hohman was a Roman Catholic. An earlier printing project to *TLLF* was *Land und Haus Apotheke* (The Field and House Pharmacy Guide), 1818.

His last known printing project was *Aufblick der Seele in den Himmel* (The Soul's upward Glance into Heaven), 1842. Heindel speculates on page 46 of his *Hexenkopf* book that Hohman passed away in Reading on 19 April 1845. Nothing is known about his earlier life in the Old World.

I.N.R.I.: This is abbreviation for the Latin found on the titulus board of Christ's cross: **I**esus **N**azernus **R**ex **I**udaeorum -- Jesus of

Nazareth, King of the Jews. It is employed as a formula in many traditional *zauberzetteln* (See ZAUBERZETTEL)

IRON: *Fe* in chemistry's Table of Elements. Iron is the metal in sympathy with the planet Mars; it is useful for protection and defense. Throughout the centuries iron has been credited with the ability to break magical currents and thereby destroy spells and curses. Horseshoes, crosses of iron, genuine iron nails, chains, tines, and other implements and devices can be used to seal out negative energies and foil psychic invasions. Too much iron used as a talisman can also be a bad thing, drawing in bellicose situations or accidents to one's person or immediate environment.

KABBALA: *The received tradition*, or Kabbala (also spelled, Kabbalah, Cabala, etc.) is Jewish theosophy. It is the science that studies the connections between the visible and invisible worlds. The roots of Kabbala can be found in pre-Judaic sources such as can be traced to Persia and India.

The *Sepher Yetzirah*, *Bahir*, and the *Zohar* are traditionally the main books of Kabbalistic theory. The latter work is a commentary on the Pentateuch and is made up of smaller books such as the *Book of Secrets*, the *Secret of Secrets*, and the *Mysteries of the Pentateuch* all of which are attributed to the 2nd century rabbi Simon ben Yohai. The main symbol or depiction of the Kabbalistic conception of the universe is the Tree of Life, which has ten "spheres" or *Sephiroth* (the plural of *Sephira*), or "jars."

God is always creating. Creation did not end on "the sixth day" but is a continual process. If God were to cease the act of perpetual creation and sustenance of the universe, *all* things would cease to exist. God's creative energies 'pour' down the Tree making manifest the various levels of Creation. God is both Being and Non-Being: *Ein*, *Ein Soph*, and *Ein Soph Aur*. From the eternal unmanifest Godhead proceeds the manifested ten Sephiroth: The Crown, Wisdom, Intelligence, Love, Justice, Beauty, Firmness,

Splendor, Foundation, and the Kingdom. Lewis Spence, in his *The Encyclopedia of the Occult* quotes a Dr. Ginsburg regarding the legendary origins of Kabbala:

> The Kabala...was first taught by God Himself to a select company of angels, who formed a theosophic school in Paradise. After the Fall, the angels most graciously communicated the heavenly doctrine to the disobedient child of earth, to furnish the protoplasts with the means of returning to their pristine nobility and felicity. – Lewis p. 241

Esotericist Mark Stavish wrote the following regarding the practical applications of Kabbala in his paper *"Drawing down the Life of Heaven: Magic in the Renaissance"*:

> Within qabala, the possibilities of magic are clearly stated, particularly through the use of Divine Names. However, magic was considered to be a rare event, only performed by a pious person in times of emergency, and at physical and spiritual risk to himself. – Stavish p. 8

Indeed this is the case, and it still remains true, especially in the case of practitioners of Braucherei. Healing is one thing, but outright conjuration was (and still is among traditional practitioners) never engaged except under tough circumstances. In fact, it has been pointed out repeatedly in *The Red Church* that a good many Pow-Wow doctors do not consider what they do to be "magic."

Sympathetic medicine is a mere vestibule to a larger structure where magical practice finds its dwelling. "Hex doctors" were more adventurous than the average person (so inclined) who may have practiced a few Pow-Wow charms. The problem with magic today is that it has become the answer to everything. The shelves of book dealers are full of works that encourage *a-spell-a-day* treatment of the magical art that trivializes the practice. The authors of such books seek to 'infuse' the reader's life with "magic". Magic becomes entertainment and a way to alleviate ennui and to provide a sense of meaning that has been lost having thrown the baby of religion out with the bath water.

Real magic is awfully hard work. Doing something in a conventional manner is much easier. At the root of this trivialization lurks the specter of Aleister Crowley who declared that just about any act whatsoever is an act of "magick". During the Renaissance and the Early Modern period Christian thinkers took a genuine interest in Hebrew Kabbala and created Christian Kabbala – often spelled "Cabala" to distinguish it from the solely Judaic practice.

Among the Germans who helped develop the Christian discipline were: Johann Reuchlin who was the source for the formula YHShVH, being the name of Jesus as developed from the Tetragrammaton YHVH. Also among these were Johann Trithemius, Cornelius Agrippa, Paracelsus, and later Jacob Boehme.

KELPIUS, JOHANN: Kelpius was a brilliant young mystic who immigrated to Pennsylvania from Germany under William Penn's general invitation to settle in the Commonwealth. Johann Kelpius was born in Halwagen in 1673. His father was a clergyman, and young Johann had mystical leanings since childhood. He graduated from the University of Altdorf with a degree in theology and joined Johann Jacob Zimmerman's *Chapter of Perfection*.

Kelpius was deeply moved by the writings of Jacob Boehme, and was displeased with the state of the reformed churches. The Chapter left Germany and sailed to England with a one year 'layover' before heading directly to the Colonies. At that time the Chapter was in the company of the English theosopher Jane Lead and the Philadelphian Society.

The ten-month journey to America began on a horrid note with a storm that almost sunk the ship before even leaving English waters. An astute astrologer, Kelpius marked the margins of his journal with planetary positions for each entry. The Chapter was Millenialist in character and eagerly awaited the Second Coming; this was the primary reason for their astrological practice, in order to calculate when Christ might yet return.

Zimmerman died before the voyage began, and Kelpius was enlisted as leader of the Chapter. Once having reached Pennsylvania, the Chapter came to Germantown, and then made settlement in the woods near the banks of the Wissahickon. The city of Philadelphia now occupies the area when the "monks" lived. They wished to be distant to the world, and retreated into the wilderness.

Due to a line in *Revelation*, their settlement became know as "the Woman in the Wilderness"; they were also called "the monks of the Wissahickon" as well as "the monks of the Ridge". These titles were given to the Chapter by other settlers; indeed, once in Pennsylvania they had no name for themselves as they wished to avoid sectarianism. All denominations were welcome at their devotions and meetings; even the Indians were welcome as they were seen as possessing great wisdom in their ways.

They celebrated the anniversary of their arrival with a bonfire every St. John's Eve. The number 40 was sacred to them, being of prime importance in Scripture. These Protestant "monks" were celibate and wore a habit reminiscent of the ones worn by Franciscans. There are always nearly 40 men in the settlement, and their communal dwelling was a cabin of 40' X 40'.

The Behmenist influence of the group was apparent in their belief that God employs nature to trigger spiritual revelation; and that God reveals Himself through nature. This is what theologians call "Natural Theology". In the context of Christian theosophy, it can truly be said that they were *panentheistic*: that is to say, God's energies are immanent in nature, but the Godhead itself is transcendent, invisible, and beyond both being and non-being. Kelpius died at the age of 35. It was his belief that he would be bodily 'translated' into Heaven just as the prophet Enoch was. As his health rapidly decreased due to tuberculosis, he realized that he would leave this world like every other "son of Adam."

Prior to his death Kelpius asked his friend Daniel Geissler to sink a small box of unknown contents in the Schuylkill River. Geissler did not immediately do this, hiding the box near the river's bank. Somehow Kelpius knew that the task was not completed and ordered Geissler to sink the box. The shaken Geissler retrieved the box and finally threw it into the Schuylkill; he reported that when it hit the water the box exploded and *"out of the water came flashes of lightening and peals like unto thunder."* Today there are people who believe that Kelpius discovered the Philosopher's Stone, and that it still lies at the bottom of the river.

LIME, unslaked: quicklime or calcium oxide (CaO). Quicklime is crushed lime that has been roasted in a furnace to free it of carbon dioxide; it absorbs water very quickly and is used in plasters and mortar. Quicklime is occasionally referenced in the older remedy books as a binding agent, such as in a concoction for repairing broken glass located in *Egyptian Secrets*, p51.

LIVERGROWN (See AAGEWACHSE)

MAGIC: According to Henry Cornelius Agrippa,

> Magic is a faculty of wonderful virtue, full of most high mysteries, containing the most profound contemplation of most secret things, together with the nature, power, quality, substance, and virtues thereof, as also the knowledge of whole nature, and it doth instruct us concerning the differing, and agreement of things amongst themselves, whence

it produceth its wonderful effects, by uniting the virtues of things through the application of them one to the other, and to their inferior suitable subjects, joining and knitting them together thoroughly by the powers, and virtues of the superior bodies.
The Three Books of Occult Philosophy, Book I, Chapter I, p5; Donald Tyson (ed). Llewellyn Publications, St. Paul, MN. 2000.

The above is one of the most eloquent and lucid descriptions of magic anywhere, encapsulating as it does the hermetic maxim "As above, thus below." Magic is, therefore, a technology whereby a 'body' of greater influence moves one of a lesser in a universe where all things are interconnected. See SYMPATHY.

Paracelsus describes magic as "*a most necessary and pure Art; not defiled nor corrupted with any Ceremonies or Conjurations, as Nigromancy*" [that is, 'black magic' -- see HEXEREI]. *The Archidoxes of Magic*, p82. For Paracelsus, magic was at its purest when pursued as alchemy or alchemically based sympathetic remedies. He despised the usual work of ceremonial magic, with its complex circles, conjurations, consecrations, and the like.

Some modern practitioners have taken to spelling 'magic' in any number of fanciful ways; this trend seems to have been inaugurated by the Edwardian magician Aleister Crowley, who made it chic to spell magic with a "k" -- 'magick'. This he did in order to differentiate his version of the magical Art from that of Houdini-like stage magic. In fact, magick is just an archaic spelling, along with words like *physick*, and *musick*, etc.

It is now not uncommon to see such silly orthographies as *majik*, or *majick* -- the practitioner of such being a *majikian*. As mentioned in the chapter on hexerei, not all Brauchers agree that they practice 'magic'. Like Paracelsus, they may indeed be practicing a purer Art, but identify it under another name (unlike Paracelsus). The spelling preferred by practitioners of the Art will usually identify their philosophical allegiance. Neo-pagans, Thelemites, Wiccans, etc. tend to prefer the pseudo-archaic (in context) Crowleyite spelling; whereas, those who spell it without the 'k' tend to be traditionalists.

The more novel orthographies are pursued by those wishing to make further distinctions between their own practice and that of others. Personally, the author finds deviating from conventional spelling to be a useless exercise. A similar phenomenon can be seen with the various spellings for the word *kabbala* (i.e., kabbalah, cabbala, qabbalah, and also kabalah, cabala, and qabalah, etc); See KABBALA.

More recently it has also become fashionable to spell the word "Witch" in any manner possible, which also will indicate some sort of philosophical divergence from the perceived norm (wytch, wycce, wicche, etc.) See HEXEREI

MAGIC SQUARES: There are two different types of squares: the ones that exist for "recreation" (i.e., as the fun mathematical puzzles they are) and the ones that have actual occult application. Magic squares can be made in different "orders" – for example, the Saturn Square belongs to the 3rd Order because it has three rows and three columns; the Square of the Moon belongs to the 9th as it has nine rows and nine columns, and so on.

Regardless of how many rows or columns, all of the numbers will add up the same up, down, backwards, or diagonally. Magic squares can also be in the form of letters instead of numbers, such as the SATOR square. When used magically the squares act as sympathetic 'keys' to influence a thing or situation with the power that the squares are connected to.

A Square of Jupiter can be used for the loosening of fetters, gain, employment, and general expansion of one's interests; where as a Square of Saturn will restrict and bind. Word squares are palindromes, which may or may not have obvious literal meaning.

MEASURING: is also known as 'taking the measure'. Measuring is a very old form of sympathetic magic whereby a part of a person's essence is bound up in and identified with a length of twine, yarn, or string. Taking a person's measure is mainly used for beneficent purposes, such as transferring illness from the patient into the string – because the measure is *like* the person. It can be, and unfortunately has been, used in hexerei for sending contagion to a person through the *like* object – much as with the so-called "voodoo doll".

Measuring children was very common as it is believed that as the child grows, he or she will out gown the measure, and therefore the disease or illness tied into it. The string or yarn used in Braucherei is almost always red – red is life, energy, and blood. Conversely, red is also a sign of inflammation, as well as death and disease by extension. Black in a negative context would be a sign of something already dead and rotting.

To make the measure, the length of string is used as a measuring tape: first from the crown of the head to the sole of the foot is measured out; then from the tip of the middle finger of one out stretched arm/hand to the other. The measure can also include the circumferences of the head, chest, and limbs. Each measure is marked by binding a knot in the string where the measure stops. That is: if the string measures a person from top-to-bottom a knot gets tied into the string at the foot; then that knot is used as the starting point for the measure between the finger tips. The last knot of each measure is the starting point of any new measure taken until the process is finished.

Diseases such as marasmus were treated this way for children. For adults the measure was often left to rot or otherwise fall to pieces: it might be buried underneath the eaves of a house near a rain spout or hung near a busy stove or up inside a fire place; sometimes they were tied to busy gates or hung in trees on certain days or at certain lunar phases. A simple form of measuring children is the very common practice of having a child stand erect with her or his back to a lintel, where someone will then make a notch or a mark in the wood at the crown of the head. Most people do this just for fun, to show the child how much he or she has grown. This sort of measuring can also be used sympathetically *when done with the intention* to have the child out grown an illness or condition.

MERCURY: The substance of Mercury is the principle of the Mind, and is the quintessence of all things: it is Spirit and Life Force. In spagyric medicine Mercury is the alcohol used in extractions and as the basis for tinctures. In archaic medicine, the raw element of mercury sometimes found its way into various preparations – many of these were crude (and highly poisonous), folksy variations on alchemical mineral preparations.

Mercury has also been used in folk charms such as Brauche bags, where the liquid metal was placed in a vial and then into the bag to accompany the zauberzettel. Sometimes the vial alone was used and hidden in the structure to be protected. In later times, the liquid metal was replaced by the so-called Mercury Dime as a safe proxy. In Afro-Caribbean traditions, the metal is sometimes poured into a hollowed nutmeg and sealed up to be used in a similar manner to the Pennsylvania German Brauche bag.

MAGNUS, ALBERTUS: (1193 – 1280) Albertus Magnus, Count of Bollstädt, was born in Lauingen, Swabia. He was a Dominican hieromonk and taught in the schools of Ratisbon, Cologne, and Hildesheim. The famous scholastic theologian Thomas Aquinas was one of his students.

Albertus seems to have been a "renaissance man" well prior to the Renaissance. His scientific probing and deep knowledge of chemistry (for that time) earned him the reputation of being a sorcerer. That Albertus knew "white" or "natural magic" is almost a dead certainty; that he may have actually practiced it is very probable. Knowledge of natural magic was part and parcel of an educated man's studies of that era. Natural magic is the result of how God has put together the natural world; it is the utilizing of its hidden, and little understood laws. For this reason, the medieval clergy saw nothing untoward in its study and application.

It is this type of "magic" that forms part of the foundation for Braucherei. The other part is charming and prayer in God's name. Albertus, being well educated, was most likely familiar with the operations of the "black arts" – being the coercion of spirits and demons. So-called black magic has been confused with "devil worship."

Much later on the alchemist and magician Paracelsus, however, would not entertain the use of conjury as he opined that natural magic, elevated *via* the alchemical art, was the most sublime of operations. Such is the contentious nature of spirit conjuration. Whether or not Albertus practiced any form of conjury is unknown, but mostly unlikely.

Many manuscripts have been attributed to his hand throughout the centuries. The text known as the *Egyptian Secrets* is most certainly not of his doing; this also includes *The Book of Secrets of Albertus Magnus*.

MARY, The Virgin: (German: Jungfrau Maria) There are many Braucherei charms that call upon the aid of the Virgin Mary, mother of Jesus Christ. Seeing that Braucherei is pre-Protestant, this is not such a strange feature, as it must seem to some who forget that, to this very day, there are such people as German Catholics.

Mary, being the "anti-type" of Eve, is considered to be our *spiritual mother* in as much as Jesus is our brother. It was through Mary's assent that God fulfilled His plan of redemption for Mankind by incarnation through her womb. It is by her womb, then, that some Braucherei charms invoke blessing for the patient. Because she gave birth to the Second Person of the Trinity, the Eastern Church calls her *Theotokos* (i.e., God Bearer).

It is unfortunate that some who subscribe to New Age or Neo-Pagan beliefs have tried to make Mary into a "goddess". Mary is not an object of worship as some Protestants (and Neo-Pagans) have opined. In Catholic theology she is offered a form of veneration called *hyperdulia*, while all other saints and angels receive the veneration called *dulia*. Worship, called *latria*, is reserved for God alone.

Despite her gift of grace and some of the outward trappings of her images, she is not a "Goddess". In some magical systems images of Mary, along with images of the classical Goddess Diana, and those of God's Wisdom personified as "Sophia" (See SOPHIA) are all allegorical usages only.

MOUNTAIN MARY: (Also *die Berg Maria*, German; and *Barricke Mariche*, Pennsylvania Deitsch) "Mountain Mary" (b.1749? - d.1819) is the folk name for one Anna Maria Jung (Jungin), a Braucherin, who lived in the hills of Oley near Pikeville, PA. She was famous for her garden of healing herbs and her great Christian faith, which earned her the title of "holy woman" or "saint" by those who knew of her great compassion and healing work. She lived in seclusion on her mountain tending the medicinal garden and spending long hours in prayer. Her healing "incantations" were various Biblical passages. According to Kriebel ("Powwowing: A Persistent American Esoteric Tradition" p.5) Maria was married, or engaged, to one Theodore Benz who fought in the Continental Army; her life was marked by much personal suffering during the years of the Revolution. She left this world in 1819, curiously the same year that Hohman's *The Long Lost Friend* (See HOHMAN, JOHN GEORGE) was ready for publication.

MOTHER PAINS (FITS): Labor pains, contractions. *Mutterweh*.

NAMES OF GOD: The title for this entry is a bit of a misnomer. God has no "Name" *per se*. What ritualistic "name" the Hebrews did have was lost with the ancient *cohens* or priests in the Temple. However, what we do have now are many, many titles for God, which read like job descriptions. It is by these so-called names that we come to know the many facets of God's grace or active energies in the world. It is also by these Names that we can ask for God's blessing (or even curse) upon any given situation or person. Spirits can be bound and coerced by these names, such as in the act of exorcism -- or, alternately, in acts of conjuration. Of course, in the later situation binding spirits in God's name does not necessarily indicate His seal of approval upon the said conjuration. God cannot be coerced.

Unlike the Pagan Gods, the True God is not overmastered and bound by any other force higher than His own Godhead. The Pagan deities could always be at the beck and call of a sly conjuror that might discover his/her/its secret name. When we call upon God, whether by the old Hebrew titles or through the name of Jesus, He comes to us out of Love and not because He is coerced to do so.

The fact that not every act of Braucherei or magic comes to fruition ought to be demonstrative of this. The only reason we can call upon God at all is because we are fashioned in the Divine Image. The 'spark' within us is what provides the *sympathy* (See SYMPATHY) and the privilege of calling upon the Almighty. Past masters of the magical art who have reached high levels of inner wisdom and enlightenment (that is, initiation) have discovered God's secret name. Such a master is called in Hebrew the *Baal Shem* -- that is, "the Master of the Name". This "name" is not the one used in the old Temple by the High Priest, but a "name" or *energy* imparted to the magician's innermost being as a gift of Divine grace.

NEURALGIA: this is a chronic nerve disorder that produces much pain and discomfort, usually in the facial area. Neuralgia is involved in such illnesses as shingles, herpes, and sciatica. The nerves affected by neuralgia are responsible for the sensation of temperature, pressure, and touch. Normally innocuous activities such as washing the face can bring about an attack of neuralgia.

NACHT ENGSCHT: Pennsylvania German dialect for "nightmare". Nightmares are caused by daily stress, matters of conscience, and also by spiritual oppression. The latter can be caused by discarnate souls seeking to make contact, or by spiritual powers that attempt to siphon off life-energy while one sleeps (a type of vampirism). Unintentional projections of others' jealousies and angers can reach one during sleep, as well as the purposefully directed "curse" by way of someone's sorcery.

Previous burial practice was to bury the dead facing east, to meet the sunrise and, thereby, symbolically their resurrection. It was considered unlucky for a living person's bed to face east for this reason; facing west was no better, as this is how heretics and the excommunicated were buried. Therefore, many a bed was arranged for the head to point north – to sleep in the manner that dead people are laid out was a way to invite potential nightmares and bad luck.

NARCOTICS (Opium & Laudanum): In the old house and farm books (which combine both Brauche charms as well as more mundane advice for running a household), opium based narcotics were often prescribed for many aches and pains. The drug known as Laudanum was quite popular during the Victorian era, but definitely not unknown prior to that time. In fact, it was the German magician-alchemist Paracelsus (see PARACELSUS) who discovered the analgesic properties of this tincture and gave it its present name, which is said to be derived from two Latin words: *laudare* (to praise) and *labdanum* (a plant extract).

Outside of opium-derived medicines, there were little in way of sedatives and painkillers up until quite recently. Laudanum is an alcoholic tincture of opium, of which there are several types. This product is still available today, but as one can imagine, it is very tightly controlled. True Laudanum is a tincture of opium with 10 milligrams of morphine per milliliter. A well-known Laudanum-like drug today is Paregoric, know also as "camphorated opium tincture" or *tincture opii camphorate*.

NITRIC SPIRIT: (See AQUAFORTIS)

OX-GALL: gall from cows mixed with alcohol creating an ink. Remedy books were often full of sundry household 'tips' besides straight healing work. Recipes for inks, glues, dyes, food preservation, basic first aid, animal feed, leather working, etc. were included in these texts. The *hausmittel* book was meant to be wholly utilitarian and not a piece of mysticism.

PARACELSUS, Theophrastus Bombastus von Hohenheim: Paracelsus (1493 – 1541), a Swiss-German born alchemist who was a contemporary of Cornelius Agrippa [see AGRIPPA]. He held degrees in medicine, and his etiological theories and treatments for disease were revolutionary for their time and bought him no end of trouble for running against the grain of that era's medical establishment. Paracelsus *despised* Galenic medicine, which he found to be crude and useless. It would not be a stretch to say that Paracelsus is the grandfather of homeopathic medicine.

Because of his great proven prowess in healing, he was made the Official Physician of Basil, Switzerland. He enjoyed this post for only a year; his medical theory and praxis was so alien to his contemporaries that he was threatened with arrest, and escaped Switzerland. After the Basil debacle, he settled in Salzburg, where he died on 24 September 1541. Paracelsus held lofty and sublime ideals for the magical-medical art (there was no division between the two).

If there was anything that he disliked *more* than the medicine of Galen, it was the practice of "conjury" or ceremonial magic. Ceremonial magic, in his estimation, was crude, superstitious, and unnecessary – it was a pox mark on the sublime art of magic. For Paracelsus, magic was a holy gift from God, and not to be abused by the work of sorcery.

The manufacture of pure alchemical remedies, the production of planetary talismans, and the working of sympathetic medicine was truly a way to serve God through the Work of Mercy. Paracelsus was equally scathing towards the clergy of his day (both Catholic and Reformed), criticizing their "blessings" and religious ceremonies (such as the use of "holy water") as "superstition"; and he also taunted them with the challenge to do *any* of the wonders that Christ said a true disciple can perform (**John 14:12**). It's small wonder that his arrest was sought.

> Philosophy informs us that the world is made out of the will of God. If, then, all things are made out of will, it logically follows that the causes of all internal diseases are also originating with the will. All diseases, such as are not caused by any action coming from the outside, are due to perverted action of the will in man, such as is not in harmony with the laws of Nature or God. – Paracelsus (as quoted by Franz Hartmann); Hartmann p.204

Don Yoder's Pow-Wow informant from the 1960's, "Aunt" Sophia Bailer, made a similar statement. All her life she enjoyed great health, which she attributed to living in the ways of God. She earnestly believed that if people lived according to nature and God's ways, they would rarely suffer ill health. It is the author's personal opinion that all aspiring Brauchers need to read the works of Paracelsus.

PENTAGRAM (See HEXENFOOS)

PETSCHAFT: Petschaft is a metal stamper. In mundane usage it is the sort of tool used to impress images on wax seals; otherwise, it stamps ink images. In short, a petschaft is a simply a stamper, a stamping tool. In Braucherei, however, a petschaft is a stamper that is specially crafted to bear a talismanic image. This image is then transferred (stamped) onto the ailing part of a patient's body. The medium may be special ink or soot from the flame of a blessed candle. See Part III Chapter 5 for specific directions on the making and use of the petschaft.

PINE TAR: Pine Tar is a sticky substance made by the carbonization of pinewood. Its primary use has been that of a preservative for wood, sometimes called "Stockholm Tar". When Pine Tar is found in old colonial era and 19th century household manuals, its use was that of an antiseptic for the hooves of cattle and horses. Pine Tar has also been used as an ingredient in medicinal soaps for assorted skin conditions, such as psoriasis.

POW-WOW: also spelled *Powwow*. According to Dr. Kriebel in his book *Powwowing Among the Pennsylvania Dutch*, Preface:

> It is important to distinguish Pennsylvania Dutch Powwowing from the "Powwows" of the various indigenous peoples known as American Indians or Native Americans. There may be some etymological connection – perhaps settlers who were not Pennsylvania Dutch observed these practices and saw them as similar to those of the indigenous people – but the origin of the term "Powwow" as applied to Brauche remains obscure.

Monroe Aurand Jr. was of the opinion that the term derived from the Algonquin languages as the word *powan* meaning a medicine man or 'shaman' of one sort or another. However, according to a friend of mine who has had generational Braucherei in his family, the practice was called "Pow-Wow" even back in Germany. Being that his family is not Pennsylvania German, but German immigrants from a much later date, this is very interesting. According to his Braucher uncles, they never knew the practice as anything but "Pow-Wow".

PSALMS, the: called in Hebrew: *Tehillim*, meaning "praises". The English word derives from the Greek *psalmoi*, meaning to sing to the accompaniment of a harp. The Psalms are used quite extensively by some Braucherei practitioners. The *Book of Psalms* contains 150 (or 151) songs, most of which have a specific meaning or purpose assigned to it in folk religious practice.

The actual numbering of the Psalms differs between the Masoretic (Hebrew) and Septuagint (Greek) texts. Traditionally, Protestants have relied on the Masoretic numbering, where as the Orthodox and Catholics have used the Septuagint numbering. An appendix of the oft-times dreaded *The Sixth and Seventh Books of Moses* (see entry for this title below) has a very workable method for employing the Psalms in sympathetic cures: *"Sefer Schimmusch Tehillim, or Use of the Psalms for the Physical Welfare of Man: A fragment out of the Practical Kabala, together with an Extract from a Few other Kabalistical Writings"*: translated by Godfrey Selig (1788).

The Psalm work in this present volume of *The Red Church* draws extensively on this appendix of *The Sixth and Seventh Books of Moses*. An example of this sort of usage: to protect one's self from persecution he or she "prays this Psalm [Psalm 11] daily with feelings of devotion, and with it keep constantly in mind the holy name of **Pele**, that is, Wonderful…"

QUINSY: is known also as peritonsillar abscesses (PTA) which are puss sacs located beside the tonsils, being a complication of an acute tonsillitis.

RED, the color: *rot, rote*. Red is the most common color used in Braucherei practice; it is also the most mentioned color in Braucherei charms and prayers. The symbolism is very plain and obvious, if dual: red is heat; therefore, it is also 'fire' and 'life' and 'blood'. Opposite of that, red is also the 'fire' of corruption (as distinguished from black, which is death and decomposition). Corruption in this context is the breakdown of the flesh suffering inflammation.

In the traditional Braucherei worldview, all inflammation and burns from external fire must be treated immediately some that the *fire* does not "set" deeper into the body, destroying more tissue (and, ultimately, bone). In Christian symbolism, red is the color of redemption, the blood of Christ; this ties the color back into its positive manifestations life-giving warmth and action.

In the making of Braucherei talismans and other operational devices (such as the red string used in curing rotlauf) the color functions the same way: it can either impart action and energy, or it can be used as a sympathetic 'sponge' to remove a condition such as an inflammation or rash.

ROMANUSBUCHLEIN, The: Also known as *The Romanus*. This is, according to Don Yoder, the main text that Hohman freely borrowed from when compiling *The Long Lost Friend*. The definitive, but sadly out of print, commentary on *The Romanus* was done by Adolf Spamer: *Romanusbüchlein: Historisch-philogischer Kommentar zu einem deutschen Zauberbuch*, 1958. An early print date for *The Romanus* seems to be 1788. Johann Scheible included *The Romanus* in his encyclopedic *Das Kloster*.

ROTLAUFE (WILDFEIER): Also as *rotlauf, rotlaufa,* and *wildfire*; erysipelas. The word *rotlauf* literally means "red-walk" and refers to the spreading action of inflammation. There are a great many Brauche charms and sympathetic operations that are devoted to the curing of rotlauf. Inflammations due to dermatitis, 'angry' wounds, infection, fever, and all "hot" swellings, also called *heisch*, fall into the category of "rotlauf." Anti-inflammation charms will personify the affliction as something "red" – a red woodland, a red church, a red dragon (*drach*), etc.

Sometimes the cure itself will involve red objects, most commonly a red string. A very common rotlauf charm starts out *"I saw a red woodland [or "wald"]; I went into the red woodland and saw a red church…"* etc. There are several variations on this one charm alone that appear in previous books and manuals of sympathetic medicine and Pow-Wow.

READ FAST, to be: Being "read fast" is an unfortunate condition where one is bound in a sort of demonic possession by having read too many of the 'wrong' books – being, for example, books of magic such as *The Sixth and Seventh Books of Moses*. There is a difference of opinion towards these tomes: either actually practicing any of their contents will entrap one in demonic enslavement, or simply just owning the same will alone be sufficient for that entrapment.

A truly "read fast" person will quickly degenerate, and working with these books will be a sole preoccupation (an obsession). Such an individual will eventually end up destroying him or herself and possibly everyone within the practitioner's sphere of influence. A read-fast person will be a transmitting device for evil, regardless of his or her wishes or conscious intentions.

If the condition is caught early on, it is possible to reverse the procedure by way of literally "reading out" of the books, reading each word backwards from cover-to-cover starting with the very last word all the way back to the very first. This is a lot like following a trail of bread crumbs in order to get out of a labyrinth. While on a certain level this may make an effective ritual for beginning the process of exorcism, the corruption is truly within the heart and not the book *per se*.

It is the heart that needs the work where as the book would be simply have been a trigger for pre-existing evils that had not been purged.

RUKSCHTEE: is a rounded stone used for pain relief and the relaxing of an ill person so that they may be able to get to sleep. Brendle and Unger, 1935, p.72, have this to say regarding the virtues of this stone and others related to it:

> Smooth or round, or even jagged blackstones were looked upon as "thunder stones" **gwidder schtee, dunner schtee** and were believed to fall from heaven with the peal of thunder. They were carefully preserved in the house being regarded as a protection against lightning. They were not uncommonly seen in homes as late as thirty years ago [*author: this time marker places the practice somewhere around 1900*]. Some of them probably were Indian stones. The idea back of the rukschtee seems to lie in the similarity of its roundness to the round head of man.

From a sympathetic point of view, Brendle and Unger may have a point about the connection between the shape of the human head and the shape of a rounded stone. However, it is also likely (in the opinion of the author) that aside from its shape, this rounded "rest" stone may have some Biblical backing in the form of Jacob's Pillow.

> And Jacob went out from Beer-sheba, and went toward Haran. And he lighted upon a certain place, and tarried there all night, because the sun was set; and he took of the stones of that place, and put them for his pillows, and lay down in that place to sleep. And he dreamed, and behold a ladder set up on the earth, and the top of it reached to heaven: and behold the angels of God ascending and descending on it. And behold, the Lord stood above it, and said, I am the Lord God of Abraham thy father, and the

God of Isaac: the land whereon thou liest, to thee will I give it, and to thy seed; And thy seed shall be as the dust of the earth, and thou shalt spread abroad to the west, and to the east, and to the north, and to the south; and in thee and in thy seed shall all the families of the earth be blessed. And behold, I am with thee, and will keep thee in all places wither thou goest, and will bring thee again into this land; for I will not leave thee, until I have done that which I have spoken to thee of. And Jacob awakened out of his sleep, and he said, Surely the Lord is in this place; and I knew it not. And he was afraid, and said, How dreadful is this place! This is none other but the house of God, and this is the gate of heaven. And Jacob rose up early in the morning, and took the stone that he had put for his pillows, and set it up for a pillar, and poured oil upon the top of it. **Genesis 28:10-18** KJV

SACRAMENTALS: In the Roman Catholic Church, these are ceremonies for the purpose of private devotion. They are called "sacramentals" in order to differentiate them from sacraments proper. Unlike the recognized Seven Sacraments of the Church, there is no limit to the number of sacramentals. According to Church theology, the number of Sacraments cannot be increased as they were instituted by Christ Himself.

Also unlike the Sacraments, sacramentals do not produce sanctifying grace. There are six divisions or types of sacramentals being: *orans* (public or private prayer), *tinctus* (holy water or holy oils), *edens* (blessed food), *confessus* (a general admission of sin -- outside of the sacrament of Confession), *dans* (alms), and *benedicens* (various blessings -- candles, ashes, etc.). Sacramentals can be either acts (general confessions, pilgrimages, good works, etc.) or objects, such as holy medals or *ex votos*.

Although the practice of Braucherei far out dates the Protestant Reformation, it has filled in the gap left by the extraction of

Catholic sacramental rites and usages. Without these sorts of minor personal rituals the whole of the Church would be focused entirely onto a cult of priestcraft, cutting the laity out wholly from any bodily or spiritual healings to be had from active religious participation. Therefore, by the above definition practices such as Braucherei, Mexican curanderismo, English cunning work, and Italian benedicaria or benedictus, etc. are all forms of folkish sacramentals.

ST. ANTHONY'S FIRE: Ergotism, ergot poisoning, ergotoxicosis. This is poisoning from the ingestion of the fungus *Claviceps purpurea*, which is sometimes found on rye. The poison causes convulsions that were at one time mistaken for demonic possession.

ST. BARTHOLOMEW'S DAY: August 24. St. Bartholomew may have been Nathaniel in the New Testament. The name Bartholomew is really a title "Son of Tolmai". According to hagiographers he was either flayed alive or beheaded. He is the patron saint of butchers.

ST. GERTRUDE'S DAY: March 17. St. Gertrude of Nivelles (b. 626 – d. March 17, 659). Gertrude was abbess of the double monastery at Nivelles, built by her mother Ida. This monastery serviced the Irish missionary monks who were sent to convert the Germanic tribes. St. Gertrude has several patronages, among these is gardening. Good weather on her feast day indicates the beginning of spring planting.

She is also patron of the newly deceased, which in medieval symbolism are depicted as mice. Votive offerings of mouse figurines have been offered to Gertrude for her prayers for the souls in Pergatory. Along with SS. Christopher and Nicholas, she is a patron of travelers. The medieval custom of drinking *Gertudenminte* before traveling acted as a sacramental protection for the journey ahead.

ST. JAMES DAY: The Feast of St. James the Greater, July 25. James (son of Zebedee and Salome) and his brother John were called "Boanerges" by Jesus, meaning "Sons of Thunder" – perhaps due to having 'thundering' voices and tempers. James is the patron of hat makers and rheumatoid sufferers.

ST. JOHN'S EVE: This is the evening of June 24th, which is really a celebration of both the Summer Solstice (*Sonnenwende*) and the Nativity of St. John. This is the ultimate time to try for illnesses. It is a time of purification where bonfires (*Sonnenwendefeuer*) are lit in order to acknowledge the zenith of the Sun's power and a symbol of Christ's Light.

In old European Catholic observance, the local priest and celebrants create the bonfire, which is then blessed. A brief liturgy is held with hymns to St. John. The Rosary is then recited as the people circumambulate the fire clockwise. Worn out sacramentals, such as scapulars, are ritually (and respectfully) destroyed in the fire. It has also been the custom for younger people to jump the fire. These were often rather large conflagrations, so it would take an athletic and brave person to do this.

The smaller, more private fires are better suited to this. On the Day of St. John, it is traditional to collect St. John's Wort (see above in "A Braucher's Pharmacopoeia"). The traditional (pre-Vatican II) Catholic hymn sung to the blessing of the fire is *"Ut queant laxis"* the words to which are:

> Ut queant laxis resonare febris, mira gestorum famuli tuorum, solve poluti labii reatum, sancte Johannes.
> Or
> So that these your servants may, with all their voice resound your marvelous deeds, clean the guilt from our stained lips; Oh, Saint John.

To truly understand the significance of St. John's Eve in Northern Europe, Scandinavia, the nights are *very* bright during the summer months, and are called "White Nights" for this reason. The fires celebrate the intensity and duration of the sun's light during this time of year. Of course, the area of the world that the later "Pennsylvania Dutch" came from is not that far north and does not have practically broad-daylight at night such as Scandinavia does.

ST. MARTIN'S DAY: *Martinstag* (German), *Martinsdaag* (PA German); *Martinmass* (British), November 11. In Europe St. Martin's Day occupied a Halloween-like spot. There is no traditional celebration of "Halloween" in Europe, which was a Celtic development known as Samhain. It is not, however, Germanic. In Germany today American-style Halloween is becoming popular. Up until quite recently this was not the case.

On the day of St. Martin children would go on "trick or treating" jaunts somewhat similarly, but not identically, to what we see in the States. A period of fasting began on the day after Martinstag and lasted for 40 days. Feasting was a prelude to the fast, with the traditional fare being roasted goose. St. Martin of Tours was a Roman soldier who died on 8 November 397 AD. He was born in what is now Hungary. He had a vision that he had clothed a naked Jesus with his cloak, and his path on the Way was set from then on.

ST. VITUS' DANCE: *Chorea* (Greek for "dance"). The "dance" refers to the quick movements of the hands and feet of those who suffer from the condition. It appears as a complication of other diseases such as rheumatic fever.

SALT: Alchemically speaking, salt is one of three major substances that make up Creation. Salt is substance, and is the "body". It is also Will and Wisdom: *"Let your speech always be with grace, seasoned with salt…"*— **Colossians 4:6**; also, see **Matthew 5:13** and **Mark 9:50**. In spagyric medicine (plant-based alchemy), salt refers to the mineral salts extracted from plant matter. Salt is a holy substance, it can cleanse and also make things sterile. "Holy water" is made with blessed salt; and ceremonial magicians cleanse their ritual spaces with salt water. Rings of salt are protective, when seeking shelter from a spiritual or psychic attack. Salt scattered on the floors of a house and then swept out from the front door to the back door clears away negative energies (as well as salt-water based floor washes). Sea water, being saline, holds a psychic charge that still fresh water cannot, and is responsible for much paranormal activity. The sea is therefore a giant trap or container for much of this sort of energy. Salt water becomes a type of "spirit trap" in this instance.

SALT PETRE (Saltpeter): a crucial ingredient in black gunpowder, being *potassium nitrate*, KNO_3. The name saltpeter comes from the Latin *sal petrae*, which can be translated as either "salt stone" or "salt of Petra"; it is also known as nitrate of potash. Saltpeter has been used as an additive in military rations thought to have anaphrodisiacal properties (to lower the libido of servicemen).

SATOR SQUARE, the: (See MAGIC SQUARES)

SECUNDINES: (*Secundinae*) this is a Latin term meaning "following" and refers to afterbirth: placenta, umbilical cord, etc. This term is used in some older charm and house books for formulae to expel afterbirth.

SEGENBUCH: Literally, a "blessing book" or book of blessings -- *segen*-- this term is sometimes used interchangeably with *zauberbuch* (a book of charms; pl. *zauberbücher*, and *segenbücher*).

SEVENTY-SEVEN, the number: The number 77 appears quite frequently in Brauche charms, such as the dispelling of 77 types of fever, 77 types of rheumatism. Numerologists refer to doubled numbers as "master numbers." In Braucherei, odd numbers are preferable. All charms receive blessings in at least threes, sometimes in fives, and also in sevens and nines. To understand 77 it is only necessary to understand the single number seven. Seven is symbolic of God's perfection, sovereignty, and holiness. The Almighty blessed the Seventh Day. The menorah has seven branches, one for each day. There are seven Archangels (which may derive from the Zoroastrian seven Amesh Spenta.

Luke's Gospel demonstrates that Jesus was destined for His role as all great men of the Bible generated in multiples of seven: seven generations starting with Adam, Enoch at seven, Abraham at 21, David at 35, and Jesus at 77. Seventy-seven, therefore, can be seen as one of Jesus' numbers. There were the seven churches in Asia; the seven joys and sorrows of the Virgin (Catholicism); seven corporal acts of mercy and seven spiritual; there are seven virtues and seven deadly sins. Also there are seven heavens in the apocryphal *Ascension of Isaiah*, and in Matthew 18:21 we are enjoined not to forgive just seven times, but 77. This number has been called a number of manifestation, somehow embodying the Law of Attraction.

SHEKINAH: ùëéðä: God's Presence – derived from the Hebrew root-word *shakan* having the meaning "to indwell" or "to settle upon." In the Hebrew language the word Shekinah is grammatically *feminine*. Because of this, and because the Shekinah is the vehicle or *vessel* of God's Presence, being His "Glory" (as in "the Glory of the Lord"); it is sometimes seen as being a *feminine* manifestation of the Divine.

In the ancient world "femininity" in the theological or esoteric sense meant that something was a passive vehicle for a "masculine" actor or initiator. Today, these terms are needlessly charged with emotionalism and hysterics. Hermetic treatise such as *The Kybalion* spell out quite clearly what it means for something to be either "masculine" or "feminine" – in much the same way poles of a magnet are either "positive" or "negative". The politicizing of these terms is a tragedy, and has ended up twisting and reinterpreting many ancient ideas simply to suit the times. Gustav Davidson in his *A Dictionary of Angels* says that the Shekinah is

...the female manifestation of God in man, the divine *inwohnung* (indwelling).

The Shekinah is the liberating Angel, manifesting in her male aspect as Metatron. In the cabala, she is the 10th sefira Malkuth, otherwise the Queen.

The 16th century mystic Rabbi Isaac Luria wrote a hymn addressing the Shekinah is the Sabbath Bride, using all feminine pronouns. According to the *Encyclopedia Judaica*, the Shekinah is the Divine Presence, God's immanence in the world. Numerous appearances of the Shekinah are recorded in the Old Testament.

> And they took their journey from Succoth, and encamped in Etham, in the edge of the wilderness. And the LORD went before them by day in a pillar of a cloud, to lead them the way; and by night in a pillar of fire, to give them light; to go by day and night: He took not away the pillar of the cloud by day, nor the pillar of fire by night, *from* before the people. **Exodus 13:20-22 KJV**

> Then a cloud covered the tent of the congregation, and the glory of the LORD filled the tabernacle. And Moses was not able to enter into the tent of the congregation, because the cloud abode thereon, and the glory of the LORD filled the tabernacle. **Exodus 40:34-35 KJV**

In the book of **John 2:19-21**, Jesus answers His detractors with the enigmatic statement that if the temple is destroyed that He will raise it up in three days. The Shekinah dwelled (*mishkan*) on the Mercy Seat, between the wings of the golden cherubim in the Holy of Holies during Yom Kippur. The Temple, in this context, is Jesus' body; the inference being that the Presence dwells in Him. Christians, as members of the body of Christ by virtue of baptism, sympathetically partake of this Presence as well. Scripture is full of echoes. Mary's pregnancy with Jesus earned her the title of *Theotokos* ("God bearer") in later Christian theology. Mary's womb was a temple housing the pre-natal presence of Christ.

SIX AND SEVENTH BOOKS OF MOSES, The: Here is the granddaddy of all hex books, traditionally dreaded, with Brauchers seldom admitting to owning a copy themselves. In fact, most traditional practitioners today do not own one. Now, with the traditional hex doctors of yesteryear, however, that was another story.

As the name implies, the volume is supposed to be the secret collection of books supplementing the Pentateuch (that is, the first five books of the Old Testament) whose authorship is ascribed to Moses. It has also been believed by some that there are three more books being the Eighth, Ninth, and Tenth books. It is said that these 'extra' Mosaic texts contain the magic used by Moses against the Egyptians. However, a quick look at *The Sixth and Seventh Books* (abbreviated here on as TSSBM) will satisfy most readers that it is no such animal.

Yet, despite its seemingly false advertising, it is a valuable companion if only for the advanced Psalmic sympathetic remedies contained in its appendices. The sinister reputation of TSSBM derives from its blatant conjurations of various infernal agencies. But, these sorts of magical operations need to be kept in context. On the one hand, some such workings of magic have a definite "Faustian" character, where the magician swaps his soul for knowledge, power, or whatever.

On the other hand, conjurations of this type often have 'higher' purposes such as is found in the grimoire called *The Book of Abramelin*, where a magician will deliberately call upon satanic powers <u>in order to defeat</u> them, thereby strengthening his will and spiritual character. The magical operations in TSSBM are mainly in the latter category. It must be said that these sorts of 'operations' are not the whole of the text. Past editions of this book have been next to unusable: the magical seals, diagrams, figures, etc. are mostly illegible and, therefore, useless. However, Joseph Peterson has reworked TSSBM into a volume any old-time hex doctor would have given his right arm for: the figures are completely cleaned up, copious foot notes and other documentation, modernized spelling, and many, many other features that make TSSBM truly accessible, perhaps for the first time since it was translated into English well over a century a go.

According to Peterson, the very first mention of this book appeared in 1734. Then the antiquarian Johann Scheible collected together various related texts, which he then published in 1849, with TSSBM as its sixth chapter.

> The core of 6/7Moses can be traced back to the Latin magical text Liber Razielis, in a section ascribed to Moses It is related to the well-known Hebrew magical text Sefer Raziel HaMalach [*The Book of the Angel Raziel*], thought to have been composed or compiled in the thirteenth century.
> (Peterson, 2008, p IX) – brackets mine

and

> *6/7Moses is in fact based largely on Books 6 and 7 of the Latin Raziel.* (Peterson IX)

According to some traditions of Kabbalah, Raziel is the archangel (or one of the cherubim) who is the keeper of divine secrets; he taught Adam and Eve the holy magic after their fall so that they would have a sort of spiritual 'road map' back to paradise, and also to have a tool of survival in a new, harsh world.

TSSBM is full of seemingly unpronounceable incantations based upon a variety of sources such as Hebrew, Greek, and Latin (see BARBAROUS INTONATION):

The Most High Words of God
The Binding of the Spirits, from Moses, Aaron, and Solomon
Zijmuorsobet, Noijm, Zavaxo, Quehaij, Abawo, Noquetonaij, Oasaij, Wuram, Thefothoson, Zijoronaijwetho, etc.

For the work taught in *The Red Church*, this depth of esoteric study is not necessary, and books such as TSSBM are deep waters, indeed. It was believed (and still is by some) that books such as these lead one into "being read fast" (see entry in this glossary), and therefore bound to powers of darkness. Some practitioners today state that the only book one needs is the Bible, and that all others are of dubious merit.

The author cannot argue against this point, as it takes much spiritual discernment to wade through texts such as TSSBM, which are best left alone by most. Perhaps there are those who will say that *The Red Church* falls into this category as well, but please be reassured that the work taught in these pages is dedicated to the craft of blessing.

SOPHIA: This is a concept that comes directly from theosophy of the 17th and 18th centuries. Its foremost exponent was the mystic Jacob Boehme. Heavy doses of early Protestant Christian theosophy, Pietism, and possibly Rosicrucianism found their way into early colonial Pennsylvania by way of the Wissahickon hermits, and later the Ephrata Cloister.

It is quite possible that some of this mysticism leaked out into the general population via the "householders" who were lay people associated with the Cloister. Other avenues are not out of the question. Sophia is the "feminine" expression of the Logos, which is Christ. Sophia is the Greek word for "wisdom", meaning God's Wisdom that is attested to throughout the Old and New

Testaments. Proponents of "Sophianic" Christianity warn against taking the mystical language of theosophy too literally and anthropomorphically. God's Virgin Wisdom draws suffering souls to repentance and wholeness in Christ. Some theosophists conflate the Virgin Sophia with the Virgin Mary, indeed their symbols mix, and the anthropomorphic depictions of Sophia are reminiscent of Catholic imagery of Mary.

The Reformation dumped the Blessed Virgin and all of the Saints in favor of a starker, barebones Christianity. Considering the excesses of the Catholic Church of that period, that overhaul was quite understandable. However, the Reformers also threw out any recognition of female warm-heartedness and motherhood within the Godhead.

It is this author's personal opinion that we cannot have a whole Christianity without God's Motherhood. Christ calls us to wholeness, and how can that be accomplished by denying the "mothering" warmhearted tenderness of God's love and mercy? This, more than anything else, has lead to people fleeing the Christian Church in favor of Neo-paganism.

The Christian religion is a very deep well and has all the elements for a wholesome mystical life, satisfying on all levels, without having to go outside of The Way. The Reverend James Wesley Stivers in his *The Mother Heart of God: A Study on the Pneumatic Role of the Woman* writes the following:

> The Greeks personified Wisdom and worshipped Sophia as a goddess. In Greek mythology she shares a place in the crowded pantheon and is often forgotten because other Greek deities see, to be far more adventurous and interesting.
>
> Second century, Christian Gnostics also worshipped Sophia. Since Sophia was female, her adoration

was condemned by some in the Early Church as idolatry. But in the light of what we now know, was that a fair accusation? If our God lacks the feminine principle, are we really worshipping the true God? -- Stivers pp 50-51.

Sophia is not "a being" outside of the Holy Trinity. Unlike the answer to this problem provided by the Shakers, who discarded Trinitarianism in favor or a dual Godhead, Sophia is in fact a personification of the Holy Ghost. Stivers makes a very convincing argument for the "feminine" nature of the Holy Ghost throughout his aforementioned book.

The Trinity is the ultimate family unit – the Godhead is a divine community. God's "three-ness" is dynamism and a profound wholeness. The all-masculine imagery of the Trinity is a mistake, and it has lead to many other errors. *All of this aside, past practitioners of Braucherei have been pretty mainstream in their Christianity with very, very few who have heard or read of "Sophia".* These mystical subjects, such as Christian theosophy, are valuable antidotes to the decay that has set into the mainstream churches, and can provide a fresh perspective and new vigor for revival of an *operative and experiential* Christian faith – a powerful faith without "fundamentalism" or its equally ugly opposite of a faithless, non-evangelical, quasi-atheistic humanism dressed up in Jesus-clothes, such as some "churches" have become.

When considering the strong theosophical current of the early sectarian Pennsylvania Germans, and that some of them were directly engaged in subjects such as alchemy, astrology, and "magical" faith healing, it is quite appropriate to address these matters within the broader examination of Braucherei. **(See SHEKINAH)**

SULPHUR: The medicinal use of sulphur is as an external antiseptic. Alchemically, sulphur is symbolic of Love; and it is the invisible Fire, or soul-essence – it is consciousness itself. In spagyric medicine is the essential oils contained within the plant matter. Sulphur, as brimstone, makes several appearances in both the Old and New Testaments as the element of punishment and cleansing. Divine Love burns out the infection of sin to create resurrection, salvation, and wholeness.

SWEENY: This word is an English corruption of the German word "schwinden" (meaning to atrophy or to waste away). Another related word is "Schwindsucht" or tuberculosis (consumption). Sweeny is the name that is used to describe any condition of injury resulting in atrophy.

SYMPATHY: For a thing to be "in sympathy" with another thing means that it somehow *like* that thing; that the two things share a connection. In music, this likeness is called *resonance*. In a universe where all things are connected in way or another, that universe's various aspects will have higher or lower degrees of resonance between those aspects.

Sympathy is used to great advantage in sorcery where a piece of clothing worn by someone, imbued with that individual's perspiration, skin flakes, or other bodily fluids, along with the electromagnetic energies of the body make the cloth a good proxy for the actual person. Blood, hair, nail clippings, and so on, retain their connection to the individual from which they came. Paracelsus called the virtue in these things *mumia*.

Mumia is the vitality that clings to such objects and connects them back to their place of origin. Among the practitioners of *the religion of Scientism*, such thinking is seen as "superstitious." However, thankfully, real practitioners of *Science*, who maintain open minds, have found that the universe is, indeed, a very odd place. Quantum physics has opened up the gates that let us out of the parochial clock-work world-view. The views of progressive physicists are now looking more like those of the "shamans" of old rather than of their Victorian ancestors.

According to the Doctrine of Signatures, the *likeness* of things can be discovered by observation. Over the centuries complex tables of this knowledge have been accumulated: plants, animals, planets, minerals, Zodiac signs, lunar phases, seasons, etc. and how these are all interconnected in their degrees of likeness. Iron, for example, is in sympathy with Mars, which is in sympathy with the sign of Aries; therefore, iron has a strong affinity with fire. Iron can be used to draw away rheums and balance out cold/wet conditions.

The herb Lungwort, because of the spots on its leaves, gives the plant the resemblance of diseased lungs. As it turns out, Lungwort is rather good for treating lung ailments. In magic the mandrake root has been used as a doll to contain protective spirits. Mandrake root resembles the human body, looking like a little person. This sympathy makes it an ideal vessel for such spirits, or for treating a patient by proxy of the doll.

In Braucherei, all of the above types of sympathies have been utilized. The greatest sympathy, however, is the likeness between God and humanity. Without this sympathy, nothing else can be done. When a Braucher Pow-Wows, he places himself in sympathy with the patient, having first aligned himself with Christ. In Christian believe, all believers are in sympathy with each other as we have all undergone the same baptism. It is for this reason that in traditional Braucherei practice, the full baptismal name is needed before proceeding with the Pow-Wow. Natural Magic is the knowledge and use of sympathies.

TEHILLIM (See PSALMS)

TETTER: is a blanket-term for any itchy skin eruption: eczema, psoriasis, herpes, etc. In the Pennsylvania German dialect it is called *ausfaahres*, or *ausfauhres*.

TEUFELSBRIEF: There are very few references to the teufelsbrief, which finds its opposite in the himmelsbrief (see HIMMELSBRIEF).

A teufelsbrief is literally a "devil's letter", which would be a means of cursing a person instead of blessing them. Despite extensive research, no such document has been discovered by the author labeled with that name. However, it is almost certain that these curse-letters were perhaps little more than ill wishing written down as a zauberzettel (see ZAUBERZETTEL) and then hidden upon the person or property of the one to be 'cursed'.

Almost certainly these 'letters' would contain conjurations of demonic agencies to torment the unfortunate recipient of the teufelsbrief. This author has read of some misguided interpretations of the teufelsbrief by the satanistically minded, thinking it some sort of "devil's blessing" for his disciples – a sort of Black Mass-like parody of the himmelsbrief. This 'brief' *never* functioned that way.

To be sure, no teufelsdiener (i.e., an evil Witch or Satanist) in his right mind would want to be on the receiving end of such 'blessings'. In fact, the traditional practitioner of hexerei was extremely careful to decontaminate his or her surroundings and person, knowing the deadly nature of the physical and spiritual poisons they used. To purposely hang a teufelsbrief in a home or upon some parcel of land would spiritually condemn the property.

As mentioned in the entry for the HIMMELSBRIEF, these letters have some elements of our modern day "chain letters" – i.e., if one does not obey these dictates and pass it around, the receiver shall be damned, or the recipient of bad luck. Chain letters with a vicious streak, such as they usually have, do function in a way as sorts of teufelsbriefe. *The only proper response to a letter 'from the devil' is a good, holy and purifying fire.*

This author sincerely suggests that all chain letters need to stop at the end of a match. The most insidious of these letters are the ones that ill-wish the breaker of the chain *in God's name*. The purpose of these letters is purportedly holy and wholesome, but it is not.

THREE, the number: In the practice of Braucherei there is no more important number than *three*. Almost every operation is done in three or multiples of three. When in doubt, always Pow-Wow three times. In Kabbalah, theosophy, and other mystical disciplines, the number three is part of the sequence of core esoteric numbers from one to ten. All other numbers beyond ten are just higher cycles of the first 'decade'. Three is the Holy Trinity, the "Three Highest Names". In Christian art, the Trinity is abstractly symbolized as a triangle. Three is dynamism, wholeness, and balance. The Rosicrucian Franz Hartmann defines the Trinity as:

> The All. The whole of the Universe. Everything is a trinity, and Three is the number of *Form*. Every conceivable thing consists of *Matter* and *Motion* in *Space*, and the three are forever one and inseparable. "God" is a Trinity, and the Universe must necessarily be a Trinity. Everything is a product of *thought*, *will*, and *substance* (form); i.e., Mercury, Sulphur, and Salt, -- *Cosmology*, p.8

The three divisions of the human body are the head, the breast, and the belly according to Agrippa. There are three dimensions (although science does speculate on there being more), Three Fates (Lachesis, Clotho, and Atropos), Three Graces (Euphrosyne, Aglaia, and Thalia), Three Norns (Verthandi, Uthr, and Skuld), Three Furies (Alecto, Tisiphone, and Megaera); the deities of the ancient Egyptians and Celts were grouped in threes, as well as the triplicities of Hecate, Diana, and the Celtic Brigit (and the Morrigan).

The twelve signs of the zodiac are grouped in threes according to the four elements (each element having three signs). According to some early Church Fathers, there were three Magi that visited the infant Christ (**see THREE KINGS**). Part One of *Cosmology*, speaking in reference to the number three requests the reader that he

Try to find spiritually the Fire and the Water, which is the Prima Materia of the Spiritus Universi, in which the Gold is consumed and from whence the latter, after the Putrefaction is over, resurrects into a new life. *Cosmology* p.3

"The General Brauche Circuit" begins with the triple invocation of *Water* and *Fire* in the name of the Virgin and the Holy Trinity. These *principles* when seen through the lens of Christian theosophy take on a whole 'new' meaning and significance.

THREE KINGS, The:

Now when Jesus was born in Bethlehem of Judea in the days of Herod the king, behold, there came wise men [*magoi*] from the east to Jerusalem, saying "Where is he that is born King of the Jews? For we have seen his star in the east, and are come to worship him." When Herod the king had heard these things, he was troubled, and all Jerusalem with him. And when he had gathered all the chief priests and scribes of the people together, he demanded of them where Christ should be born. And they said unto him, in Bethlehem of Judaea: for it is written by the prophet; and thou Bethlehem, in the land of Judah, art not the least among the princes of Judah: for out of thee shall come a Governor, that shall rule my people Israel. Then Herod, when he had privily called the wise men [*magoi*], enquired of them diligently what time the star appeared. And he sent them to Bethlehem, and said, "Go and search diligently for the young child; and when you have found him, bring me word again, that I may come and worship him also." When they had heard the king, they departed; and lo, the star, which they saw in the east, went before them, till it came and stood over where the young child was. When they saw the star, they rejoiced with exceeding joy. And when they were come into the house, they saw the young child with Mary his mother, and fell down, and worshipped him: and when they had opened their treasures. They presented unto him gifts; gold, and frankincense, and myrrh. And being warned by God in a dream that they should not return to Herod, they departed into their own country another way. **Matthew 2:1-12 KJV** [Note: bracketed italics mine]

And thus is the Biblical account of the Magi (magicians) who visited Christ. As can be seen from the above passages, there is no mention of the number of Magi (Greek: *magoi*) who were on the journey. Various Church Fathers mention three as the number, due (perhaps) to the number of gifts presented.

The word used to describe these sages is, indeed, *magus*. A magus was a member of a priestly caste in ancient Persia, who where (among other things) philosophers, astrologers, and 'medicine men,' doubtless the latter is a loaded term, but such was their function. Like all priests, they mediated between God and the people. It is said that these priests were "fire worshipers" which is a misnomer – fire was a symbol for God and the Supreme Good, just as it is with modern Zoroastrians.

Considering the threefold nature of God, the artistic usage of "three" magi is understandable, if debatable. The word "magus" appears in other passages in the New Testament as a term of abuse for the condemnation of Elymas and Simon Magus, where the word is selectively translated as "sorcerer" in English versions. After reading through *The Red Church*, it ought to be clear that there is a rather curt dividing line between vulgar "sorcery" and its exalted sister "magic."

In the West, at least since the 8th century, the "three" are known as Caspar (Gaspar), Melchior, and Balthazar. However, other Christians have different names. Among the Syrians they are: Larvandad, Gushnasaph, and Hormisdas. Considering the Syrians' proximity to the ancient Persian cultural area, these names are quite plausible – although when looked at closely, they seem to be merely titles.

For Ethiopian Christians they are: Hor, Karsudan, and Basanata; and for Armenians: Kagba, Badadakharida, and Badadilma. However, for our uses in Braucherei, the traditional Western names are what are found in the zauberzetteln and Brauche charms. Often in the former, only the initials are used creating a sort of 'runic-looking' inscription: CMBCMBCMB, etc.

As for the star, a few skeptics (and modern astrologers) have tried to explain it away as a physical phenomenon possibly being a conjunction of Jupiter in Saturn (7 B.C.), or Jupiter in Venus (6 B.C.). Of course, that begs the question of how the star *moved*. That is to say, it was neither a comet nor a star.

THREE KINGS' WATER: This is water that has been blessed on Epiphany. It is said to hold 'extra' special properties not held in other blessed water. *The Sixth and Seventh Books of Moses* mentions the use of this water as part of a purification ceremony for inviting angelic presences and fighting demonic ones.

As with many of the old grimoires, these books of magic were written by priests and monks, and it this is clear enough from some of the directions for various operations, such as having to celebrate Mass prior to an act of conjuration. It was also taken for granted that such a priest will make a special batch of holy water on Epiphany. This author has heard that there is another formulation for "Three Kings' Water" that is independent of the aforementioned, but it is most likely not the candidate for the water mentioned in the grimoires.

UFFGELESE (See CONTAGION)

UTICARIA (See WEIBELSUCHT)

VENETIAN SOAP: (*Sapo Castiliensis*) "Venetian" is another term designating "castile" soap, which is made from olive oil and sodium hydroxide (alkaline ash). This is a very hard (durable), cleansing vegetable-based soap, which sometimes doubled as a laxative – in the same manner as Epsom salts.

VERDIGRIS: (from French *Vert de Grise* – the "Green of Greece") The resulting green patina of brass, copper, or bronze when exposed to the elements is called verdigris. Chemically, verdigris is copper acetate (Cu2), and was once used widely as a pigment. In the old house and charm books verdigris, along with other dyeing agents such as blue vitriol (see BLUE VITRIOL) are listed as ingredients in various unguent formulae. Sometimes verdigris is used as an anti fungal, but copper is also toxic.

WALPURGISNACHT: is the German name for May Eve – the evening of April 30th. Traditionally, this is a night when many different spirits are supposed on the prowl: spirits of the dead, demons, devils, nature spirits and the like. May Eve is often described as being one of two 'liminal' points in the year when the 'veil is thin' between this world and the spirit world.

Walpurgisnacht is the threshold of summer, with the next day being May Day – a popular fertility festival of old. Scholars such as Carlo Ginsburg (author of *Night Battles* and *Deciphering the Witches' Sabbath*) have demonstrated how various indigenous strains of vestigial European 'shamanism' have shaped thought and practice surrounding these liminal points in the year, such as Walpurgisnacht, All Hollow's Eve (Halloween, the other 'thin' eve – especially in Celtic cultural areas), the Ember days, Christmas Eve, New Years, midsummer, etc.

According to Ginsburg's thesis (and this is a *very* over-simplified distilling), these supernaturally active points in the calendar are indicative of traditional spiritual battles held between the powers of Light and Darkness; that is to say, the fight between the spirits of fertility and infertility: summer vs. winter; life vs. death. Some spiritually sensitive people (called 'shamans' today) would go into a trance during these times and fight along side with the powers of Light to ensure the growth of plants for good harvests during the year.

Those people who fought along side of the powers of Darkness to cause infertility, distress, and death were said to be the "Witches". When our ancestors converted to Christianity, these trance-battles continued but were reshaped by the new religion. Post-pagan shamans (or as some would refer to as "white Witches") would see these spirit battles as the powers of Christ and His angels defeating those of the Devil: for the Pennsylvania Dutch had a saying that Witches exist *"fa die leid gwele"*—that is, to torment people.

Aside from these spirit journeys, May Eve is/has been traditionally marked in the Germanic world by the lighting of bonfires. Walpurgis Night receives its name from St. Walpurga, a Benedictine nun, who was canonized on May 1st by Pope Adrian II in the year 870. St. Walpurga was born in 710 AD, Devonshire, England, and died February 25th, 870 AD in Heidenheim, Germany. She was sister to saints Willibald and Winibald. Her earthly remains are said to exude a healing oil (actually this fluid is more like water than oil) called "Oil of Saints" to this very day.

Due to the supernatural activity ascribed to this evening, an alternate name for it is *Hexennacht*, or Witches' Night. Geographical loci (points of liminality) such as the Brocken in Germany, or the Hexenkopf (**see HEXENKOPF**) in Williams Township, Pennsylvania, have been known for being sites of preternatural phenomena on nights such as Walpurgisnacht.

WIEBELSUCHT: a sensation like bugs crawling on the skin – related to the sensations of hives.

WHITE VITRIOL: White vitriol is zinc sulfate ($ZnSO_4$). White vitriol was used as a mordant for dyeing, and also for the preservation of leather. In archaic medicine it was used for its purgative action when ingested, and also as an astringent (hence its archaic use for abscess washes). Like blue vitriol, it too is poisonous. Presently, it is used as a zinc source for various pet and barnyard feeds.

WINDGALLS: This is usually a benign condition in horses, also called "windpuffs". Windgalls are puffy, cyst-like swellings which occur around a horse's fetlock joins (the legs). When lameness occurs along with windgalls, it is potentially problematic. These puffs can disappear spontaneously, and are seen in larger, heavier horses. Braucherei can be used to reduce the swellings, which was mostly a concern when the horse went lame.

WITCHCRAFT (See HEXEREI)

WOMB DISEASE: In German this would be a score of different terms relating to afflictions of the womb or the *mudder*. Brendle and Unger catalogue a few of these: *muddergichtre* (womb gout), *mutterweh* (womb pain), *mutterkrankheit* (womb sickness), and *muttergrimmen* (womb colic). The euphemism "ihre zeit" (her time) for menstruation has been used in connection with afflictions of the womb: too much bleeding, not enough bleeding, pain, etc.

WORMS: In folk medicine "worms" (German *warm*) have a lengthy and complex history. Generally, when speaking of "worms" we can safely assume that the usual meaning (especially of late) designates the infestation of intestinal worms, for which there are countless herbal remedies to expulse these being called *vermifuges*. However, "worm" has also broadly referred to any sort of footless or crawling parasite (real or imagined) as the cause of disease. These creatures have ranged from the common earthworm to "dragons" (*drache* in German, or *wyrm* in archaic English) otherwise called "serpents" (see The BRAZEN SERPENT). *Drache* can also have the double meaning of "devil".

Here we can recall the words of **Revelation 12:9** that describes the devil as the great dragon "[who] *was cast out, that old serpent, called the devil, and Satan, which deceiveth the whole world...*" (see The DEVIL). Charms and prayers to control the skin disease of rotlaufe, or any other reddish inflammation, sometimes personify and address the illness as a "red dragon". Even today, many will speak of the common fungal infection as "ring worm" when there is no real "worm" involved. Some acts of Witchcraft have been credited with the ability to place various noxious creatures *into* the body of a human or animal victim; in some of these cases the creatures placed within are described as worms.

WOUND WOOD (See ASH TREE)

WYRD: is an old Germanic concept, but it is **not** a term that is used in traditional Braucherei. Of course, the word itself is Old English, and it is from *wyrd* that we get our modern English word "weird". Among the ancient Norse, the word was *Urdr* or *Urd*, personified this was the name of one of the three Norns: *Urdr, Verdandi, and Skuld* being past, present, and future. Wyrd/Urd derive from the proto-German *wurþiz*, and farther back to the Indo European **wert* meaning "to turn".

The Latin word *vertere* is also related to "wyrd" by way of this descent. In Old English there is also the word *weorþan* meaning "to become". All of the above is in reference to what we can call the dynamics of the "web" of existence: all things and all actions are interconnected. This is the true meaning of "Fate", but it is not a Fate of predestination.

Despite the absence of this word in the vocabulary of Braucherei, we can see some echoes of wyrd-like ideas in Germanic strains of

Christian thought, being Divine Providence. Although the ancient heathen gods were not greater than Fate itself, we can see in the Triune God of Christianity the Master or overseer of the 'web' itself – in fact, its Creator and captain. In the Christian religion a human creature is endowed with free will, but that will is circumscribed by certain of God's laws (e.g., physical nature) – the ancients would have called these primal laws *orlay* or *örlog*.

A Germanic heathen would describe each of one's personal actions as "laying a deed in the Well of Wyrd", thus building up the momentum of one's "fate". In the Far East this is analogous to the concept of *karma*. *Providence* comes from the Latin *providencia*, meaning foresight with an aim to provide and sustain. God is the Creator and Sustainer of creation. The practice of Braucherei, like its wicked sibling hexerei, has ramifications for both the practitioner and the patient. The affect of each deed of healing or hexing leads to yet more effects. Nothing exists in alone, and as the saying goes, Nature abhors a vacuum.

ZAUBERZETTEL: This is a combination of two German words: *zauber* (meaning 'sorcery' or in this case a 'charm') and *zettel* (a slip of paper). A zauberzettel is, therefore, a small slip of paper used as a talisman. These slips (the plural being *zauberzetteln*) usually consist of small, rune-like inscriptions of Biblically related symbols (See I.N.R.I.) and passages of scripture, along with the possible addition of crosses, the hexenfoos, etc. These are usually hidden in the same manner as Brauche bags (See BRAUCHE BAGS) in homes, barns (and other outbuildings), and upon one's person.

When they are secreted away in a dwelling they are affixed in an unseen place *without the use of metal* (such as pins and clips). The cramped writing on these "papers", as noted above, tends to be rather indecipherable. This is not a matter of haste on the part of the past practitioners as it is the employment of symbol making, when the known is made mysterious (See BARBAROUS INTONATION and BARBAROUS MANIPULATION). The zauberzettel is also known as *annängsel*, which refers to a written talisman that is placed upon, or worn by, the patient.

ZWISCHENTRAGER: A go-between used in order to remove illness or malevolent energies (curses) – a vehicle for carrying contagion.

Appendix II
Use of the Psalms and the Names of God from Scripture

This is a listing of all Psalms in numerical order along with their sympathetic uses according to the *Sepher Schimmusch Tehillim* as translated by Godfrey Selig appearing in *The Sixth and Seventh Books of Moses*. It is this author's opinion that this section of the above mentioned book is its most useful chapter – especially if you are not going to go any deeper into that work. *The Red Church* only gives the proper workings of a few of these Psalms – that is, the directions for the accompanying prayers, Name of God, and other directions as listed in the *Sepher*. For further information on these uses, you will need a copy of *The Sixth and Seventh Books of Moses*. Joseph Peterson's revision of this book is incomparable – a truly superior effort.

Psalm 1: for pregnancy and fears of premature delivery
Psalm 2: for danger at sea (storms); also for headache
Psalm 3: for severe backache and headache
Psalm 4: for bad luck
Psalm 5: for gaining favor in business
Psalm 6: for eye diseases
Psalm 7: for protection from enemies and conspiracies
Psalm 8: for securing good will
Psalm 9: for restoring health to male children (and also for protection against enemies)
Psalm 10: for use against unclean spirits
Psalm 11: for safety against evil schemes and persecution
Psalm 12: same use as Psalm 11
Psalm 13: for safety against physical torments and dangers for 24 hours
Psalm 14: for retaining favor and for freedom from mistrust and slander

Psalm 15: for use against evil spirits, insanity, and depression
Psalm 16: for discovering the name of a thief
Psalm 17: for safety during travel
Psalm 18: for protection against a direct, immanent physical threat
Psalm 19: for help during a long and dangerous recuperation or confinement
Psalm 20: for remaining safe from danger
Psalm 21: for dangerous storms at sea
Psalm 22: for protection against harm during travel
Psalm 23: for receiving an answer to a question through dreams or visions
Psalms 24 & 25: for dangers of nature – especially the danger of floods
Psalm 26: same as Psalms 24 & 25; also against imprisonment
Psalm 27: for being well received by strangers
Psalm 28: for being reconciled with an enemy
Psalm 29: for casting out evil spirits
Psalm 30: for use against evil occurrences
Psalm 31: for negating slander
Psalm 32: for receiving compassion and grace
Psalm 33: for use against tragedies – especially children
Psalm 34: for gaining favor with authority figures
Psalm 35: for success in lawsuits
Psalm 36: for use against evil and slander
Psalm 37: for protection during intoxication
Psalms 38 & 39: for use against slander that has gotten one in trouble
Psalm 40: for deliverance from wicked spirits and temptation
Psalms 41, 42, & 43: for enemies who have caused one to be mistrusted
Psalm 44: for being safe from enemies
Psalms 45 & 46: for making peace between husband and wife
Psalm 47: for being esteemed
Psalm 48: for use against envy
Psalms 49 & 50: for use against fever

Psalm 51: for healing one's conscience
Psalm 52: for use against slander
Psalms 53, 54, & 55: for protecting against persecution
Psalm 56: for freedom from the effects of lust, envy, and to clear one's head of these temptations
Psalm 57: for being fortunate in all undertakings
Psalm 58: for use against dog (or other animal) attack
Psalm 59: for freeing against evil inclinations
Psalm 60: for use by a soldier going into battle
Psalm 61: for blessing a new house
Psalm 62: for the pardon of wrong doings
Psalm 63: for use against being taken advantage of
Psalm 64: for safe seafaring
Psalm 65: for good fortune in all undertakings
Psalm 66: for use against evil spirits
Psalms 67 & 68: for severe fever, and also for imprisonment
Psalms 69 & 70: for overcoming evil habits
Psalm 71: for liberating one wrongly imprisoned
Psalm 72: for finding favor and remaining within it
Psalm 73: for keeping faith
Psalm 74: for defeating persecution
Psalm 75: same as Psalm 74
Psalm 76: for averting danger from water
Psalm 77: for not being overtaken by enemies
Psalm 78: for being loved by authority figures
Psalm 79: for use against fatal enemies
Psalms 80 & 81: for saving against unbelief
Psalm 82: for helping in business – especially on behalf of another
Psalm 83: for safety during war
Psalm 84: for the removal of bad odors during illness
Psalm 85: for reconciliation between friends – also good for harmony in church congregations
Psalms 86, 87, & 88: for general wellbeing
Psalm 89: for saving a person from a wasting disease; also to liberate a friend in prison
Psalm 90: for safety from wild animals or spirits

Psalm 91: for one afflicted by an evil spirit or incurable disease
Psalm 92: for attaining high honors
Psalm 93: for one in a suit with an unjust opponent
Psalm 94: for relief from tenacious enemies
Psalm 95: for backsliding believers
Psalms 96 & 97: for causing joy in one's family
Psalm 98: for causing peace in one's family
Psalm 99: for increasing one's piety
Psalm 100: for overcoming enemies and obstacles
Psalm 101: for gaining release from obsession and evil spirits
Psalms 102 & 103: for barren women
Psalms 104: for negating or destroying an evil influence
Psalms 105, 106, & 107: for fevers – 105 is used for a fever of three days; 106 for a fever of four days; and 107 for a daily fever
Psalm 108: for blessing upon coming or going from home
Psalm 109: for use against a tenacious enemy; also for acquiring friends
Psalms 110 & 111: for use in having enemies ask one for forgiveness; 111 for the acquiring of friends (no Name of God used)
Psalms 112 & 113: for growing in influence and power; also for stopping heresy
Psalm 114: for success in trade or business
Psalm 115: for when engaging non-believers in debate
Psalm 116: for securing against violent death
Psalm 117: for forgiveness in breaking a vow
Psalm 118: for silencing heretics and scoffers
Psalm 119: *Aleph*: for convulsions; *Beth*: for good memory, a clear heart; *Gimel*: for an injured eye; *Daleth*: for an injury to the left eye – also for troubles with occupation or residence; *He*: for refraining from committing sins; *Vau*: for securing the good service of subordinates; *Zain*: for the healing of depression and also stitches in the side; also for use when one has been mislead by evil counsel; *Cheth*: for severe pains in the upper body; *Teth*: for kidney and liver dysfunction; also for pain in the hips; *Yod*: for gaining grace and favor with God and people; *Caph*: for a hot swelling on the right side of the nose; *Lamed*: for obtaining a favorable hearing in court;

Mem: for pain in the limbs; especially for paralysis in the right arm or hand; *Nun*: for protection in travel; *Samech*: for use when asking favors of superiors; *Ain*: for curing pain in the left arm and hand; *Pe*: for a hot swelling on the left side of the nose; *Tsaddi*: for use when being induced to make decisions that one knows to be bad; *Koph*: for the cure of pain or injury to the left leg; *Resh*: for a painful boil in the right ear; *Shin*: for use against a severe headache; *Tau*: for a painful boil in the left ear

Psalm 120: for gaining favor in court; also for protection against animal and insect pests while traveling

Psalm 121: for safety while traveling at night alone

Psalm 122: for finding favor with a person of great authority

Psalm 123: for use when employees or helpers have abandoned the job

Psalm 124: for use when about to cross a dangerous body of water or before boarding a ship

Psalm 125: for use when about to travel in a hostile country

Psalm 126: for protection of new born children

Psalm 127: same as Psalm 126

Psalm 128: for the protection of a pregnant woman

Psalm 129: for ensuring that one always does good works

Psalm 130: for leaving a war besieged area in safety

Psalm 131: for placing in check the spirit of overweening pride

Psalm 132: for staying true to one's promises

Psalm 133: for retaining the love and friendship of others

Psalm 134: for help in academic studies and intellectual work

Psalm 135: for the sincere repentance of sin

Psalm 136: same as Psalm 135

Psalm 137: for removing hate, envy and malice from the heart

Psalm 138: for producing love and friendship

Psalm 139: for increasing love among married people

Psalm 143: for removing hatred between man and wife

Psalm 144: for healing a broken arm

Psalm 145: for protection against ghosts, demons, and unclean spirits

Psalm 146: for use in helping to heal wounds made by weapons

Psalm 147: for use in the curing of deadly bites and wounds
Psalms 148 & 149: for use in curbing the spread of fire
Psalm 150: for use in thanksgiving for having been brought safely through great danger

Appendix III
Pennsylvania German and Standard German Pronunciation Guide

Unless familiar with the Pennsylvania Dutch dialect specifically, and standard High-German generally, the pronunciation of the words associated with traditional German folk magic and medicine may not be immediately apparent for those new to the subject. Therefore, this appendix is provided in order to make the subject a little more accessible. For those of you who shall take on Braucherei practice in earnest, knowing the correct pronunciation of the German is a must.

As noted in the history section of this book, the Germans who became the Pennsylvania Dutch emigrated mainly from the Palatine. The dialect of that area of Germany being called Pfälzisch, which is much closer to High German than other dialects such as Swabian, Barvarian, Swiss German, Plautdietsch, etc. Unlike High German, this dialect has a number of peculiarities that off set it: a simplified grammar, various vowel shifts, and different idiomatic expressions.

Pennsylvania Dutch has become even farther removed from High German than its Pfälzisch parent having developed *in situ* vocabulary and idioms neither found in the former nor the latter. The Pennsylvania dialect has many English loan words. The Germans who came to America in the 17th and 18th centuries did so prior to the Industrial Revolution. As a result, their vocabulary was deprived of the technical terminology which was developing in the Old World during those decades. Therefore, they borrowed freely from English to fill in the gaps.

Some words in Deitsch vocabulary are unique to it, being neither English nor Continental German. Other differences between

Pennsylvaanisch Deitsch and Old World Pfälzisch have occurred mainly in pronunciation, making some of its variants unintelligible to modern speakers of standard High German.

As for the spelling of Deitsch:
Pennsylvanian Dutch was very rarely written down in the early years. It has always been mainly a spoken rather than written language. As a result, numerous variations in spelling have taken place on those occasions when it was written. Today, as in the past, those who speak the language have taken to using phonetic American English spelling conventions to write down the dialect.

As you can imagine, there are countless ways in which to spell phonetically, and this has added to the confusion when trying to read Deitsch. Alternate to phonetic spelling are the Buffington-Barba conventions preferred by scholars and academics in order to standardize Deitsch for its preservation and continuation. This system applies standard High German spelling conventions to the dialect, and it is what is presented below.

Pennsylvaanisch Deitsch Pronunciation

Vowels
The vowels come in two types, short and long.

Short:
A -- short 'a' sounds like the 'o' in the English word *cot*.
AE -- is pronounced like the 'a' in the word *cat*.
E -- this is like the 'e' in the words *bet* or *bed*.
I -- like the 'i' in *kid*.
O -- sometimes this letter is said like the 'ou' in *bought* or the 'u' in *tuck*.

Long:

Generally, any vowel followed by and 'h' is pronounced as a long vowel. Also, the letter H is usually silent when it comes after a vowel.

AA -- as the 'aw' in the English word *awe*.
AE -- as the 'a' in the English word *trade*.
E -- sometimes written as **EE** is the same as long **AE** above.
O -- long **O** is written also as **OO** and **OH**. This is pronounced in the same way as the 'oa' in the English word *oat* or the interjection '*Oh!*'
U -- also seen as **UH** is like the 'oo' in *smooth*.
UU – same as **U** and **UH** above.

<u>Diphthongs</u>
AU -- this is a sound that is not really found in mainstream English. It is a sound that is somewhere between the 'ou' in the word *house*, and the 'o' in the *toss*.
EI -- the same as in standard German: *ein*, *dein*; or as in the English 'i' in *spice*.
OI -- the same as the English 'oi', as in *oil*.

The Consonants
The following are the same as in English: **b***, **ck**, **d***, **f**, **g***, **k**, **l**, **m**, **n**, **p**, **t**, **x***, **y***.
***B** -- at the end of a word **B** sounds like 'p'
BB – sounds like 'pp'
BH -- pronounced like English 'p'
***D** -- at the end of a word **D** sounds like 't'
DD – sounds like 'tt'
CH -- this makes two different sounds: in standard German this would be the difference between the CH in *ich* and the **CH** in *buch*. The former is more of an aspirant, like a strongly pronounced 'h'; the latter is more like the Scottish word *loch*.
***G** -- at the end of a word **G** sounds like 'k'; also, when G stands in-between two vowels it sounds like the 'y' in *yes*
GG -- the double 'g' that sometimes sits in the middle of words is barely pronounced; it is almost a glottal stop.
GH -- pronounced like English 'k'

H -- like English 'h' at the beginning of a word; see note above under the heading of Long Vowels for **H**.
J -- as in standard German, **J** is pronounced like **Y**: *ja* or *yah*.
R -- sometimes this is rolled lightly at the beginning of words and in-between vowels. **R** at the end of words makes an English 'ah' sound. For example: *Er* = ah, *fer* = fah, *der* = dah; however, unlike English, the sound is not drawn out.
S -- and also SS is much like the English 's', but not like the 'z' sound in *hose*.
SCH -- this sound is always 'sh' as in *ship*.
TSCH -- this is like the 'ch' in *charge* or *church*. It stands in also for the 'j' in English words such as *jump*.
V -- sounds like English 'f'
W -- sounds like English 'v'
*****X** -- this is always the 'ks' sound, never as a 'z'.
*****Y** -- **Y** is always a consonant that makes the 'y' as in *yes*.
Z -- this makes the sound 'ts', as in *cats*.

Standard German Pronunciation

The pronunciation of Standard German (High German) is similar to that of Deitsch.

Vowels
Short:
A – like the 'u' in *cut*
E – 'e' as in the English *bet*
I – 'i' as in *kitten*
O – the 'o' in *toss*
U – the 'u' in *brush*
Long:
A – also seen as **AA**, and **AH** – pronounced like the 'a' in *papa*
E – also seen as **EE, EH**, and **ÄH** – pronounced like 'ay' in *say*
I – also as **IH** and **IE** -- like the 'ee' in *see*
O – also as **OH**, or **OO** – as in the 'o' in the English word *so*

U – also as **UH** – as in the 'ue' in *clue*
Umlauts:
The sounds represented by these vowels are not heard in English (at least not in any mainstream English)
Long:
Ö – also as **ÖH** – this is sounded by pronouncing the German long **E** with lips rounded while also sounding out the German long **O**.
Short:
Ö – sounded out by pronouncing German short **E** with rounded lips while sounding out the German short **O**
Long:
Ü -- also as **ÜH** – this sound will not be found in English; it is like the 'ue' in the French word *rue* -- German long **I** pronounced with rounded lips
Short:
Ü – also as **Y** – this is sounded as the German short **I** with lips rounded while sounding the German short **U**

Diphthongs
AI – also as **EI**, **AY**, **EY**; this pair is sounded like the word *eye* in English
AU – this is pronounced like the 'ou' in *out*
ÄU – this is pronounced 'oi' as in *oil*

Consonants
The consonants of Standard German are the same as those of Deitsch, with the additions of:
QU – pronounced as kv
GN, **KN**, and **PF** are all pronounced as discrete letters. For example, unlike in the modern English a word beginning with the letters **KN** would not have a silent 'k' such as is found in the words knight, and knowledge. The same applies to the other two combinations.

A Basic Fraktur Alphabet									
A, a	B, b	C, c	D, d	E, e	F, f	G, g	H, h	I, i	J, j	K, k
𝔄, a	𝔅, b	ℭ, c	𝔇, d	𝔈, e	𝔉, f	𝔊, g	ℌ, h	ℑ, i	ℑ, j	𝔎, k
L, l	M, m	N, n	O, o	P, p	Q, q	R, r	S, s	T, t	U, u	V, v
𝔏, l	𝔐, m	𝔑, n	𝔒, o	𝔓, p	𝔔, q	ℜ, r	𝔖, s	𝔗, t	𝔘, u	𝔙, v
W, w	X, x	Y, y	Z, z	ch	ck					
𝔚, w	𝔛, x	𝔜, y	𝔷, z	ch	ck					

To see the differences between standard High German and Pennsylvaanisch Deitsch, below is the Lord's Prayer in both translations.

Pennsylvaanisch Deitsch: Unser Vadder

Unser Vadder im Himmel,
Dei Naame loss heilich sei,
Dei Reich loss komme.
Dei Wille loss gedu sei,
uff die Erd wie in Himmel.
unser deeglich Brot gebb uns heit,
Un vergewwe unser Schulde,
wie mir die vergewwe wu uns schuldich sinn.
Un fiehr uns net in die Versuchung,
awwer hald uns vum Iewile.
Fer die iss es Reich, die Graft,
un die Hallichkeit in Ewichkeit.
Amen.

Standard High German: Vater Unser

Vater unser im Himmel,
geheiligt werde dein Name,
Dein Reich komme.
Dein Wille geschehe,
wie im Himmel, so auf Erden.
Unser tägliches Brot gib uns heute,
und vergib uns unsere Schuld,
wie auch wir vergeben unseren Schuldigern.

Und führe uns nicht in Versuchung,
sondern erlöse uns von dem Bösen.
Denn Dein ist der Reich, und die Kraft
und die Herrlichkeit in Ewigkeit.
Amen.

Appendix IV
Planetary Hours

Planetary Hours of the Day

Hour	Sunday	Monday	Tuesday	Wednesday	Thursday	Friday	Saturday
1	Sun	Moon	Mars	Mercury	Jupiter	Venus	Saturn
2	Venus	Saturn	Sun	Moon	Mars	Mercury	Jupiter
3	Mercury	Jupiter	Venus	Saturn	Sun	Moon	Mars
4	Moon	Mars	Mercury	Jupiter	Venus	Saturn	Sun
5	Saturn	Sun	Moon	Mars	Mercury	Jupiter	Venus
6	Jupiter	Venus	Saturn	Sun	Moon	Mars	Mercury
7	Mars	Mercury	Jupiter	Venus	Saturn	Sun	Moon
8	Sun	Moon	Mars	Mercury	Jupiter	Venus	Saturn
9	Venus	Saturn	Sun	Moon	Mars	Mercury	Jupiter
10	Mercury	Jupiter	Venus	Saturn	Sun	Moon	Mars
11	Moon	Mars	Mercury	Jupiter	Venus	Saturn	Sun
12	Saturn	Sun	Moon	Mars	Mercury	Jupiter	Venus

Planetary Hours of the Night

Hours	Sunday	Monday	Tuesday	Wednesday	Thursday	Friday	Saturday
1	Jupiter	Venus	Saturn	Sun	Moon	Mars	Mercury
2	Mars	Mercury	Jupiter	Venus	Saturn	Sun	Moon
3	Sun	Moon	Mars	Mercury	Jupiter	Venus	Saturn
4	Venus	Saturn	Sun	Moon	Mars	Mercury	Jupiter
5	Mercury	Jupiter	Venus	Saturn	Sun	Moon	Mars
6	Moon	Mars	Mercury	Jupiter	Venus	Saturn	Sun
7	Saturn	Sun	Moon	Mars	Mercury	Jupiter	Venus
8	Jupiter	Venus	Saturn	Sun	Moon	Mars	Mercury
9	Mars	Mercury	Jupiter	Venus	Saturn	Sun	Moon
10	Sun	Moon	Mars	Mercury	Jupiter	Venus	Saturn
11	Venus	Saturn	Sun	Moon	Mars	Mercury	Jupiter
12	Mercury	Jupiter	Venus	Saturn	Sun	Moon	Mars

Bibliography

This bibliography contains all of the works cited in *The Red Church*, as well as some that were not. It would have been ideal to list every work that I have come across over the years that has touched upon the subject of Braucherei (even if only peripherally), but that would make a daunting, and redundant, reading list. A few titles here do, indeed, fall into the realm of the peripheral, but within the context of Pow-Wow illuminate the subject further.

Agrippa of Nettesheim, Henry Cornelius; Donald Tyson, ed. *Three Books of Occult Philosophy*. St. Paul, MN: Llewellyn Publications, 2000.

Anonymous. *Meditations on the Tarot: A Journey into Christian Hermeticism*. Rockport, MA: Element Books Ltd., 1985.

Aurand Jr., A. Monroe. *The Realness of Witchcraft in America*. Lancaster: The Aurand Press, no date.

-- *Popular Home Remedies Superstitions of the Pennsylvania Germans*. Lancaster: The Aurand Press, no date.

Andrews, E. Benjamin. *History of the United States, from the Earliest Discovery of America to the End of 1902*. New York, Charles Scribner's Sons, 1904.

Bach, Jeff. *Voices of The Turtledoves: The Sacred World of Ephrata*. The Pennsylvania State University Press, 2003.

Backus, Rev. Dr. William. *The Healing Power of the Christian Mind: How Biblical Truth Can Keep You Healthy*. Minneapolis, MN: Bethany House Publishers, 1996.

Bailer, Aunt Sophie. "Witches... I Have Known." *The Pennsylvania Dutchman* (May 1952): 8.

-- "How to Stop a Witch." *The Pennsylvania Dutchman* (May 1952): 8-9.

-- "How I Learned Powwowing." *The Pennsylvania Dutchman* (June 1952): 8.

Bailes, Frederick. *Basic Principles of the Science of Mind: 12 Lesson Home Study Course*. Camarillo, CA: DeVors & Company. 2004.

Barr, James. *Biblical Faith and Natural Theology*. Oxford University Press, Clarendon Paperbacks, 1994.

Barth, George. *The Mesmerist's Manual of Phenomena and Practice; with Directions for Applying Mesmerism to The Care of Disease*. 1850.

Beidelman, William. *The Story of the Pennsylvania Germans, embracing an account of their Origin, their History, and their Dialect*. Easton, PA: Express Book Print, 1898.

Beissel, James D. *Powwow Power: A True Story of A Powwow Relative and Other Related Events*. Willow Street, PA: Crystal Educational Counselors, 1998.

Bell, Adam. "1929 York Murder Trial Kept Nation Spellbound." Patriot-News, 31 October 1995, A1

Benner, Craig. *Low Dutch Morning Star*. Gettysburg, PA: Dickinson-Longabaugh Press, 2006.

Blanchard, Robert, ed. *Black Book of Dr. Faust -- Dr. Johannes Faust's Miracle and Magic Book, or The Black Raven, or Also Named The Threefold Coersion of Hell*. Second Edition. Palm Springs, CA:

International Guild of Occult Sciences, College and Research Society, 1992.

Boehme, Jacob. *Signature of All Things (Signatura Rerum)*. New York, NY: Cosimo Classics, 2007.

Boyer, Dennis. *Once Upon A Hex: A Spiritual Ecology of The Pennsylvania Germans*. Oregon, WI: Badger Books, Inc., 2004.

Bourgeois, Robert L. "Psychokinesis and Contact with an Artificial Spirit: A Replication of the Philip Phenomena." Franklin Pierce College, 1994.

Brendle, Thomas R.; Claude W. Unger. *Folk Medicine of the Pennsylvania Germans: The Non-Occult Cures*. New York: Augustus M. Kelley Publishers, 1970. (Reprint of 1935 ed.)

Caine, Kenneth Winston, et al. *Prayer, Faith, and Healing: Cure Your Body, Heal Your Mind, and Restore Your Soul*. Rodale, Inc., 1999.

Carus, Dr. Paul. *The History of the Devil and The Idea of Evil*. New York: Gramercy Books, 1996.

Dieffenbach, Victor C. "Powwowing among the Pennsylvania Germans." *Pennsylvania Folklife* (Winter 1975-1976, Vol. XXV, No.2): 29

Diffenderffer, Frank Ried. *Immigration into Pennsylvania through the Port of Philadelphia, 1700 – 1775, Part II: The Redemptioners*. Lancaster, PA: Published by Author, 1900.

Dluge Jr., Robert L. "My Interview with a Powwower." *Pennsylvania Folklife* (Summer 1972, Vol. XXI, No.4): 39

Dossey, Larry. *Healing Words: The Power of Prayer and the Practice of Medicine.* San Francisco: Harper, 1993.

Egle, William A. *The History of the Commonwealth of Pennsylvaniam Civil, Political, Military, from its Earliest Settlement to the Present Time, including Historical Descriptions of Each County in the State, Their Towns, and Industrial Resources.* 3rd edition. Philadelphia: E.M. Gardner, 1883.

Ellis, Bill. *Lucifer Ascending: The Occult in Folklore and Popular Culture.* The University Press of Kentucky, 2004.

Erb, Peter. *Jacob Boehme: The Way to Christ.* New York: Paulist Press, 1977.

Eshleman, Frank H. *Historic Background and Annals of The Swiss German Pioneer Settlers of South-Eastern Pennsylvania, and of Their Remote Ancestors, from The Middle of The Dark Ages, down to The Time of The Revolutionary War.* Lancaster, PA: publisher unknown, 1917.

Fischer, Elizabeth W. "'Prophecies and Revelations': German Cabalists in Early Pennsylvania." *Pennsylvania Magazine of History and Biography* 109 (July 1985): pp 299-333.

Fleetwood, Rev. John. *The Life of Our Blessed Lord and Saviour Jesus Christ: and the lives and sufferings of His holy apostles and evangelists, with an introduction to the American edition to which is added, the lives and labors of eminent Christians and martyrs from the Crucifixion to the Reformation, and a history of the Jews from the earliest ages to the present time.* Philadelphia, PA: Bradley & Co., 1870.

Gandee, Lee R. *Strange Experience: The Autobiography of a Hexenmeister.* Englewood Cliffs, NJ: Prentice-Hall, Inc., 1971.

Gichtel, Johann Georg; Arthur Versluis, ed. *Awakening to Divine Wisdom: Christian Initiation into Three Worlds*. (Great Christian Spirituality) Grail Publishing, 2004.

Gossner, Johannes. *The Heart of Man: Either a Temple of God or The Habitation of Satan; Represented in Ten Emblematical Figures Calculated to Awaken and Promote A Christian Disposition*. No publisher, date. (English trans. Reading, PA., 1822). Translated from Gossner's *Herz des Menschen, ein Tempel Gottes, oder eine Werkstätte des Satans* (1812).

Grieve, Mrs. M. *A Modern Herbal: The Medicinal, Culinary, Cosmetic and Economic Properties, Cultivation and Folk Lore of Herbs, Grasses, Fungi, Shrubs and Trees with All Their Modern Scientific Uses*. New York: Dover, 1971.

Haag, Earl C. *A Pennsylvania German Reader and Grammar*. University Park, PA. Keystone Books, The Pennsylvania State University Press, 1982.

Hand, Wayland D. ed. *American Folk Medicine: A Symposium*. Berkeley: University of California Press, 1976.

Hark Ann. *Blue Hills and Shoofly Pie in Pennsylvania Dutchland*. New York: J.B. Lippincott Co., 1952.

-- *Hex Marks the Spot: In Pennsylvania Dutch Country*. New York: J.B. Lippincott Co., 1938.

Hartmann, Franz. *Cosmology, or Universal Science, Cabala, Alchemy containing the Mysteries of the Universe regarding God, Nature, Man, the Macrocosm and Microcosm, Eternity and Time explained according to the religion of Christ by means of the secret symbols of the Rosicrucians of the sixteenth and seventeenth centuries: copied and translated from an old German manuscript, and provided with a dictionary of occult terms*. Pomeroy, WA: Health Research. Originally published: Boston, MA: Occult Publishing Co., 1888.

-- *The Life of Phillippus Theophrastus Bomast of Hohenheim: known by the name of Paracelsus and the substance of his teachings concerning cosmology, anthropology, pneumatology, magic and sorcery, medicine, alchemy and astrology, philosophy and theosophy*. London: Kegan Paul, Trench, Trubner & Co. Ltd.

Heindel, Ned D. *Hexenkopf: History, Healing and Hexerei*. Easton, PA: Williams Township Historical Society, 2005.

Herr, Karl. *Hex and Spellwork: The Magical Practices of the Pennsylvania Dutch*. Boston: Weiser Books, 2002.

Hohman, John George. *Pow-Wows, or Long-Lost Friend: A Collection of Mysterious and Invaluable Arts and Remedies*. (Originally printed in 1820). Pomeroy, WA: Health Research, 1971.

Hoffman, Bengt, trans. *The Theologica Germanica* of Martin Luther. New York: Paulist Press, 1980.

Ingenthron Dunn, Ella; Elmo Ingenthron. *The Granny Woman of The Hills*. Branson, MO: The Ozarks Mountaineer, 1990.

Jahn, Dr. Ulrich. *Hexenwesen und Zauberei in Pommern*. Breslan im Commissionsverlag bei W. Koebner, 1886.

Jeep, John M. (ed.) *Medieval Germany: An Encyclopedia*. New York: Garland Publishing, Inc., 2001.

Kieckhefer, Richard. *Magic in the Middle Ages*. Cambridge: Cambridge University Press, 1990.

Klees, Fredric. *The Pennsylvania Dutch*. New York: The Macmillan Co., 1950.

Koenig, Harold G. *The Healing Power of Faith: Science Explores Medicine's Last Great Frontier.* NewYork, NY: Simon & Schuster, 1999.

Korson, George. *Black Rock: Mining Folklore of The Pennsylvania Dutch.* Baltimore: The Johns Hopkins Press, 1960.

Kriebel, Dr. David W. "Powwowing: A Persistent Healing Tradition." *Pennsylvania German Review*, Fall 2001, 14-22.

-- *Powwowing Among the Pennsylvania Dutch: A Traditional Medical Practice in the Modern World.* Penn State University Press, 2007.

Krieger, Dolores. *The Therapeutic Touch: How to Use Your Hands to Help or to Heal.* New York: Simon & Schuster, 1979.

Kusler, Ruth Weil. *Tender Hands: Ruth's Story of Healing.* Germans from Russia Heritage Collection. Fargo: North Dakota State University Libraries, 1998.

Lewis, Arthur H. *Hex: A Spell-binding Account of Witchcraft and Murder in Pennsylvania.* New York: Pocket Books, 1970.

Lick, D.E. and Rev. Thomas R. Brendle. "Plant Names and Plant Lore among the Pennsylvania-Germans." *The Pennsylvania German Society Proceedings and Addresses*, Vol 30, October 6, 1922. Reading, PA: Published by the Society, 1923; copyright 1926. Part 3, pp 1 – 300.

Lisiewski, Joseph C. *Ceremonial Magic & the Power of Evocation.* Tempe, AZ: New Falcon Publications, 2004.

Magnus, Albertus. *Albertus Magnus Egyptian Secrets: White and Black Art for Man and Beast, Revealing The Forbidden Knowledge and Mysteries of Ancient Philosophers.* New York: Empire Publishing Company, no date.

-- ; Michael R. Best; Frank H. Brightman, eds. *The Book of Secrets of Albertus Magnus: Of The Virtues of Herbs, Stones, and Certain Beasts, Also a Book of the Marvels of the World.* Boston: Weiser Books, 1999.

Mannix, Daniel Pratt. *The Healer.* New York: E.P. Dutton, 1971.

Marion, Jim. *Putting on the Mind of Christ: The Inner Work of Christian Spirituality.* Charlottesville, VA: Hampton Roads Publishing Co. Inc., 2000.

Maynard Clark, Sara. "White Magic." *Bucks County Traveler*, October 1956, pp 48-49, 56.

McGuiness, J. Ross. *Trials of Hex.* Davis/Trinity Publishing Co., 2000.

Meyer, Marvin W.; Richard Smith, eds. *Ancient Christian Magic: Coptic Texts of Ritual Power.* Princeton, NJ: Princeton University Press, 1999.

McKenzie, John L., S.J. *Dictionary of the Bible.* NewYork, NY: Simon & Schuster, 1965.

Milnes, Gerald C. *Signs, Cures & Witchery: German Appalachian Folklore.* Knoxville, TN: The University of Tennessee Press, 2007.

Muhlenberg, Henry Melchior. *The Notebooks of a Colonial Clergyman: An Anthology of the Journals of Henry Melchior Muhlenberg.* Philadelphia: Muhlenberg Press, 1959.

My Self: Magazine of Applied Divine Metaphysics. January, Vol. IV, No. 5, 1934.

Nelson, E. Clifford. *The Lutherans in North America.* Philadelphia: Fortress Press, 1975.

Nolt, Steven M. *A History of the Amish*. Intercourse, PA: Good Books, 1992.

-- *Foreigners in Their Own Land: Pennsylvania Germans in the Early Republic*. University Park, PA: The Pennsylvania State University Press, 2002.

Nyce, James Martin. *Convention, Power and the Self in German Mennonite Magic*. Doctoral thesis, Brown University, May, 1987.

Oyer, John S.; Robert S. Kreider. *Mirror of The Martyrs. Stories of courage, inspiringly retold, of 16th century Anabaptists who gave their lives for their faith*. Intercourse, PA: Good Books, 2003.

Paracelsus; Robert Turner, trans. *The Archidoxes of Magic*. Berwick, ME: Ibis Press, 1975.

Müller-Ebeling, Claudia, et al. *Witchcraft Medicine: Healing Arts, Shamanic Practices, and Forbidden Plants*. Rochester, VT: Inner Traditions, 1998.

Page, Sydney H.T. *Powers of Evil: A Biblical Study of Satan & Demons*. Grand Rapids, MI: Baker Books, 1995.

Parsons, William T. *The Pennsylvania Dutch: A Persistent Minority*. Boston, MA: Twayne Publishers, 1976.

Peterson, Joseph ed. *Sixth and Seventh Books of Moses: Or, Moses' Magical Spirit Art Know as the Wonderful Arts of the Old Wise Hebrews, Taken from the Mosaic Books of the Kabbalah and the Talmud, for the Good of Mankind*. Berwick, ME: Ibis Press, 2008.

Richman, Irwin. *The Pennsylvania Dutch Country*. San Francisco: Arcadia Publishing, 2004.

Rippley, LaVern. *Of German Ways*. Minneapolis, MN: Dillon Press, Inc., 1970.

Russell, James C. *The Germanization of Early Medieval Christianity: A Sociohistorical Approach to Religious Transformation*. New York: Oxford University Press, 1994.

Ryrie, Charles Caldwell. *The Miracles of Our Lord*. Nashville, TN: Thomas Nelson Publishers, 1984.

Sachse, Julius F. *The German Sectarians of Pennsylvania: A Critical and Legendary History of the Ephrata Cloister and the Dunkers*. Philadelphia: author, 1899-1900.

Santee, Frederick L. *The Devil's Wager: A Faustian Drama of The Second Fall and A Second Redemption*. Hicksville, NY: Exposition Press, 1979.

Schultz, Monika. *Beschwörungen im Mittelalter: Einführung und Überblick*. Heidelberg: Universitätsverlag C. Winter, 2003.

Shaner, Richard H. *Hexerei: A Practice of Witchcraft Among the Pennsylvania Dutch*. Indiana, PA: A.G. Halldin Press, 1973.

Snellenburg, Betty. "Four Interviews with Powwowers." *Pennsylvania Folklife*. (1969) 18.4: 40-45.

Spamer, Adolf. *Romanusbüchlein: Historisch-philogischer Kommentar zu einem deutschen Zauberbuch*. Berlin: Akademie-Verlag, 1958.

Stavish, Mark. "Pow-Wow, Psalms, and German Magical Folklore." Mezlim, Samhain, 1993.

-- *Kabbalah for Health & Wellness*. Woodbury, MN: Llewellyn Publications, 2007.

Stivers, John Wesley. *The Mother Heart of God: A Study on the Pneumatic Role of the Woman*. Andover, KS: Stivers Publications, 1997.

Strasser, Dr. Brendan. "Pennsylvania German Mysticism & Folk Spirituality." Presentation. Allentown Art Museum, Wednesday, 3 November 1999.

Strobel, Lee. *The Case for Faith: A Journalist Investigates the Toughest Objections to Christianity*. Grand Rapids, MI: Zondervan, 2000.

Stoudt, John Joseph. *Sunbonnets and Shoofly Pies: A Pennsylvania Dutch Cultural History*. New York: A.S. Barnes and Co., 1973.

The Sixth and Seventh Book of Moses: Or Moses' Magical Spirit Art Know as the Wonderful Arts of the Old Wise Hebrews, Taken from the Mosaic Books of the Cabala and the Talmud for the Good of Mankind. Montana, Kessinger Publishing Company, no date.

Treben, Maria. *Health from God's Garden: Herbal Remedies for Glowing Health and Well-Being*. Rochester, VT: Healing Arts Press, 1988.

Versluis, Arthur. *Theosophia: Hidden Dimensions of Christianity*. New York: Lindisfarne Press, 1994.

-- *Wisdom's Children: A Christian Esoteric Tradition*. State University of New York Press, 1999.

Wager, Susan. *A Doctor's Guide to Therapeutic Touch: Enhancing the Body's Energy to Promote Healing*. New York: A Perigree Book, 1996.

Walters, Raube. *The Hex Woman*. New York: The Macaulay Co., 1931.

Weaver, William Woys, trans. *Saurer's Herbal Cures: America's First Book of Botanic Healing*. New York: Routledge, 2001.

Wilby, Emma. *Cunning Folk and Familiar Spirits: Shamanistic Visionary Traditions in Early Modern British Witchcraft and Magic*. Portland, OR: Sussex Academic Press, 2005.

(von) Worms, Abraham; Steven Guth, trans; Georg Dehn, ed. *The Book of Abramelin: A New Translation; Being a complete and modern translation from various extant manuscripts, including a previously unpublished fourth part*. Lake Worth, FL: Ibis Press, 2006.

Wust, Klaus. *The Saint-Adventurers of the Virginia Frontier*. Edinburg, VA: Shenandoah History Publications, 1977.

Yoder, Don. *The Pennsylvania German Broadside*. Pennsylvania State University Press, 2005.

Yoder, Don; Thomas E. Graves. *Hex Signs: Pennsylvania Dutch Bar Symbols & Their Meaning, Revised & Expanded 2nd Edition*. Mechanicsburg, PA: Stackpole Books, 2000.

Yoder, Don; Barbara Duncan. *Amish Folk Medicine: Simple Secrets to a Healthier Body, Mind, and Soul*. Lincolnwoood, IL: Publication International, Ltd., 1999.

Zook, et al. *Hexology: The History and The Meaning of the Hex Symbols*. Lancaster, PA: publisher unknown, 1978.

Index

A

Aadorn, 336
AAGEWACHSE, 145, 209-212, 365, 385, 426
Aaron, 380, 451
Abate, 237, 311
Abawo, 451
Abbiss, 332
Abdansdaag, 253, 365
Abdansdaek, 253
ABDANSDAK, 365
Abdanstag, 365
Abednego, 367
Abia Am, 259
Abide, 228, 237, 390, 409
Abnemmes, 88, 145, 212-213, 248, 366
Abraham, 441, 447, 494
Abscesses, 145, 195, 235, 330-331, 438
Active Prayer, 113, 406
Acts, 46, 63, 92, 112, 127, 136, 139, 395, 433, 442, 447, 464
Adam Kadmon, 184, 186
Adhesion, 211
Admiral
    Penn, 44
    Sir William Penn, 44
Adolf Spamer, 94, 439
Adolph Spamer, 296
ADONAI
    Shamayyim, 191
ADONAY, 293
Adoshem, 188
Afriass, 259
Afro-Caribbean, 430
Agania, 279
AGLA, 293

Aglaia, 457
Agrimonia, 326
AGRIMONY, 259, 326, 403
Agrippa of Nettesheim, 95, 483
Ailments, 146, 169, 184, 212, 253-254, 258, 290, 323, 328, 334, 344, 382, 392-393, 402, 406, 455
Ain, 471
Akkadian, 189
Alam, 302
Aland, 208, 334
Alant, 334
Alantwurzel, 208
Albert Einstein, 108
Albertus Magnus Egyptian Secrets, 85, 91, 365, 371, 383, 421, 489
Alboa, 288
Alchemy, 305, 368, 427, 445, 453, 487-488
Aldifraa, 340
Alecto, 457
Aleister Crowley, 353, 424, 427
Aleph, 470
Aletris, 204
Alexander Mack, 66
Alfred Jenanyen, 354
Algonquin Indian, 382
All
    Hollow, 461
    Saints, 401
Alleluia, 102
Allen, 359, 415
Allentown Art Museum, 493
Allergic, 230, 240
Allium, 335
Almighty King, 141
Alpha, 281, 284
Alsace, 41, 47, 63
ALUM, 234, 367-368, 376

Amacha, 302
Amara Tonta Tyra, 265
Amber-tinted, 345
American
    Bruachers, 86
    Elder, 333
    English, 474
    Folk Medicine, 487
    Indian, 81, 383
    Indians, 46, 342-343, 346, 437
    Protestant, 57
    Revolution, 56
American-style Halloween, 445
Americana, 301, 357
Amerindian, 151
Amesh Spenta, 447
Amish Folk Medicine, 494
Amishmen, 316
Ammann, 65
Ammon Aurand, 88
Among Germanic, 192
Amongst Lutherans, 54
Amschala, 302
Anabaptism, 62-63
Anabaptist, 52, 62-64, 71
Ananiah, 278
ANANIAS, 367-368
Ancient
    Christian Magic, 490
Andorn, 336
Andover, 493
Andrew Lenhart, 88
Andrews, 483
Angel Raziel, 93, 450
ANGELICA, 205, 259, 326
Angelika, 326
Angelus Silesius, 99
Anglo-Catholicism, 356
Anglo-Saxon, 127
Anglo-Saxons, 43
ANIMAL PARTS, 368
Animals, 133, 149, 151, 155, 173-174, 192, 230, 244, 258, 294, 301-302, 314, 328, 334, 391, 415-416, 419, 455, 469
Ann Hark, 292-293
Anna Maria Jung, 432
Annania, 279
Annängsel, 148, 269-270, 368, 466
Anthemis, 329
Anthology, 490
Anti-Catholicism, 57-58
Anti-inflammation, 440
Anti-Theft Amulets, 284
Anton
    LaVey, 76, 411
    Mesmer, 110
Apologia, 150
Apoplexia, 145, 224, 368
APOPLEXY, 226, 368
Apostles, 56, 68, 173, 207, 238, 298, 486
Apostolic Succession, 72
Appalachia, 125, 382
Appalachian, 382, 490
AQUAFORTIS, 368, 435
Arabic, 137
Aralia, 204-205, 343
Aramaic, 137
Archangel Gabriel, 296
Archangels, 293, 447
Archbishop of Cologne, 367
Archidoxes of Magic, 427, 491
Archives of
    American Art, 353
Arctium, 204, 221, 256, 328
AREPO, 281
ARETO, 281
Argon, 256
Aries, 290-291, 328, 455
Arise, 223, 309
Aristolochia, 219, 344
Arkansas, 354
Armenians, 460
Armentown, 48

Arnold Reinmann, 353
Artemisia, 219-220, 240, 264, 301, 340
Arthur
    Edward Waite, 123
    H.
        Hex, 489
        Lewis, 309
    Lewis, 88
    Versluis, 135, 487
Artificial Spirit, 485
Asarum, 336
Ascension of Isaiah, 447
ASH TREE, 195, 197, 368, 464
Asia, 447
Assembly, 46, 67
Associated Brethren, 59
Asteroth, 298
Asterott, 297
Astrological, 177-179, 254, 273, 328, 338, 425
Atestoos, 259
Atrophy, 145, 212, 366, 454
Atropos, 457
Aufblick, 87, 421
Auge, 297
August Gottlieb Spanenberg, 59
Augustus M. Kelley Publishers, 485
Aunt
    Sophia Bailer, 151, 156, 436
    Sophie, 157, 484
Aurand Jr., 437, 483
Ausführlich, 47
Austria, 59, 366, 397
Austrian Tyrol, 63
Auswachs, 146, 406
Avesta, 79
Avicenna, 405
Ayurvedic, 405
Azaria, 279
Azariah, 277-278, 367-368

B

Baal Shem --, 433
Babylonian, 396
Bach, 373, 483
Backus, 111, 116, 483
Badadakharida, 460
Badadilma, 460
Baden, 41, 47, 372
Bahir, 422
Bailer, 151, 157, 436, 484
Bailes, 484
Balder, 75, 386-387
Balsam of Gilead, 338
Balthazar, 277, 460
Baltimore, 354, 489
Baptism, 55-56, 61-63, 66, 307, 313, 419, 448, 455
Baptist, 66-67, 110, 344
Baptists, 52, 66, 373
Barbara Duncan, 494
Barbarous
    INTONATION, 369-370, 450, 465
    MANIPULATION, 370, 465
Barjesus, 139
BARN SIGN, 317, 319, 322, 371
Barr, 484
Barricke Mariche, 432
Barth, 108, 110, 484
Bartholomew, 443
Barvarian, 64, 473
Basanata, 460
Basic Principles, 484
Basil, 435
Bavaria, 397
Bayerische Staatsbibliothek, 97
Bearberry, 249
Beast, 80, 197, 232, 266, 363, 371, 489
Beauty, 228, 358, 422
Becher, 202

Becker, 66, 372
BEDGOBLIN, 266, 371
Bedseecher, 332
Beelzebub, 69, 297-298
Beer-sheba, 441
BEES, 289, 370, 374
BEESERGUCK, 374, 403
BEETS, 204, 327, 375
Behmenist, 373, 425
Beidelman, 46, 57, 83, 484
Beifuss, 340
Bein, 235
BEISSEL, 52, 60, 95-96, 307, 313, 372-374, 419, 484
Belgic Conference, 54
Belief, 54, 60, 62-64, 68, 86, 116, 154, 230, 304, 332, 340, 351, 369, 373, 375, 390, 393, 402, 412, 425-426
Bell, 484
Belschnickel, 397
Belznickel, 397
Benedictine, 462
Benedikt, 327
Bengt, 488
Benner, 318-319, 484
Berg Maria, 432
Bericht, 47
Berkeley, 487
Berlin, 353, 492
Berthelsdorf, 59
Berwick, 351, 491
Berwick-Bloomsburg-Danville, 359
Bessarabia, 58
Bessiabato, 256
Beth, 470
Bethlehem of
    Judaea, 458
    Judea, 458
Betty
    Addis of Cumberland, 354
    Snellenburg, 122
Betula, 327

Biblical
    Faith, 484
    Study of Satan, 491
Biblically, 465
Biblionomancy, 303
Bill
    Beissel, 96
    Ellis, 307, 420
Binah, 186
Binding, 123, 426, 429, 433, 451
Binds, 81, 99, 120, 124
Biography, 486
BIRCH, 207, 327, 370
Birke, 327
Bis, 231
Bishop of Myra, 397
Bitterselaat, 332
Black
    Art, 115, 141-142, 371, 489
    Book of Dr. Faust -- Dr. Johannes Faust, 484
    Rock, 489
    Sabbath, 124
Blackberry, 220
Blanchard, 484
Bleeding, 124, 145, 198-199, 201, 203-204, 254, 261, 343, 360, 376, 389, 463
Bless, 72, 171, 188, 198, 202, 207, 250, 254, 257, 263, 265, 274, 310, 319, 368, 408
Blessed
    Mother, 201
    THISTLE, 327-328, 333
    Virgin Mary, 260
BLOOD
    LETTING, 375, 392
    MAKING, 375
BLOODLETTING, 215, 375, 381, 405
Bloodstone, 202-203, 377-378
Bloomsburg, 351, 358
Bloss, 205

Blow, 206-207, 214, 237, 242-243, 375
BLOWING FIRE, 375
Blue
    Hills, 487
    VITRIOL, 376, 461, 463
Blumen, 103
Blutreinigungsmitteln, 215, 328, 377
Blymire, 88-90, 159
Blymires, 89
Boanerges, 444
Body of Christ, 84, 448
Boehme, 321, 358, 373, 424, 451, 485-486
Bohemia, 60
Bohemian Brethren, 59
Boils, 145, 195, 234, 328-330
Boischtuck, 346
Bone, 51, 71, 75, 142, 166, 169-171, 174, 179, 184, 209, 221, 223, 237, 243, 250, 263, 368, 375, 378, 391, 402, 408, 439
Bone-sprain, 75
Bones, 140-141, 184, 212, 319, 357, 378, 391
Book
    House, 355
    of
        Abramelin, 93, 449, 494
        Concord, 54
        Daniel, 277, 367
        Psalms, 438
        Ruth, 97, 303
        Secrets of Albertus Magnus, 91, 431, 490
        Shadows, 362
Boston, 372, 488, 490-491
Bourgeois, 485
Bowels, 146, 238, 330, 343
Boyer, 485
Bradley, 486
Braght, 42, 63

Brain, 186, 188, 216, 299
Branson, 488
Brassica Rapa, 327
Brauche
    Bag, 270, 285-286, 288, 379, 418, 430
    Bible --that, 155
    Remedies, 225
    STICK, 379-380
Brauche-psalm, 215
Braucher
    Dr. Peter Saylor, 300
    Pow-Wows, 455
BRAUCHEREI, 39, 108, 113, 119-120, 124, 126, 135-136, 145, 147, 149-151, 153-154, 156-158, 160, 163, 173, 177, 184-185, 188, 190-194, 199-200, 203, 230, 238, 240, 266, 269, 271, 276, 280, 285, 287-288, 304, 316, 319, 322-324, 349, 351, 365, 368, 370-371, 374, 376, 379-384, 386, 390-392, 394, 402, 408, 410-411, 423, 429, 431-433, 437-439, 442-443, 446, 453, 455, 457, 460, 463-465, 473, 483
Braucherin, 170, 360, 432
Brauching, 125, 132, 150, 161, 172, 179, 184, 193, 210, 224, 242, 254, 264, 269-270, 323, 376, 402-403, 406, 415
BRAZEN SERPENT, 383, 464
Breining, 205
Brennessel, 341
Breslan, 488
Brethren World Assembly, 67
Bride, 321, 408, 448
Briefe, 269-270, 276-278, 307, 309, 311, 419-420
Brimming, 248
Britain, 44, 103, 355, 382
British
    Isles, 106
    Navy, 44

Brocken, 130, 415, 462
Brot, 478
Brother
    House, 373
    Ludwig, 60
Brothers Grimm, 397
Brown University, 491
Bruache, 75, 92, 97-98, 106
Bruacher Nelson D. Rehmeyer, 88
Bruacherin Ruth Weil Kusler, 72
Bruachers, 71, 84, 86, 91-92, 95, 97
Bruckelesch, 342
Brunn, 206
Bryaceae, 339
Bryant Holman, 151
Bucks County Traveler, 490
Buffington-Barba, 474
Bur, 328
BURDOCK, 204-205, 221, 256, 328-329, 375
Bureau of Consumer Protection, 158
Burning, 63, 121, 137-138, 140, 204, 240, 341, 348, 368
Burs, 328
Bury, 89, 196, 207, 239, 245, 248, 252-253, 292, 294, 328, 434
Burying, 245, 253
Buschmoos, 339
Buschwawsem, 339
Byrd, 114
Böhme, 135
Bösen, 479
Böser Blick, 374, 403

ℭ

C. S. Lewis, 386
CA, 484
Cabala, 190, 422, 424, 428, 448, 487, 493
Caesar, 352
Caine, 485
Calendar of Saints, 59

Calendarium Naturale Magicum Perpetuum, 412
Calendula, 338, 341
Calvary Holiness Church, 67
Calvinist, 42
Camarillo, 484
Cambridge University Press, 488
Campania, 282
Campher, 329
CAMPHOR OIL, 325, 329
Cana, 389
Canaan, 140
Canada, 49, 59, 79
Canadensis, 219, 333, 342
Cancer, 326
Candied, 328, 331
Candlemass, 401, 408
Candor, 317
Canons of Dortrecht, 55
Capricorn, 184
Capricornian, 184
Capsella, 205, 220
Carbenia, 327
CARDIOLOGY, 209, 365, 385
Carlisle, 55
Carlo Ginsburg, 461
Carolina, 47, 61, 65
Carolinas, 49
Carus, 386-387, 485
Caspar Schwenkfeld, 67
Catawissa, 351
Catherine July, 49
Catholic
    Brauchers, 149
    Church, 53, 58, 60, 67, 77, 442, 452
    Dutchmen, 53
Catholicism, 52, 56, 58, 67, 79, 401, 447
Cats, 95, 174, 356-357, 361-362, 476
CELANDINE, 330
Celibacy, 373

Celtic
    Brigit, 457
    Christianity, 408
Celts, 457
Centarium Erythraea, 240
Centaurea, 234
Ceremonial Magic, 304, 367, 427, 436, 489
Ceremonies, 427, 436, 442
Chain, 307, 420, 456
Chamacha, 302
CHAMOMILE, 211, 291, 329
Chant, 103, 168-170, 174, 210
Chaos Theory, 108
Chapter of
    Isaiah, 372
    Perfection, 424
Charity, 99, 140, 312, 373
Charles
    Caldwell, 492
    II, 44-45
    LaMotte, 352
    Scribner, 483
Charlottesville, 490
Charm, 74-75, 91, 98, 101, 103, 106, 154, 164, 166-167, 174, 195-197, 199, 201-202, 206, 210, 214-217, 220-221, 225, 230, 232-234, 236, 238, 241-246, 250-251, 254-255, 262-267, 270-279, 283-285, 287, 299, 301-303, 319, 376, 379, 383-384, 392, 408, 440, 446, 461, 465
Charmer, 124
Charmers, 124
Charms, 74-75, 79, 85-86, 91-92, 96-98, 100-101, 103, 106, 108, 135, 145-147, 149-152, 156-157, 166, 174, 178, 188, 191, 193-195, 200-201, 212, 214, 216, 225, 231, 240, 249-251, 261, 264, 269, 271, 275-276, 278, 284, 286, 368, 370, 374, 376, 379, 384, 391, 395, 403, 406,
418, 423, 430-432, 434, 439-440, 446, 460, 464
Chelidonium, 330
Chemically, 461
Cherub, 398
Cheth, 470
Chi-Rho, 319
CHICK WEED, 330
Chicken, 252, 319, 330
Chickweed, 234-235, 330
Children, 51, 63, 69, 88, 115, 122-123, 127, 161, 209-210, 212-213, 240, 277-278, 312, 316, 332, 354, 356, 365-368, 380, 397, 407, 429-430, 445, 467-468, 471, 493
Chimaphila, 219, 342
Chinese, 346, 405
Chokhmah, 186
Chorea, 445
Christ
    Child, 397
    Himself, 161, 312, 442
    Jesus, 260
    Wunde, 198
Christ-like God of Light, 387
Christendom, 78, 263, 319
Christi, 200, 297, 344, 413
Christian
    Church, 312, 452
    Esoteric Tradition, 493
    Gnostics, 452
    Hermeticism, 483
    Initiation, 487
    Kabbala, 424
    Kabbalah, 190, 276
    Mind, 116, 483
Christianization, 73
Christmas
    Day, 66
    Eve, 461
Christo, 247
Christo-paganism, 100
Christology, 398

Christopher
    Saur, 68
    Schulz, 68
Christos -- Christ, 191
Christus, 53, 235-236
Chrysanthemum Parthenium, 220
Church
    Dutch, 39, 419
    Fathers, 457, 459
    of
        Satan, 411
        United Brethren, 66
    People, 52
Church-State, 55, 62
Churchianity, 70
Cinnamonum, 329
Cinquefoil, 344
Circabato, 256
Circuit, 108, 150, 160, 163-165, 168, 170-172, 194, 209, 212-213, 215, 225, 235, 241, 243-244, 249-250, 264, 406, 458
Circuits, 168-170, 173-175, 194
Civil War, 352
Clarendon Paperbacks, 484
Classical
    Diana, 130
Classis of Amsterdam, 55
Classist, 354
Claude
    Unger, 325
    W. Unger, 485
Claudia, 491
Claviceps, 443
Clotental, 288
Clotho, 457
CLOVES, 330, 336
Clyde Pharr, 354
Cnicus Benedictus, 327
Cocalico Creek, 373
Cochlearia, 337
Cocks Comb, 331

Coetus, 55
Colds, 145, 205, 326, 334, 340, 406
Colic, 145, 209-211, 326, 329, 335, 338, 365, 463
Collection of Mysterious, 488
College, 55-56, 354, 357, 485
Cologne, 366-367, 430
Cologneand Hildesheim, 91
Colonel, 109
Colonial
    America, 42, 56
    Assembly of Pennsylvania, 46
    Clergyman, 490
    Pennsylvania, 58, 451
Colonies, 47-49, 56, 58, 60, 346, 372-373, 424
Colorado, 59
Colored, 285-286, 374, 379
Colossians, 445
Coltsfoot, 291, 331
Colyn, 367
Combined, 91, 156, 325, 343, 355, 367, 369, 381
Combining, 256, 369
COMFREY, 331
Commandment, 276, 298
Commiphora Opobalsammum, 338
Commission, 72, 80, 363
Commissionsverlag, 488
Commonwealth of Pennsylvania, 158-159
Community, 59, 61, 64, 82, 84, 125, 127-128, 132, 137, 362, 371, 373, 410, 453
Company, 43, 90, 374, 423-424, 484, 489, 493
Compendium of Dogmatic Theology, 68
Conestoga, 60
Conewago, 58
Confession, 64, 442
Confessors, 67

502

Congregational Christian Churches, 56
Congregations of Pennsylvania, 55
Conjuration, 95, 97, 125, 154, 197, 264, 295, 297, 304-305, 371, 395, 423, 431, 433, 460
Conjurations, 93, 369, 427, 449, 456
Conjury, 304-305, 394-395, 431, 436
Conrad
    Beissel, 52, 60, 372, 374
    Colyn of Ulm, 367
Conservative Grace Brethren Churches, 67
Consonants, 137, 475, 477
Consult, 126, 178, 276, 324, 345
Contact, 100, 109, 138, 158, 161, 167-168, 170, 257, 341, 354-355, 396, 408, 434, 485
CONTAGION TARGET, 160, 253, 378, 391-392, 415
Contemporary
    Comparisons, 100
    Jewish, 138
Continent, 48, 56
Continental
    Army, 432
    German, 473
Convention, 76, 99, 491
Convulsions, 145, 224-225, 402, 443, 470
COPPERAS, 392
Coptic
    Christian Egyptian, 101
    Christians, 318
    Texts of Ritual Power, 490
CORIANDER, 331
Corinthians, 141
Cornelius Agrippa, 95, 123, 366-367, 424, 426, 435
Cornish, 366
Corns, 146, 249, 253, 345
Cornwall, 213

Corpses, 138, 334, 392, 394
Corpus Schwenkfeldianorum, 68
Corruption, 135, 241, 397, 439-440, 454
Cosimo Classics, 485
Cosmetic, 487
Cosmology, 385, 457-458, 487-488
Costa Rica, 65
Count
    Nicholas, 60
    Nikolaus, 59
    of Bollstädt, 91, 430
    Zinzendorf, 59, 67
Covenant, 308, 420
Cover, 51, 99, 228, 245, 333, 341
COXCOMB, 331
Craft, 71, 136-137, 149, 177, 289, 291, 355, 451
Craig Benner, 318
Creation, 59, 79, 81, 107-108, 137, 159, 186, 197, 287-288, 305, 308-309, 322, 369, 374, 410, 420, 422, 445, 465
Creative Energies, 72, 186, 422
Creator of All, 276
Creed, 56, 68, 77, 173, 231, 238, 262
Crimean Peninsula, 58
Crisco, 330, 339
Critical, 64, 408, 492
Cross, 45, 57, 122, 155-156, 165, 172, 190, 194, 199, 210, 217, 220, 222, 225, 233, 235-236, 247, 263, 273, 282-284, 288, 291, 348, 390, 392-394, 401, 408-409, 411, 421, 471
Crossing, 165, 169, 393, 399
Crowleyite, 428
Crown, 45-46, 68, 148, 210, 222, 263, 340, 422, 429-430
Crucifixion, 199, 273, 377, 393, 486
Crystal Educational Counselors, 484
Cucurbita, 342

Culinary, 487
Culpepper, 327-328, 330, 338-339, 343
Cultivation, 487
Cunning
    Folk, 494
    Work, 443
Curanderismo, 79, 151, 443
Cures, 69, 115, 213, 248-249, 339, 382-383, 438, 485, 490, 494
Curieuse Nachricht, 47
Curiosity, 131
Currently, 50, 54, 59, 67, 137, 253, 324, 381, 416
Curry, 88, 90, 159
CuSO4, 376
Cyclopedia of Working Braucherei, 193
Cydonia, 239, 302
Czar Alexander II, 58
Czarina Catherine II, 58
Czech Republic, 60

D

D.
    E. Lick, 325
    O. You, 159
Daisy Dietrich, 97, 406, 408
Dakotas, 51
Dale, 360
Daleth, 470
Dame
    Elder, 333
    Holle, 333
    Venus, 130
Damned, 119, 312, 320, 456
DANCE, 445
Dandelion, 219, 332, 403
Daniel
    Falkner, 47
    Geissler, 426
    Pratt, 490

Danish, 333
Darkness, 94, 132-133, 155, 228, 284, 387, 390, 396, 403, 409, 451, 462
Das Kloster, 94, 439
Datt, 164, 174
Datura, 346
David, 319, 395, 412, 447, 489, 495
Davis, 490
Day of
    Judgment, 314
    St. John, 444
De Signatura Rerum, 135
DEAD, 90, 123, 130, 138-140, 152, 197, 204, 226, 236, 252, 259, 263, 289, 302, 334, 387, 389, 392, 394-395, 416, 429, 431, 434, 461
Deal Democrat, 353, 356
Dear God, 407
Death, 67, 88, 135, 199, 261-262, 278-279, 294, 335, 343, 352, 355, 358, 368, 372, 393, 408-409, 417, 426, 429, 439, 462, 470
Decalogue, 308
December, 114, 362, 397
Deciphering, 461
Decius, 366
Decocted, 328, 330-331, 336, 338-341, 343
Defenseless Christians, 63
Degrees of Power, 124-125, 410
Dei
    Hand, 165-166, 169-170, 174, 243, 250
    Naame, 478
    Reich, 478
    Wille, 478
Deib, 297
Deifelbiss, 332
Deifelsabbisswarzel, 332
Dein
    Reich, 478
    Wille, 478

Deitsch, 50, 410-411, 432, 473-474, 476-478
Deity, 120, 179, 287, 334, 386, 408
Delaware, 42-44, 49, 65
Demonology *****
Demons, 388, 390, 431, 461, 471, 491
Den, 87, 201-202, 206, 279, 297, 421
Denn Dein, 236, 479
Dennis, 485
Depression, 265, 344, 360, 405, 468, 470
Der
    Lange Verborgene
        Freund, 85, 420-421
        Schatz, 85, 420
Detoxifying, 204, 377
Deus, 189
Deuteronomy, 198
Deutsch, 50
DEVIL, 69-70, 82, 107, 115-116, 121, 126, 130, 139, 142, 155, 204, 231, 248, 259, 298-299, 326, 332-333, 357-358, 384-385, 395-398, 400, 431, 456, 462, 464, 485, 492
Devon, 103
Devonshire, 462
DeVors, 484
Devotion, 60, 98-99, 438, 442
Diabetics, 326
Dialect, 41, 50, 91, 326-347, 365, 368, 403, 407, 410, 418, 434, 455, 473-474, 484
Diana, 130, 432, 457
Dianthus, 330
Dich, 199, 254, 279, 297
Dickinson-Longabaugh Press, 484
Die
    Bibel, 97
    Rosenfar, 103
Diebstahls, 297

Dieffenbach, 378, 485
Dietsch, 50
Diffenderffer, 485
Different, 39, 46, 63, 65, 67, 103, 106, 112, 114-116, 124, 133, 136, 141, 147, 156, 159, 172-174, 213, 238, 242, 245, 261, 274, 285, 303, 309, 317, 333, 339, 351, 369, 388, 395, 400, 403, 428, 460-461, 463, 473, 475
Dig, 226, 292
Diminish, 191, 207, 287, 393, 402, 404
Dioletian, 63
Diphthongs, 475, 477
Diseases, 111, 258, 290, 326, 334, 340, 343-344, 375, 400, 406, 429, 436, 445, 467
Distilled, 328-331, 333, 335, 337, 339, 347-348
Divination, 97, 125, 127, 139, 158, 292, 296, 303
Divine
    Feminine, 190
    Image, 433
    Intervention, 113, 115
    Liturgy, 369
    Love, 454
    Names, 423
    Presence, 448
    Providence, 113, 465
    Services, 76
    Wisdom, 487
Divining, 129
Dluge Jr., 485
DNA, 82
Doctor Santee, 362
Doctrine of Signatures, 455
DOG, 88, 175, 262, 292, 294, 313, 326, 399-400, 469
Dogs, 174, 367, 399
Dolores Krieger, 109, 111, 116
Dominican, 91, 430

Don, 76, 85, 87, 113, 124, 153, 156, 195, 207, 234, 286, 317, 356, 410, 420, 436, 439, 494
Donald Tyson, 95, 427, 483
Doogie Houser, 352
Dora, 109
Dort, 64, 206
Dortrecht Confession, 64
Dosage, 113, 205, 333, 338, 343, 345
Dossey, 486
Douay-Rheims, 277, 368
Doubtless, 388, 416, 459
Dover, 487
Dr.
    Brendan Strasser, 418
    David W., 489
    Dolores Krieger, 109, 111
    Fred Santee, 359
    Frederick
        LaMotte Santee of Wapwallopen, 381
        Santee, 351
    Ginsburg, 423
    Guerusey, 353
    Kriebel, 437
    Lenhart, 89
    Paul Carus, 386
    Peter Saylor, 132, 300
    Randolf Byrd, 114
    Robert Fludd, 110
    Santee, 346, 351, 358, 361
    Saylor, 132
    Ulrich, 488
    William, 483
Dracaena Draco, 333
Drache, 258, 464
DRAGON, 228, 240, 333, 400, 408, 440, 464
Drain, 153, 164, 204, 239, 253, 402
Drawing, 211, 218, 231, 299-300, 310, 376, 391, 422-423
Dresden, 59

DROPSY, 328, 337, 339-340, 400
Dryopteris, 335
Duke of York, 43, 45
Dumb Supper, 395
Duncan Fishwick, 282
DUNG, 400
Dunkards, 66
Dunker Brethren, 67
Dunkers, 66, 492
Durch, 200, 241, 297
Durham, 415
Dutch
    Catholic, 63
    Country, 62, 90, 130, 292, 309, 323, 351, 418, 487, 491
    Director-General, 43
    West India Company, 43
Dutchmen, 51, 53
Dutchy, 316, 319
Dysentery, 339, 342-343, 347

E

E.
    Benjamin, 483
    Clifford, 490
    M. Gardner, 486
    P. Dutton, 490
Earl C. A Pennsylvania German Reader, 487
Earliest Settlement, 486
Early
    Church, 453, 457
    Modern British Witchcraft, 494
    Pennsylvania, 486
    Republic, 491
Ears, 145, 205
Earth, 80-81, 90, 98, 112, 191, 197, 216, 223-224, 229, 261-262, 292, 312-313, 388, 399, 408-409, 412, 423, 441-442

East, 44, 103, 111, 155, 173-174, 296, 299, 343, 394, 434, 442, 458, 465
Easter
    Egg, 116
    Sunday, 407
Eastern
    Church, 432
    Orthodox Churches, 121
    Orthodoxy, 186
Easton, 484, 488
Easy, 148-149, 174, 186, 289, 320, 335
Eat, 80, 227, 232, 243, 248, 283, 302, 402
Eberbach, 372
Ecgitar, 256
Economic Properties, 487
Ecumenical Creeds, 54
Eden, 80, 94, 261, 385
Edgar, 359-360
Edinburg, 494
Edith Rundle of Allentown, 354
Edition, 51, 309, 331, 356, 484, 486, 494
Edna
    Kishbaugh, 359
    Williams, 359
Eduardo, 151
Edwardian, 131, 427
Eedann, 336
Eel Chad, 257-258
Egypt, 308, 318, 353, 380, 419
Egyptian
    Christians, 318
    Secrets of Albertus Magnus, 145
Egyptians, 449, 457
Ehrenpreis, 344
Ein
    Geringer, 60
    Soph Aur, 422
Einführung, 492

Einz, 273
Eiris, 74
Eisegraut, 347
Eisenkraut, 347
EL
    -- God, 189
    Elyon, 191
    Salvador, 65
    SHADDAI, 227-228
Elast Lamach, 302
ELCA, 54, 59
Elder Mother, 333-334
Elderberry, 219, 334
Elecampane, 205, 208, 259, 334-335
Elector of Saxony, 67
Electrical, 64, 196
Eleven, 115, 292
Elf
    Dock, 208, 334
    Wort, 208, 334
Elias, 262
Elion, 189
Elisha, 107
Ella, 488
Ellis, 307, 420, 486
Elmo Ingenthron, 488
Elmwood, 301
Elohim, 189, 293
Elymas, 459
Elyon, 189, 191
Elypolis, 265
Elysburg, 351
EMANUEL, 293
Ember Days, 192, 401, 461
Emden, 45
Emma, 494
Emmanuel, 191
Emperor Constantine, 413
Encyclopedia Judaica, 448
Energy, 110-113, 115, 136, 152, 156, 160, 164, 168, 171-172, 177, 191, 195, 291, 303, 378, 391, 429, 433, 439, 446, 493

England, 45, 48, 51, 56, 103, 106, 317, 353, 371, 424, 462
Englewood Cliffs, 486
English
    Witchcraft, 135
Enlighten, 127, 265, 409
Enlightenment, 78, 433
Enoch, 426, 447
Entzian-Wurtzel, 336
Enzian, 336
Ephesians, 132
Ephrata Cloister, 52, 373, 451, 492
Epiphany, 460
Epistle of James, 303
Epsom, 461
Equisetum, 249, 337
Erb, 486
Erd, 478
Erden, 478
Ere, 357
Ergotism, 443
ERICHTHONIE, 102
Erysipelas, 146, 240, 402, 439
Es Wasser, 163, 174
Esch, 368
Esche, 368
Eschebaam, 368
Eshleman, 486
Esoteric, 91, 94, 272, 287-288, 291, 316, 319, 353, 412, 432, 447, 451, 457, 493
Esoterically, 386
Esotericist Mark Stavish, 423
Estebany, 109-110
Eternal Hunter, 397
Eternity, 487
Etham, 448
Etheric Fluid, 110-111
Ethiopian
    Christians, 460
    Lutherans, 77
Ethnicity, 77, 81, 318
Etymological Origins of Witch, 127

Etymology, 127
Eucharist, 55, 76
Eucharistic, 54
Eugenia, 330
Euphrosyne, 457
Europa, 342
Europe St. Martin, 445
European
    Catholic, 444
    Christian, 280
    Theosophical, 355
Europeans, 192
Evangelical
    Catechism, 56
    Lutheran Church, 54, 59
Eve of St. John, 192
Everinia, 339
Evil, 110-111, 120, 129-131, 135, 141-142, 192, 228, 263, 266, 273, 283, 298, 303, 317, 333-334, 340, 345, 358, 361, 374, 386-387, 390, 394-398, 403, 409-410, 414-415, 440, 456, 467-470, 485, 491
Ewichkeit, 478
Ewigkeit, 479
Ewigyeager, 397
Exaltation, 401
Examination, 418, 453
Examine, 169, 186, 295
Example, 51, 67, 77, 97, 101, 113, 130, 132-133, 137, 184, 272-273, 288-292, 294-295, 305, 307, 310, 324, 354, 370, 374, 376, 378, 384, 388, 391, 397, 405, 428, 438, 440, 455, 476-477
Examples, 46, 75, 100, 106, 112, 269, 271, 307, 347, 375, 392, 420
Excessive, 131, 253-254, 346
Excrement, 400
Exodus, 56-57, 137, 298, 380, 448
Exorcism, 154, 261, 264-266, 269, 273, 275-276, 283, 301, 372, 433, 440

Extract, 211, 249, 281, 333, 434, 438
Eye Troubles, 145, 214
Ezekiel, 98, 199, 272, 376

F

Face, 80-81, 90, 131, 134, 155, 165-166, 168, 173, 288, 292-293, 299, 366, 387, 399, 434
Faith, 46, 53, 56, 67-68, 77, 79, 84, 114, 126, 137, 159, 267, 280, 371, 381, 386, 389, 393, 409, 411, 432, 453, 469, 484-485, 489, 491, 493
Fall, 80, 115, 124, 131, 177, 189, 197, 203, 228, 242, 254, 326, 334, 340, 357, 381, 397, 401, 423, 429, 440-441, 450, 483, 489, 492
Falscher Ketzer, 231
False Sarsaparilla, 343
Familial, 125, 150
Familiar Spirits, 494
Far East, 465
Fargo, 489
Fate, 79, 124, 464-465
Father
    Christmas, 397
    Felix Grosser, 281
    God, 165, 191, 211, 221, 225, 254-255, 260, 263, 360, 408
    James H. Flye, 354
Fatigue, 153, 160-161, 258-259
Faust, 358, 412-413, 484
Faustian Drama of The Second Fall, 357, 492
FDA, 359
Feast of St.
    Brigid, 408
    James, 443
    John, 345
Feasting, 445
February, 407, 462

Federal Government, 354
Feet, 89, 148, 155, 158, 163, 165, 172, 210, 228, 242, 252, 263, 300, 308, 335, 345, 378, 390, 412, 445
Feier, 163
Feldteufel, 372
Fellowship of Grace Brethren Churches, 67
Fenchel, 335
Fenichel, 335
FENNEL, 335
Fer, 320, 476, 478
FERHEXT, 374, 402
Fern, 335
FERNS, 335
FeSO4, 392
Fetid, 406
Feuer, 279
Fever, 101-102, 191, 215-217, 220, 243, 283, 328, 332, 336, 400, 403-404, 440, 445-446, 468-470
Feverfew, 220, 291
Fevers, 96, 145, 215-218, 220, 238, 240, 283, 327-328, 334, 403-404, 470
Few, 41, 45, 53, 71, 95, 97, 113, 125, 127, 130, 136, 141, 147, 156, 158-159, 170, 177-178, 189-190, 210, 233, 240, 251-252, 261, 269, 272-273, 276-278, 280, 282, 286, 288, 293, 297, 304, 309-310, 321, 323-324, 335, 338, 347, 356, 359-361, 370, 379, 381, 386, 403, 405, 407, 411, 418-419, 423, 438, 453, 455, 460, 463, 467, 483
FIEWER, 145, 215, 328, 403
Filii, 284
Fimffingergraut, 344
Finns, 43, 47
Fire of
    Love, 408
    Wrath, 408
First

Book of Botanic Healing, 494
Quarter, 178
World War, 51
Fischer, 486
Fits, 225, 317, 359, 433
Five
    Books of Moses, 413
    Holy Wounds, 191, 263, 267
    Virtues, 412
    Wounds
        of Christ, 199
        Star, 411
Flatten, 275
Fleetwood, 486
Flesh, 128, 132, 141, 212, 221, 237, 243, 257, 263, 266, 312, 341, 366, 374-375, 439
Florat, 288
Florida, 65
Flower of Life, 319
Foeniculum, 335
Folk
    Lore of Herbs, 487
    Medicine, 69-70, 96, 151, 218, 326, 370, 385, 391, 403, 463, 485, 487, 494
    Spirituality, 70-71, 77-78, 493
Folklore, 122, 340, 359, 385, 397, 486, 489-490, 492
FOOT, 66, 75, 136, 166, 170, 172, 190, 197, 201, 228, 300, 341, 348, 408, 411, 413, 429, 450
Forbidden Plants, 491
Formulae, 86, 97, 145-146, 193, 251, 277, 327, 332, 337, 341, 343, 370, 376, 378, 392, 420, 446, 461
Fort Christina, 43
Foundation, 45, 50, 53, 68, 82, 91, 106, 154, 166, 253, 305, 397, 408, 423, 431

Four
    Directions, 394
    Evangelists, 279, 394
    Gospels, 303
    HUMORS, 375, 377, 405
    Interviews, 122, 492
    Winds, 394
Fourth
    Book of Occult Philosophy, 95, 98, 367
    Coalition, 42
Fr. Flye, 354-355
Fraktur, 309-310, 373
France, 41
Franciscans, 425
Franconia, 47
Frank
    Brightman, 490
    Ried, 485
Franklin
    College, 55
    Pierce College, 485
Franz Hartmann, 133, 436, 457
Fraxinus, 368
Fred Santee, 355, 359
Frederick Santee, 351-352
Fredna, 351, 361-362
Fredric, 488
Freiburg, 353
French Vert de Grise, 461
Freya, 396
Friday, 192, 197, 218, 235, 247, 288, 293, 301, 368, 401
Friedrich, 110
Friedsam Gottrecht, 372
Friend, 58, 85-89, 91, 94, 115, 145, 150-151, 230, 269, 273-274, 278, 359, 362, 420-421, 426, 432, 437, 439, 469, 488
Frija, 75
Fruits, 325, 377
Fujita Scale, 124
Fulda, 74

Full Moon, 178, 235, 287-288, 310
Functionalism, 82
Fungi, 487
Futhark, 277

G

G-d, 188
Gabriel Thomas, 44
Gaelic, 408
Galen, 375, 405, 436
Galenic, 435
Gall, 392, 435
Gallic Wars, 352
Gamache, 93
Gandee, 140, 147-148, 234, 288, 367, 375-376, 486
Garden Benedict, 327
GARLIC, 259, 335-336
Gaspar, 460
Gates of Life, 393
Gathas, 79
Gatorade, 218
Gay Dutch, 419
Geboth Gottes, 297
Gedächtnestag, 68
Geier, 372
Geilsschwanzgraut, 337
Geissler, 426
Geistes, 166, 206, 255, 349
Gemini, 326
GENERAL
    BRAUCHE CIRCUIT, 108, 150, 160, 163, 209, 212, 215, 225, 241, 243, 249-250, 406, 458
    Circuit, 264
    Lunar Influences, 180
    Planetary Influences, 181
    Washington, 373
    Zodiac Influences, 182
Genesis, 79-80, 442
GENTIAN, 259, 336

Gentianaceae, 336
Georg
    Dehn, 494
    Waitz, 74
George
    Barth, 108
    Hohman, 58, 85, 392
    Michael Weiss, 55
Georgia, 61, 65
Gerald C.
    Milnes, 382
    Signs, 490
German
    Anabaptists, 63
    Appalachian Folklore, 490
    Brauchen, 382
    Cabalists, 486
    Catholic, 57-58
    Catholics, 48, 57-58, 431
    Christian, 321
    Magical Folklore, 492
    Mennonite Magic, 491
    Quitten, 239
    Reformed
        Marshall College, 55
        Seminary, 55
    Seventh-Day Baptists, 52
    Tausenguldenkraut, 240
    Ways, 492
German-American Catholic, 57
German-Americans, 51
German-ness, 407
German-speaking Pennsylvania Catholics, 57
Germanicizing, 77
Germanies, 41
Germanization, 492
Germantowns, 46
Germanyand, 106
Gertrude, 443
Gertudenminte, 443
Geselschaft, 297

Gettysburg, 484
Gewalt, 297
GEWECKS, 146, 240, 249, 406
Gewürznelke, 330
Gichtel, 487
GIFTICHE LUFT, 406
Gimel, 470
Ginger, 291, 336
Ginsburg, 423, 461-462
Glechoma, 233
Gleddegraut, 328
Gleene, 342
Glory, 67, 71, 197, 223, 226, 229, 349, 399, 409, 447-448
Glossary of Braucherei, 365
Glowing Health, 493
Glückstern, 412
Gnostic Christians, 385
Gnowwelloch, 335
Goat of Satan, 384
God
    Bearer, 432, 449
    Himself, 86, 92, 262, 308, 420, 423
    of Isaac, 442
God-question, 116
Goddess Diana, 432
Godfrey Selig, 94, 438, 467
Godhead, 186, 422, 426, 433, 452-453
Gods, 116, 140, 189, 387, 433, 465
Goethe, 412
Gold, 226, 290, 307-308, 312-313, 355, 419-420, 458-459
Golden
    Calf, 77
    SUNDAY, 407
Golgotha, 277
Good
    Books, 491
    Friday, 192, 197, 301, 368
    of Mankind, 491, 493
Gordebenedikt, 327

Goshenhoppen, 58
Gospel of John, 303
Gospels, 303, 387-389
Gossner, 487
Gotha, 59
Gott, 206, 231, 254, 297, 407
Gottes Hand, 165
Gourmet, 99
Governor, 458
Gradually, 56, 122, 168
Graft, 478
Grammar, 352, 473, 487
Grand
    Rapids, 491, 493
    Secret, 279
Grandmas, 125
Grandpappy, 292-294
Granny Woman of The Hills, 488
Grant, 44, 258, 284, 409
Grasses, 487
Graves, 317-318, 321, 494
Grease, 240, 244-245, 293
Great
    Christian Spirituality, 487
    Commission, 72, 363
Greater Sanicle, 342
Greece, 353, 375, 461
Greek Christos, 385
Greeks, 413, 452
Green
    Thursday, 332
Grim Reaper, 396
Grimr, 396
Groggy Rustic, 415
Grossdaadi Grundsau Lodge, 407
Grosse Sanickel, 342
Ground Ivy, 222, 233-234, 259, 336
GROUNDHOG
    DAY, 407
    Lodges, 407
Grundbein, 342
Grundelreewe, 336
Grunderman, 336

Grundsau
    Lodge, 407
    Lodges, 407
Grünstadt, 41
GSCHWAER, 146, 195, 233
Guadalupe, 79
Guardian Angels, 221, 237, 260, 304
Guide, 87, 163, 284, 365, 421, 473, 493
Gushnasaph, 460
Gustav Davidson, 447
Gwaersnegelin, 330
Gwittegortschel, 239
Gypsies, 383
Gypsy King of Egypt, 308, 419

H

H. P. Blavatsky, 353
Ha Shem, 188
Haag, 487
Haegtessa, 128
HAERZSCHLAEK, 145, 224
Hail Mary, 262
Haisch, 410
Half-Anabaptists, 65
Hallichkeit, 478
Halloween, 191, 401, 445, 461
Halloween-like, 445
Halwagen, 424
Hammer, 204, 297-298
Hampton Roads Publishing Co. Inc, 490
Hananiah, 367
Hand of God, 165
Hang, 213, 218, 242, 246, 256-257, 456
Hanover, 413
Hans Reist, 65
Haran, 441
Hare Krishnas, 361
Hark Ann, 487
Harper, 486

Harrisburg, 90
Hartmann, 133-134, 436, 457, 487
Harvard
    University, 352
    Yearbook, 355-356
Harz Mountains, 415
Hasba, 246
Haselwurz, 336
Hasselwatzel, 336
Hasselwortsel, 336
Hast, 157, 205-206, 208, 210, 223, 228-229, 260, 263, 299-300, 311, 409
Hatte, 201
Hauntings, 326, 381
Haus
    Apotheke, 87, 421
    Freund, 85
Haus-Freund, 420
Haute Cuisine, 99
Havamal, 128
Hawkweed, 288, 339
Head, 89, 131, 148, 163-166, 168-170, 174-175, 177, 186, 210, 212, 220-223, 242, 244, 252, 256, 263, 265, 287, 290, 301, 328, 347, 379, 412, 414, 429-430, 434, 441, 457, 469
Headache, 145, 220-223, 327-328, 348, 467, 471
Heal, 72, 74, 102-103, 107, 154, 164, 192, 197, 200-201, 212, 222, 237, 367, 471, 485, 489
Healer, 109-111, 115, 160, 249, 381, 408, 490
Healing
    Arts, 387, 491, 493
    Power, 116, 483, 489
    Words, 486
    Work, 72, 149, 173, 177, 432, 435
Health Research, 488
Healthcare Research, 114

Healthier Body, 494
Hear, 52, 129, 157, 228, 257, 399
Heart
    of Man, 409, 487
    Troubles, 145, 224, 227
Heathenism, 71, 73, 100, 414
Heavenly Father, 284
Heavens, 191, 224, 447
Hebrew
    Bible, 395
    Kabbala, 424
    Names of God, 369
    Tree of Life, 369
Hebrews, 189, 408, 433, 491, 493
Hecate, 457
Hedge, 128, 130, 416
HEIBS, 410
Heidel, 414
Heidelberg Catechism, 54, 56
Heidenheim, 462
Heiland Jesus Christ, 297
Heilige
    Geist, 297-298
    Jungfrau Maria, 297
    Schrift, 97, 99
Heiligen Geistes, 166, 206, 255, 349
Heilnecke, 342
Heindel, 87, 300, 415, 421, 488
HEISCH, 146, 240, 244, 406, 410, 440
Hell, 122, 278-279, 298, 300, 312, 358, 368, 409, 413, 484
Helmot, 110
Hemorrhages, 331, 344
Henken, 235
Henri Gamache, 93
HENRICUS CORENELIUS, 366
Henry
    Cornelius Agrippa of Nettesheim, 95
    Hudson, 43
    Melchior Muhlenberg, 53, 490

Herbal
    Cures, 339, 494
    Remedies, 193, 208, 323, 344, 403-404, 463, 493
Herbalists, 204, 381
Herbs, 72, 98, 145, 218, 240, 259, 287, 289, 305, 323-325, 341, 345, 347, 378-379, 432, 487, 490
Heresy, 61, 123, 470
Herod, 458-459
Herpes, 146, 233, 434, 455
Herrlichkeit, 479
Herrn, 279, 297
Herrnhut, 59
Herz Mountain, 130
Hess, 88, 90
Hesse, 41
Hessia, 321
Hex
    Doctor, 89, 95, 125-127, 299, 359, 362, 410, 450
    Grex, 316
    Marks The Spot, 487
    Murder, 87, 96, 158-159, 323, 371
    Sign, 318-319, 371, 382, 410, 418
    Signs, 316-318, 320, 382, 410-411, 418, 494
    Symbols, 494
    Woman, 493
HEX-FEET, 320
Hexagraut, 346
Hexefoos, 273, 277, 309, 317
Hexekimmel, 346
Hexekraut, 344
HEXEN, 128, 132, 411, 416-417
Hexenfiess, 411
HEXENFOOS, 156, 190, 194, 199, 411, 418, 437, 465
Hexenkopf Mountain, 300
Hexenmeister
    Lee Gandee, 140, 375

Hexennacht, 462
Hexenwesen, 488
Hexerei, 72, 119-121, 128-129, 136, 141-142, 157, 298, 304, 306, 326, 351, 362, 382-383, 395, 410, 415-418, 427-429, 456, 463, 465, 488, 492
Hexology, 494
Hezekiah, 190
Hicksville, 492
Hidden Dimensions of Christianity, 493
HIDE-BOUND, 419
Hier, 297
Hieracium Pilosella, 288, 339
High
    German, 50, 74, 128, 374, 410, 473-474, 476, 478
    Germans, 51
    Priest, 92, 433
    Priestess, 361
High-German, 473
Higher Power, 154
Highest Names, 101, 154, 171-172, 194, 198, 202, 207, 210, 218, 225, 230, 243, 248, 250, 264, 273, 277, 287, 296, 302, 394-395, 457
Hildesheim, 91, 430
Himmel
    Drin, 407
    Reuch, 231
Himmelsbrief, 142, 145, 270, 307-310, 312, 368, 405, 419-421, 455-456
Himmelsbriefe, 87, 146, 159, 214, 280, 286, 307, 419-421
Himself, 46, 64, 69, 76, 85-86, 88, 91-92, 109, 121, 126, 132, 156-157, 161, 199, 262, 294, 304, 308, 312, 332, 351-353, 355-356, 366, 373, 391, 401, 420, 423, 425, 442, 455
Hindus, 391
Hinkeldarem, 330

Hippocrates, 405
Historian Richard Kieckhefer, 96
Historic Background, 486
Historical Descriptions of Each County, 486
Historically, 77, 91, 369
Historisch-philogischer Kommentar, 94, 296, 439, 492
History of
    Braucherei, 39, 351
    Magic, 264
HITZ, 215, 403
HNO3, 368
Hoffman, 488
Hohenheim, 69, 435, 488
HOHMAN, 58, 85-87, 90, 93-96, 101, 221, 230, 243, 269, 273-274, 278, 374, 392, 420-421, 432, 439, 488
Holda, 130, 414
Holland
    Dutch Reformed, 55
Hollander, 50
Hollanders, 50
Hollerbeera, 333
Hollow, 88, 351, 461
Holstein, 47, 307, 310, 313, 419
Holunder, 333
Holy
    Apostle, 216
    Guardian Angels, 221
    Name of EL SHADDAI, 227
    of Holies, 448
    Roman Emperor, 41
    Saint John, 248
    Spirit, 101, 154, 165, 191, 318, 387
Thistle, 327
Thursday, 260
Trinity, 84, 96, 266-267, 311, 393, 400, 453, 457-458

Virgin Mary, 262, 298
Homan, 86, 420
Hoodoo, 93, 285, 379, 382
Hopewell Township, 88
Hopkins, 352-353, 489
Hor, 460
HOREHOUND, 331, 336-337
Hormisdas, 460
Horse, 61, 74-75, 109, 174, 213, 337, 366, 378, 400, 463
Horseradish, 256, 291, 332, 337
Horseshoes, 422
Horsetail, 249, 337
Houdini-like, 427
House Pharmacy Guide, 87, 421
How
    Biblical Truth Can Keep You Healthy, 483
    I Learned Powwowing, 484
Hudson River, 48
Huflattuich, 331
Hulda, 130
Huldrych Zwingli, 55
Humorism, 405
Hungarian, 109
Hungary, 445
Hunting, 89, 325, 351
Hus, 60
Hutschefuss, 331
Hylde Moer, 333
Hypericum, 344-345
Hölle, 297
Höllen, 279

Iewile, 478
Ihesous Xristos Theou Yios Soter, 385
Ihm, 206, 235-236
Ihr, 206, 231, 297
Illinois, 65
Illness, 97, 112-113, 145, 147, 160, 167, 173, 188, 199, 209, 212-213, 219, 227, 229, 258, 264, 276, 285, 289, 323, 362, 380, 385, 391, 402, 405-406, 408, 415, 429-430, 464, 466, 469
Illnesses, 145, 184, 192, 205, 213, 215, 224, 248, 337, 341, 381, 434, 444
Im Namen Gottes, 205-206
Imbolc, 408
Immigration, 401, 485
Imperatoria, 339
Important Note, 172, 304
IN THE NAME of God, 101, 165, 191, 206, 225, 230, 254-255, 263, 266, 296, 311, 313
India, 43, 422
Indian, 46, 81, 131, 382-383, 405, 441
Indiana, 65, 492
Indians, 46, 48, 131, 342-343, 346, 425, 437
Indo European, 385, 396, 464
Industrial
    Resources, 486
    Revolution, 381, 473
Inflammation Charm, 210, 250
Inflammations, 338, 342, 439
Influence, 86, 95, 115-116, 132, 135, 140, 184, 317, 374, 382, 385, 425, 427-428, 440, 470
Ingenthron Dunn, 488
Injun, 360
Inner
    Traditions, 491
    Work of Christian Spirituality, 490

J

I.
    N. R. I., 277, 421, 465
ICHTHONIE, 102
Ida, 443
Ideally, 290
Idisi, 74
Iehovah, 189

Inquisitor of Cologne, 367
Intelligence, 422
Intercourse, 60, 491
International Guild of Occult Sciences, 485
Interview, 131, 161, 485
Introduction, 112, 119, 151, 157, 169, 193, 421, 486
Introductory, 94, 227-228
Inula Helenium, 205, 208, 334
Invaluable Arts, 488
Iowa, 65
Ipecac, 359
Ireland, 48
Irish, 70, 77, 366, 443
Iron
    Herb, 347
    Weed, 234, 347
Irwin, 491
Isaiah, 372, 396, 447
Israel, 138, 140, 380, 384, 458
Italian Catholic Churches, 77
Italy, 282
Iwwerbariyaleit, 48

J

J.
    B. Lippincott Co., 487
    J. J. Amen, 280
    P. Collipp, 115
    Ross, 490
Jacob
    Boehme, 321, 358, 373, 424, 451, 486
    Martin, 374
    Yoder, 273
    Zook, 410
Jah, 190, 220, 257
Jahn, 488
Jakob Ammann, 65
Early Medieval Christianity, 492
    Powwow Power, 484

Martin Nyce, 124
Jamestown, 346
Jan
    Hus, 60
    Luyken, 63
Jane Lead, 424
Janee, 359
January, 46, 62, 490
Jeep, 74, 488
Jeff, 483
Jehovah, 189, 229
Jerusalem, 92, 412, 458
Jesu Blut, 344
Jesuit, 58
Jesus
    Christ
        ERICHTHONIE
Jesus-clothes, 453
Jewish, 138, 147, 276, 280, 282, 319, 383, 418, 422
Jews, 140, 276-277, 312, 383, 413, 422, 458, 486
Jim Thorpe, 351
Johann
    Adam Gruber, 60
    Georg Hohman, 420
    Jacob Zimmerman, 424
    Kelpius, 424
    Konrad, 372
    Reuchlin, 424
    Scheible, 93-94, 439, 450
    Trithemius, 424
Johanna Nickel, 94
Johannes Hannes, 205
Johanneskraut, 344
John
    Baptist, 110
    Blymire, 88-90, 159
    Cabot, 43
    Colhane, 354
    Curry, 88, 90, 159
    Engle, 66
    George Hohman, 58, 85

Graphaeus of Antwerp, 95
Hannes, 206
Jeep, 74
Joseph Stoudt, 318
Stout, 415
Wesley, 493
Jordan, 248, 265, 311
Joseph
   Lisiewski, 304
   Peterson, 92, 450, 467
Joshua Kocherthal, 47-48
Journals of Henry Melchior Muhlenberg, 490
Journey, 47, 75, 77, 261-262, 417, 425, 443, 448, 459, 483
Juan Zaragoza, 354
Judah, 458
Judaic, 424
Judaism, 73, 147, 188, 190, 319, 412
Judas, 300
Judeo-Christian, 276
Judge, 197, 226, 302, 374
Julius F. The German Sectarians of Pennsylvania, 492
July, 49, 205, 235, 253, 327, 330, 338, 365-366, 443, 486
June, 192, 326, 330, 340, 401, 444, 484
Jungefrau Maria, 297
Jungfraa Maria, 164
Jungfrau Maria, 297, 431
Jungin, 432
Juniper, 215, 249, 301, 333, 337-338
Juniperus, 337
Jupiter, 135, 428, 460
Justice, 53, 87, 298, 302, 386, 422
Justification, 53, 107, 421

K

Kabala, 423, 438
Kabalistical Writings, 438
KABBALA, 422-424, 428

Kabbalism, 147
Kabbalist, 185
Kabbalistic Tree of Life, 186
Kackaabula, 246
Kagba, 460
KAI, 367
KALTFIEWER, 145, 215, 403
Kamille, 329
Kamp, 201
Kampf, 202
Kansas City Statement of Faith, 56
Karbs, 342
Kariander, 331
Karl Herr, 147, 154, 159, 319, 419
Karsudan, 460
KasHaS, 246
Katherine, 72-73
Kedar, 373
Keenichslichter, 340
Kelpius, 372, 424-426
Kenneth Winston, 485
Kentucky, 65, 486
Kenyon, 353
Keshaphim, 137-138
Kether, 186
Kettle, 359
Kex, 247
Keys, 264, 428
Keystone Trail Inn, 407
Kidneys, 167, 326-327, 335, 337, 342, 344
Kieckhefer, 96-97, 488
King
   Charles II, 44
   David, 395
   James Version, 138
   Louis XIV, 42
   Nebuchadnezzar, 368
   Saul, 138, 140
   Solomon, 86
Kingdoms, 107
Kings, 138, 223-224, 277, 307, 310, 411, 457-458, 460

Kirche, 241
Kiss, 224
KJV, 69, 107, 150, 157, 442, 448, 459
Klaus, 494
Klees, 488
Kleiner Odermennig, 326
Klette, 328
Kletten, 256, 328
Knautia, 333
KNO3, 446
Knoblauch, 335
Knopt, 89
Knowledge, 50, 54, 76, 81, 91, 93, 98, 108, 115, 160, 178, 276, 284, 293, 324-325, 355, 365, 370-371, 379, 390, 426, 430-431, 449, 455, 477, 489
Knoxville, 490
Kobold, 371-372
KOC, 245
Koenig, 489
Koenigsberg Fire Brief, 307, 311, 419
KONRAD, 372
Koph, 471
KOPPSCHMAERZE, 145, 220
KOPPWEH, 220
Koriander, 331
Korson, 489
Kraft, 231, 479
Krampus, 397
Kranke, 236
Kreuz, 235
Kriebel, 89, 382, 432, 437, 489
Krieger, 109, 111, 116, 489
Kris Kringle, 397
Krist Kindel, 397
Krüge, 201
Kulblume, 332
Kunz, 109
Kusler, 72, 103, 211, 489
Kutztown University, 407
Königswollenkraut, 340

Kürbis, 342

𝔏

La Gallina Negra, 417
Labor, 256-257, 260, 312, 433
Lachesis, 457
Lady Holda, 414
Lahme, 236
Lake Worth, 494
Lamb of Christ, 384
Lamed, 470
Lammas, 401
Lancaster
    County, 55
    Theological Seminary, 55
Land Lord, 116
Large, 51, 61, 161, 171-172, 174, 204, 213, 219, 233, 276, 282, 286, 312, 325, 333, 345, 351, 366, 379, 413-414, 444
Larvandad, 460
Last
    Great Frontier, 489
    Judgment, 262
    Quarter, 178
Latin
    Lutherans, 77
    Raziel, 94, 450
    Tridentine Mass, 369
    Vulgate, 271, 277, 368
Latinate, 130, 282
Latinate-type, 191
Latinist, 354
Latria, 121, 432
Laudanum, 434-435
Laudanum-like, 435
Lauingen, 91, 430
LaVern, 492
Law of Attraction, 447
Laws of God, 307
Layman Conrad Templeman, 55
Lebanon County, 158, 373

Lee
    Gandee, 140, 234, 288, 367, 375
    R.
        Gandee, 147
        Strange Experience, 486
Leg, 85, 168, 172, 213, 235-236, 254, 391, 421, 471
Legend, 131, 214, 308, 357-359, 420
Legendary History, 492
Legion, 148, 306
Lehigh Valley, 131
Lenhart, 88-89
Lenne Lennape, 359
Leo, 226, 338
Lester Breininger, 320
Lethargy, 258
Letter of Protection, 307, 313, 419
Letters, 45, 145-146, 184, 188, 190, 270-272, 274, 277, 280-281, 283, 291, 307, 309-310, 313, 354, 368, 385, 412, 419-420, 428, 456, 477
Levant, 195, 242, 244
Leviathan, 79
Leviticus, 138
Lewis Spence, 423
Liber Razielis, 93, 450
Liberation, 74
Liberty, 45, 52, 58, 61, 287
Libra, 253
Lice, 258, 347
Licensing, 159
Lichte, 297
Lichtmess, 408
Lick, 325, 328, 335, 340, 342, 346, 489
Liewwer Gott, 407
Life
    Force, 430
    of
        Heaven, 423
        Our Blessed Lord, 486
Lift, 88, 380, 399
Light
    Bringer, 294, 386
    of Christ, 344
Lightmass, 408
Lilienzeit, 261
Lilith, 372
Limb, 75, 85, 236-238, 421
LIME, 426
Lincolnwoood, 494
Lindisfarne Press, 493
Lisiewski, 304-305, 489
Little
    League, 125
    Sanicle, 342
Liturgy, 54, 76, 97, 369, 444
Liver, 171, 209, 300, 326, 332, 337-338, 340-341, 365, 404, 470
Livergrown, 145, 209, 365, 385, 426
Living Spirit, 152
Llewellyn Publications, 427, 483, 492
Lloyd, 352
Lodges, 407-408
Logos, 142, 451
London, 45, 48, 488
Long
    Lost Friend, 58, 85, 87-88, 91, 94, 145, 230, 269, 273-274, 278, 420-421, 432, 439
    Vowels, 476
Long-Lost Friend, 488
Lord
    God of Abraham, 441
    Jesus Christ, 210, 226, 248, 260, 262
    of Heaven, 197
    Peter, 264
Loss Uns Deitsche, 407
Love Feast, 66
Low
    Dutch Morning Star, 318,

484
German, 50, 127
Lucifer Ascending, 420, 486
Lucky Star, 412
Lunar Phase, 288, 370
Lungegraut, 338
Lungenkraut, 337-338
Lungs, 145, 169, 205, 258, 300, 302, 326, 338, 343-344, 347, 455
LUNGWORT, 338, 455
Lupus, 324
Luther, 53, 55-56, 60, 199, 372, 488
Lutheran
    Book of Worship, 69
    Christians, 53
    Church, 53-54, 59
Lutheran-Reformed, 52-53
Lutheranism, 42, 53-54, 67, 70
Lutherans, 47, 52-54, 77, 392, 490
Lycopodium, 339
Lying, 44, 46, 90, 140, 175, 203, 210, 320

𝔐

M. Grieve, 234, 327, 332, 334, 340, 347
Macrocosm, 487
Madaginery, 307, 314, 419
Magan David, 319, 412
Magazine of Applied Divine Metaphysics, 490
Magdeburg
    Himmelsbrief, 307, 312, 419
Magi, 277, 310, 411, 457, 459
Magia de Furto, 296
Magian, 396, 412
MAGIC
    BALSAM, 338
    Book, 358, 484
    SQUARES, 428, 446
Magical

Practices, 177, 488
    Spirit Art Know, 491, 493
Magicians, 121, 123-124, 138, 184, 300, 353, 367, 369-370, 380, 446, 459
Magism, 139
Magnetism, 110-111, 391
Magnets, 112
MAGNUS, 85, 91-92, 145, 269, 343, 346, 365, 367, 371, 383, 421, 430-431, 489-490
Majesty, 280
Making Christianity, 76
Mal Amen, 202
Malaria, 216, 404
Malkuth, 186, 448
Man, 60, 80, 82, 85-90, 99, 109-111, 129, 134, 139, 159, 178, 184, 186, 197, 236, 254-255, 258, 266, 279, 308, 311, 346, 352, 357-358, 361, 363, 371, 380, 384-385, 409-410, 412-413, 420-421, 430-431, 436-438, 441, 448, 471, 487, 489
Mandrake, 294, 455
Maneuvering, 145
Mankind, 312, 382, 431, 491, 493
Mannheim, 41
Mannix, 490
Manual of Phenomena, 108, 484
Map of Pennsylvania, 44
March, 44, 354, 401, 443
Marder, 372
MARIGOLD, 338-339
Marion, 490
Mark Stavish, 423
Market Church, 413
Marktkirche, 413
Marrubium, 336-337
Marshall College, 55
Martial, 285, 289
Martin
    Boehm, 66
    Luther, 53, 55, 488

521

Martinmass, 445
Martinsdaag, 445
Martinstag, 445
Martyrs Mirror, 42, 63, 373
Marvels, 490
Marvin W., 490
Mary Slusser Kishbaugh, 359
Maryland, 44, 49, 65, 354
MAS MAS MAS, 232
Mash, 222, 239
Masoretic, 438
Mass, 76, 81, 86, 133, 327, 333, 369, 404, 460
Massage, 108, 158, 211, 235, 383
Masses, 76
Master, 95, 161, 299, 382, 387, 410, 433, 446, 465
MASTERWORT, 259, 291, 333, 339
Material, 112, 152, 159, 269, 285-286, 306, 325, 379
Matricaria, 329
Matt, 133, 150, 157
Matter, 50, 67, 76, 83, 86, 133, 136, 152, 157, 189, 219, 234, 287, 301, 305, 312, 319, 346, 379, 445, 454, 457, 465
Mauch Chunk, 351
Maul, 205
Maundy Thursday, 263, 332
May
    Day, 461
    Eve, 130, 132, 401, 461-462
Maynard Clark, 490
McGuiness, 490
McKenzie, 388, 490
Mechanicsburg, 494
Medical
    Times, 115
Medieval
    Germans, 401
    Germany, 74, 488
Meditations, 483

Mediterranean Pagan, 399
Meerrettich, 337
Meeschderwarzel, 339
Megaera, 457
Mehrreddich, 337
Mein Schlund, 206
Meisterwurz, 339
Melchior, 53, 277, 460, 490
Men, 85, 90-91, 101, 124, 132, 139, 147, 150, 158, 195, 242-244, 277, 300, 302, 314, 355, 357, 363, 380, 390, 397, 425, 447, 458-459
Menno Simons, 63
Mennonite Churches, 65
Menschen, 487
Mentha Pulegium, 205
Mention, 79, 85, 93, 95, 133, 160, 197, 248, 254, 338, 359, 361, 450, 459
Mephistopheles, 412-413
Mercersberg Movement, 55-56
Mercurial, 294
Mercury
    Dime, 430
    Dimes, 203, 285-286, 379
    Headed Dime, 287
Mercy Seat, 448
Merseburg Incantations, 74, 100
Meshach, 367
MESHIACH -- Messiah, 191
Mesmer, 110-111
Mesmerism, 108, 383, 406, 484
Mesmerist, 108-109, 484
Messiah, 191, 385
Messias, 191
Metatron, 448
Methods, 98, 108-109, 112, 142, 148, 152, 160, 230, 253, 343, 370, 405
Metumbor, 265
Mexican
    Curanderismo, 151, 443
    Curanderos, 151

Mexico, 78-79, 160, 417
Meyer, 490
Mezlim, 492
Michael
    R. Best, 490
    Schlatter, 55
Michigan, 65
Microcosm, 487
Middle
    Ages, 51, 488
    East, 343
    English, 127
    High German, 128
    Way, 52, 68
Midwives, 381
Military, 42, 354, 446, 486
Mill Creek, 373
Millenialist, 425
Milnes, 382, 490
Milton Hill, 320
Mind of Christ, 490
Mining Folklore of The Pennsylvania Dutch, 489
Ministerium, 54-55
Minneapolis, 483, 492
Minnesota, 65
Minor, 161, 270, 273, 297, 330, 443
Miracle, 164, 351, 380, 484
Miracles of Our Lord, 388, 492
Miratus, 354
Mirror of The Martyrs, 491
Mirrors, 293-294, 306
Misael, 278-279, 368
MISAIL, 367
Mishael, 367
Mission, 58, 60, 73
Missouri Synod, 54
Mithraism, 100
Mithras, 280
Mittelalter, 492
Modern
    English, 128, 416, 464, 477
    World, 489

Monika, 492
Monroe Aurand Jr., 437
Montana, 65, 493
Moon, 135, 178, 184, 192, 195, 214-215, 226, 235, 237, 240, 246, 249, 251, 253-254, 264, 276, 287-288, 290, 293, 298, 301, 310-311, 326, 330, 345, 406, 415, 428
Moravia, 60, 63
Moravian
    Church, 59-61
    Star, 316
    Synod, 59
Moravians, 52, 59
Morning
    Star, 318-319, 412, 484, 495
    Stars, 319
Morrigan, 457
Mosaic Books, 491, 493
Mosaical Philosophy, 110
Moses Changes Water, 92
Mosquitoes, 233, 404
MOSS, 339
Most High Words of God, 451
Mostard, 341
Mother
    Earth, 261
    Goose, 414
    Heart of God, 452, 493
    Mary, 202, 360
    Nature, 374
    of God, 266
    PAINS, 433
Motherhood, 452
Mount of Olives, 313
Mountain Mary, 432
MOUSE EAR, 288, 339-340
Mouth, 101, 145, 150, 203, 205-207, 210, 267, 326, 337, 341, 347, 389
Mugwort, 219-220, 326, 340
Muhlenberg Press, 490

Mullein Tea, 340
Mumia, 111-112, 115, 391-392, 454
Mund Fauling, 205
Munich Handbook, 97
Murder, 87, 90, 96, 158-159, 323, 371, 484, 489
Muss, 202
MUSTARD SEED, 341
Muster, 267
Mutter
    Jesu Christi, 297
    Maria, 202
Mutterweh, 146, 254, 433, 463
Mysteries of
    Ancient Philosophers, 371, 489
Mystery Religions, 100
Mysticism, 60, 435, 451, 493
Märter, 297
Müller-Ebeling, 347, 491
Münster, 63
Müntze, 240

𝔑

NACHT ENGSCHT, 434
Nagel, 297
Name of
    God, 101, 165, 188-189, 191, 206, 223, 225, 230, 254-255, 263, 266, 272, 296, 311, 313, 467, 470
    Power, 185
    Ship Date of Arrival No. of Passengers, 49
Namen Gottes, 165, 205-206, 255, 349
Names of God, 184, 188-189, 369, 395, 433, 467
Nancy, 48-49
Nanny, 386
Napoleonic Wars, 42
NARCOTICS, 434

Narration, 103
Narrative, 75, 101, 214, 243
Nashville, 492
Nassau, 47
Nasty, 42, 230, 307, 400
Nathaniel, 443
National Institute, 114
Native
    Americans, 437
Nativity of
    Mary, 302
    St. John, 444
Natural
    Magic, 81, 91, 95, 136, 305, 367, 431, 455
    Theology, 321, 425, 484
Navaho, 128
Navajo, 137, 417
Navy, 44, 49, 354
Nazareth, 60, 195, 210, 244, 277, 312, 422
Nazism, 394
Near East, 394
Nebraska, 59
Negelin, 330
Nehushtan, 383-384
Neither, 99, 114, 130, 150, 152, 161, 191, 228, 312, 320, 323, 338, 460, 473
Nelson
    D. Rehmeyer, 88, 158
    Rehmeyer, 89-91, 96, 351
Neo-pagan, 191, 432
Neo-paganism, 452
Neo-pagans, 360, 411, 428, 432
Nepeta Hederacea, 222, 336
Nescopeck, 351
Nescopeck-Berwick, 360
Netherlands, 41, 43
NETTESHEIM, 95, 366, 483
NETTLE, 226, 341, 377
Neu-Eingerichtetes Gesang-Buch, 68
NEURALGIA, 327, 346, 348, 434

Neustadt, 41
New
    Age, 116, 151-152, 304, 308, 319, 432
    England, 51, 317
    Falcon Publications, 489
    Jersey, 43
    Moon, 178, 226
    Netherlands, 43
    Sweden, 42-43
    Testament, 66, 111, 139, 388, 443, 459
    Testaments, 275, 451, 454
    Translation, 494
    World, 41, 43, 47, 49-50, 58, 129
    Years, 461
    York
        City, 76
        State, 46
Newburgh, 48
NewYork, 489-490
Next, 48, 51, 61, 63, 79, 112, 127, 134, 138, 149-151, 158, 163, 169, 186, 197, 216, 222, 234, 249-250, 254, 256, 311, 328, 373, 395, 450, 461
Nicene Creed, 56
Nicholas, 60, 397, 443
Nicknamed, 66, 354
Night Battles, 461
Nightmares, 434
Nigromancy, 427
Nine Worlds, 369
Nineteenth, 57
Ninte, 239
Ninth, 449
NITRIC SPIRIT, 435
Nivelles, 443
Noijm, 451
Noll, 89
Nolt, 57, 491
Non-Being, 422, 426

Non-Occult Cures, 485
Noquetonaij, 451
Norns, 457, 464
Norse, 368, 464
North
    America, 43, 47, 53-54, 490
    American Union, 79
    Carolina, 61, 65
    Dakota State University Libraries, 489
    Dakotan, 72
    Door, 155
Northern
    Europe, 387, 444
    Lehigh County, 230
Nosebleed, 203-205, 270
Notebooks, 362, 490
November, 88-89, 91, 335, 445, 493
Numerologists, 446
Nun, 462, 471
Nutting, 317

O

Oak Moss, 339
Oasaij, 451
Observe, 70, 110, 141, 160, 194, 197, 251, 275, 289, 317, 413
Obviously, 96, 293
Occult, 93, 95, 98, 134, 158, 194, 355, 358, 366-367, 423, 427-428, 483, 485-488
Occultist Arthur Edward Waite, 123
October, 87, 335, 346, 353, 421, 484, 489-490
Odd, 88, 103, 108, 200, 211, 271, 285, 323, 357, 379, 385, 392, 446, 454
Oddly, 126, 396
Odermennig, 326
Oderminnich, 326
Odin, 75, 130
Offenders, 139

Officer Andrea Kohut, 158
Official Physician of Basil, 435
Ohio, 65
Oil of Saints, 462
Oklahoma, 65
Olandswartzel, 334
Old
    English, 127-128, 401, 464
    German Baptist Brethren, 67
    High German, 74, 128
    Nick, 351, 396
    Order
        Mennonites, 61, 64-65, 316
        River Brethren, 67
    Reformed, 56
    Scratch, 396
    Slavonic, 369
    Testament, 92, 137-139, 395, 448-449
    Wise Hebrews, 491, 493
    World Pfälzisch, 474
Omega, 281-282, 284
Omnipotence, 409
One
    Power, 116
Onion, 207-208, 252
Ontario, 65
Operation of
    Braucherei, 147
    Pow-Wow, 153
Ophite, 385
Opium, 434-435
Opposite, 100, 188, 250, 265, 410, 439, 453, 455
Orangeville, 358
Order Mennonites, 61, 64-65, 67, 316
Oregon, 485
Orient, 140
Oriental, 139
Orthodox
    Churches, 77, 121
    Jewish, 147
Osiris, 318
Oskar Estebany, 109
Ossig, 67
Otermenig, 326
Ouija, 141, 351
Our
    Father, 281-282, 373, 387
    Lord, 191, 197, 260, 262, 320, 388, 492
Outside of Pennsylvania Dutch, 125
Overseer, 386, 465
Overview of Braucherei Practice, 69
Overviews, 52
OX-GALL, 435
Oxford University Press, 484, 492
Oyer, 491
Ozarks Mountaineer, 488

P

PA German, 445
Pacts, 121
Paeonia, 226
Pagan Gods, 433
Pain, 106, 170, 196, 198, 206-207, 220, 223, 225, 235, 237-238, 260, 334, 341, 343-344, 346, 375-376, 378, 381, 392, 402, 408, 434, 441, 463, 470-471
Palatinate, 42, 47, 50
Palatine, 41, 47-48, 50, 372, 473
Palatines, 47, 58
Palestine, 77, 387
Palm Springs, 484
Papacy, 58
Papal, 55
Papus, 98
Par, 247
Paracelsian, 111-112
PARACELSUS, 69, 110-111, 115-116, 248, 269, 290-291, 305, 391,

400, 424, 427, 431, 434-436, 454, 488, 491
Paraclete, 387
Paradise, 94, 221, 423, 450
Paraguay, 65
Paregoric, 435
Parents, 59, 122, 161, 227, 353, 359
Paris, 367
Parsley, 219
Parsons, 491
Passau, 64
Past, 45, 52, 65, 73, 75, 82, 95, 107-108, 112, 126, 129, 150, 157, 159-160, 177-178, 209, 307, 323, 341, 343, 347, 351, 359-360, 379, 381, 392-393, 403, 405, 433, 450, 453, 464-465, 474
Pater Noster, 281-283
Path, 68, 141, 305, 409, 445
Patriachen, 297
Patriarchs, 298
Patriot-News, 484
Patris, 284
Paul, 55, 58, 132, 139-140, 255, 282, 386, 427, 483, 485, 488
Paulist Press, 486, 488
Pay, 88, 177-178, 287, 325
Pazzuoli, 282
Peace of Westphalia, 42
Peaceful, 42, 142, 372
Pele, 438
PENDOT, 79
Pennsylvaanisch Deitsch Pronunciation, 474
Pennsylvania
    Beautiful, 317
    Deitsch, 411, 432
    Department of Transportation, 79
    Dutch
        Bar Symbols, 494
        Barn Symbols, 317
        Brauchers, 417
        Bruacherei, 95
        Bruachers, 95
        Christian, 371
        Country, 487, 491
        Cultural History, 493
        Folk Spirituality, 70
        Powwowing, 437
        Witch-tales, 129
        Witchcraft, 417
    Dutchland, 487
    Dutchman, 151, 484
    Folklife, 378, 485, 492
    German
        Brauche, 430
        Broadside, 87, 420, 494
        Christians, 386, 395
        Mysticism, 493
        Protestant, 57
        Review, 489
        Society Proceedings, 489
        Witches, 411
    Magazine of History, 486
    Ministerium, 54
Pennsylvania-Germans, 489
Pennsylvanian Dutch, 474
Pensylvania, 47
Pentagram of Man, 413
Pentateuch, 92, 413, 422, 449
Pentecost, 401
People, 41-42, 47-48, 50-53, 59, 61-63, 65-67, 70, 72, 76, 78, 80-84, 87, 89, 91, 98, 107-108, 137, 139-141, 147, 152-154, 158, 160, 174, 177, 210, 213, 215, 218, 223, 229, 266, 307, 316, 320, 339, 344, 351, 357-358, 361, 366, 369, 373, 383-384, 396, 404, 414, 416-417, 419, 426, 430-431, 434, 436-437, 444, 448,

451-452, 458-459, 462, 470-471
Perchta, 130
Pergatory, 443
Perigree Book, 493
Persia, 422, 459
Persian Magian, 396
Persians, 366
Persistent
    American Esoteric Tradition, 432
    Healing Tradition, 489
    Minority, 491
Person, 64, 70, 78-79, 82, 86, 89, 103, 108-109, 112-114, 121-122, 125, 129, 134-135, 137-138, 141-142, 145, 148, 150, 153-154, 156-158, 161, 163, 167-173, 177, 188, 191, 198-199, 201, 205-207, 212, 214, 223, 225, 232, 238, 242-243, 250, 253, 260, 263, 265-266, 269, 273, 278-279, 283, 285, 294, 301, 303, 305-306, 308-309, 312, 324-325, 359-360, 376, 378-379, 381, 389, 391, 394-395, 402-403, 410, 417, 422-423, 429, 432-434, 440-441, 444, 454-456, 465, 469, 471
Personal, 136-137, 141, 153-155, 159, 177, 193, 281, 284, 305, 316, 360-362, 374, 377-378, 388, 432, 436, 443, 452, 465
Pestilence
    Charms, 276
    LETTER, 308, 405, 419
Peter
    Becker, 66, 372
    Pan, 308
    Saylor, 132, 300, 415
Peterson, 92-93, 450, 467, 491
Petra, 446
Petroselinum, 219
Petschaft, 148, 288-291, 374, 437
Pfälzisch, 41, 50, 473-474
Pharaoh, 92, 380

Pharisees, 69
Pharmacopeia, 259, 323
Pharmacopoeia, 444
Pharmakeia, 139
Philadelphia German Catholics, 58
Philadelphian Society, 424
Philip
    Phenomena, 485
    William Otterbein, 55
Philistines, 138
Philosopher, 426
Philosophy, 95, 98, 110-111, 366-367, 427, 436, 483, 488
Phrygian, 287
Physical Welfare of Man, 438
Pierce, 217, 485
Pietism, 55, 66, 373, 451
Pietist Conrad Beissel, 52
Pietistic, 52, 71
Pietists, 59
Pikeville, 432
Pilate, 300
Pillow, 155, 168, 172, 196, 441
PINE TAR, 437
Pipisissewa, 219
Pipsissewa, 219, 342
Piscean, 184
Pisces, 184
Pissbett, 332
Plain People, 52, 62, 67, 80, 419
Planet, 98, 179, 261, 273, 290, 294, 398, 422
Planetary Hours, 289, 293, 481
Plant
    Lore, 489
    Names, 489
Plantago, 221
Plattdietsch, 50
Plautdietsch, 473
Plead, 208
Plymouth Rock, 41, 47
Pneumatic Role, 452, 493
Pocket Books, 489

Poison, 135, 231-232, 301, 330, 336, 376, 443
Poisoned, 140, 404, 406
Poland, 41
Pole Star, 155
Polish Catholics, 70
Political, 45-47, 58, 62, 261, 353, 486
Politics, 353, 356, 372
Polypodiaceae, 335
Polytrichaceae, 339
Pomeroy, 488
Pommern, 488
Pompeii, 282
Poor Sam, 356
Pope Adrian II, 462
Popular Culture, 486
Port
    Clinton, 351
    of Philadelphia, 49, 485
Portland, 494
Portuguese, 70
Positive, 115, 156, 287, 439, 447
Post-pagan, 462
Potentilla, 347
Pottendorf, 59
POW-WOW, 58, 69-70, 75, 81, 84-85, 88, 96-97, 101, 108, 110, 113, 125-126, 147, 149-153, 155-157, 160-161, 177-178, 188, 191, 193, 230, 238, 254, 269, 292, 304-305, 313, 323-324, 349, 371, 374-375, 377-378, 381-383, 385, 392, 419, 423, 436-438, 440, 455, 457, 483-484, 492
Pow-Wower
    Aunt Sophia Bailer, 151
    Marie May, 158
    Robert Dluge, 161
Pow-Wowers, 93, 122, 124, 158-160, 377, 492
Pow-Wows, 85, 437, 455, 488
Powers, 86, 92-94, 116, 121, 123, 126, 128, 132, 134, 142, 163, 264, 266, 300, 372, 385, 387, 396, 399, 402, 414, 417, 427, 434, 449, 451, 462, 491
Powwow Power, 96, 313, 484
Powwow-Doctor, 162
Powwower, 113, 125, 151, 158, 161, 485
Powwowers, 93, 122, 124, 158-160, 377, 492
Powwowing Among, 437, 485, 489
Powwows, 85, 437, 455, 488
Practical Kabala, 438
Practice of
    Braucherei, 145, 177, 323, 391, 410, 442, 457, 465
    Medicine, 486
    Witchcraft Among, 492
Practitioners of Pow-Wow, 371, 385
Prague, 60
Praise, 141, 208, 279, 344, 368, 434
Praised, 70, 229
Pray, 84, 157, 173, 208, 222-223, 257, 261, 275, 306, 309, 313-314, 384, 409
Prayers, 72, 96-98, 108, 113, 145, 147-150, 156-157, 174, 179, 188, 191, 193-194, 200, 227, 229, 233, 238, 240, 261, 264, 269, 291, 295, 310, 319-320, 406, 418, 439, 443, 464, 467
Praying, 72, 139, 197, 207-208, 222, 227, 261
Presbyterian, 54
Presence, 43, 48, 50, 53-54, 61, 128, 131, 149, 190, 282, 378, 388, 447-449
Preston Barba, 320
PRICKLY ASH, 342
Priests, 51, 92, 97, 264, 386, 433, 458-460
Prima Materia, 458
Primarily, 42, 212, 280, 338, 347,

529

366, 368, 372, 379
Princeton University Press, 490
Professor
    Bill Ellis, 307
Promote Healing, 493
Prophecies, 486
Propheten, 297
Prophets, 262, 298
Proponents, 452
Proprietary, 44
Protection, 101, 145-146, 149, 156, 158, 161, 257, 261, 264, 279, 284, 307, 313, 318, 340, 399, 413-414, 419, 422, 441, 443, 467-468, 471
Protestant
    Brauchers, 201
    Christian, 451
    Reformation, 442
Protestantism, 78
Protestants, 42, 63, 66, 432, 438
Proto Indo European, 385, 396
Proto-Germanic, 127
Proverbiis, 354
Providence, 113, 120, 395, 465
Psalm Remedy, 207, 220, 222, 226, 257
Psalmic, 193, 449
PSALMS, 94, 193, 220, 226, 257, 261, 438, 455, 467-470, 472, 492
Psi, 307
Psychokinesis, 485
Public Ledger, 51
Pulmonaria, 337-338
Pulverize, 256
PUMPKIN, 342
Purification, 192, 342, 408, 444, 460
Puteoli, 282
Putrefaction, 458
Pyrex, 219
Pythagoreans, 413
Pythoness, 138

Q

Quakerism, 45
Quakers, 45-46
Quantum Mechanics, 108
Quatember Times, 401
Quatemberzeiten, 401
Quator Tempora, 401
Queen
    Anne, 48, 56
    Jezebel, 138
Quehaij, 451
Quem, 354
Quicklime, 426
Quince, 239
QUINSY, 206, 343, 438
Quite, 45, 47, 53, 59, 62-63, 70, 73, 75, 96, 98, 108, 122, 155, 174, 193, 204, 226, 230, 243, 249, 253, 261, 270, 280, 282, 289, 291, 299, 304, 306, 361, 367, 371-372, 383, 387, 394-395, 399, 403, 410, 434-435, 438, 445-447, 451-453, 460
Quosum, 246

R

Rabbi Isaac Luria, 448
Rabbinical, 226
Rabbis, 136, 190, 304
Rabhq, 246
Radical Pietism, 373
Radicula, 337
RADISH, 345
Ragnarok, 387
RAIN-WORM OIL, 343, 346
Ranunculus, 330
Raphael, 190, 221, 293, 295
Raphanus, 345
Ratisbon, 91, 430
Raube, 493
Raubsville, 132
Raute, 240

Raziel, 93-94, 450
Reader, 87, 99, 106, 145, 153-154, 386, 424, 457, 487
Reading, 87, 97, 124, 131, 204, 304, 412, 421, 440, 459, 483, 487, 489
Real Presence, 54
Realness of Witchcraft, 483
Recipe, 205, 219, 240, 333, 336, 338, 340, 344, 346
Recipes, 86, 145, 258, 435
Red
    Altar, 241, 250
    Beet, 327, 345
    Book, 241, 250
    Church, 71, 87, 91, 94, 97-98, 136, 150, 152, 241, 250, 269, 287, 304, 323-325, 349, 383, 386, 416, 420, 423, 438, 440, 451, 459, 467, 483
    Lion, 88
    Wald, 75, 241, 250
Red-walk, 240-241, 439
Redemptioners, 485
Reflexology, 108
Reformation, 54-55, 59, 62, 67-68, 442, 452, 486
Reformed
    Church, 42, 52, 54-56, 67
    Ministerium, 55
Reformers, 452
Reforms, 55, 60, 62
Rehmeyer, 88-91, 96, 158, 351
Reich, 111, 478-479
Reiki, 108, 151, 406
Reinmand, 353
Religious Transformation, 492
Remedies, 89, 112, 193, 204, 208, 212-213, 225, 230, 234, 244, 251-252, 287, 323-325, 343-344, 346-347, 359, 368, 376, 382, 402-405, 427, 436, 449, 463, 483, 488, 493
Remedy, 76, 88-89, 96, 195-196, 198, 202, 204-205, 207, 209, 211-212, 214-218, 220-222, 225-226, 230, 232-235, 238-241, 244-246, 248-249, 251-254, 256-257, 259, 290, 309, 324, 326, 331, 336-337, 339-340, 342-343, 348, 366-367, 376-377, 400, 426, 435
Remote Pow-Wowing, 173
Renaissance, 423-424, 430
Rents, 48
Resh, 207, 471
Resurrection, 155, 318, 434, 454
Rettich, 345
Rev, 483, 486, 489
Revealing The Forbidden Knowledge, 371, 489
Revelation, 412, 425, 464, 495
Revelations, 281, 486
Reverend
    James Wesley Stivers, 452
    Thomas R. Brendle, 325
Revolution, 56-57, 373, 381, 432, 473
Rhabarber, 346
Rheum, 290, 346
Rheumatism, 146, 235, 238, 326-327, 329, 334, 341-342, 348, 446
Rheums, 290, 328, 455
Rhinanthus Crista-galli, 331
Rhine Valley, 41
Rhinebeck, 48
RHUBARB, 346, 359
Rhubicac, 346, 359
Richard
    Backhouse, 415
    E. Wentz, 70
    H. Hexerei, 492
    Smith, 490
    Wentz, 70
Richman, 491
RICHTHONIE, 102
Rieb, 327
Right, 89, 121-122, 125, 154, 156, 158, 165-172, 175, 186, 188, 195,

198, 200-203, 206-207, 210, 213, 215, 222, 228, 230, 236, 242, 250, 256, 265, 299, 302, 322, 346, 372, 393, 401, 450, 456, 470-471
Rings, 203, 262, 288, 446
Rippley, 492
Rites, 369, 443
River Brethren, 66-67
Robert
    L., 485
    S. Kreider, 491
    Turner, 491
Rochester, 491, 493
Rock, 41, 47, 131, 229, 327, 331, 344-345, 378, 398, 414-415, 489
Rockport, 483
Rockwell, 357
Rockwellesque, 357
Rodale, 485
Roll, 223, 257
Rom, 383
Roman
    Catholic
        Church, 442
        Classicist, 354
    Catholicism, 56
    Catholics, 46, 56-58
    Empire, 73
    Light Bringer, 294
Romans, 371
Romanus Book, 383, 420
ROMANUSBUCHLEIN, 383, 421, 439
Romanusbüchlein, 85, 94, 296, 439, 492
Rome, 55, 353
Roots, 58, 71, 73, 77, 81, 95, 101, 106, 204, 219, 233-234, 280, 289, 326, 328, 331, 334-336, 340-341, 366, 369, 383, 422
Rosary, 227, 444
Rosen, 103
Rosicrucian Franz Hartmann, 457

Rosicrucianism, 451
Rosicrucians, 487
Rotas, 281
Roten Schaden, 215, 403
Rothlaufstein, 242
Rotlauf, 240-242, 244-245, 439-440
ROTLAUFE, 146, 161, 240, 326, 402, 410, 439, 464
Rotrieb, 327
Rotterdam, 48, 56
Roughwood Collection, 162
Routledge, 494
Royal
    Art, 305
    Navy, 49
Rubus, 220
Ruhe, 297, 372
RUKSCHTEE, 196-197, 202, 441
Rulership, 112, 178
Russell, 492
Russia Heritage Collection, 489
Russian, 58, 70
Russification, 58
Ruta, 240
Ruth
    Frey, 408
    Strickland-Frey, 274
    Weil Kusler, 72, 103, 211
    Weil-Kusler, 383
Rye, 256, 443
Ryrie, 388, 492
Rätsch, 347
Rübe, 327

S

S A T O R, 280
Sabaoth, 190-191, 288
Sabbatarian, 373
Sabbath
    Bride, 448
    Queen, 130
Sachse, 492

SACRAMENTALS, 150, 442-444
Sacraments, 56, 61, 442
Sacred World of Ephrata, 483
SADAI, 293
SADAY, 293
Saint
    Andrew Oct, 49
    John, 248, 444
    Nicholas, 397
    Nicosius, 214
Saint-Adventurers, 494
Saints, 59, 79, 99, 265, 401, 432, 452, 462
SALATHEEL, 293, 295
Salathiel, 189
Salem, 90
Salome, 443
SALT PETRE, 446
Saltpeter, 368, 446
Salvation, 66, 85, 98-99, 208, 223, 229, 387, 399, 454
Salzburg, 435
Sambuca Canadensis, 219
Sambucus, 333
Samech, 471
Samhain, 191, 445, 492
Samtblume, 338
Samuel, 138
San Francisco, 486, 491
Sanicle, 219, 326, 342-343
Sanicula, 219, 342
Santa Clause, 397
Santee, 346, 351-352, 355, 358-359, 361-362, 381, 492
Santees, 351
Sapo Castiliensis, 461
Sara, 490
Sarah, 243
SARSAPARILLA-ROOT, 343
Sassafras, 204-205, 218, 343, 375
Sassafrasbaam, 343
Satanas, 297
Satanic Panic, 71

Satanism, 79
Satanist, 456
Satanists, 411
Satanologies, 398
Satans, 487
SATOR Square, 280, 282, 428, 446
Saturday, 311-312, 401
Saturdays, 314
Saturn Square, 428
Saturnine, 273
Sauerkraut, 52
Saul, 138, 140
Saurer, 494
Savior Jesus Christ, 191, 197, 298
Saviour Jesus Christ, 486
Sawdust, 354
Saxony, 50, 59, 67
Saylor, 132, 300, 415
Saylors, 126, 160
Scabiosa, 234, 332
Scandinavia, 444-445
Scandinavian, 77
Scandinavians, 43
Schadet, 235
Schaftheu, 337
Scheible, 93-94, 439, 450
Scheide, 164
Schellegraut, 330
Schlag, 297
Schlangewurtzel, 344
Schleitheim Confession, 64
SCHLIER, 146, 195, 233
Schof, 337
Scholars, 126, 281, 401, 461, 474
Schpickliesche, 342
Schtinckros, 338
Schuld, 478
Schulde, 478
Schuldigern, 478
Schultz, 492
Schuster, 489-490
Schuylkill River, 426
Schwaer, 195

Schwartsholler, 333
Schwarze Peter, 397
Schwarzenau German Baptist Brethren, 66
Schweckfelder, 52
Schwenkfeld, 67-68
Schwenkfelder, 68
Schwenkfelders, 53, 67-68
Schwindsucht, 366, 454
Science of Mind, 484
Scientism, 454
SCORPION OIL, 325, 343
Scotch-Irish, 47
Scots-Irish, 125, 382
Scottish, 475
Scriptural, 273, 278
Sea, 75, 80, 92, 207, 236-237, 242, 260, 380, 390, 446, 467-468
Seal, 165-172, 257, 275, 278, 288, 290-292, 333, 378, 392, 412-413, 422, 433
Seat, 155, 169, 258, 448
Second
    Century, 100-101, 452
    Coming, 425
    Edition, 484
    Fall, 357, 492
    Person, 432
Secret of Secrets, 422
Secrets of Sympathy, 95, 307, 419
Secundinae, 446
SECUNDINES, 446
Secure, 275, 283, 302
Seeing, 138, 324, 398, 431
Seele, 87, 421
Seemingly, 61, 70, 74, 112, 209, 365, 378, 449-450
Sefer
    Raziel HaMalach, 93, 450
    Schimmusch Tehillim, 438
Sega, 231
SEGENBUCH, 446
Seikarrebs, 342

Seite, 200
Selah, 222-223, 228, 258, 399
Seldom, 84, 92, 449
Self, 98, 135, 360, 377, 438, 490-491
Selig, 94, 227, 438, 467
Semi-audible, 156-157
Semitic, 137, 190
Senf, 341
Sennen, 366
Sepher
    Schimmusch Tehillim, 94, 227, 467
    Yetzirah, 422
Sephira, 185, 422
Sephiroth Kether, 186
September, 55, 68, 302, 333, 352, 401, 435
Septuagint, 438
Seraph, 398
Serbian, 70
Serve, 55, 97, 164, 224, 365, 436
Seven
    Sacraments, 442
Seventh
    Book of Moses, 493
    Books, 92, 269, 288, 293, 295, 438, 440, 449, 460, 467, 491
    Day Baptists, 373
SEVENTY-SEVEN, 446-447
Severity, 122, 210
Sew, 217, 256-257, 283, 286-287
SHADAI, 293
SHADDAI
    El Chai, 191
    Thy, 223
Shadrach, 367
Shakers, 79, 453
SHALOM -- Peace, 190
Shaman, 437
Shamanic Practices, 491
Shamanistic Visionary Traditions, 494

Shaner, 141-142, 492
Sharp, 195, 248, 292, 339
Sheep, 208, 337, 397
SHEKINAH -- Dwelling Place, 190
Shelter, 284, 446
Shenandoah History Publications, 494
Shepherd, 205, 220, 393
Shew, 229, 380
Shiatsu, 151
Shield of David, 412
Shin, 190, 471
Shoofly
    Pie, 316, 487
    Pies, 493
Shrubs, 487
Shunning, 64
Sickness, 255, 278, 372, 398, 403, 407, 463
Sie, 202
Sigils, 92, 193
Signatura Rerum, 135, 485
Signature of All Things, 485
Signs, 92, 107, 148, 178-179, 184, 273, 291, 316-321, 382, 410-411, 414, 418-419, 455, 457, 490, 494
Silesia, 41, 47, 321
Silesian, 67
Simon Magus, 139, 459
Simons, 63
Simony, 139
Sinthgunt, 75
Sinusitis, 169, 290
Sir Francis Galton, 114
Sister House, 373
SIX AND SEVENTH BOOKS OF MOSES, 449
Sixteen, 109
Sixth, 92-93, 269, 288, 293, 295, 422, 438, 440, 449-450, 460, 467, 491, 493
Sixty, 60
Skin, 112, 128, 196, 216, 237, 240, 258, 326-327, 329, 331, 334, 341, 343-344, 375, 391, 419, 437, 454-455, 463-464
Skippack, 55, 59
Skuld, 457, 464
Small Catechism, 56
Snake Bite, 146, 230, 232, 384
SNAKEROOT, 219, 344
Snellenburg, 122, 492
SO4, 367
Society of Schwenkfelders, 68
Sociohistorical Approach, 492
Sohn, 297
Sohnes, 166, 206, 255, 349
Sola
    Fide, 53
    Gratia, 53
    Scriptura, 54
Solar Plexus, 156, 167, 169, 265
Solomon, 86, 451
Solus Christus, 53
Sonand Holy Ghost, 103
Sonnenwende, 192, 444
Sonnenwendefeuer, 444
Sons of Thunder, 444
Sophia Bailer, 151, 157, 436
Sophianic Christianity, 358, 452
Sophiology, 373
Sorcery, 86, 99, 137, 139-140, 301-302, 304, 434, 436, 454, 459, 465, 488
Sore, 101, 206-207, 224, 233, 235-236, 246-247, 334-335, 343-344, 347, 368, 402
Sores, 145-146, 195, 205, 233-235, 327-328, 330-331, 337, 367
Soter, 191, 385
Soul, 60, 81, 87, 91, 93, 111, 135-136, 142, 208, 223, 261, 263, 265-266, 351, 357-359, 361, 397, 399, 421, 449, 485, 494
South
    America, 160

Pacific, 354
Southern
    Germans, 130
    Medical Journal, 114
Sovereign, 116
Space, 74, 283, 319, 324, 457
Spamer, 94, 296, 439, 492
Spanish, 42, 70, 357
SPEEDWELL, 344
Spell-binding Account of Witchcraft, 489
Spellwork, 147, 319, 370, 488
Spirit of God, 69, 81
Spirits, 123, 130-133, 138-141, 263, 266, 273, 278, 283, 293, 304, 306, 333-334, 340, 358, 361, 371-372, 387, 390, 395-397, 431, 433, 451, 455, 461-462, 467-471, 494
Spiritual
    Discernment, 94, 136, 451
    Ecology of The Pennsylvania Germans, 485
    Subjects, 114
Spiritus
    Sancti, 284
    Universi, 458
Spleen, 171, 404
Splendor, 423
Spot, 200, 203, 241, 247, 250, 361, 445, 487
Sprach, 199, 206
Sprains, 146, 235-236, 329
Spread, 52-53, 63, 65, 106, 327, 341, 420, 442, 472
Spricht, 297
Square of
    Jupiter, 428
    Saturn, 429
Squares, 286, 428-429, 446
Squeeze, 170, 250, 275
Sras, 259
Srus, 259
St.
    Abdan, 253, 365
    Anthony, 240, 334, 443
    BARTHOLOMEW, 443
    Francis Regis Mission, 58
    Gertrude of Nivelles, 443
    Jacob, 205
    JAMES DAY, 443
    JOHN, 192, 264, 279, 291, 326, 340, 344-345, 425, 444
    Lucy, 401
    Luke, 279
    Mark, 279
    Martin of Tours, 445
    Mary, 302
    Matthew, 279
    Paul, 58, 132, 140, 282, 427, 483
    Peter, 264, 267
    Thomas Aquinas, 91
    VITUS, 445
    Walpurga, 462
Standard
    German Pronunciation Guide, 473
    High German, 50, 374, 410, 474, 478
Star of
    Bethlehem, 412-413
    David, 412
State Attorney General, 158
Statement of Faith, 56
States, 46, 54-55, 59, 65, 78, 82, 234, 318, 361, 421, 445, 483
Stavish, 423, 492
Stechapfel, 346
Stehen, 297, 411, 418
Stein, 131
Stellaria, 234, 330
Steps, 122, 142, 168, 194, 241, 247, 251
Sterne, 297
Steven

Guth, 494
M. A History, 491
Nolt, 57
Stockholm Tar, 437
Stoic, 387
STOMACH AND BOWELS, 146, 238
Stone, 131, 160, 196-197, 203, 213, 228, 242, 319, 377-379, 411, 426, 441-442, 446
Stones, 196-197, 203, 213, 337, 345, 366, 378, 441, 490
Stories, 99, 132, 214, 389, 397, 491
Storl, 347
Story of Healing, 103, 489
Stoudt, 318-319, 493
Strange Experience, 147, 234, 367, 375, 486
Strasser, 418, 493
String Theory, 108
Strobel, 493
Stroke, 195, 197, 224, 236-237, 292, 368, 392
Students, 91, 95, 398, 416, 430
Study Scripture, 305
Subratum, 256
Succoth, 448
Sufi, 353
SULPHUR, 453-454, 457
Summer Solstice, 444
Sun Signs, 178
Sunbonnets, 493
Sunday, 76, 125, 226, 311-312, 314, 407
Sunk, 207, 236, 260, 425
Sunna, 75
Superintendent General, 308, 420
Supernal Triad of Kether, 186
Supper, 54, 395
Supreme
    Being, 107
    Good, 143, 459
Susan, 493

Suspend, 223, 226, 288
Susquehanna River, 66, 351
Sussex Academic Press, 494
Swabia, 91, 430
Swabian, 473
Sweden, 42-43
Swedes, 42-43, 47
Swedish Bitters, 377
Sweeny, 237, 378, 454
Sweep, 163-164, 166-168, 170, 172, 174, 303
Swelling, 195, 244, 341, 378, 400, 404, 410, 470-471
Swellings, 146, 240, 244, 334, 346-347, 440, 463
Swiss
    German, 473, 486
    Mennonite, 65
Swiss-German, 64, 435
Switzerland, 41, 48, 62-63, 321, 397, 435
Sybil Leek, 355, 360
Sympathetic
    Alignments, 177
    Medicine, 39, 107-108, 290, 390, 394, 423, 436, 440
Sympathy, 39, 57, 95, 107, 112, 196, 213, 247, 290, 307, 392, 408, 410, 419, 422, 427, 433, 454-455
Symphytum, 331
Symposium, 487
Syrians, 460
Syrup, 239, 334-338
Syzygium, 330

T

Tabernacle, 190, 448
Table of Elements, 422
Talismans, 125, 145, 148-149, 184, 189, 193, 269, 271, 276, 278, 285, 317, 368, 374, 406, 418, 436, 439
Talismantia of Working Braucherei,

269
TALKING, 197
Talmud, 491, 493
Tamaqua, 351
Tao, 354
Taraxacum, 219, 332
Tarot, 483
Tau, 207-208, 393, 471
Tav, 282
Tay-oh, 354
Teas, 205, 218-219, 259, 286, 332, 403
Technological Society, 82-83
Teeth, 146, 223, 246, 339, 398, 404
Tehillim, 94, 227, 438, 455, 467
Tell, 78, 154, 161, 197, 221, 293-296, 360, 381, 415
Tempe, 489
Tempel Gottes, 487
Temple of
    God, 487
    Osiris, 318
Tender Hands, 103, 489
TENET, 281-282
Tennessee, 65, 490
Tenth, 449
TESET, 281
Testaments, 97, 275, 452, 454
Teth, 470
Tetragrammation, 284
Tetragrammaton, 184, 188-190, 293, 412, 424
Tetter, 146, 233, 369, 455
Teufel Beelzebub, 297
TEUFELSBRIEF, 142, 455-456
Teufelsflucht, 344
Teuton, 386
Teutonic, 253, 293, 386, 394
Texas, 51, 65
Textus Vulgatus, 271
Thal, 206
Thalia, 457
Thefothoson, 451

Thelemites, 370, 428
Theodore Benz, 432
Theologica Germanica of Martin Luther, 488
Theological, 55, 74, 121, 304, 414, 447
Theologically, 386
Theology, 54, 68, 106, 154, 321, 360, 386, 398, 424-425, 432, 442, 449, 484
Theophrastus Bombastus, 435
Theosis, 121
Theosopher Jacob Boehme, 358
Theosophia, 493
Theosophical Society of England, 353
Theotokos, 432, 449
Therapeutic Touch, 108, 111, 115-116, 151, 489, 493
Thesis, 462, 491
Thielman J., 63
Thievery, 292, 300
Thirty Years War, 42
Thomas
    Aquinas, 91, 430
    E. Graves, 494
    Nelson Publishers, 492
    R. Brendle, 325, 489
THONIE, 102
Thor, 394, 396
THORNAPPLE, 346
Thorndike, 264
Thoroughly Christian, 75
Three
    Angels, 103
    Books of Occult Philosophy, 95, 366-367, 427, 483
    Divine Persons of One Holy God, 84
    Fates, 457
    Furies, 457
    Golden Hairs, 397
    Graces, 457
    Holy Children, 277-278,

368
  Kings Water, 310, 460
  Norns, 457, 464
  Worlds, 487
Throat, 101, 145, 205-206, 308, 335, 337, 343-344, 347, 402
Throne, 313, 408
Thursday, 216-217, 260, 263, 332
Tiefe, 236, 297
Till Eulenspiegel, 397
Time, 41, 45, 47, 58-59, 62-64, 72, 80, 85, 88, 91, 97, 100, 106, 114-115, 122, 142, 151, 153, 155, 159, 167-168, 170-173, 178, 184, 188, 191-192, 194-197, 202, 210, 214, 229-230, 233, 237, 239, 242, 252-255, 258, 270, 274, 276, 281, 290, 295-296, 300, 309-310, 320-321, 323-324, 329-330, 335, 339-340, 344, 346, 352-355, 361, 366, 369-370, 374, 381, 387-388, 392, 398, 400, 407-408, 412, 415, 421, 424, 430, 434-435, 441, 443-445, 450, 458, 463, 486-487
Timing, 173, 177-178, 184, 191
Tincture, 218-219, 249, 329, 339, 343, 345-347, 434-435
Tiphareth, 186
Tisiphone, 457
Titram, 265
Todte, 236
Toleration Act, 45
Tom Graves, 317
Tomatoes, 354
Toothache, 146, 246-247, 342
TORMENTIL, 333, 336, 347
Tormentill, 347
Tower of London, 45
Toys, 141
Traditional
  Brauchers, 149
  Catholic, 390
  Medical Practice, 489

Trage, 279
Transfiguratio Christi, 413
Transfiguration of Christ, 413
Treaty of Ryswick, 42
Treben, 493
Tree of Life, 184-186, 369, 422
Trees, 197, 266, 378, 391, 430, 487
Trench, 488
Trials of Hex, 490
Tribalism, 81
Trinitarian, 61, 166
Trinitarianism, 453
Trinity
  Episcopal, 76, 81
  Publishing Co., 490
Triune God of Christianity, 465
Trubner, 488
True
  God, 385, 433, 453
  Laudanum, 435
  Story of A Powwow Relative, 484
Truth, 99, 178, 228, 293, 316, 413, 483
Tsaddi, 471
Tuesday, 289-290, 292
Tumors, 146, 240, 406
Tumult, 41
Turnip, 327, 345
Turnips, 327
TURPENTINE, 347, 402
Turpentine-based, 347
Tussilago, 331
Twayne Publishers, 491
Twelve Apostles, 207
Twenty, 52
Twilight, 387
Tycho Brahe, 412
Tyrol, 63, 334
Tyson, 95, 427, 483
Tzevaot, 190

U

Uber Stock, 131
UCC, 56
UFFGELESE, 461
Ukraine, 58
Ulcerations, 145, 195, 343
Ulmus, 301
Unclean, 138, 224, 387, 390, 467, 471
Underworld, 399, 414, 417
Underworlds, 414
Union, 52-53, 55, 60, 65, 79
Unitas Fratrum, 60
United
    Brethren Church, 56
    Church of Christ, 56
    Lutheran Church, 54
    Methodist Church, 56
    State, 353
    States Government, 46
    Zion Church, 67
Unity of
    Brethren, 60
    God, 280
Universal
    Man, 184, 186
    Science, 487
Universe, 136, 140, 308, 412, 422, 427, 454, 457, 487
University
    of
        Altdorf, 424
        Berlin, 353
        Cologne, 367
        Dole, 123
    Park, 487, 491
    Press of Kentucky, 486
Universitätsverlag C. Winter, 492
Unser Vadder, 478
Urban, 81, 351, 355, 357-358, 361, 367
Urd, 464
Uriel, 221, 293, 295
Urim, 138
Urinary, 146, 167, 248-249, 326, 337-338, 342
Ursinus College, 56
Urtica, 226, 341

V

Valentinus, 265
Valkyries, 414
Vaseline, 341
Vater Unser, 478
Vaters, 166, 206, 255, 349
Vatican, 62
Vau, 188, 470
Vegetarianism, 373
VENETIAN SOAP, 461
Venusberg, 130
Verbal
    Charms, 103, 261, 368
    Healing Charms, 195
Verbascum Thapsus, 340
Verbena, 347
Verdandi, 464
VERDIGRIS, 461
Verna, 352
Veronica, 344
VERRENKDER, 146, 235
Versluis, 135-136, 487, 493
Versuchung, 478-479
Verthandi, 457
VERVAIN, 347-348
Vicks, 329
Victor
    C., 485
    Dieffenbach, 378
Victorian, 114, 131, 367, 392, 395, 434, 454
Victorian-scientific, 108
Victory, 393, 409, 414
Vigaro Tanet, 256
Vihi Noam, 227-228

Vikings, 43
Village, 59, 351-352, 355, 361, 373
Vinegar, 222, 330-331, 334, 336-337
Vineland, 43
Vinland, 43
Violating, 307-308
Virgin
    Sophia, 452
    Wisdom, 452
Virgina, 65
Virginia
    Frontier, 494
    Snakeroot, 219
Virgo, 342
Vlecq, 55
Vodka, 345
Vogelmiere, 330
Voices of The Turtledoves, 483
Volga River, 58
Volla, 75
Volume, 97, 109, 114, 205, 438, 449-450
Votive, 443
Vowels, 137, 188, 474-477
Vulgar Latin, 370
Vulgate, 271-272, 277, 368

W

W.
    B. Yeats, 353
    J. McKnight, 354
    Koebner, 488
Wacholder, 337
Wager, 357-358, 492-493
Waite, 123
Wal-Mart, 79
Wallace Nutting, 317
Wallwort, 331
Wallwurtz, 331
Walpurgis Night, 462
Walpurgisnacht, 130-131, 461-462
Walters, 493
Wand, 254, 296
Waning
    Crescent, 178
    Gibbous, 178
Wapwallopen, 351-352, 354, 361, 381
War of
    Augsburg, 42
    Spanish Succession, 42
Wardings, 301
Warts, 113, 146, 184, 192, 249-253, 330, 366, 390, 394, 406
Wasp, 231
Wasser, 163, 174, 200-202, 399
Water, 84, 92, 129, 152, 160, 163, 168, 172, 196, 201-202, 205, 215, 217-220, 233-234, 238-239, 248-249, 253-255, 258, 262, 283, 286, 296, 310, 312, 326, 328, 330-339, 341, 343-348, 368, 389-391, 399-400, 404, 424, 426, 436, 442, 446, 458, 460, 462, 469, 471
WAX, 288-290, 370, 374, 437
Waxing
    Crescent, 178
    Gibbous, 178
Way of Christ, 410
Waystou, 302
Weaver, 107, 234, 332-333, 339, 494
Wednesday, 293, 401, 493
Week, 46, 173, 254, 287, 357, 401
Weihfasten, 401
Well of Wyrd, 124, 465
Well-Being, 261, 469, 493
Wellness, 492
Welsh, 47, 366
Wentz, 70
Werkstätte, 487
Wermuth, 240, 301
Wespi, 231
West
    Camp, 48
    Virginia, 49

Western
    Canada, 59
    Civilization, 75
    European, 401
Westphalia, 42, 321
White
    Beet, 327
    Magic, 490
    Man, 346
    Nights, 445
    Sabbath, 124
    VITRIOL, 335, 463
Whitsunday, 401
Wicca, 127, 316, 355, 358-359
Wiccan, 119, 156, 360-361
Wiccans, 191, 370, 411, 428
WIEBELSUCHT, 410, 463
Wilbert Hess, 88, 90
Wilby, 494
Wild Hunt, 130, 397
Wilde Jaeger, 397
Wilderness, 373, 384, 425, 448
WILDFEIER, 240, 439
Wildisassefrillwatzel, 343
Wilhelm Reich, 111
Wilhelms of Williams Township, 160
Wilkes-Barre, 352, 358
William
    Backus, 111, 116
    Beidelman, 57
    H. Allen, 359
    James Beissel, 95
    Penn, 44-47, 58, 424
    Wilson Beissel, 307, 313, 419
    Woys Weaver, 234, 332-333, 339
Williams Township Historical Society, 488
Willibald, 462
Wilmington, 43
Wilt, 223, 228-229
WINDGALLS, 463

Winged Liberty Head, 287
Winibald, 462
Winston-Salem, 61
Winter Solstices, 192
Wintergreen, 301, 342
Wintergrie, 342
Wisconsin Synod, 54
Wisdom, 294, 375, 377, 384-385, 414, 422, 425, 432-433, 445, 451-452, 487, 493
Wise Men, 139, 195, 244, 277, 380, 458
Wisonsin, 65
Wissahickon, 425, 451
Witch
    Finders, 410
    Master, 382, 410
    of
        Endor, 138, 140
        Rehmeyer, 88, 351
    Queen, 334
Witch-finder, 381
Witch-haunted, 415
Witch-induced, 326
Witch-lore, 415-416
Witch-mountains, 130
Witch-ness, 119
Witch-passages, 138
Witch-spirits, 415
Witchcraft 39, 87, 89, 113, 119-120, 122, 125, 127, 132-133, 135-138, 142, 145, 263, 304, 316, 318, 326, 347, 355, 359, 366, 395, 416-419, 463-464, 483, 489, 491-492, 494
    Medicine, 347, 491
    Sauer, 326
Witchcrafts, 273, 278, 283, 292
Witchdom, 122, 401
Witched, 89, 129, 248, 294
Witchery, 135, 248, 382, 415-416, 490
Witches 84, 124, 128-130, 133, 137-138, 157, 292, 317-318, 346, 357,

390, 410-411, 414-418, 461-462, 484
    of Mexico, 417
Witching, 128-129, 296, 351
Woden, 130, 293, 387, 396-397
Wolfsthurn Manual, 96, 247, 265
Wollengraut, 340
Wolleschtengel, 340
Woman, 72, 76, 122, 138, 140, 243, 245, 255-258, 324, 340, 342, 358, 392, 425, 432, 452, 471, 488, 493
WOMB DISEASE, 463
Women, 51, 54, 124-125, 146, 178, 243, 253, 256-257, 264, 314, 329, 331, 345, 357, 363, 394, 470
Woodbury, 492
Wooden, 234, 275, 277, 286, 397
Words of Power, 369
Work of
    Mercy, 410, 436
    Salvation, 387
World
    Tree, 369
    War
        I, 51, 131
        II, 90
Worm, 258, 366, 374, 400, 463-464
Worms, 146, 212, 258-259, 326, 328, 347, 366, 463-464, 494
Wormwood, 220, 240, 301, 338
Worn, 218, 246, 257, 285, 340, 370, 379, 393, 400, 425, 444, 454, 466
Worship, 54-55, 69, 84, 121, 276, 298, 397, 415, 431-432, 458
Wort, 192, 208, 264, 291, 326, 334, 344-345, 347, 444
Worte, 279
Wound Wood, 197-198, 368, 464
Wounds of Christ, 60, 199-201
Written
    Charm of Exorcism, 273, 283
    Charms of Protection, 284
    Hebrew, 188
Wunden, 200
Wuram, 451
Wust, 494
WWII, 52, 90, 353
WYRD, 124, 464-465
Württemberg, 47

X

Xaa, 259
Xanthoxylum Americanum, 342

Y

Yahweh, 138, 189
Yang, 412
Year, 42, 45, 49, 64, 68, 88, 95, 110, 178, 191-192, 296, 301, 388, 407, 415, 424, 432, 435, 445, 461-462
Yellow Rattle, 331
Yesod, 186
Yggdraisil, 369
Yin, 412
Yod
    Heh Vau Heh, 188
Yoderite, 126
Yohai, 422
Yom Kippur, 448
York Hex Murder Trial, 159

Z

ZAESCHMERZE, 146, 246
ZAEWEH, 146, 246
Zahnwehgelbholz, 342
Zain, 470
Zauberbuch, 94, 296, 439, 446, 492
Zauberei, 488
Zauberzettel, 101, 269-271, 277-278, 285, 368, 379, 422, 430, 456, 465-466
Zauberzetteln, 110, 223, 269, 271,

543

276, 278, 285-287, 379, 403, 422,
460, 465
Zavaxo, 451
Zebedee, 443
Zijmuorsobet, 451
Zijoronaijwetho, 451
Zimmerman, 424-425
Zinzendorf, 59-61, 67
Zion, 67, 224
ZnSO4, 463
Zodiac
    Man, 178
    Women, 178
Zohar, 422
Zondervan, 493
Zook, 410, 494
Zoroastrian, 447
Zoroastrians, 459
Zur Tradition, 94
Zurich Counsil, 62
Zwingli, 55
Zwischentrager, 112, 466

"*I am the root of David, and the bright and morning star.*"
Revelation 22:16

www.ingramcontent.com/pod-product-compliance
Lightning Source LLC
Chambersburg PA
CBHW030403250426
43670CB00049B/71